Masterpi

Greek literature

Homer: Tyrtaeus: Archilochus: Callistratus: Alcaeus: Sappho: Anacreon: Pindar: Aeschylus: Sophocles: Euripides Aristophanes: Herodotus: Thucydides: Xenophon: Plato: Theocritus: Lucian, with biographical sketches and notes

John Henry Wright

Alpha Editions

This edition published in 2019

ISBN : 9789353927028

Design and Setting By
Alpha Editions
email - alphaedis@gmail.com

As per information held with us this book is in Public Domain.
This book is a reproduction of an important historical work. Alpha Editions uses the best technology to reproduce historical work in the same manner it was first published to preserve its original nature. Any marks or number seen are left intentionally to preserve its true form.

MASTERPIECES OF GREEK LITERATURE

HOMER: TYRTAEUS: ARCHILOCHUS: CALLISTRA-
TUS: ALCAEUS: SAPPHO: ANACREON: PINDAR:
AESCHYLUS: SOPHOCLES: EURIPIDES:
ARISTOPHANES: HERODOTUS: THU-
CYDIDES: XENOPHON: PLATO:
THEOCRITUS: LUCIAN

WITH BIOGRAPHICAL SKETCHES AND NOTES

SUPERVISING EDITOR

JOHN HENRY WRIGHT, LL.D.

PROFESSOR OF GREEK IN HARVARD UNIVERSITY

HOUGHTON, MIFFLIN AND COMPANY
Boston: 4 Park Street; New York: 85 Fifth Avenue
Chicago: 378-388 Wabash Avenue
The Riverside Press, Cambridge

CONTENTS

[The names of translators are given in *italics*.]

	PAGE
INTRODUCTION	vii

HOMER.
   INTRODUCTORY NOTE 1
   ILIAD. *Bryant.*
      Meeting of Hector and Andromachè 2
      The Death of Hector 6
      The Mourning for Hector 19
   ODYSSEY. *Worsley.*
      Odysseus in the Cave of Polyphemus 22

TYRTAEUS.
   INTRODUCTORY NOTE 46
   MARTIAL ELEGY. *Campbell* 46

ARCHILOCHUS.
   INTRODUCTORY NOTE 48
   TO HIS SOUL. *Hay* 48

SCOLIA.
   INTRODUCTORY NOTE 50
   A SCOLION OF CALLISTRATUS. *Conington* 50
   A SCOLION OF HYBRIAS THE CRETAN. *Campbell* . . 51
   THE SWALLOW SONG. *Symonds* 51

ALCAEUS.
   INTRODUCTORY NOTE 53
   WINTER. *Symonds* 53

SAPPHO.
   INTRODUCTORY NOTE 55
   HYMN TO VENUS. *Merivale* 55
   TO A LOVED ONE. *Phillips* 56
   "INTER IGNES LUNA MINORES." *Arnold* 57
   TO AN UNCULTURED LESBIAN WOMAN. *Symonds* . . 57
   A GIRL IN LOVE. *Moore* 58
   ONE GIRL. *Rossetti* 58
   TO EVENING. *Appleton* 59

ANACREON.
   INTRODUCTORY NOTE 60
   ANACREONTICS. *Moore.*
      Old Age 60

CONTENTS

The Wiser Part	61
To a Swallow	62
Love's Assault	62
The Pet Dove	63
The Portrait	65
Drinking Song	66
Music and Love	67
Nature's Gifts	68

SIMONIDES OF CEOS.

INTRODUCTORY NOTE	69
DANAË AND HER BABE ADRIFT. *Symonds*	70
ON THOSE WHO DIED AT THERMOPYLAE. *Sterling*	71

PINDAR.

INTRODUCTORY NOTE	72
FIRST PYTHIAN ODE. *West*	74
FROM PINDAR'S FOURTH PYTHIAN ODE. *Myers*	82

AESCHYLUS.

INTRODUCTORY NOTE	85
PROMETHEUS BOUND. *Mrs. Browning*	88

SOPHOCLES.

INTRODUCTORY NOTE	136
ANTIGONE. *Plumptre*	138

EURIPIDES.

INTRODUCTORY NOTE	191
HERACLES. *Browning.*	
The Fate of Heracles	193
The Madness of Heracles	197
ALCESTIS. *Browning*	201

ARISTOPHANES.

INTRODUCTORY NOTE	249
THE BIRDS. *Frere*	251
THE FROGS. *Frere*	286

HERODOTUS.

INTRODUCTORY NOTE	292
EXTRACTS FROM THE HISTORY. *Rawlinson.*	
The Taking of Babylon	293
Persian Customs	295
The Nile	297
Egyptian Customs	304
Crocodiles and the Hippopotamus	306
Sesostris	308
The Pyramid of Cheops	312
The Battle of Marathon	314

THUCYDIDES.

INTRODUCTORY NOTE	319

CONTENTS

EXTRACTS FROM THE HISTORY OF THE PELOPONNESIAN WAR.
  Jowett.
 The Plague at Athens 320
 Public Funeral at Athens 327
 The Siege of Plataea 332
 The Retreat from Syracuse 337

XENOPHON.
 INTRODUCTORY NOTE 350
 MEMORABILIA. *Dakyns.*
  Socrates and Aristodemus 351
  The Choice of Heracles 355
  Socrates and Chaerecrates 360
 ANABASIS. *Dakyns.*
  The Battle of Cunaxa 365
  The First Glimpse of the Sea 368

PLATO.
 INTRODUCTORY NOTE 371
 NOTE ON SOCRATES 373
 GORGIAS. *Jowett.*
  The True Politician 374
 CRITO. *Jowett* 377
 PHAEDO. *Jowett.*
  The Death of Socrates 395
 THE REPUBLIC. *Jowett.*
  The Ship of State 401
  The Allegory of the Cave 408

DEMOSTHENES.
 INTRODUCTORY NOTE 417
 ORATION ON THE CROWN. *Lord Brougham* . . . 418

THEOCRITUS.
 INTRODUCTORY NOTE 429
 IDYL I. THE DEATH OF DAPHNIS. *Calverley* . . 430
 IDYL VII. HARVEST HOME. *Calverley* . . . 435
 IDYL XV. THE FESTIVAL OF ADONIS. *Arnold* . . 438

LUCIAN.
 INTRODUCTORY NOTE 444
 TIMON OF ATHENS. ACT. III. *Sheldon* . . . 445
 A DIALOGUE OF THE DEAD. *Sheldon* 453
 PEREGRINUS. *Sheldon* 454

INTRODUCTION

THE idea of collecting and publishing representative selections of Greek literature is not a new one with us of the twentieth century. Especially in the later periods of the life of the Greeks and Romans such selections were made in the Florilegia that have come down to us, and in other earlier and later collections and compilations that are now lost. These were made primarily for the use of students, but the needs and tastes of other readers were also consulted.

The chief value of a good collection of specimens is that a book of them gives, in concrete examples, a summary view of the various sorts of literature. And if the extracts are accompanied by suitable introductory biographical notes, wherein, with other information, the relation of the different forms of literary expression to each other and of their development are duly set forth, we have in the work what is in effect a useful illustrated history of literature. But with these advantages we must not fail to recognize that there are disadvantages in a book of selections of Greek prose and poetry. These disadvantages are due, in part, to the fact that the book is a book of extracts and fragments, and, in part, to the fact that a book for English readers can contain only translations. The task of selecting the extracts, especially from a literature so abundant, varied, and rich as is Greek literature, is at once easy and difficult. It is easy because of the great wealth of material at our disposal; difficult because of the necessity, for lack of space, of omitting much that has as strong a claim to admission as most that is actually admitted. Indeed, a dozen books of Greek masterpieces might be prepared, each one of which would be as representative as any of the others. The chief disadvantage, then, of a single volume of selections, like the present one, is that it must be incomplete. Extracts and fragments for the most part can alone be given, and fragments, though interesting in themselves, can afford no idea of the complete works from which they are taken. Furthermore, Greek literature itself, owing to the marvellous organic development through which it came into being, is, as it were, itself a literary whole, and a book of minor extracts, being in itself only a fragment of something greater, can hardly be completely satisfying.

The fact that a book intended for English readers must be a collection of translations is likewise a disadvantage. "No work of genius," as Mr. Lowell says, "can be adequately translated, because every word of it is permeated with what Milton calls 'the precious life-blood of a master spirit,' which cannot be transfused into the veins of the best translation." No translation of a piece of literary art can ever be entirely satisfactory. The original work has a distinct individuality that it is impossible to reproduce, an individuality which is determined not only by the substance of thought embodied in it, but by the æsthetic form in which it is cast and the language in which this thought finds expression. Indeed, a perfect translation is as impossible as the duplication of an individuality, and approximations to perfect translation are difficult in proportion to the richness and complexity of the original. A great painting may be copied, — translated, as it were; but even here, where the medium of translation is the same as that which was used in the original, color and drawing, how inadequate and disappointing the result! Still more is this the case when the medium of translation is something wholly different from the original medium, as when a work in one language is translated into another of alien spirit and genius. In all translations something is lost, something is added. If all the thoughts of the original are preserved, something of the color, form, atmosphere necessarily disappears; and when the translation is made from Greek into a language like English, — at once rich and poor, brilliant and bizarre, particolored and bald, each word in its vocabulary surcharged with manifold meanings and associations, — it is inevitable that even at the hands of the most competent and careful of translators much should be imported into the translation that was not in the original, the language of which is, above all, simple, direct, vivid, "fitting aptest words to things," only the translucent veil of thought, not its cumbrous garment..

But translations have been made, and many of them are as successful as the limitations and conditions of the problem will allow. The requisites of what may be called a successful translation are twofold: not only scholarship to know, and fully and delicately to appreciate, all that was in the original — substance of thought, form, tone, color; but also creative literary power, often the poetic gift, so to render the original into English phrase that it may produce on the unlearned modern reader the entire effect, so far as may be, that it produced on the readers for whom it was first designed. In translations to be included in a book of masterpieces these two conditions should be fulfilled, and when we have at our command versions by masters in English expression, great poets and prose writers of the time, these should be chosen in preference to others. Such choices have been made in the selections included in this volume.

Though all translation, certainly from the æsthetic point of view, is disappointing and inadequate, there are other points of view from which good translations are of the highest importance and value. For persons who have not easy access to the original fountains, they are convenient as a sort of substitute for those clear springs of utterance. They swiftly bring the modern reader at least to the crude thought of the original, to the bare facts there recounted, and where these are, as so often, thoughts of wisdom and facts of vast significance, their value is incontestable. Perhaps one may not go quite so far as Emerson in saying that "What is really best in any book is translatable, — any real insight or broad human sentiment," remembering Emerson's other saying, "I confide in your scholarly character that you spurn translations and read Greek." It still remains true that the best translations preserve for such as read with open and discerning minds very much "that was in their originals to enlarge, liberalize, and refine the mind." Some English translations, too, have a value which is not dependent upon their relation to their originals. They gain this by their own native charm, being themselves English classics. Such is Pope's *Iliad*, of which Bentley said, "It is a pretty poem, but must not be called Homer." Paraphrases of this character are of course in no sense substitutes for the original. All translations, however, whether mere

INTRODUCTION xi

echoes, or whether fairly successful and adequate or the contrary, if they possess an independent literary quality, have the merit of guiding the sympathetic and ambitious reader to the original. It is to be hoped that this will be the outcome for many readers of these pages.

In the present volume the attempt has been made, and in my opinion happily made, to group together a considerable number of representative passages, each of distinct intrinsic interest, from Greek poetry and prose, mainly of the classical age, in the best available translations; the translations, so far as possible, come from the hands of acknowledged masters of English speech. The selections from each author are accompanied by brief biographical sketches and other notes in which the place of the author in Greek literature is sketched, and other pertinent information is given.

We have here representation of nearly all the classes of extant Greek poetry. Three memorable passages from the *Iliad* which recount scenes in the life of Hector and the mourning for him (in Bryant's translation), followed by one book of the *Odyssey* — Odysseus and Polyphemus — (in Worsley's version) open the volume and give us a glimpse of epic poetry. What we call lyric poetry is represented in selections from Tyrtaeus and Archilochus, in three interesting specimens of Scolia, and in entire poems or fragments of Alcaeus, Sappho, Simonides of Ceos, and Pindar. Then follow Mrs. Browning's *Prometheus Bound* of Aeschylus and Plumptre's *Antigone* of Sophocles, each entire. These, with selections from the *Mad Heracles* and nearly the whole of the *Alcestis* of Euripides, in Mr. Browning's transcripts, stand for Greek tragedy. Scenes from the *Birds* and the *Frogs* of Aristophanes, the two most important of the plays of this writer, in Frere's paraphrases, show the reader Greek comedy at its best.

Greek classical prose, on the other hand, is represented, first, by short extracts from the historians Herodotus and Thucydides, and from Xenophon, the essayist and bright story-teller, with a few scenes from the pages of Plato, poet and philosopher in one, Jowett's classic versions being used for Thucydides and Plato. Several of these passages from Xenophon and Plato have reference to that most unique and striking personality in ancient thought, the Athenian Socrates. Then follows, in Lord Brougham's spirited rendering, a brief extract from the speech of Demosthenes *On the Crown*, a speech of which David Hume said "that it is the most perfect production of the human intellect." The poetry of the post-classical age is represented by three of the *Idyls* of Theocritus, and by eight or ten of the little pieces which have been, though incorrectly, ascribed to Anacreon. The book closes with three selections from Lucian, a prose writer of the second century of our era, who, in his satirical *Dialogues*, marks a new departure in literature and seems in many ways to link together the ancient and the modern world.

This volume and other books like it will appeal to readers of various classes. We may read literature for the information on matters of fact that it affords, or for the æsthetic pleasure and quickening that it yields, or for the new light it casts on human life, or for its effect upon our manner of thinking and upon our expression of thought; we may read it also as students

INTRODUCTION xiii

of great achievements in thought, or as lovers of the beautiful, the knowledge of which elevates and ennobles life, of things that "soothe the cares and lift the thoughts of men." The reasons why Greek literature in particular, which is represented in this volume, has this universal appeal, are numerous. The literature of the Greeks, in its varied types, in its perfection of form, and in the richness and fruitfulness of its content, was the most significant contribution made by the ancient world to civilization. It impressed itself on Rome, both in the models it furnished and in the ideas it conveyed, and the rediscovery of it after the Dark Ages was one of the chief causes of that new birth or awakening of the human spirit which in its results means the modern world. The chief instrument of the liberal education of the people of Rome and Byzantium, it became not long after the Renaissance one of the most important elements in the systems of the higher education as these were framed on the Continent and in England. Its influence, then, has been both direct and indirect in contributing to the creation of that great unseen world of ideas and ideals in which all generous souls now live and long have lived, and will live in time to come. It is impossible for us to know this world or to know ourselves, who are a part of it, or our work, which is conditioned by it, without some knowledge of the sources from which arose this mighty fabric, which

"like a dome of many colored glass,
Stains the white radiance of eternity."

Greek literature owes its commanding place in the realm of the spirit to several causes. It is the adequate expression in uttered words — as Greek art is the expression in plastic forms — of ideals of thought.

The thought is large and free and fine and enlightening, beholding the things of the spirit as they are, "steadily" and "whole," and the expression of the thought is as perfect as human speech can make it, helped as this expression here is by a language that is marvellous and unmatched in its power, delicacy, and range. Greek poetry is thus what Wordsworth says all poetry is, —

"Wisdom married to immortal verse."

Here is above all a noble originality. Practically everything in Greek poetry, forms of art and themes, and for that matter almost everything in European literature, is original in Greece, and so far as we know has no organic or derivative connection with anything outside of Greece, except now and then some minor matter or *motif*— as, perhaps, the strophic forms of poetry from the Babylonians and flute music from Phrygia. The Greeks inherited, it is true, from their ancestors certain poetic impulses and forms, but as Greek poetry dawns upon us in Homer it is something wonderfully in advance of the crude Indo-European beginnings such as we infer these to have been from Sanskrit literature. The Greeks borrowed, it is also true, but in borrowing they so transformed and recreated what they borrowed, transfiguring it into a larger life, that it seems to be and to the eye of the soul really is a new creation. The author of the Platonic *Epinomis* felt this truth, which finds illustration not only in literature but in all other forms of artistic expression, when he said, "Whatever the Greeks take over from the foreign world they fashion into something far more beautiful." Other nations have struck out on new lines in many things, but in none has the world ever beheld such a transcendent wealth of original tendencies, impulses, products. Think of what — to speak of forms of poetry only — we owe in their beginnings to the Greeks: epic poetry, lyric poetry, tragedy, comedy. These comprise nearly the whole of poetry, and these were not only initiated by the Hellenic people, but were brought to such completeness and perfection of growth that subsequent poetic achievement, at least in the ancient world, was hardly more than an intended imitation, or an unconscious echo, of the voices and notes of Hellas.

But originality is not enough. Originality, except in things themselves nobly worth while, may be a bane and not a benefit. The originality of the Greeks led to the production of works of poetic art which in themselves, on their own intrinsic merits, stand supreme. It is the manifold and universal excellence of the several kinds of Greek poetry — their perennial freshness, vigor, spontaneous vitality, their lucidity and their enkindling light — more than anything else that establishes the claim of Greek literature to its high place in the traditions and elements of civilization.

Greek literature — poetry, and to a certain extent prose also — has these peculiar excellences to so signal a degree, because it stood, as no other literature has since stood, in intimate relations with the whole of the life whence it sprung. Greek civilization had a solidarity and unity, and withal a noble simplicity, that gave to all parts and elements of it a vital interrelation and connection. Life, the whole life of the city-state, and sometimes of the whole nation, was the poet's inspirer, regulator, test. The poet was the consummate product, the epitome, as it were, of his age, not a wandering voice: he sang the true heart of the people, whether in their higher aspirations or in their grosser desires. And just here lies much of the meaning of Greek poetry for the student of humanity. It is the spontaneous and universal expression of the life and character of the Greeks; it is the comprehensive interpretation of the essential qualities of the race; in it is sounded the diapason of the capacities of this people; it is, as Sir Richard Jebb has said, the "index of their capacity." Literature, especially poetry, is national life expressed, not, as to-day, an individual's "criticism of life."

How does this relation show itself? In the first place, in the universality of Greek poetry, and in its infinite variety within certain grand types, which had been developed by the reaction of poets on their environment. Besides the great branches of poetic art, with the scant fragments of which we are familiar, it must be remembered that every class in society had its peculiar form of poetic utterance. The originals are gone, leaving only scant allusions to them in such writers as Athenaeus and Plutarch: there was poetry for each time of life, from cradle songs to dirges for the aged dead; each occupation had its peculiar poetry — watchmen, waterdrawers, shepherds, weavers, harvesters, soldiers. There were choral songs, in part rude and improvised, in part original artistic creations of famous poets, in part re-fashioned by great poets from rude popular originals. In the glad festivals of Dionysus there were choral songs of great variety, from two kinds of which Attic drama, both tragedy and comedy, in an unprecedented development, drew its origin. Plutarch tells of the hymn of invocation to Dionysus, sung by the women of Elis at Olympia; we read of the free and unrestrained songs of guilds of roving beggars, sung at spring and autumn gatherings. It was songs of this character that gave rise to the idea of responsive recitation, which when accompanied by intricate dance movements led to the highly artistic framework of subsequent choral poetry with its elaborate correspondences and symmetries. Especially interesting are the songs that were sung at convivial gatherings; traces of such songs are found in all branches of the Hellenic stock, as the elegiac verses of the Ionians, and the scolia which were popular with the Athenians in the classical age. Examples of the latter are given in the following pages.

The use of poetry in Greek education, indeed its almost exclusive use here, is another evidence of the intimate relation and interrelation of poetry and life. Plato tells us that " Homer is the teacher of Greece." At school, so soon as the boy could read he was introduced to the poets, and the purpose of this study was a moral one, having regard to the precepts of the poets, and to the praises of the great men of old, " in order," says Plato, " that the boy may emulate their examples and strive to become such as they." Precisely the reasons that we of to-day urge for the study of the Bible were by the Greeks urged for the study of Homer, and many more. A striking passage in Plato's *Laws* sets forth the practice of the Greeks of his day in reference to the use of poetry in education: " We have a great many poets writing in hexameter [Homer, Hesiod, Theognis], trimeter [the dramatists and others], and all sorts of measures — some who are serious, others who aim only at raising a laugh; and all mankind declare that the youths who are rightly educated should be brought up in them and saturated with them; some insist that they should be constantly hearing them read aloud, and always learning them, so as to get by heart entire poets; while others select choice passages and long speeches, and make compendiums of them, saying that these ought to be committed to memory, if a man is to be made good and wise by experience and learning of many things." The object of this literary study, as already suggested, was not to impart learned lore, to delight and enrich the imagination, to refine the taste, but to shape character. Aeschines, the orator, expresses the same conception when he says: "I recite these verses, for I maintain that the reason why we learn by heart in boyhood the sentiments of the poets is that when we are men we shall put them into practice."

These citations from Plato and Aeschines suggest the remark that the views expressed by the Greeks in general on the function of poetry are an interesting confirmation of what has been said about the intimate connection between Greek literature and life. And the gradual change in these views reflects the gradual change that took place in this relation. For after the loss of national liberty at Chaeronea there came about a disassociation of all the finer elements of Greek life from each other, and we trace the sad development of individualism, sectionalism, party narrowness, begun earlier, which finally broke up the fabric of Hellenic society. In a familiar passage in the *Frogs* of Aristophanes there is a scene between Aeschylus and Euripides, who are represented as engaging in a poetical contest in the lower world, the victor in which is to be released and to revisit Athens. The dialogue opens thus: "Tell me," says Aeschylus, "for what qualities we should admire a poet." "For wit and useful wisdom," replies Euripides, with the approbation of Aeschylus, "for making men better." The same thought reappears in the words of the orator Hyperides — "How can we live beautifully unless we know the beautiful things in life?" For is not poetry among the most beautiful things in life? Plato, as is well known, would exclude the poet from his ideal state. But even this exclusion is evidence of the position and power of Greek poetry among the Greek people, and it is accompanied by interesting modifications. It is mainly, says Plato, because men believe in the literal truth of immoral myths and legends that they are injured by poetry. To a noble and true poetry he raises no objection. The poet and the law-giver are rivals, the latter striving to set in action the noblest of dramas, and the poet must not address the citizens in a manner out of harmony with the institutions of the state. There must be a censorship of poetry, and the poet must sing only of high thoughts and deeds. But even in Aristotle we note the beginning of a change of opinion as to the chief object of poetry, — a slight but a significant change. For him the chief use of poetry is that it affords a "noble pleasure;" and this double view is reflected in the sentiment of Sir Philip Sidney that the end of poetry is "delightful teaching," poetry being the "sweet food of uttered knowledge." A century after Aristotle, a great scholar, — perhaps the first great scholar in the modern sense of this word, Eratosthenes of Cyrene, — declares with emphasis that the end of poetry is not instruction or edification, but pleasure, or beguiling delight. And this view leads on to the further degradation of the conception of the office of poetry, until men say that the chief reason for studying poetry is to have something to quote!

Such was Greek poetry to the Greeks themselves in the classical age. What may it be to us? Has it a message for modern ears,— a message that we may spell out in the pages of this book of selections from Greek poetry,— and what is that message? We may answer this question in many ways, but mainly as students of human achievement and as lovers of the beautiful. The survivals of antiquity, especially the literature of Greece, interest us and should demand our devotion because they are the tokens and memorials of human life and spirit, brilliant, beautiful, powerful, pregnant in meaning for later times — it "contains the future as it came out of the past;" — memorials of memorable epochs, bright and happy moments in the history of humanity when the individual was at his best and uttered himself as seldom since, in spite — and perhaps because — of the vast enrichment and expansion of our modern world. As the man of science delights in nature because she speaks of herself, so the student of literature delights in the poetry of the Greeks because it reveals the soul of man in its radiant and wondrously gifted youth. And so when we are asked whether modern poetry has not much to offer that is better than Greek poetry, and are told that it suits our times, being ampler and deeper in sentiment, and at least equally happy in marrying sense and verse, we can only reply that the thoughtful really live in no one time above another; they are citizens of all time, and must find their own, what they need for the enlargement and awakening of their souls, in the poetry of Athens equally with that of Weimar and Paris and London and Boston. And to the second contention we can only answer that modern poetry is in no sense a substitute for Greek poetry. It has, it is true, much that Greek poetry has not; so has Greek poetry much, very much, that finds no echo nor counterpart in modern verse. Modern poetry, modern literature, is supplementary to that of the Greeks. And the liberal soul that covets earnestly the best gifts, and all the best gifts, will seek and study and cultivate them both, with equal assiduity and strong endeavor.

It remains for me to add that the selections in this volume were made, and the biographical and other notes written, by Miss Clara Hitchcock Seymour, B. A., of Bryn Mawr College, and that she had in her task, which she has executed with both taste and skill, the counsel of her father, the distinguished Hillhouse Professor of Greek in Yale University. My share in the work has been merely to contribute this brief Introduction.

JOHN HENRY WRIGHT.

October 29, 1902.

HOMER

THE name Homer now stands for ancient Greek epic poetry. We know nothing of the man and his life. In times past, scholars asked with regard to his birthplace, but now they ask rather where epic poetry had its rise. The earliest Greek epics seem to have been sung in Thessaly, south of Mount Olympus, where was the fabled home of the gods; and the muses were called Pierian, from Pieria in Macedonia, not far to the north. But epic poetry was brought to its perfection by Ionian Greeks, on the western coast of Asia Minor. Thirty years ago many scholars believed the whole story of the Trojan war, on which both the Iliad and the Odyssey are based, to be a mere figment of the imagination, developed perhaps from misinterpreted expressions relating to the Dawn; but the excavations of the last quarter of the nineteenth century showed that, rather more than a thousand years before the beginning of our era, powerful and wealthy cities with mighty walls stood where Homer placed Mycenae and Troy, the homes of Agamemnon, "king of men," and the old king Priam. So we need not doubt that the Trojan war was a real war, though doubtless the poems exaggerate the numbers of those who took part in it. Achilles and Agamemnon may have been real men, though "Homer" was a poet and not a historian.

How much of the poems, as we have them, is due to any one poet, no one can say. Doubtless the poet who gave them their unity used very freely older lays and poetic material of every sort, adapting this to his use, while the bards who followed our Homer added verses, brief passages, or even whole lays. Before the age when writing was used for literary purposes, the sense of literary property was not strong, and each bard or "rhapsode" felt at liberty to modify and to add. But that a true and great poetic genius put the poems into essentially their present form, fewer doubt now than a quarter of a century ago. This poet probably lived as early as the ninth century before our era. Other scholars would hold that the poems are the product of three or four poets in different ages, — the later poet extending and developing the plan of his predecessors. The earliest of these may have lived as early as the tenth century, and the latest in the eighth century B. C.

The translations from the Iliad are by William Cullen Bryant; that from the Odyssey by Philip Stanhope Worsley.

MEETING OF HECTOR AND ANDROMACHÈ

From the Sixth Book of the Iliad, verses 390-502; in Bryant's translation, verses 505-633.

In the first of the four great battles of the Iliad, the Trojans are hard pressed, and Hector, the bravest and mightiest of the sons of King Priam, returns to the city from the battle on the plain, to bid the Trojan matrons offer vows to the goddess Pallas Athena for the safety of the city, and to urge his brother Paris to return to the fight. From the house of Paris, Hector turns to his own home, that he may see his wife, Andromachè.

This evidently is intended by the poet to be the last meeting between Hector and Andromachè before his death, although in the present form of the Iliad, Hector might have returned to his home at the close of this day of battle.

                    HECTOR left in haste   505
The mansion, and retraced his way between
The rows of stately dwellings, traversing
The mighty city. When at length he reached
The Scaean gates, that issue on the field,
His spouse, the nobly dowered Andromache,   510
Came forth to meet him — daughter of the prince
Eëtion, who, among the woody slopes

MEETING OF HECTOR AND ANDROMACHE

Of Placos, in the Hypoplacian town
Of Thebè, ruled Cilicia and her sons,
And gave his child to Hector, great in arms. 515
She came attended by a maid, who bore
A tender child — a babe too young to speak —
Upon her bosom — Hector's only son,
Beautiful as a star, whom Hector called
Scamandrius, but all else Astyanax — 520
The city's lord — since Hector stood the sole
Defence of Troy. The father on his child
Looked with a silent smile. Andromache
Pressed to his side meanwhile, and, all in tears,
Clung to his hand, and, thus beginning, said: 525
  "Too brave! thy valor yet will cause thy death.
Thou hast no pity on thy tender child,
Nor me, unhappy one, who soon must be
Thy widow. All the Greeks will rush on thee
To take thy life. A happier lot were mine, 530
If I must lose thee, to go down to earth,
For I shall have no hope when thou art gone, —
Nothing but sorrow. Father have I none,
And no dear mother. Great Achilles slew
My father when he sacked the populous town 535
Of the Cilicians, — Thebè with high gates.
'T was there he smote Eëtion, yet forbore
To make his arms a spoil; he dared not that,
But burned the dead with his bright armor on,
And raised a mound above him. Mountain-nymphs, 540
Daughters of Aegis-bearing Jupiter,
Came to the spot and planted it with elms. —
Seven brothers had I in my father's house,
And all went down to Hades in one day.
Achilles, the swift-footed, slew them all 545
Among their slow-paced bullocks and white sheep.

My mother, princess on the woody slopes
Of Placos, with his spoils he bare away,
And only for large ransom gave her back.
But her Diana,[1] archer-queen, struck down
Within her father's palace. Hector, thou
Art father and dear mother now to me,
And brother and my youthful spouse besides.
In pity keep within the fortress here,
Nor make thy child an orphan — nor thy wife
A widow. Post thine army near the place
Of the wild fig-tree, where the city walls
Are low and may be scaled. Thrice in the war
The boldest of the foe have tried the spot —
The Ajaces[2] and the famed Idomeneus,
The two chiefs born to Atreus,[3] and the brave
Tydides,[4] whether counselled by some seer,
Or prompted to the attempt by their own minds."

    Then answered Hector, great in war : " All this
I bear in mind, dear wife; but I should stand
Ashamed before the men and long-robed dames
Of Troy, were I to keep aloof and shun
The conflict, coward-like. Not thus my heart
Prompts me, for greatly have I learned to dare
And strike among the foremost sons of Troy,
Upholding my great father's fame and mine ;
Yet well in my undoubting mind I know
The day shall come in which our sacred Troy,
And Priam, and the people over whom
Spear-bearing Priam rules, shall perish all.

  [1] Diana's arrows carried a swift and painless death to women.
  [2] Ajax son of Telamon and Ajax son of Oïleus.
  [3] Agamemnon, king of Mycenae and commander-in-chief of the Greeks, and his brother Menelaüs, whose wife Helen was the cause of the war.
  [4] Diomede, the son of Tydeus.

MEETING OF HECTOR AND ANDROMACHE 5

But not the sorrows of the Trojan race,
Nor those of Hecuba herself, nor those
Of royal Priam, nor the woes that wait
My brothers many and brave — who all at last,
Slain by the pitiless foe, shall lie in dust — 580
Grieve me so much as thine, when some mailed Greek
Shall lead thee weeping hence, and take from thee
Thy day of freedom. Thou in Argos then
Shalt, at another's bidding, ply thy loom,
And from the fountain of Messeïs draw 585
Water, or from the Hypereian spring,
Constrained unwillingly by some cruel lot.
And then shall some one say that sees thee weep,
' This was the wife of Hector, most renowned
Of the horse-taming Trojans, when they fought 590
Around their city.' So shall some one say,
And thou shalt grieve the more, lamenting him
Who haply might have kept afar the day
Of thy captivity. O let the earth
Be heaped above my head in death before 595
I hear thy cries as thou art borne away!"
   So speaking, mighty Hector stretched his arms
To take the boy; the boy shrank crying back
To his fair nurse's bosom, scared to see
His father helmeted in glittering brass, 600
And eyeing with affright the horse-hair plume
That grimly nodded from the lofty crest.
At this both parents in their fondness laughed;
And hastily the mighty Hector took
The helmet from his brow and laid it down 605
Gleaming upon the ground, and, having kissed
His darling son and tossed him up in play,
Prayed thus to Jove and all the gods of heaven:
   "O Jupiter and all ye deities,

Vouchsafe that this my son may yet become 610
Among the Trojans eminent like me,
And nobly rule in Ilium. May they say,
'This man is greater than his father was!'
When they behold him from the battlefield
Bring back the bloody spoil of the slain foe, 615
That so his mother may be glad at heart."
 So speaking, to the arms of his dear spouse
He gave the boy; she on her fragrant breast
Received him, weeping as she smiled. The chief
Beheld, and, moved with tender pity, smoothed 620
Her forehead gently with his hand and said:
 "Sorrow not thus, beloved one, for me.
No living man can send me to the shades
Before my time; no man of woman born,
Coward or brave, can shun his destiny. 625
But go thou home, and tend thy labors there, —
The web, the distaff, — and command thy maids
To speed the work. The cares of war pertain
To all men born in Troy, and most to me."
 Thus speaking, mighty Hector took again 630
His helmet, shadowed with the horse-hair plume,
While homeward his beloved consort went,
Oft looking back, and shedding many tears.

THE DEATH OF HECTOR

From the Twenty-second Book of the Iliad, verses 188-515; in Bryant's translation, verses 233-636.

On the third great day of battle, Patroclus, the comrade and dearest friend of Achilles, is slain by Hector. This leads Achilles, who has been "sulking in his tent," to return to the fray. Our scene opens near the close of the fourth day of battle, on the twenty-seventh day of the action of the Iliad. Hector is pursued by Achilles. The other Trojan warriors have

THE DEATH OF HECTOR

been slain or have fled into the city walls. Hector's aged father and mother, Priam and Hecuba, are standing on a tower by the Scaean gate, looking on.

STILL, with quick steps, the fleet Achilles pressed
On Hector's flight. As when a hound has roused
A fawn from its retreat among the hills, 235
And chases it through glen and forest ground,
And to close thickets, where it skulks in fear
Until he overtakes it, Hector thus
Sought vainly to elude the fleet pursuit
Of Peleus' son. As often as he thought, 240
By springing toward the gates of Troy, to gain
Aid from the weapons of his friends who stood
On the tall towers, so often was the Greek
Before him, forcing him to turn away.

. . . .
When the twain had come
For the fourth time beside Scamander's springs, 260
The All-Father raised the golden balance high,
And, placing in the scales two lots which bring
Death's long dark sleep, — one lot for Peleus' son,
And one for knightly Hector, — by the midst
He poised the balance. Hector's fate sank down 265
To Hades, and Apollo left the field.
 The blue-eyed goddess Pallas [1] then approached
The son of Peleus with these wingèd words:
 "Renowned Achilles, dear to Jupiter!
Now may we, as I hope, at last return 270
To the Achaian army and the fleet
With glory, Hector slain, the terrible
In war. Escape he cannot, even though
The archer-god Apollo fling himself

---

[1] Pallas was hostile to the Trojans because of the slight put upon her charms by Paris, in awarding the golden apple to Aphrodite.

With passionate entreaty at the feet 275
Of Jove the Aegis-bearer. Stay thou here
And breathe a moment, while I go to him
And lure him hither to encounter thee."
 She spoke, and he obeyed, and gladly stood
Propped on the ashen stem of his keen spear; 280
While, passing on, Minerva overtook
The noble Hector. In the outward form
And with the strong voice of Deïphobus,[1]
She stood by him and spake these wingèd words:
 "Hard pressed I find thee, brother, by the swift 285
Achilles, who, with feet that never rest,
Pursues thee round the walls of Priam's town.
But let us make a stand and beat him back."
 And then the crested Hector spake in turn:
 "Deïphobus, thou ever hast been dear 290
To me beyond my other brethren, sons
Of Hecuba and Priam. Now still more
I honor thee, since thou hast seen my plight,
And for my sake hast ventured forth without
The gates, while all the rest remain within." 295
 And the blue-eyed Pallas spake again:
 "Brother, 't is true, my father, and the queen
My mother, and my comrades, clasped my knees
In turn, and earnestly entreated me
That I would not go forth, such fear had fallen 300
On them all; but I was grieved for thee.
Now let us combat valiantly, nor spare
The weapons that we bear, and we shall learn
Whether Achilles, having slain us both,
Will carry to the fleet our bloody spoil, 305
Or die himself, the victim of thy spear."
 The treacherous goddess spake, and led the way;

[1] Hector's brother, who wedded Helen after Paris' death.

THE DEATH OF HECTOR

And when the advancing chiefs stood face to face,
The crested hero, Hector, thus began:
 "No longer I avoid thee as of late, 310
O son of Peleus! Thrice around the walls
Of Priam's mighty city have I fled,
Nor dared to wait thy coming. Now my heart
Bids me encounter thee; my time is come
To slay or to be slain. Now let us call 315
The gods to witness, who attest and guard
The covenants of men. Should Jove bestow
On me the victory, and I take thy life,
Thou shalt meet no dishonor at my hands;
But, stripping off the armor, I will send 320
The Greeks thy body. Do the like by me."
 The swift Achilles answered with a frown:
 "Accursed Hector, never talk to me
Of covenants. Men and lions plight no faith,
Nor wolves agree with lambs, but each must plan 325
Evil against the other. So between
Thyself and me no compact can exist,
Or understood intent. First, one of us
Must fall and yield his life-blood to the god
Of battles. Summon all thy valor now. 330
A skilful spearman thou hast need to be,
And a bold warrior. There is no escape,
For now doth Pallas doom thee to be slain
By my good spear. Thou shalt repay to me
The evils thou hast done my countrymen, — 335
My friends whom thou hast slaughtered in thy rage."
 He spake, and brandishing his massive spear
Hurled it at Hector, who beheld its aim
From where he stood. He stooped, and over him
The brazen weapon passed and plunged to earth. 340
Unseen by royal Hector, Pallas went

And plucked it from the ground, and brought it back
And gave it to the hands of Peleus' son,
While Hector said to his illustrious foe :
    " Godlike Achilles, thou hast missed thy mark ;   345
Nor hast thou learned my doom from Jupiter,
As thou pretendest. Thou art glib of tongue,
And cunningly thou orderest thy speech,
In hope that I who hear thee may forget
My might and valor. Think not that I shall flee,   350
That thou mayst pierce my back ; for thou shalt send
Thy spear, if God permit thee, through my breast
As I rush on thee. Now avoid in turn
My brazen weapon. Would that it might pass
Clean through thee, all its length ! The tasks of war
For us of Troy were lighter for thy death,   356
Thou pest and deadly foe of all our race ! "
    He spake, and brandishing his massive spear
Hurled it, nor missed, but in the centre smote
The buckler of Pelides. Far away   360
It bounded from the brass, and he was vexed
To see that the swift weapon from his hand
Had flown in vain. He stood perplexed and sad ;
No second spear had he. He called aloud
On the white-bucklered chief, Deïphobus,   365
To bring another ; but that chief was far,
And Hector saw that it was so, and said :
    " Ah me ! the gods have summoned me to die.
I thought my warrior friend, Deïphobus,
Was by my side ; but he is still in Troy,   370
And Pallas has deceived me. Now my death
Cannot be far, — is near ; there is no hope
Of my escape, for so it pleases Jove
And Jove's great archer-son, who have till now
Delivered me. My hour at last is come ;   375

THE DEATH OF HECTOR

Yet not ingloriously or passively
I die, but first will do some valiant deed,
Of which mankind shall hear in after time."
   He spake, and drew the keen-edged sword that hung,
Massive and finely tempered, at his side, 380
And sprang — as when an eagle high in heaven,
Through the thick cloud, darts downward to the plain
To clutch some tender lamb or timid hare,
So Hector, brandishing that keen-edged sword,
Sprang forward, while Achilles opposite 385
Leaped toward him, all on fire with savage hate,
And holding his bright buckler, nobly wrought,
Before him. On his shining helmet waved
The four-fold crest; there tossed the golden tufts
With which the hand of Vulcan lavishly 390
Had decked it. As in the still hours of night
Hesper goes forth among the host of stars,
The fairest light of heaven, so brightly shone,
Brandished in the right hand of Peleus' son,
The spear's keen blade, as, confident to slay 395
The noble Hector, o'er his glorious form
His quick eye ran, exploring where to plant
The surest wound. The glittering mail of brass
Won from the slain Patroclus [1] guarded well
Each part, save only where the collar-bones 400
Divide the shoulder and the neck, and there
Appeared the throat, the spot where life is most
In peril. Through that part the noble son
Of Peleus drave his spear; it went quite through
The tender neck, and yet the brazen blade 405
Cleft not the windpipe, and the power to speak

[1] Hector when he slew Patroclus stripped him of his armor, which had been given him by Achilles, and put it on himself.

Remained. The Trojan fell amid the dust,
And thus Achilles boasted o'er his fall:
  "Hector, when from the slain Patroclus thou
Didst strip his armor, little didst thou think   410
Of danger. Thou hadst then no fear of me.
. . . .
Foul dogs and birds of prey shall tear thy flesh;
The Greeks shall honor him with funeral rites."
  And then the crested Hector faintly said:
  "I pray thee by thy life, and by thy knees,
And by thy parents, suffer not the dogs   420
To tear me at the galleys of the Greeks.
Accept abundant store of brass and gold,
Which gladly will my father and the queen
My mother give in ransom. Send to them
My body, that the warriors and the dames   425
Of Troy may light for me the funeral pile."[1]
  The swift Achilles answered with a frown:
  "Nay, by my knees entreat me not, thou cur,
Nor by my parents. I could even wish
My fury prompted me to cut thy flesh   430
In fragments, and devour it, such the wrong
That I have had from thee. There will be none
To drive away the dogs about thy head,
Not though thy Trojan friends should bring to me
Tenfold and twentyfold the offered gifts,   435
And promise others, — not though Priam, sprung
From Dardanus, should send thy weight in gold.
Thy mother shall not lay thee on thy bier,
To sorrow over thee whom she brought forth;
But dogs and birds of prey shall mangle thee."   440

---

[1] Burial was regarded by the Greeks as a sacred duty. The soul had no rest in the realms of the dead so long as the body remained unburied. *Cf.* the same belief expressed in the *Antigone*, p. 139.

THE DEATH OF HECTOR

And then the crested Hector, dying, said:
"I know thee, and too clearly I foresaw
I should not move thee, for thou hast a heart
Of iron. Yet reflect that for my sake
The anger of the gods may fall on thee, 445
When Paris and Apollo strike thee down,
Strong as thou art, before the Scaean gates."

Thus Hector spake, and straightway o'er him closed
The night of death; the soul forsook his limbs,
And flew to Hades, grieving for its fate, — 450
So soon divorced from youth and youthful might.
Then said the great Achilles to the dead:

"Die thou; and I, whenever it shall please
Jove and the other gods, will meet my fate."

He spake, and plucking forth his brazen lance 455
He laid it by, and from the body stripped
The bloody mail. The thronging Greeks beheld
With wonder Hector's tall and stately form,
And no one came who did not add a wound;
And looking to each other thus they said: 460

"How much more tamely Hector now endures
Our touch than when he set the fleet on fire!"

Such were the words of those who smote the dead.
But now, when swift Achilles from the corpse
Had stripped the armor, he stood forth among 465
The Achaian host, and spake these wingèd words:

"Leaders and princes of the Grecian host!
Since we, my friends, by favor of the gods,
Have overcome the chief who wrought more harm
To us than all the rest, let us assault 470
The town, and learn what they of Troy intend; —
Whether their troops will leave the citadel
Since he is slain, or hold it with strong hand,
Though Hector is no more. But why give thought

To plans like these while yet Patroclus lies 475
A corpse unwept, unburied, at the fleet?
I never will forget him while I live
And while these limbs have motion. Though below
In Hades they forget the dead, yet I
Will there remember my belovèd friend. 480
Now then, ye youths of Greece, move on and chant
A paean, while returning to the fleet.
We bring great glory with us; we have slain
The noble Hector, whom, throughout their town,
The Trojans ever worshiped like a god." 485
He spake, and planning in his mind to treat
The noble Hector shamefully, he bored
The sinews of his feet between the heel
And ankle; drawing through them leathern thongs
He bound them to the car, but left the head 490
To trail in dust. And then he climbed the car,
Took in the shining mail, and lashed to speed
The coursers. Not unwillingly they flew.
Around the dead, as he was dragged along,
The dust arose; his dark locks swept the ground. 495
That head, of late so noble in men's eyes,
Lay deep amid the dust, for Jove that day
Suffered the foes of Hector to insult
His corse in his own land. His mother saw,
And tore her hair, and flung her lustrous veil 500
Away, and uttered piercing shrieks. No less
His father, who so loved him, piteously
Bewailed him; and in all the streets of Troy
The people wept aloud, with such lament
As if the towery Ilium were in flames 505
Even to its loftiest roofs. They scarce could keep
The aged king within, who, wild with grief,
Struggled to rush through the Dardanian gates,

THE DEATH OF HECTOR

And, rolling in the dust, entreated all
Who stood around him, calling them by name:
  "Refrain, my friends, though kind be your intent.
Let me go forth alone, and at the fleet
Of Greece will I entreat this man of blood
And violence. He may perchance be moved
With reverence for my age, and pity me
In my gray hairs; for such a one as I
Is Peleus, his own father, by whose care
This Greek was reared to be a scourge to Troy,
And, more than all, a cause of grief to me,
So many sons of mine in life's fresh prime
Have fallen by his hand. I mourn for them,
But not with such keen anguish as I mourn
For Hector. Sorrow for his death will bring
My soul to Hades. Would that he had died
Here in my arms! this solace had been ours,
His most unhappy mother and myself
Had stooped to shed these tears upon his bier."
  He spake, and wept, and all the citizens
Wept with him. Hecuba among the dames
Took up the lamentation and began:
  "Why do I live, my son, when thou art dead,
And I so wretched? — thou who wert my boast
Ever, by night and day, where'er I went,
And whom the Trojan men and matrons called
Their bulwark, honoring thee as if thou wert
A god. They glory in thy might no more,
Since fate and death have overtaken thee."
Weeping she spake. Meantime Andromache
Had heard no tidings of her husband yet.
No messenger had even come to say
That he was still without the gates. She sat
In a recess of those magnificent halls,

And wove a twofold web of brilliant hues,
On which were scattered flowers of rare device;
And she had given her bright-haired maidens charge
To place an ample caldron on the fire, 546
That Hector, coming from the battlefield,
Might find the warm bath ready. Thoughtless one!
She knew not that the blue-eyed archer-queen,[1]
Far from the bath prepared for him, had slain 550
Her husband by the hand of Peleus' son.
She heard the shrieks, the wail upon the tower,
Trembled in every limb, and quickly dropped
The shuttle, saying to her bright-haired maids:
"Come with me, two of you, that I may learn 555
What now has happened. 'T is my mother's voice
That I have heard. My heart leaps to my mouth;
My limbs fail under me. Some deadly harm
Hangs over Priam's sons; far be the hour
When I shall hear of it. And yet I fear 560
Lest that Achilles, having got between
The daring Hector and the city gates,
May drive him to the plain alone, and quell
The desperate valor that was ever his;
For never would he keep the ranks, but ranged 565
Beyond them, and gave way to no man's might."
  She spake, and from the royal mansion rushed
Distractedly, and with a beating heart.
Her maids went with her. When she reached the tower
And throng of men, and, standing on the wall, 570
Looked forth, she saw her husband dragged away
Before the city. Toward the Grecian fleet
The swift steeds drew him. Sudden darkness came
Over her eyes, and in a breathless swoon
She sank away and fell. The ornaments 575

[1] Pallas Athena (Minerva).

Dropped from her brow, — the wreath, the woven
    band,
The net, the veil which golden Venus gave
That day when crested Hector wedded her,
Dowered with large gifts, and led her from her home,
Eëtion's palace. Round her in a throng   580
Her sisters of the house of Priam pressed,
And gently raised her in that deathlike swoon.
But when she breathed again, and to its seat
The conscious mind returned, as in their arms
She lay, with sobs and broken speech she said :   585
  "Hector, — O wretched me! — we both were born
To sorrow : thou at Troy, in Priam's house,
And I at Thebè in Eëtion's halls,
By woody Placos. From a little child
He reared me there, — unhappy he, and I   590
Unhappy! O that I had ne'er been born!
Thou goest down to Hades and the depths
Of earth, and leavest me in thine abode,
Widowed, and never to be comforted.
Thy son, a speechless babe, to whom we two   595
Gave being, — hapless parents! — cannot have
Thy loving guardianship now thou art dead,
Nor be a joy to thee. Though he survive
The cruel warfare which the sons of Greece
Are waging, hard and evil yet will be   600
His lot hereafter; others will remove
His landmarks and will make his fields their own.
The day in which a boy is fatherless
Makes him companionless; with downcast eyes
He wanders, and his cheeks are stained with tears.   605
Unfed he goes where sit his father's friends,
And plucks one by the cloak, and by the robe
Another. One who pities him shall give

A scanty draught, which only wets his lips,
But not his palate; while another boy, 610
Whose parents both are living, thrusts him thence
With blows and vulgar clamor: 'Get thee gone!
Thy father is not with us at the feast.'
Then to his widowed mother shall return
Astyanax in tears, who not long since 615
Was fed, while sitting in his father's lap,
On marrow and the delicate fat of lambs.
And ever when his childish sports had tired
The boy, and sleep came stealing over him,
He slumbered, softly cushioned, on a couch 620
And in his nurse's arms, his heart at ease
And satiate with delights. But now thy son
Astyanax,[1] — whom so the Trojans name
Because thy valor guarded gate and tower, —
Thy care withdrawn, shall suffer many things. 625
While far from those who gave thee birth, beside
The roomy ships of Greece, the restless worms
Shall make thy flesh their banquet when the dogs
Have gorged themselves. Thy garments yet remain
Within the palace, delicately wrought 630
And graceful, woven by the women's hands;
And these, since thou shalt put them on no more,
Nor wear them in thy death, I burn with fire
Before the Trojan men and dames; and all
Shall see how gloriously thou wert arrayed." 635
 Weeping she spake, and with her wept her maids.

[1] Astyanax means *Defender of the City*. See p. 3, line 521. Sons often were named from some distinction of the father.

THE MOURNING FOR HECTOR

From the Twenty-fourth Book of the Iliad, from verse 718 to the end; in Bryant's translation, verses 911-1022.

Old Priam, attended by Hermes (Mercury), the herald of the gods, has gone to the tent of Achilles, who is moved with compassion and gives up to him the body of Hector. On Priam's return, he is met at the city gate by the Trojan people.

THE throng gave way and let the chariot pass;
And having brought it to the royal halls,
On a fair couch they laid the corse, and placed
Singers beside it, leaders of the dirge,
Who sang a sorrowful, lamenting strain,   915
And all the women answered it with sobs.
White-armed Andromache in both her hands
Took warlike Hector's head, and over it
Began the lamentation midst them all:
  "Thou hast died young, my husband, leaving me   920
In this thy home a widow, and one son,
An infant yet. To an unhappy pair
He owes his birth, and never will, I fear,
Bloom into youth; for ere that day will Troy
Be overthrown, since thou, its chief defence,   925
Art dead, the guardian of its walls and all
Its noble matrons and its speechless babes,
Yet to be carried captive far away,
And I among them, in the hollow barks;
And thou, my son, wilt either go with me,   930
Where thou shalt toil at menial tasks for some
Pitiless master; or perhaps some Greek
Will seize thy little arm, and in his rage
Will hurl thee from a tower and dash thee dead,
Remembering how thy father, Hector, slew   935
His brother, son, or father; for the hand
Of Hector forced full many a Greek to bite

The dust of earth. Not slow to smite was he
In the fierce conflict; therefore all who dwell
Within the city sorrow for his fall. 940
Thou bringest an unutterable grief,
O Hector, on thy parents, and on me
The sharpest sorrows. Thou didst not stretch forth
Thy hands to me, in dying, from thy couch,
Nor speak a word to comfort me, which I 945
Might ever think of, night and day, with tears."
So spake the weeping wife; the women all
Mingled their wail with hers, and Hecuba
Took up the passionate lamentation next:
  " O Hector, thou who wert most fondly loved 950
Of all my sons! While yet thou wert alive,
Dear wert thou to the gods, who even now,
When death has overtaken thee, bestow
Such care upon thee. All my other sons
Whom swift Achilles took in war he sold 955
At Samos, Imbrus by the barren sea,
And Lemnos harborless. But as for thee,
When he had taken with his cruel spear
Thy life, he dragged thee round and round the tomb
Of his young friend, Patroclus, whom thy hand 960
Had slain, yet raised he not by this the dead;
And now thou liest in the palace here,
Fresh and besprinkled as with early dew,
Like one just slain with silent arrows aimed
By Phoebus, bearer of the silver bow." 965
  Weeping she spake, and woke in all who heard
Grief without measure. Helen, last of all
Took up the lamentation, and began:
  " O Hector, who wert dearest to my heart
Of all my husband's brothers, — for the wife 970
Am I of godlike Paris, him whose fleet

THE MOURNING FOR HECTOR

Brought me to Troy, — would I had sooner died!
And now the twentieth year is past since first
I came a stranger from my native shore,
Yet never have I heard from thee a word 975
Of anger or reproach. And when the sons
Of Priam, and his daughters, and the wives
Of Priam's sons, in all their fair array,
Taunted me grievously, or Hecuba
Herself, — for Priam ever was to me 980
A gracious father, — thou didst take my part
With kindly admonition, and restrain
Their tongues with soft address and gentle words.
Therefore my heart is grieved, and I bewail
Thee and myself at once, — unhappy me! 985
For now I have no friend in all wide Troy, —
None to be kind to me: they hate me all."
    Weeping she spake: the mighty throng again
Answered with wailing. Priam then addressed
The people: "Now bring wood, ye men of Troy, 990
Into the city. Let there be no fear
Of ambush from the Greeks, for when of late
I left Achilles at the dark-hulled barks,
He gave his promise to molest no more
The men of Troy till the twelfth morn shall rise." 995
    He spake, and speedily they yoked the mules
And oxen to the wains, and came in throngs
Before the city walls. Nine days they toiled
To bring the trunks of trees, and when the tenth
Arose to light the abodes of men, they brought 1000
The corse of valiant Hector from the town
With many tears, and laid it on the wood
High up, and flung the fire to light the pile.
    Now when the early rosy-fingered Dawn
Looked forth, the people gathered round the pile 1005

Of glorious Hector. When they all had come
Together, first they quenched the funeral fires,
Wherever they had spread, with dark-red wine,
And then his brothers and companions searched
For the white bones. In sorrow and in tears   1010
That streaming stained their cheeks, they gathered
      them,
And placed them in a golden urn. O'er this
They drew a covering of soft purple robes,
And laid it in a hollow grave, and piled
Fragments of rock above it, many and huge.   1015
In haste they reared the tomb, with sentries set
On every side, lest all too soon the Greeks
Should come in armor to renew the war.
When now the tomb was built, the multitude
Returned, and in the halls where Priam dwelt,   1020
Nursling of Jove, were feasted royally.
Such was the mighty Hector's burial rite.

ODYSSEUS IN THE CAVE OF POLYPHEMUS

The Ninth Book of the Odyssey; Worsley's translation.

Odysseus (Ulysses) here begins the story of his wanderings and adventures on his return from Troy. This story is called the "Apologue of Alcinous," being told to Alcinous, king of the Phaeacians, a people who dwelt in fairyland on an island which the later Greeks identified with Corfu. On the night following the relation of this story, Odysseus, after ten years at the siege of Troy and ten years of wanderings, is carried by the Phaeacians to Ithaca, his home.

THEN said Odysseus: Thrice-renownèd king,
Sweet is it minstrelsies like these to hear,
Framed by a bard who like the gods can sing.
Find me a joy to human heart more dear
Than is a people's gladness, when good cheer   5

ODYSSEUS IN THE CAVE OF POLYPHEMUS 23

Reigns, and all listening pause in deep delight,
While in mid-feast the bard his song doth rear,
What time the board with all good things is dight,
And for each guest the herald fills the wine-cup bright.

Methinks that nothing can more lovely be!   10
But thou my soul art turning to a tale
Heavy with heartache even in memory.
Ah! which then first, if I uplift the veil,
Which of my sorrows shall I last bewail? —
Woes in such number the celestials poured.   15
First I my name unfold that when from bale
Resting hereafter, to my land restored,
I, though far off, may greet your faces at my board.

I, then, Odysseus am, Laertes' son,
For all wise policies a name of fear   20
To men; my rumor to the skies hath gone.
And sunward Ithaca my country dear
I boast. Hill Neritus stands waving there
His green trees visible for many a mile,
Centre of soils divine, which clustering near,   25
Stars of the blue sea, round about him smile,
Dulichium, Samé steep, Zacynthus' wood-crowned isle.

Thus lies the land high-tabled in the main
Westward; the others take the morning sun;
Rough, but a good nurse, and divine in grain   30
Her heroes. Never can I gaze upon
Land to my mind so lovely as that one,
Land not to be forgotten — aye, though me
Calypso in her caves would fain have won,
And Circe, deep-embowered within the sea,   35
Held me with artful wiles her own true love to be.

Never could these the inward heart persuade,
Never make sweet the cold unfaithfulness.
More than all pleasures that were ever made
Parents and fatherland our life still bless. 40
Though we rich home in a strange land possess,
Still the old memories about us cling.
But hear, while I the bitter woes express,
Which, as from Troia I my comrades bring,
Zeus, the Olympian Sire, around my life did fling. 45

Me winds to Ismarus from Ilion bear,
To the Ciconians. I their town lay waste,
And wives and wealth with my companions share,
That none for me might sail away disgraced.
Anon I urged them with quick feet to haste 50
Their flight, but they, infatuate fools, forbore —
There the red wine they ever dreaming taste,
While carcasses of sheep lie many a score,
And trailing-footed beeves, slain, on the barren shore.

But all this while, on other works intent, 55
Loudly the Cicons to the Cicons call,
Who more and braver hold the continent.
These both from horseback cope with heroes tall,
Or foot to foot can make their foeman fall.
Wrapt in the morning mist they loom in view, 60
Thick as the leaves and flowers ambrosial,
Children of Spring. Onward the dark fate drew,
Big with the woes which Zeus had destined for our due.

Hard by the swift ships, each in ordered line,
With steely spears the battle they darrayne.[1] 65
While toward the zenith clomb the day divine,
We, though much fewer, their assault sustain.

[1] Darrayne, i. e. *set in array.*

ODYSSEUS IN THE CAVE OF POLYPHEMUS

But when, toward loosing of the plough, did wane
The slanting sun, then the Ciconian host
Turned us to flight along the shadowy plain. 70
Six of our comrades from each ship were lost,
But we the rest fled safely from the Thracian coast.

Then on our course we sail, distressed in heart,
Glad of our lives, yet grieving for the dead;
Natheless we list not from that shore depart, 75
Ere thrice with cries we hailed each fallen head
Of those whose blood the fierce Ciconians shed
In the wide plain. Ere yet we ceased to weep,
Zeus on our fleet the rage of Boreas dread
Launched, and with black clouds veiled the earth and deep, 80
While the dark Night came rushing from heaven's stormy steep.

Headlong the ships were driven with tattered sails.
These having furled we drave our keels ashore,
Fearing destruction from the raving gales.
Two nights and days we eating our heart's core 85
Lay till the third light beauteous Dawn upbore;
Then we the masts plant, and the white sails spread,
And sitting lean to the laborious oar.
Wind and good pilotage the brave barks sped;
Soon had I scatheless seen my native earth ahead, 90

But me the current and fell Boreas whirled,
Doubling Malea's cape, and far astray
Beyond the rude cliffs of Cythera hurled.
So for nine days along the watery way,
Teeming with monsters, me the winds affray 95
And with destruction ever seem to whelm:

But, on the afternoon of the tenth day,
We reached, borne downward with an easy helm,
Land of the flowery food, the Lotus-eating realm.

Anon we step forth on the dear mainland, 100
And draw fresh water from the springs, and there,
Seated at ease along the silent strand,
Not far from the swift ships our meal prepare.
Soon having tasted of the welcome fare,
I with the herald brave companions twain 105
Sent to explore what manner of men they were,
Who, on the green earth couched beside the main,
Seemed ever with sweet food their lips to entertain.

Who, when they came on the delightful place
Where those sat feeding by the barren wave, 110
There mingled with the Lotus-eating race;
Who nought of ruin for our comrades brave
Dreamed in their minds, but of the Lotus gave;
And whoso tasted of their flowery meat
Cared not with tidings to return, but clave 115
Fast to that tribe, for ever fain to eat,
Reckless of home-return, the tender Lotus sweet.

These sorely weeping by main strength we bore
Back to the hollow ships with all our speed,
And thrust them bound with cords upon the floor,
Under the benches: then the rest I lead 121
On board and bid them to the work give heed,
Lest others, eating of the Lotus, yearn
Always to linger in that land, and feed,
Careless for ever of the home-return: 125
Then, bending to their oars, the foamy deep they spurn.

ODYSSEUS IN THE CAVE OF POLYPHEMUS

Thence we sailed onward overwhelmed in heart,
And to the land of the Cyclopes came,
An undiscerning people, void of art
In life, and tramplers on the sacred claim 130
Of laws which men for civil uses frame.
Scorners of common weal no bounds they keep,
Nor learn with labors the rude earth to tame;
Who neither plant nor plough nor sow nor reap;
Still in the gods they trust, still careless wake and
    sleep. 135

There all good fruits on the spontaneous soil
Fed by the rain of Zeus for ever grow;
Unsown, untended, corn and wine and oil
Spring to their hand; but they no councils know
Nor justice, but for ever lawless go. 140
Housed in the hills they neither buy nor sell,
No kindly offices demand or show;
Each in the hollow cave where he doth dwell
Gives law to wife and children, as he thinketh well.

Skirting their harbor, neither near nor far, 145
A little island lies, with forest crowned,
Wherein wild goats in countless numbers are;
Since there no track of mortal men is found
Who hunt in hardship over mountain ground,
And never plough hath pierced the woodland glen.
Unvisited it lies the whole year round, 151
None their tame flocks amid those pastures pen,
Feeding wild goats, and widowed of the race of men.

Not to Cyclopian brood doth appertain
Skill in the seas, or vermeil-painted fleet 155
Of barks, which, sailing o'er the azure main,
Pass and repass wherever seemeth meet,

And all the covenants of men complete;
Nor have they shipwrights who might build them such;
Else would they soon have colonized this seat. 160
Not worthless is it, but at human touch
Would take the seasons well, and yield exceeding much.

Fast by the margin of the hoary deep
Lie soft well-watered meadows. There the vine
Would bloom for ever. If to plough and reap, 165
Observant of the hours,[1] one's heart incline,
Black with fertility the soil doth shine.
Smooth is the haven, nor is need at all
Of anchor, cable, and shore-fastened line.
Floating in shelter of the firm sea-wall 170
Sailors at will may wait till prosperous breezes call.

There a white waterfall beneath the cave
Springs forth, and flashes at the haven-head;
Round it the whispering alders darkly wave.
Thitherward sailing through the night we sped, 175
Yea, some divinity the swift ships led
Through glooms not pierceable by power of eye.
Round us the deep night-air swung listless, dead;
Nor moon nor stars looked down from the wide sky,
Hid by the gross cloud-curtain brooding heavily. 180

No mariner beheld the nearing strand,
Helmsman expert or wielder of the oar,
Nor marked the long waves rolling on the land.
Still with a steady prow we onward bore
Till the keels grated on the shelving shore. 185
Then we the sails take down, and, past the line

[1] *Hours*, in the Greek sense, *seasons*.

ODYSSEUS IN THE CAVE OF POLYPHEMUS

Of ripple, landing from the waters hoar,
Along the margin of the deep recline,
And sound asleep wait dreaming for the Dawn divine.

But when the rosy-fingered Dawn came on, 190
Child of the mist, we wondering rose apace
The beauteous island to explore anon.
And lo! the Nymphs inhabiting the place
Stirred in our sight the creatures of the chase,
That so my comrades might have food to eat. 195
Straight to the ships for bows and spears we race,
And, parted in three bands, the thickets beat;
Soon did the god vouchsafe large spoil exceeding sweet.

Me twelve ships followed, and for each we won
Nine goats; but for myself I chose out ten. 200
Thus all day long, till falling of the sun,
We sat there feasting in the hollow glen;
Cheer'ly I ween the red wine circled then;
Since of the liquor there remained much more
Sealed safely in the ships; for when our men 205
Sacked the Ciconian citadel, good store
Of wine in earthen vessels to our fleet they bore.

And on the land of the Cyclopes near
We looked, and saw their smoke, and heard their hum.
Also the bleatings of their flocks we hear, 210
Till the ambrosial Night made all things dumb.
But when the rosy-fingered Dawn was come,
I called my friends, and said: "Stay ye the rest,
While I go forward to explore with some,
Mine own ship's crew, what folk this shore infest, 215
Despiteful, wild, unjust, or of a gentle breast."

Forthwith I march on board, and bid my crew
With me their captain the tall bark ascend,
And the stern-cables vigorously undo.
They to their several tasks with zeal attend; 220
Then, sitting, to the oars' long sweep they bend,
And smite in unison the billows hoar.
Right quickly to the continent we wend;
And lo! a huge deep cave our eyes before,
Shaded about with laurels, very near the shore. 225

And all around the flocks and herds recline,
Parked by a rough-hewn fence of mountain stone,
All overhung with oak and towery pine.
There dwelt the monstrous keeper all alone,
Who in his breast no kindred ties did own, 230
But far apart, ungodly ways pursued;
Sight not resembling human flesh and bone,
But like a mountain-column, crowned with wood,
Reigning above the hills in awful solitude.

Then of my comrades I the rest command 235
To guard the well-benched ship, remaining there,
But I the while with my twelve bravest land,
And of dark wine an ample goatskin bear,
Which Maron, venerable priest and seer
Of lord Apollo, the divine defence 240
Of Ismarus, because we held him dear,
Son of Euanthes, gave us to take thence,
Whom with his wife and child we saved in reverence.

Deep-foliaged grove his dwelling doth enfold,
Phoebus Apollo's, who there keeps his shrine. 245
Rich gifts he gave me — talents seven of gold
Which curiously was wrought and well did shine,

And bowl of silver, and twelve jars of wine,
Which in his halls lay hidden out of view,
Mellow with age, unmingled, sweet, divine;   250
Known but to him the priest and other two,
His wife and chief house-dame, of all his retinue.

When they the red wine drank, he filled one cup,
Which when in twenty measures he did pour
Of water, and the scent divine rose up,   255
'T were hard to hold one's cravings any more.
Thereof a goatskin filled I with me bore,
And in a wallet did provision crowd,
For my brave heart at once foreboded sore
How I a man should meet, unpitying, proud,   260
Lawless and void of right, with giant strength endowed.

Soon to the cave we came, nor him there found,
Who 'mid the pastures with his flocks did stay.
We then the crates admire with cheeses crowned,
And the pens, packed with kids and lambs, survey
Where in his place each kind distinguished lay.   265
Here rest the firstlings, there the middle-born,
And further on the yeanlings. Brimmed with whey
Pails, ranged in ordered rank, the walls adorn —
Wherein his flocks he wont to milk at eve and
    morn.   270

With strong persuasion me my friends besought
To steal some cheeses, and return with haste
To the swift ship, and thither having brought
Both kids and fat lambs, from their pens displaced,
Sailing to vanish o'er the watery waste.   275
I, to our loss, would not persuaded be,
Wishing to see him and his cheer to taste,

If chance he lend me hospitality —
Alas! to my poor friends no welcome host proved he!

    We then for holy offerings kindle flame, 280
    Eat of the cheeses, and till eventide
    Wait. Then with flocks and herds the Cyclops came
    Bearing a mighty pile of pinewood dried,
    Wherewith his evening meal might be supplied.
    Down with a crash he cast it in the cave; 285
    We to the deep recess ran terrified.
    Anon his flocks within the walls he drave,
But to the males a place without the courtyard gave.

    Forthwith a rock stupendous with his hands
    He lifted, and athwart the entrance flung. 290
    Firm-rooted o'er the cave's deep mouth it stands.
    Not two-and-twenty wagons, four-wheeled, strong,
    Ever could move the mighty bulk along.
    Then sat he down and milked each teeming ewe
    And she-goat, and anon their eager young 295
    Under the dams disposed in order due;
And all the while thick bleatings rang the wide cave through.

    Half the white milk he curdled, and laid up
    On crates of woven wicker-work with care;
    And half he set aside in bowl and cup 300
    To stand in readiness for use, whene'er
    Thirst should invite, and for his evening fare.
    Thus he his tasks right busily essayed,
    And at the last a red flame kindled there;
    And, while the firelight o'er the cavern played, 305
Us crouching he espied, and speedy question made.

ODYSSEUS IN THE CAVE OF POLYPHEMUS

"Strangers, who are ye? from what strand unknown
Sail ye the watery ways? After some star
Of purpose, or on random courses blown
Range ye like pirates, whom no perils bar,   310
Who risk their own lives other men to mar?"
So made he question and our dear heart brake,
Scared at the dread voice searching near and far,
The rough rude accent, and the monstrous make.
Natheless, though sore cast down, I thus responding
   spake: 315

"We sons of Argos, while from Troy we keep
Straight homeward, driven by many storms astray,
Over the wide abysses of the deep,
Chance on another course, a different way.
Haply such doom upon us Zeus doth lay.   320
Also of Agamemnon, Atreus' son,
Soldiers we are, and his command obey
Whose name rings loudest underneath the sun,
City so vast he sacked, such people hath undone.

"So in our wanderings to thy knees we come   325
If thou the boon of hospitality
Would'st furnish to our wants, or render some
Of those sweet offices which none deny
To strangers. Thou at least the gods on high
Respect, most noble one! for theirs are we,   330
Who now poor suppliants on thy help rely;
Chiefly revere our guardian Zeus, for he
Avenger of all such is ever wont to be!"

So did I speak: he ruthlessly replied:
"O fool, or new from some outlandish place,   335

Who by the fear of gods hast me defied!
What then is Zeus to the Cyclopian race,
Matched with whose strength the blessèd gods are
 base?
Save that I choose to spare your heads, I trow
Zeus will not much avail you in this case.   340
But tell me where your good ship ye bestow,
At the land's end or near, that I the truth may know."

Thus spake he, urging trial of our state,
Nor caught me, in experience manifold
Well versed. With crafty words I answered
 straight: 345
" Mighty Poseidon, who the earth doth hold,
Near the far limits which your land enfold,
On the sharp rocks our vessel did impel.
Thither a great wind from the deep us rolled.
I with these comrades from the yawning hell   350
Of waters have alone escaped, the tale to tell."

He nought replied, but of my comrades twain
Seized, and like dog-whelps on the cavern-floor
Dashed them: the wet ground steamed with blood
 and brain.
Straight in his ravin limb from limb he tore   355
Fierce as a lion, and left nothing o'er;
Flesh, entrails, marrowy bones of men just killed,
Gorging. To Zeus our hands, bemoaning sore,
We raised in horror, while his maw he filled,
And human meat devoured, and milk in rivers
 swilled.   360

After his meal he lay down with the sheep.
I, at the first, was minded to go near

And in his liver slake my drawn sword deep;
But soon another mind made me forbear;
For so should we have gained destruction sheer, 365
Since never from the doorway could we move
With all our strength the stone which he set there.
We all night long with groans our anguish prove,
Till rosy-fingered Dawn shone forth in heaven above.

At dawn a fire he kindled in the cave, 370
And milked the famous flocks in order due,
And to each mother her young suckling gave.
But when the morning tasks were all gone through,
He, of my wretched comrades seizing two,
Gorged breakfast as became his savage taste, 375
And with the fat flocks from the cave withdrew.
Moved he the stone, and set it back with haste,
Lightly as on some quiver he the lid replaced;

Then toward the mountain turned with noise; but I
Sat brooding on revenge, and made my prayer 380
To Pallas, and resolved this scheme to try:
For a huge club beside the sheepfold there,
Green olive-wood, lay drying in his lair,
Cut for a staff to serve him out of doors,
Which we admiring to the mast compare 385
Of some wide merchantman with twenty oars,
Which the divine abysses of the deep explores.

Therefrom I severed as it were an ell,[1]
And bade my comrades make it smooth and round.
Then to a tapering spire I shaped it well, 390
And the green timber in the flame embrowned
For hardness; and, where dung did most abound,

[1] For *ell*, the Greek says *fathom*.

Deep in the cave the pointed stake concealed.
Anon my comrades cast their lots all round,
Which should with me the fiery weapon wield,   395
And twirl it in his eye while sleep his huge strength
   sealed.

Then were four chosen — even the very same
Whom I myself should have picked out to be
My comrades in the work — and me they name
The fifth, their captain. In the evening he   400
Came, shepherding his flocks in due degree,
Home from the hills, and all his fleecy rout
Into the wide cave urged imperiously,
Nor left one loiterer in the space without,   404
Whether from God so minded, or his own dark doubt.[1]

Soon with the great stone he blocked up the cave,
And milked the bleating flocks in order due,
And to each mother her young suckling gave.
But when the evening tasks were all gone through,
He of my wretched comrades seizing two   410
Straight on the horrible repast did sup.
Then I myself near to the Cyclops drew,
And, holding in my hands an ivy cup
Brimmed with the dark-red wine, took courage and
   spake up:

"Cyclops, take wine, and drink after thy meal   415
Consumed, of human flesh, that thou mayest know
The kind of liquor wherein we sailors deal.
This a drink-offering have I brought, that so
Thou mightest pity me and let me go
Safe homeward. Thou alas! with fury extreme   420

[1] I. e. for Odysseus' sake, or a mere presentiment of ill.

Art raving, and thy fierceness doth outgrow
All bounds of reason. How then dost thou dream
Others will seek thy place, who dost so ruthless seem?"

He then received and drank and loudly cried
Rejoicing: "Give me, give me more, and tell 425
Thy name, that some good boon I may provide.
True, the rich earth where the Cyclopes dwell,
Fed by the rain of Zeus, in wine doth well,—
But this is nectar, pure ambrosia's soul."
So spake he. Thrice I gave the fatal spell; 430
Thrice in his foolishness he quaffed the whole.
Then said I, while his brain with the curling fumes
 did roll:

"Cyclops, thou askest me my name renowned —
Now will I make it known; nor thou withhold
That boon whereto thy solemn troth is bound — 435
Hear then; My name is Noman. From of old
My father, mother, these my comrades bold,
Give me this title." So I spake, and he
Answered at once with mind of ruthless mould:
"This shall fit largess unto Noman be — 440
Last, after all thy peers, I promise to eat thee."

Therewith his head fell and he lay supine,
Tamed by the stroke of all-subduing sleep;
And the vast neck heaved, while rejected wine
And morsels of men's flesh in spasms did leap 445
Forth from his throat. Then did I rise, and deep
In the live embers hid the pointed stake,
Urging my comrades a good heart to keep.
Soon the green olive-wood the fire did bake;
Then all aglow with sparkles I the red brand take. 450

Round me my comrades wait. The gods inbreathe
Fierce ardor. In his eye we thrust the brand,
I twirling from above and they beneath.
As when a shipwright at his work doth stand
Boring ship-timber, and on either hand 455
His fellows, kneeling at their toil below,
Whirl the swift auger with a leathern band
For ever; — we the weapon keep whirling so,
While round the fiery point red blood doth bubbling
 flow.

And from the burning eyeball the fierce steam 460
Singed all his brows, and the deep roots of sight
Crackled with fire. As when in the cold stream
Some smith the axe untempered, fiery-white,
Dips hissing; for thence comes the iron's might;
So did his eye hiss, and he roared again. 465
Loudly the vault rebellowed. We in flight
Rushed diverse. He the stake wrenched forth
 amain,
Soaked in the crimson gore, and hurled it mad with
 pain;

Then, bursting forth into a mighty yell,
Called the Cyclopes, who in cave and lair 470
'Mid the deep glens and windy hill-tops dwell.
They, trooping to the shriek from far and near,
Ask from without what ails him: "In what fear
Or trouble, Polyphemus, dost thou cry
Through night ambrosial, and our slumbers scare? 475
Thee of thy flocks doth mortal violently
Despoil, or strive to kill by strength or treachery?"

And frenzied Polyphemus from the cave
This answer in his pain with shrieks out-threw:

ODYSSEUS IN THE CAVE OF POLYPHEMUS   39

"Never by strength, my friends, or courage brave! 480
Noman by treachery doth me subdue."
Whereto his fellows wingèd words renew:
"Good sooth! if no man work thee injury,
But in thy lone resort this sickness grew,
The hand of Zeus is not to be put by — 485
Go, then, in filial prayer to king Poseidon [1] cry."

So they retiring; and I laughed in heart,
To find the shrewd illusion working well.
But the dread Cyclops over every part
Groped eyeless with wild hands, in anguish fell, 490
Rolled back the massive mouthstone from the cell,
And in the door sat waving everywhere
His sightless arms, to capture or repel
Any forth venturing with his flocks to fare —
Dreaming to deal with one of all good prudence bare.

Seeking deliverance 'mid these dangers rife, 495
So deadly-near the mighty evil pressed,
All thoughts I weave as one that weaves for life,
All kinds of scheming in my spirit test;
And this of various counsels seemed the best. 500
Fat rams there were, with goodly fleeces dight
Of violet-tinted wool. These breast to breast
I silent link with osiers twisted tight,
Whereon the ill-minded Cyclops used to sleep at night.

By threes I linked them, and each middle one 505
Carried a man: one walked on either side:
Such was our plan the monster's rage to shun;
And thus three rams for each man we provide.
But I, choosing a beast than all beside

[1] Polyphemus was the son of Poseidon and a nymph.

Fairer, in length more large and strength of spine, 510
Under his belly in the woolly hide
Clinging with both hands resolute recline;
And thus, groaning in soul, we wait the Dawn divine.

But with the rosy-fingered Morn troop thence
The fat rams toward their pastures eagerly, 515
While bleat the unmilked ewes with udders tense,
Distressful. So their lord, while each went by,
Feeling their backs with many a bitter sigh,
Dreamed not that we clung bound beneath the
   breast.
Last came the great ram, trailing heavily 520
Me and his wool, with cumbrous weight oppressed.
Him mighty Polyphemus handling thus addressed:

"Ah! mine own fondling, why dost linger now
So late? — far other wast thou known of old.
With lordly steps the flowery pastures thou 525
First ever seekest, and the waters cold,
First too at eve returnest to the fold. —
Now last of all — dost thou thy master's eye
Bewail, whose dear orb, when I sank controlled
With wine, this Noman vile with infamy, 530
Backed by his rascal crew, hath darkened treacher-
   ously?

"Whom let not vaunt himself escaped this debt,
Nor think me quenched and poor and powerless;
Vengeance may chance to overtake him yet.
O hadst thou mind like mine, and couldst address 535
Thy master, and the secret lair confess
Wherein my wrath he shuns, then should his brain
Dashed on the earth with hideous stamp impress

ODYSSEUS IN THE CAVE OF POLYPHEMUS 41

Pavement and wall, appeasing the fell pain
Which from this Noman-traitor nothing-worth I
 drain!" 540

Thus spake he, and the great ram from his doors
Dismissed. A little outward from the cave
Borne with the flock we passed, and left his floors
Blood-stained behind, escaping a dire grave.
First mine own bands I loosened, and then gave 545
My friends their freedom: but the slow fat sheep,
Lengthily winding, to the ships we drave.
Joy stirred within our comrades strong and deep,
Glad of our help from doom, though forced the slain
 to weep.

Natheless their lamentations I made cease, 550
And with bent brows gave signal not to wail;
But with all haste the flock so fine of fleece
Bade them on shipboard set, and forward sail.
So they the canvas open to the gale
And with timed oarage smite the foamy mere. 555
Soon from such distance as the voice might hail
A landsman, and by shouting make him hear,
I to the Cyclops shrilled with scorn and cutting jeer:

"Cyclops, you thought to eat a poor man's friends
Here in your cavern by sheer brutal might. 560
Go to: rough vengeance on thy crime attends;
Since, in thy soul not reverencing the right,
Thy guests thou hast devoured in foul despite,
Even on thine own hearth. Therefore Zeus at last
And all the gods thine evil deeds requite." 565
So did I blow wind on his anger's blast.
He a hill-peak tore off, and the huge fragment cast

Just o'er the blue-prowed ship. As the mass fell,
Heaved in a stormy tumult the great main,
Bearing us landward on the refluent swell. 570
I a long barge-pole seize and strive and strain
To work our vessel toward the deep again,
Still beckoning to my crew to ply the oar ;
Who stoop to the strong toil and pull right fain
To twice the former distance from the shore. 575
Then stood I forth to hail the Cyclops yet once more.

Me then my friends with dear dissuasions tire
On all sides, one and other. "Desperate one!
Why wilt thou to a wild man's wrath add fire?
Hardly but now did we destruction shun, 580
So nigh that hurling had our bark undone.
Yea, let a movement of the mouth but show
Where through the billows from his rage we run,
And he with heads will strew the dark sea-flow,
And break our timbered decks — so mightily doth he throw." 585

So spake they, but so speaking could not turn
My breast large-hearted; and again I sent
Accents of wrath, his inmost soul to burn :
"Cyclops, if mortal man hereafter, bent
To know the story of this strange event, 590
Should of thy hideous blindness make demand,
Asking whence came this dire disfigurement,
Name thou Laertes-born Odysseus' hand,
Waster of walls, who dwells in Ithaca's rough land."

Then did he groaning in these words reply : 595
"Gods! the old oracles upon me break —

That warning of the antique prophecy
Which Telemus Eurymides once spake —
Skilled seer, who on our hills did auguries take,
And waxed in years amid Cyclopian race.
Of all these things did he foreshadowings make,
And well proclaimed my pitiable case,
And how this lightless brow Odysseus should deface.

" But always I some great and beauteous man
Expected, one in awful strength arrayed,
So to assail me as the legend ran.
Now one unworthy by unworthy aid
Doth blind me helpless, and with wine waylaid,
And all-too strengthless doth surpass the strong.
But come, Odysseus, let respect be paid
To thee my guest, and thou shalt sail ere long,
By the Earth-shaker wafted, free from scathe and
    wrong.

" His child am I, my sire he boasts to be,
Who if he will, none else of mortal seed
Or of the blest, can heal my wound." Thus he:
But I made answer : " Now in very deed
I would to heaven this right arm might succeed
So surely in thy death, as I am sure
That no Poseidon even, at thy need,
Thee of thine eyelessness hath power to cure.
Know well thy fatal hurt for ever shall endure."

Then to the king Poseidon he made prayer,
Lifting his hand up to the starry sky:
" Hear now, great monarch of the raven hair;
Holder of earth, Poseidon, hear my cry,
If thou my father art indeed, and I

Thy child! Or ever he the way fulfil,
Make thou Laertes-born Odysseus die,
Waster of walls! or should the high Fates will
That friends and home he see, then lone and late and
    ill   630

"Let him return on board a foreign [1] ship,
And in his house find evil!" Thus he prayed
With hand uplifted and indignant lip;
And the dark-haired one heeded what he said.
He then his hand upon a great stone laid,   635
Larger by far than that he hurled before,
And the huge mass in booming flight obeyed
The measureless impulse, and right onward bore,
There 'twixt the blue-prowed bark descending and the
    shore.

Just short of ruin; and the foaming wave   640
Whitened in boiling eddies where it fell,
And rolling toward the isle our vessel drave,
Tossed on the mane of that tumultuous swell.
There found we all our fleet defended well,
And comrades sorrow-laden on the sand,   645
Hoping if yet, past hope, the seas impel
Their long-lost friends to the forsaken strand —
Grated our keel ashore; we hurrying leap on land.

Straight from the hollow bark our prize we share,
That none might portionless come off. To me   650
The ram for my great guerdon then and there
My well-greaved comrades gave in courtesy;
Which I to Zeus, supreme in majesty,
Killed on the shore, and burned the thighs with fire:

---

[1] The Greek says *another's ship*, i. e. let his own be lost.

ODYSSEUS IN THE CAVE OF POLYPHEMUS 45

But to mine offering little heed gave he; 655
Since deep within his heart the cloud-wrapt Sire [1]
Against both friends and fleet sat musing deathful ire.

So till the sun fell did we drink and eat,
And all night long beside the billows lay,
Till blushed the hills 'neath morning's rosy feet; 660
Then did I bid my friends, with break of day,
Loosen the hawsers, and each bark array;
Who take the benches and the whitening main
Cleave with the sounding oars, and sail away.
So from the isle we part, not void of pain, 665
Right glad of our own lives, but grieving for the slain.

[1] Zeus (Jove), the "father of both gods and men."

TYRTAEUS

MILTON says that it is the function of the poet "to inbreed and cherish in a great people the seeds of virtue and public civility." On this ground, if on no other, Tyrtaeus deserves the title of poet. He was general of the Spartans during the Second Messenian war, in the seventh century before Christ, and by his patriotic verses aroused in his fellow citizens increased courage and spirit in battle, and a larger devotion to the State in peace. His songs were long sung about the Spartan camp fires.

MARTIAL ELEGY

How glorious fall the valiant, sword in hand,
In front of battle for their native land!
But oh! what ills await the wretch that yields,
A recreant outcast from his country's fields!
The mother whom he loves shall quit her home,   5
An aged father at his side shall roam;
His little ones shall weeping with him go,
And a young wife participate his woe;
While scorned and scowled upon by every face,
They pine for food, and beg from place to place.   10

Stain of his breed! dishonoring manhood's form,
All ills shall cleave to him: affliction's storm
Shall blind him wandering in the vale of years,
Till, lost to all but ignominious fears,

MARTIAL ELEGY

He shall not blush to leave a recreant's name, 15
And children, like himself, inured to shame.
But we will combat for our fathers' land,
And we will drain the life-blood where we stand,
To save our children. — Fight ye side by side,
And serried close, ye men of youthful pride, 20
Disdaining fear, and deeming light the cost
Of life itself in glorious battle lost.

Leave not our sires to stem the unequal fight,
Whose limbs are nerved no more with buoyant might;
Nor, lagging backward, let the younger breast 25
Permit the man of age (a sight unblest)
To welter in the combat's foremost thrust,
His hoary head dishevelled in the dust,
And venerable bosom bleeding bare.
But youth's fair form, though fallen, is ever fair, 30
And beautiful in death the boy appears,
The hero boy, that dies in blooming years:
In man's regret he lives, and woman's tears;
More sacred than in life, and lovelier far,
For having perished in the front of war. 35

Translated by Thomas Campbell.

ARCHILOCHUS

ARCHILOCHUS, of the island Paros, was the first poet to use the iambic metre, which afterwards played an important part in Greek verse. His birth, at about 700 B. C., was, according to the story, foretold by the Delphic oracle; and this same oracle after his death cursed the soldier who had killed him in battle, for "slaying the servant of the Muses."

His poems we hear were largely personal attacks on the family of Lycambes, who had betrothed his daughter Neobulé to the poet and then withdrawn his consent to the marriage, and the "rage" of Archilochus was noted in ancient times. But he certainly did not limit himself to invectives, for he was held in the highest esteem by the ancients, ranking indeed second only to Homer. Of his work only a few considerable fragments are extant.

TO HIS SOUL

TOSSED on a sea of troubles, Soul, my Soul,
    Thyself do thou control;
And to the weapons of advancing foes
    A stubborn breast oppose;
Undaunted 'mid the hostile might   5
Of squadrons burning for the fight.

Thine be no boasting when the victor's crown
    Wins thee deserved renown;
Thine no dejected sorrow, when defeat
    Would urge a base retreat: 10

TO HIS SOUL

Rejoice in joyous things — nor overmuch
    Let grief thy bosom touch
Midst evil, and still bear in mind
How changeful are the ways of humankind.

Translated by William Hay.

SCOLIA

The early lyric poetry of the Greeks was made up largely of songs composed for different occasions, — marriages, funerals, celebrations of victories and the like. An important class of these were "banquet songs," — *scolia*, or catches, sung as the wine-cup passed around, — which every Athenian was assumed to be ready to sing.

Of these the most celebrated in ancient times was the following, attributed to Callistratus.

A SCOLION OF CALLISTRATUS

Harmodius and Aristogeiton conspired to slay Hipparchus and his elder brother Hippias, tyrant of Athens, during the procession at the Panathenaic festival in 514 B. C. Through a mistake they succeeded in killing only Hipparchus. Harmodius was put to death at once by the tyrant's guard, and Aristogeiton soon after. After the expulsion of Hippias in 510 B. C., Harmodius and Aristogeiton became the most popular of Athenian heroes, and through a false view of their act were celebrated as the deliverers of Athens.

In a wreath of myrtle I 'll wear my glaive,
Like Harmodius and Aristogeiton brave,
    Who, striking the tyrant down,
    Made Athens a freeman's town.

Harmodius, our darling, thou art not dead!   5
Thou liv'st in the isles of the blest, 't is said,
    With Achilles first in speed,
    And Tydides Diomede.

In a wreath of myrtle I 'll wear my glaive,
Like Harmodius and Aristogeiton brave, 10
   When the twain on Athena's day
   Did the tyrant Hipparchus slay.

For aye shall your fame in the land be told,
Harmodius and Aristogeiton bold,
   Who, striking the tyrant down, 15
   Made Athens a freeman's town.
              Translated by John Conington.

A SCOLION OF HYBRIAS THE CRETAN

My wealth 's a burly spear and brand,
And a right good shield of hides untanned,
   Which on my arm I buckle:
With these I plough, I reap, I sow,
With these I make the sweet vintage flow, 5
   And all around me truckle.
But your wights that take no pride to wield
A massy spear and well-made shield,
   Nor joy to draw the sword:
O, I bring those heartless, hapless drones, 10
Down in a trice on their marrow-bones,
   To call me king and lord.
              Translated by Thomas Campbell.

THE SWALLOW SONG

   In ancient times as well as modern, the swallow was regarded as the harbinger of spring. Every year boys went from house to house in Rhodes, announcing the welcome arrival of this bird, and begging gifts in return for their good news. This is the song that they sang.

SHE is here, she is here, the swallow!
Fair seasons bringing, fair years to follow!
    Her belly is white,
    Her back black as night!
    From your rich house
    Roll forth to us
    Tarts, wine, and cheese:
    Or if not these,
    Oatmeal and barley-cake
    The swallow deigns to take.
What shall we have? or must we hence away?
Thanks, if you give; if not, we 'll make you pay!
    The house-door hence we 'll carry;
    Nor shall the lintel tarry;
    From hearth and home your wife we 'll rob;
    She is so small,
To take her off will be an easy job!
Whate'er you give, give largess free!
Up! open, open to the swallow's call!
No grave old men, but merry children we!
        Translated by John Addington Symonds.

ALCAEUS

ALL the poets from whose works extracts have been given, with the exception of Tyrtaeus, were Ionians. But in the perfection of lyric poetry the Ionians have no place, and the Aeolians and Dorians hold the lead side by side. This difference existed between them, however, that the Aeolians sang solos, treating of their own joys and sorrows, while the Dorians composed complex odes, for a trained chorus, in celebration of public events.

Alcaeus was a noble of Mytilene, the chief town of Lesbos, who flourished as early as 612 B. C. His life was spent largely in war, party strife, and wanderings, and its character is reflected in his poems, of which only a few fragments remain.

The following poem has been imitated by Horace, in the ninth Ode of his first book.

WINTER

THE rain of Zeus descends, and from high heaven
    A storm is driven:
And on the running water-brooks the cold
    Lays icy hold:
Then up! beat down the winter; make the fire
    Blaze high and higher;
Mix wine as sweet as honey of the bee
    Abundantly;
Then drink with comfortable wool around
    Your temples bound.

We must not yield our hearts to woe, or wear
    With wasting care ;
For grief will profit us no whit, my friend,
    Nor nothing mend ;
But this is our best medicine, with wine fraught   15
    To cast out thought.
Translated by John Addington Symonds.

SAPPHO

SAPPHO, living near the time of Alcaeus, and composing verses in similar metrical and musical forms, far surpassed him. In both ancient and modern times she has been regarded as the greatest love poet of Greece. As Homer is called "The Poet," so is she "The Poetess," and Plato has an epigram —

> "Some thoughtlessly proclaim the Muses nine;
> A tenth is Lesbian Sappho, maid divine."

Little is known of her life, and the stories told of her are so inconsistent that we must rely for our knowledge of her upon her verses. She lived in Mytilene near the beginning of the sixth century before Christ, and was the leader of a coterie of women devoted to the pursuit of music and poesy. Tradition tells of her rejection of Alcaeus' love, and of her own unrequited passion for Phaon, for whose sake she leaped from the Leucadian cliff into the sea. False as these stories probably are, it is at least certain that her verses are written chiefly on one theme — that of love.

HYMN TO VENUS

IMMORTAL Venus, throned above
In radiant beauty, child of Jove,
O skilled in every art of love
    And artful snare;
Dread power, to whom I bend the knee,
Release my soul and set it free

From bonds of piercing agony
    And gloomy care.
Yet come thyself, if e'er, benign,
Thy listening ears thou didst incline   10
To my rude lay, the starry shine
    Of Jove's court leaving,
In chariot yoked with coursers fair,[1]
Thine own immortal birds that bear
Thee swift to earth, the middle air   15
    With bright wings cleaving.
Soon they were sped — and thou, most blest,
In thine own smiles ambrosial dressed,
Didst ask what griefs my mind oppressed —
    What meant my song —   20
What end my frenzied thoughts pursue —
For what loved youth I spread anew
My amorous nets — "Who, Sappho, who
    Hath done thee wrong?
What though he fly, he'll soon return —   25
Still press thy gifts, though now he spurn;
Heed not his coldness — soon he'll burn,
    E'en though thou chide."
— And saidst thou thus, dread goddess? O,
Come then once more to ease my woe;   30
Grant all, and thy great self bestow,
    My shield and guide!
            Translated by John Herman Merivale.

TO A LOVED ONE

Blest as the immortal gods is he,
The youth who fondly sits by thee,
And hears and sees thee all the while
Softly speak and sweetly smile.

[1] The chariot of Venus was drawn by doves.

TO AN UNCULTURED LESBIAN WOMAN

'T was this deprived my soul of rest,   5
And raised such tumults in my breast;
For while I gazed, in transport tost,
My breath was gone, my voice was lost:

My bosom glowed; the subtle flame
Ran quick through all my vital frame;   10
O'er my dim eyes a darkness hung;
My ears with hollow murmurs rung.

In dewy damps my limbs were chilled;
My blood with gentle horror thrilled;
My feeble pulse forgot to play;   15
I fainted, sank, and died away.
                      Translated by Ambrose Phillips.

"INTER IGNES LUNA MINORES"

THE stars around the lovely moon
Fade back and vanish very soon,
When, round and full, her silver face
Swims into sight, and lights all space.
                      Translated by Edwin Arnold.

TO AN UNCULTURED LESBIAN WOMAN

YEA, thou shalt die,
And lie
  Dumb in the silent tomb;
Nor of thy name
Shall there be any fame   5
  In ages yet to be or years to come:
  For of the flowering Rose

    Which on Pieria [1] blows,
      Thou hast no share:
    But in sad Hades' house,   10
      Unknown, inglorious
'Mid the dim shades that wander there
Shalt thou flit forth and haunt the filmy air.
Translated by John Addington Symonds.

A GIRL IN LOVE

"Oh, my sweet mother, 't is in vain,
I cannot weave as once I wove,
So 'wildered is my heart and brain
With thinking of that youth I love."
Translated by Thomas Moore.

ONE GIRL

I.

Like the sweet apple which reddens upon the topmost bough,
A-top on the topmost twig, — which the pluckers forgot, somehow, —
Forgot it not, nay! but got it not, for none could get it till now.

II.

Like the wild hyacinth flower which on the hills is found,
Which the passing feet of the shepherds for ever tear and wound,
Until the purple blossom is trodden into the ground.
Translated by Dante Gabriel Rossetti.

---

[1] The Muses received their name Pierian from Pieria on the northern slopes of Mount Olympus in Thessaly, where was their early home.

TO EVENING

O HESPERUS![1] Thou bringest all things home;
All that the garish day hath scattered wide;
The sheep, the goat, back to the welcome fold;
Thou bring'st the child, too, to his mother's side.
Translated by William Hyde Appleton.

[1] The evening star.

ANACREON

ANACREON of Teos, although an Ionian by birth, is generally reckoned with Alcaeus and Sappho among the Aeolians, because he "cultivated the lyrical stanza of personal emotion." His Ionian temperament, however, influences his verses to such an extent that they lose the intensity and sincerity of those of Alcaeus and Sappho, although they keep the grace and delicacy of style of these earlier poets.

Anacreon was essentially a court poet, although it was at a different court from time to time that he made his home, — first under the patronage of Polycrates in Samos, then with Hipparchus at Athens. He died probably at the court of a Thessalian prince at the end of the sixth century B. C. His songs rarely touched on themes more serious than love and wine, and make it hard to find the man behind the poet. The wide popularity of his verses incited many to imitate them, and most of the writings which have come down to us under his name are "Anacreontics," works of authors of unknown later periods.

The translations that follow are all from the Anacreontics, made by Thomas Moore.

ANACREONTICS

OLD AGE. ODE VII.

THE women tell me every day
That all my bloom has past away.
"Behold," the pretty wantons cry,
"Behold this mirror with a sigh;

The locks upon thy brow are few,
And, like the rest, they 're withering too! "
Whether decline has thinned my hair,
I 'm sure I neither know, nor care;
But this I know and this I feel,
As onward to the tomb I steal,
That still as death approaches nearer,
The joys of life are sweeter, dearer;
And had I but an hour to live,
That little hour to bliss I 'd give.

THE WISER PART. ODE VIII.

I care not for the idle state
Of Persia's king, the rich, the great:
I envy not the monarch's throne
Nor wish the treasur'd gold my own.
But oh! be mine the rosy wreath,
Its freshness o'er my brow to breathe;
Be mine the rich perfumes that flow,
To cool and scent my locks of snow.
To-day I 'll haste to quaff my wine,
As if to-morrow ne'er would shine;
But if to-morrow comes, why then —
I 'll haste to quaff my wine again.
And thus while all our days are bright,
Nor time has dimmed their bloomy light,
Let us the festal hours beguile
With mantling cup and cordial smile;
And shed from each new bowl of wine
The richest drop on Bacchus' shrine.
For Death may come, with brow unpleasant,
May come, when least we wish him present,
And beckon to the sable shore,
And grimly bid us — drink no more!

TO A SWALLOW. ODE X.

How am I to punish thee,
For the wrong thou 'st done to me,
Silly swallow, prating thing —
Shall I clip that wheeling wing?
Or, as Tereus [1] did, of old,   5
(So the fabled tale is told,)
Shall I tear that tongue away,
Tongue that utter'd such a lay?
Ah, how thoughtless hast thou been!
Long before the dawn was seen,   10
When a dream came o'er my mind,
Picturing her I worship, kind,
Just when I was nearly blest,
Loud thy matins broke my rest!

LOVE'S ASSAULT. ODE XIII.

I will, I will, the conflict's past,
And I'll consent to love at last.
Cupid has long, with smiling art,
Invited me to yield my heart;
And I have thought that peace of mind   5
Should not be for a smile resign'd;
And so repell'd the tender lure,
And hop'd my heart would sleep secure.

But, slighted in his boasted charms,
The angry infant flew to arms;   10
He slung his quiver's golden frame,
He took his bow, his shafts of flame,
And proudly summoned me to yield,
Or meet him on the martial field.

---

[1] Tereus cut out the tongue of his wife's sister, Philomela, to prevent her telling the wrong he had done her.

And what did I unthinking do? 15
I took to arms, undaunted, too;
Assum'd the corslet, shield, and spear,
And, like Pelides,[1] smil'd at fear.
Then (hear it, all ye powers above!)
I fought with Love! I fought with Love! 20

And now his arrows all were shed,
And I had just in terror fled —
When, hearing an indignant sigh,
To see me thus unwounded fly,
And having now no other dart, 25
He shot himself into my heart!
My heart — alas the luckless day!
Receiv'd the God, and died away.
Farewell, farewell, my faithless shield!
Thy lord at length is forc'd to yield. 30
Vain, vain, is every outward care,
The foe's within, and triumphs there.

THE PET DOVE. ODE XV.

"Tell me,[2] why, my sweetest dove,
Thus your humid pinions move,
Shedding through the air in showers
Essence of the balmiest flowers?
Tell me whither, whence you rove, 5
Tell me all, my sweetest dove."

"Curious stranger, I belong
To the bard of Teian[3] song;

---

[1] Achilles, the son of Peleus.

[2] The first six verses are addressed by a stranger to Anacreon's dove, who is bearing a note from the poet to his mistress. The dove replies.

[3] Anacreon was born at Teos.

With his mandate now I fly
To the nymph of azure eye; —
She, whose eye has madden'd many,
But the poet more than any.
Venus, for a hymn of love,
Warbled in her votive grove,
('T was in sooth a gentle lay,)
Gave me to the bard away.[1]
See me now his faithful minion, —
Thus with softly-gliding pinion,
To his lovely girl I bear
Songs of passion through the air.
Oft he blandly whispers me,
'Soon, my bird, I 'll set you free,'
But in vain he 'll bid me fly,
I shall serve him till I die.
Never could my plumes sustain
Ruffling winds and chilling rain,
O'er the plains, or in the dell,
On the mountain's savage swell,
Seeking in the desert wood
Gloomy shelter, savage food.
Now I lead a life of ease,
Far from rugged haunts like these.
From Anacreon's hand I eat
Food delicious, viands sweet;
Flutter o'er his goblet's brim,
Sip the foamy wine with him.
Then, when I have wanton'd round
To his lyre's beguiling sound;
Or with gently-moving wings
Fann'd the minstrel while he sings:

[1] Since the dove was Venus' own bird she could fitly bestow it as reward for a song.

On his harp I sink in slumbers,
Dreaming still of dulcet numbers!

"This is all — away — away —
You have made me waste the day.
How I 've chatter'd! prating crow 45
Never yet did chatter so."

THE PORTRAIT. ODE XVI.

Thou, whose soft and rosy hues
Mimic form and soul infuse,
Best of painters, come portray
The lovely maid that 's far away.
Far away, my soul! thou art, 5
But I 've thy beauties all by heart.
Paint her jetty ringlets playing,
Silky locks, like tendrils straying;
And, if painting hath the skill
To make the spicy balm distil, 10
Let every little lock exhale
A sigh of perfume on the gale.
Where her tresses' curly flow
Darkles o'er the brow of snow,
Let her forehead beam to light, 15
Burnish'd as the ivory bright.
Let her eyebrows smoothly rise
In jetty arches o'er her eyes,
Each, a crescent gently gliding,
Just commingling, just dividing. 20

But hast thou any sparkles warm,
The lightning of her eyes to form?
Let them effuse the azure rays
That in Minerva's glances blaze,

Mix'd with the liquid light that lies 25
In Cytherea's [1] languid eyes.
O'er her nose and cheek be shed
Flushing white and soften'd red ;
Mingling tints, as when there glows
In snowy milk the bashful rose. 30
Then her lip, so rich in blisses,
Sweet petitioner for kisses,
Rosy nest, where lurks Persuasion,
Mutely courting Love's invasion.
Next, beneath the velvet chin, 35
Whose dimple hides a Love within,
Mould her neck with grace descending,
In a heaven of beauty ending ;
While countless charms, above, below,
Sport and flutter round its snow. 40
Now let a floating, lucid veil
Shadow her form, but not conceal ;
A charm may peep, a hue may beam,
And leave the rest to Fancy's dream.
Enough — 't is she ! 't is all I seek ; 45
It glows, it lives, it soon will speak !

DRINKING SONG. ODE XXI.

Observe when Mother Earth is dry,
She drinks the droppings of the sky ;
And then the dewy cordial gives
To ev'ry thirsty plant that lives.
The vapours, which at evening weep, 5
Are beverage to the swelling deep ;
And when the rosy sun appears,
He drinks the ocean's misty tears.

---

[1] Venus took this name from the island of Cythera, one of her favorite haunts, near Sparta.

The moon, too, quaffs her paly stream
Of lustre, from the solar beam.
Then, hence with all your sober thinking!
Since Nature's holy law is drinking;
I'll make the laws of nature mine,
And pledge the universe in wine.

MUSIC AND LOVE. ODE XXIII.

I often wish this languid lyre,
This warbler of my soul's desire,
Could raise the breath of song sublime,
To men of fame in former time.
But when the soaring theme I try,
Along the chords my numbers die,
And whisper, with dissolving tone,
" Our sighs are given to love alone!"
Indignant at the feeble lay,
I tore the panting chords away,[1]
Attun'd them to a nobler swell,
And struck again the breathing shell;[2]
In all the glow of epic fire,
To Hercules I wake the lyre;
But still its fainting sighs repeat,
"The tale of love alone is sweet!"
Then fare thee well, seductive dream,
That mad'st me follow Glory's theme,
For thou my lyre, and thou my heart,
Shall never more in spirit part;
And all that one has felt so well
The other shall as sweetly tell!

[1] I. e., he tried new strings for his lyre.
[2] The sounding board of the early lyres was formed of a tortoise-shell.

NATURE'S GIFTS. ODE XXIV.

To all that breathe the air of heaven,
Some boon of strength has Nature given.
In forming the majestic bull,
She fenced with wreathèd horns his skull;
A hoof of strength she lent the steed,   5
And wing'd the timorous hare with speed.
She gave the lion fangs of terror,
And o'er the ocean's crystal mirror
Taught the unnumber'd scaly throng
To trace their liquid path along;   10
While for the umbrage of the grove,
She plum'd the warbling world of love.
To man she gave, in that proud hour,
The boon of intellectual power.
Then what, O woman, what for thee,   15
Was left in Nature's treasury?
She gave thee beauty — mightier far
Than all the pomp and power of war.
Nor steel, nor fire itself hath power
Like woman in her conquering hour.   20
Be thou but fair, mankind adore thee,
Smile, and a world is weak before thee!

SIMONIDES OF CEOS.

BEFORE Simonides, Greek lyric poetry had been chiefly of the personal and individual type. But the increased prominence of the national games in the sixth century B. C., and the Persian wars in the early part of the fifth century, tended to draw the Hellenes together, and to stimulate a national spirit and a national lyric.

The poet's long life covered a period of great importance to his country. Born about 556 B. C., in the age of the Tyrants at Athens, he lived to see the overthrow of the Peisistratidae, the Ionic Revolt, the two Persian invasions, and the establishment of Athens as the leader of Hellas, before his death in 467 B. C. Among his friends were all the great men of the time, — kings and tyrants like Hipparchus at Athens, and Hiero at Syracuse, and the Thessalian princes; statesmen like Pausanias of Sparta and the Athenian Themistocles; and poets like Aeschylus, Anacreon, and Bacchylides.

Simonides lived mainly at the courts of his friends, whose praises he sang in return for gifts; but he identified himself heartily with the Greeks in their struggle for freedom. The patriotic spirit of his epitaphs on those who fell in the Persian Wars has hardly been surpassed. Many of his choral odes celebrated victories in the national games. He achieved distinction in his dirges as well, and from the delicacy and tenderness of his style won from the ancients the name of *Melicertes — the sweet poet*. He was the most productive of all the Greek lyric poets.

DANAË AND HER BABE ADRIFT [1]

When, in the carven chest,
The winds that blew and waves in wild unrest
Smote her with fear, she, not with cheeks unwet,
    Her arms of love round Perseus set,
    And said: " O child, what grief is mine!   5
But thou dost slumber, and thy baby breast
    Is sunk in rest,
Here in the cheerless brass-bound bark,
Tossed amid starless night and pitchy dark.
    Nor dost thou heed the scudding brine   10
Of waves that wash above thy curls so deep,
Nor the shrill winds that sweep, —
Lapped in thy purple robe's embrace,
    Fair little face!
But if this dread were dreadful too to thee,   15
Then wouldst thou lend thy listening ear to me;
Therefore I cry, — Sleep, babe, and sea, be still,
And slumber our unmeasured ill!
    Oh, may some change of fate, sire Zeus, from thee
Descend, our woes to end!   20
But if this prayer, too overbold, offend
    Thy justice, yet be merciful to me!"

                  Translated by John Addington Symonds.

[1] Danaë was imprisoned in a tower by her father Acrisius, in consequence of an oracle which predicted that he would be slain by his daughter's son. Nevertheless Zeus visited her in a shower of gold, and she bore a son, Perseus. She and her child were then shut up in a chest by her father, and thrown out to sea.

ON THOSE WHO DIED AT THERMOPYLAE [1]

OF those who at Thermopylae were slain,
  Glorious the doom, and beautiful the lot;
Their tomb an altar: men from tears refrain
  To honor them, and praise, but mourn them not.
Such sepulchre, nor drear decay   5
Nor all-destroying time shall waste; this right have
  they.
Within their grave the home-bred glory
  Of Greece was laid: this witness gives
Leonidas the Spartan, in whose story   10
  A wreath of famous virtue ever lives.

Translated by John Sterling.

[1] When the Persians invaded Greece in 480 B. C., Leonidas, king of Sparta, went to hold the pass of Thermopylae against them. When by a circuitous route the Persians entered the pass, Leonidas dismissed his army except three hundred Spartans and seven hundred Thespians, who died on the field faithful to their trust.

PINDAR

THE different kinds of Greek literature during the classical age existed not so much side by side as successively. In modern times, Tennyson and Goethe composed not only lyric and dramatic poems, but also epics on a small scale, but in Greece no single poet tried his powers in these three classes of literature; still less did he compose not only all kinds of poetry, but also artistic and scientific prose. Probably lyric poetry, songs in praise of the gods, songs of love and of war, songs of joy and of grief, preceded epic poetry in Greece as in India; but these earliest lays have all perished. Greek lyric poetry as we know it was in its beginning when the light of epic poetry was waning, and it passed its highest glory before dramatic poetry reached its zenith. And though the drama had but a short life, its glory was passing before the historian's art was perfected, and this in turn yielded to oratory and the dialogues of Philosophy. Bucolic poetry was the only new kind of literature to be developed after the middle of the fourth century before the beginning of our era.

Greek lyric poetry had two main divisions,—the Aeolic personal poetry of Asia Minor, that of Sappho and Alcaeus, which served as a model to the Roman Horace; and the choral poetry which flourished particularly among the Dorians, and from which Attic tragedy with its choral songs was developed. To the latter division belongs the poetry of Alcman, Simonides, and Pindar.

Pindar, the greatest and the last of the great lyric poets of Greece, was almost the exact contemporary of Aeschylus, the earliest and the most lyric of the great dramatic poets. He was born near Thebes in the summer of 522 B. C., and studied music and poetry at Athens, where he must have known Aeschylus.

The works of Pindar were collected by the scholars of the Alexandrian library and divided into seventeen "books" or parts. Of these, three books are extant and probably most of a fourth, all but two or three of the forty-four odes being in celebration of victories in the national games of Greece, — the Olympian held in Elis, the Pythian at Delphi, the Isthmian at Corinth, and the Nemean at Nemea. The ode does not in any case describe the contest in which the victory was won, but only indicates it. The games, like all the festivals of the Greeks, were religious in their origin, being held in honor of some god, and the odes of victory are very like Greek hymns. The heart of each of the longer odes is formed by a myth, which if possible is connected with the family or home of the victor, or if not, at least with the foundation of the games themselves.

Not every victory could be celebrated by a Pindaric ode, and naturally Pindar's patrons were for the most part princes or men of wealth. None but men of Greek blood could take part in these Greek games, and the princes of Sicily and Cyrene seem to have been particularly eager to bind more firmly and openly the tie which bound them to their kinsmen in Greece by taking part in the contests at least by proxy, sending a saddle horse or a chariot and four horses to contend in the races. Thus Hiero of Syracuse, who was a patron of literature and drew to his court also Aeschylus and Simonides, Thero of Agrigentum, and Arcesilaus of Cyrene called the "Theban eagle" to celebrate their victories, and by his songs he built for them "monuments more enduring than brass."

FIRST PYTHIAN ODE.

In honor of a victory with the chariot in the Pythian Games won by Hiero, king of Syracuse, in 470 B. C. Reference is made to a recent volcanic eruption of Mt. Aetna, and to the newly founded city Aetna, which Hiero had recently established with a Spartan constitution, near the foot of that mountain, on the site of the modern Catania. There Hiero had made his son Deinomenes king. Matthew Arnold paraphrases part of this ode in his *Empedocles on Etna.*

HAIL, golden lyre! whose heav'n-invented string
   To Phoebus and the black-hair'd nine belongs;
Who in sweet chorus round their tuneful king
   Mix with thy sounding chords their sacred songs.
The dance, gay queen of pleasure, thee attends;   5
   Thy jocund strains her list'ning feet inspire;
And each melodious tongue its voice suspends
   Till thou, great leader of the heav'nly quire,
With wanton art preluding giv'st the sign —
Swells the full concert then with harmony divine.   10

Then, of their streaming lightnings all disarm'd,
   The smould'ring thunderbolts of Jove expire;
Then, by the music of thy numbers charm'd,
   The birds' fierce monarch drops his vengeful ire;
Perch'd on the sceptre of th' Olympian king,   15
   The thrilling darts of harmony he feels;
And indolently hangs his rapid wing,
   While gentle sleep his closing eyelid seals;
And o'er his heaving limbs in loose array
To ev'ry balmy gale the ruffling feathers play.   20

Ev'n Mars, stern god of violence and war,
   Soothes with thy lulling strains his furious breast,

FIRST PYTHIAN ODE

And driving from his heart each bloody care,
   His pointed lance consigns to peaceful rest.
Nor less enraptur'd each immortal mind
   Owns the soft influence of enchanting song,
When, in melodious symphony combin'd,
   Thy son,[1] Latona, and the tuneful throng
Of muses, skill'd in wisdom's deepest lore,
The subtle pow'rs of verse and harmony explore.

But they, on earth, or the devouring main,
   Whom righteous Jove with detestation views,
With envious horror hear the heav'nly strain,
   Exil'd from praise, from virtue, and the muse.
Such is Typhoeus,[2] impious foe of gods,
   Whose hundred headed form Cilicia's cave
Once foster'd in her infamous abodes;
   Till daring with presumptuous arms to brave
The might of thund'ring Jove, subdued he fell,
Plung'd in the horrid dungeons of profoundest hell.

Now under sulph'rous Cumae's sea-bound coast,
   And vast Sicilia lies his shaggy breast;
By snowy Aetna, nurse of endless frost,
   The pillar'd prop of heav'n, for ever press'd:
Forth from whose nitrous caverns issuing rise
   Pure liquid fountains of tempestuous fire,
And veil in ruddy mists the noon-day skies,
   While wrapt in smoke the eddying flames
      aspire,

[1] Apollo.
[2] Typhoeus or Typhon, an enemy of Zeus, is supposed by Homer to lie beneath the Cilician plain, in the "earthquake belt" of Asia Minor. But now that Mt. Aetna is an active volcano, Pindar transfers him thither, and he is said to extend from Cumae's coast (i. e. Mt. Vesuvius) to Sicily (Mt. Aetna).

Or gleaming thro' the night with hideous roar
Far o'er the redd'ning main huge rocky fragments
    pour. 50

But he, vulcanian monster, to the clouds
    The fiercest, hottest inundations throws,
While with the burthen of incumbent woods,
    And Aetna's gloomy cliffs o'erwhelm'd he glows.
There on his flinty bed out-stretch'd he lies, 55
    Whose pointed rock his tossing carcase wounds:
There with dismay he strikes beholding eyes,
    Or frights the distant ear with horrid sounds.
O save us from thy wrath, Sicilian Jove!
Thou, that here reign'st, ador'd in Aetna's sacred
    grove: 60

Aetna, fair forehead of this fruitful land!
    Whose borrow'd name adorns the royal town,
Rais'd by illustrious Hiero's gen'rous hand,
    And render'd glorious with his high renown.
By Pythian heralds were her praises sung, 65
    When Hiero triumph'd in the dusty course,
When sweet Castalia with applauses rung,
    And glorious laurels crown'd the conqu'ring
    horse.
The happy city for her future days
Presages hence increase of victory and praise. 70

Thus when the mariners to prosp'rous winds,
    The port forsaking, spread their swelling sails;
The fair departure cheers their jocund minds
    With pleasing hopes of favorable gales,
While o'er the dang'rous deserts of the main, 75
    To their lov'd country they pursue their ways.

Ev'n so, Apollo, thou, whom Lycia's plain,
  Whom Delus, and Castalia's springs obey,
These hopes regard, and Aetna's glory raise
With valiant sons, triumphant steeds, and heav'nly
    lays! 80

For human virtue from the gods proceeds;
  They the wise mind bestow'd, and smooth'd the
    tongue
With elocution, and for mighty deeds
The nervous arm with manly vigor strung.
All these are Hiero's: these to rival lays 85
  Call forth the bard. Arise then, Muse, and
    speed
To this contention; strive in Hiero's praise,
  Nor fear thy efforts shall his worth exceed;
Within the lines of truth secure to throw,
Thy dart shall still surpass each vain attempting
    foe. 90

So may succeeding ages, as they roll,
  Great Hiero still in wealth and bliss maintain,
And joyous health recalling, on his soul
  Oblivion pour of life-consuming pain.
Yet may thy memory with sweet delight 95
  The various dangers and the toils recount,
Which in intestine wars and bloody fight
  Thy patient virtue, Hiero, did surmount;
What time, by Heav'n above all Grecians crown'd,
The prize of sov'reign sway with thee thy brother
    found. 100

Then like the son of Poean didst thou war,
  Smit with the arrows of a sore disease;

While, as along slow rolls thy sickly car,
　　Love and amaze the haughtiest bosoms seize.
In Lemnos pining with th' envenom'd wound　　105
　　The son of Poean, Philoctetes,[1] lay :
There, after tedious quest, the heroes found,
　　And bore the limping archer thence away ;
By whom fell Priam's tow'rs (so Fate ordain'd)
And the long harass'd Greeks their wish'd repose
　　　　obtain'd.　　110

May Hiero too, like Poean's son, receive
　　Recover'd vigor from celestial hands!
And may the healing God proceed to give
　　The pow'r to gain whate'er his wish demands.
But now, O Muse, address thy sounding lays　　115
　　To young Dinomenes, his virtuous heir.
Sing to Dinomenes his father's praise ;
　　His father's praise shall glad his filial ear.
For him hereafter shalt thou touch the string,
And chant in friendly strains fair Aetna's future king.

Hiero for him th' illustrious city rear'd,　　121
　　And fill'd with sons of Greece her stately tow'rs,
Where by the free-born citizen rever'd
　　The Spartan laws exert their virtuous pow'rs.
For by the statutes, which their fathers gave,　　125
　　Still must the restive Dorian youth be led ;
Who dwelling once on cold Eurotas' wave,[2]

[1] The Greeks on their way to Troy abandoned Philoctetes at Lemnos, but were obliged to seek his aid.

[2] The Eurotas flows past Sparta, and Mt. Taÿgetus rises high above the city. The Spartans derived their origin from Doris on the slopes of Pindus. Amyclae was the old capital of Lacedaemon. The "Twins of Leda" were Castor and Pollux, whose sanctuary was near Amyclae.

FIRST PYTHIAN ODE

Where proud Taÿgetus exalts his head,
From the great stock of Hercules divine
And warlike Pamphylus deriv'd their noble line. 130

These from Thessalian Pindus rushing down,
The walls of fam'd Amyclae once possess'd,
And rich in fortune's gifts and high renown,
Dwelt near the twins of Leda, while they press'd
Their milky coursers, and the pastures o'er 135
Of neighb'ring Argos rang'd, in arms supreme.
To king and people on the flow'ry shore
Of lucid Amenas, Sicilian stream,
Grant the like fortune, Jove, with like desert
The splendor of their race and glory to assert. 140

And do thou aid Sicilia's hoary lord
To form and rule his son's obedient mind;
And still in golden chains of sweet accord,
And mutual peace the friendly people bind.
Then grant, O Son of Saturn, grant my pray'r! 145
The bold Phoenician[1] on his shore detain;
And may the hardy Tuscan never dare
To vex with clam'rous war Sicilia's main;
Rememb'ring Hiero, how on Cumae's coast
Wreck'd by his stormy arms their groaning fleets
    were lost. 150

What terrors! what destruction then assail'd!
Hurl'd from their riven decks what numbers died!
When o'er their might Sicilia's chief prevail'd,
Their youth o'erwhelming in the foamy tide,
Greece from impending servitude to save. 155
Thy favor, glorious Athens! to acquire

[1] I. e. the western Phoenician, or Carthaginian.

Would I record the Salaminian wave [1]
Fam'd in thy triumphs; and my tuneful lyre
To Sparta's sons with sweetest praise should tell,
Beneath Cithaeron's shade [2] what Medish archers fell.

But on fair Himera's wide-water'd shores [3]   161
   Thy sons, Dinomenes, my lyre demand,
To grace their virtues with the various stores
   Of sacred verse, and sing th' illustrious band
Of valiant brothers, who from Carthage won   165
   The glorious meed of conquest, deathless praise.
A pleasing theme! but censure's dreaded frown
   Compels me to contract my spreading lays.
In verse conciseness pleases ev'ry guest,
While each impatient blames and loathes a tedious
      feast.   170

Nor less distasteful is excessive fame
   To the sour palate of the envious mind;
Who hears with grief his neighbor's goodly name,
   And hates the fortune that he ne'er shall find.
Yet in thy virtue, Hiero, persevere!   175
   Since to be envied is a nobler fate
Than to be pitied. Let strict justice steer
   With equitable hand the helm of state,
And arm thy tongue with truth. O king, beware
Of ev'ry step! a prince can never lightly err.   180

O'er many nations art thou set, to deal
   The goods of fortune with impartial hand;

---

[1] Referring to the battle of Salamis, 480 B. C.

[2] Referring to the battle of Plataea, 479 B. C.

[3] The poet thus compares the battle of Himera, 480 B. C., won by Hiero and his brothers (sons of Dinomenes the elder) over the Carthaginians, with the battles of Salamis and Plataea.

And ever watchful of the public weal,
　Unnumber'd witnesses around thee stand.
Then, would thy virtuous ear for ever feast
　On the sweet melody of well-earn'd fame,
In gen'rous purposes confirm thy breast,
　Nor dread expenses that will grace thy name;
But scorning sordid and unprincely gain,
Spread all thy bounteous sails, and launch into the main.

When in the mould'ring urn the monarch lies,
　His fame in lively characters remains,
Or grav'd in monumental histories,
　Or deck'd and painted in Aonian [1] strains.
Thus fresh, and fragrant, and immortal blooms
　The virtue, Croesus, of thy gentle mind.
While fate to infamy and hatred dooms
　Sicilia's tyrant,[2] scorn of human kind;
Whose ruthless bosom swell'd with cruel pride,
When in his brazen bull the broiling wretches died.

Him therefore nor in sweet society
　The gen'rous youth conversing ever name,
Nor with the harp's delightful melody
　Mingle his odious inharmonious fame.
The first, the greatest bliss on man conferr'd
　Is in the acts of virtue to excel;
The second, to obtain their high reward,
　The soul-exalting praise of doing well.
Who both these lots attains, is bless'd indeed,
Since fortune here below can give no richer meed.

　　　　　　　　Translated by Gilbert West.

[1] I. e. of the Muses.
[2] Phalaris, tyrant of Agrigentum (*Girgenti*), who was said to roast men alive in a bronze bull.

FROM PINDAR'S FOURTH PYTHIAN ODE

Part of the description of the expedition of the Argonauts to Colchis for the Golden Fleece, which was in the possession of King Aietes, son of Helios, and father of Medea, who was skilled in sorcery. The Golden Fleece was the skin of the wonderful ram which had borne Phrixus from danger in Greece, and had been sacrificed by him in Asia.

AND with breezes of the South they came wafted to the mouth of the Axine[1] sea; there they founded a shrine and sacred close of Poseidon, god of seas, where was a red herd of Thracian bulls, and a new-built altar of stone with hollow top.

Then as they set forth toward an exceeding peril they prayed the lord of ships that they might shun the terrible shock of the jarring rocks:[2] for they were twain that had life, and plunged along more swiftly than the legions of the bellowing winds; but that travel of the seed of gods made end of them at last.

After that they came to the Phasis; there they fought with dark-faced Colchians even in the presence of Aietes. And there the queen of keenest darts, the Cyprus-born,[3] first brought to men from Olympus the frenzied bird, the speckled wry-neck, binding it to a four-spoked wheel without deliverance, and taught the son of Aison[4] to be wise in prayers and charms, that he might make Medea take no thought to honor her

[1] *Axine* is *inhospitable*, — the early name of the Black Sea, which was later called *Euxine*, or *hospitable*.
[2] The "justling rocks," which lay at the mouth of the Black Sea, were thought to clash together until the Argo passed through safely.
[3] Aphrodite, the Roman Venus.
[4] Jason, leader of the Argonauts.

parents, and longing for Hellas might drive her by persuasion's lash, her heart afire with love.

Then speedily she showed him the accomplishment of the tasks her father set, and mixing drugs with oil gave him for his anointment antidotes of cruel pain, and they vowed to be joined together in sweet wedlock.

But when Aietes had set in the midst a plough of adamant, and oxen that from tawny jaws breathed flame of blazing fire, and with bronze hoofs smote the earth in alternate steps, and had led them and yoked them single-handed, he marked out in a line straight furrows, and for a fathom's length clave the back of the loamy earth; then he spake thus: "This work let your king, whosoever he be that hath command of the ship, accomplish me, and then let him bear away with him the imperishable coverlet, the fleece glittering with tufts of gold."

He said, and Jason flung off from him his saffron mantle, and putting his trust in God betook himself to the work; and the fire made him not to shrink, for that he had had heed to the bidding of the stranger maiden skilled in all pharmacy. So he drew to him the plough and made fast by force the bulls' necks in the harness, and plunged the wounding goad into the bulk of their huge sides, and with manful strain fulfilled the measure of his work. And a cry without speech came from Aietes in his agony, at the marvel of the power he beheld.

Then to the strong man his comrades stretched forth their hands, and crowned him with green wreaths, and greeted him with gracious words. And thereupon the wondrous son of Helios told him in what place the knife of Phrixos had stretched the shining fell; yet he trusted that this labor at least should never be accomplished by him. For it lay in a thick wood and grasped by a terrible dragon's jaws, and he in length and thickness was larger than their ship of fifty oars, which the iron's blows had welded.

Translated by Ernest Myers.

AESCHYLUS

AESCHYLUS was born at Athens, 525 B. C. He had part in the battle of Marathon, 490 B. C., as he tells us on his tombstone, and doubtless also in the battle of Salamis, 480 B. C. He is called the Father of Greek Tragedy, since before him only one actor was employed, who, wearing various masks, held converse with the leader of the chorus. No true dramatic action was possible until the second actor was introduced. Of the ninety plays of Aeschylus, only seven have come down to us; of these the most magnificent and the most difficult to understand is the *Agamemnon*, which Robert Browning translated. Aeschylus died at Gela in Sicily in 456 B. C.

The story on which the *Prometheus Bound* is based is told in the play itself. The audience had no play-bills or information other than that which the drama supplied. Prometheus belonged to the older race of gods, — he was a Titan, — but he took the part of Zeus (Jupiter) in the latter's contest with his father Cronos (Saturn), and assisted in establishing the new dynasty. By aiding men, however, especially in conveying to them the gift of fire, which should prove for them the mother of every art, he incurred the enmity of Zeus, and is to be severely punished.

The scene of the play is laid in Scythia, near the waters of Ocean.

The *Dramatis Personae* are skilfully chosen: *Strength* and *Force*, as the roughest of Zeus's servants, bring Prometheus to the scene of his sufferings. *Hephaestus* (Vulcan), the god of fire and the patron of all work in metals, the Tubal Cain of the Greeks, binds the Titan to the rocks. The *Ocean Nymphs* hear the sound of the hammer on the

fetters, and come out of curiosity, but full of sympathy.
They are sisters of Prometheus's bride, Hesione. No others
could have formed the chorus so well, since the brothers
of Prometheus had been hurled into Tartarus, and the
higher gods of Olympus were at enmity with the Titan,
and his place of punishment had been chosen far from the
dwellings of mortals. *Oceanus* (Ocean) himself enters not
long after his daughters, and advises Prometheus to bow
before the sovereignty of Zeus. He is an excellent foil to
the chief character, since he agrees with him in his feeling,
but adapts himself to circumstances. *Io* is the only mortal
introduced in the play, and a "motive" is given for her
coming: she is wandering, tormented by the oestrus, along
the shore. She, too, is a foil to Prometheus, since her sufferings come indirectly from Zeus, but she yields helplessly,
in a manner contrasted with the Titan's stubborn resist-
ance. She is further connected with the story, since her
descendant Heracles (Hercules) is to release Prometheus.
Prometheus's sympathy for Io in her sufferings draws from
him a distinct prediction of the overthrow of Zeus and his
dynasty, and this brings upon the scene Hermes (*Mercury*),
the messenger of the gods, who threatens suffering still
more dire, if Prometheus will not tell how this disaster may
be averted. The Titan defies Zeus, and the play ends with
thunder, lightning, and earthquake.

This play was the *Prometheus Bound*. Another (no
longer extant) followed, — *Prometheus Unbound*, — in
which the Titans, who had been freed from Tartarus, served
as chorus, and Heracles (Hercules) at the bidding of Zeus
released Prometheus. How the reconciliation between Zeus
and Prometheus could be brought about without humiliation
to the king of the gods, is not easy to see. In the play
before us, Zeus is represented as a wilful and unjust tyrant.
How these ways were justified to men in the second play,
we do not know. Shelley's *Prometheus Unbound*, in which
he makes Prometheus a martyr, is wholly fanciful.

The character of Prometheus was before Milton's mind

as he depicted Satan, and by the Greek title *Prometheus Desmōtes* (*Bound*) was suggested the title of Milton's *Samson Agonistes*.

The play was presented in the great open-air theatre of Dionysus, at the foot of the Acropolis in Athens, about 470 B. C. In the time of Aeschylus the action seems to have been not on a raised stage, but in a circular "orchestra" or dancing-place. The scenery and theatrical machinery were simple. The actors wore masks, and in general Aeschylus employed but two actors for each play. In this play, one actor may have taken the parts of Strength, Oceanus, Io, and Hermes, while the actor who took the part of Hephaestus may have slipped around behind the rocks to speak the verses of Prometheus. This would require a lay figure for the Titan, but would explain how the "adamantine wedge" could be driven through his breast, and would provide a mechanical reason for the silence of Prometheus during the first scene. The dramatic reason for this silence is that the Titan will not demean himself to bandy words with his tormentors. *Force* is a "mute," a supernumerary.

In 1833, Elizabeth Barrett (Mrs. Browning) published anonymously a translation of the Prometheus, — "completed in thirteen days," she wrote in 1845 to Mr. Browning, — "the iambics thrown into blank verse, the lyrics into rhymed octosyllabics and the like." This work was afterwards suppressed, but Miss Barrett in 1845 thoroughly revised it, and published her new translation in 1850. Another slight revision was made and published in 1856. Mr. Browning wrote that Mrs. Browning was "self-taught in almost every respect," and her Greek scholarship naturally was not that of a philologist of to-day. Of a few words and phrases she failed to catch the exact meaning, and in several instances she thus lost the full connection of thought. But her poetic genius more than atoned for her lack of technical scholarship, and her translation (which follows) is accepted as a true work of art.

PROMETHEUS BOUND

PERSONS OF THE DRAMA.

PROMETHEUS. HEPHAESTUS.
OCEANUS. Io, daughter of Inachus.
HERMES.
STRENGTH and FORCE.
CHORUS of Ocean Nymphs.

[*First Scene of Prologue.*]

STRENGTH *and* FORCE, HEPHAESTUS *and* PROMETHEUS, *at the Rocks.*

Strength. We reach the utmost limit of the earth, —
The Scythian track, the desert without man.
And now, Hephaestus, thou must needs fulfil
The mandate of our Father, and with links
Indissoluble of adamantine chains 5
Fasten against this beetling precipice
This guilty god. Because he filched away
Thine own bright flower, the glory of plastic fire,
And gifted mortals with it, — such a sin
It doth behoove he expiate to the gods, 10
Learning to accept the empery of Zeus,
And leave off his old trick of loving man.

Hephaestus. O Strength and Force, for you our
    Zeus's will
Presents a deed for doing, no more ! — But *I*,
I lack your daring, up this storm-rent chasm 15
To fix with violent hands a kindred god,
Howbeit necessity compels me so
That I must dare it, and our Zeus commands
With a most inevitable word. Ho, thou !
High-thoughted son of Themis, who is sage ! 20
Thee loath, I loath must rivet fast in chains
Against this rocky height unclomb by man,

Where never human voice nor face shall find
Out thee who lov'st them ; and thy beauty's flower,
Scorched in the sun's clear heat, shall fade away. 25
Night shall come up with garniture of stars
To comfort thee with shadow, and the sun
Disperse with retrickt beams the morning-frosts;
But through all changes, sense of present woe
Shall vex thee sore, because with none of them 30
There comes a hand to free. Such fruit is plucked
From love of man ! And in that thou, a god,
Didst brave the wrath of gods, and give away
Undue respect to mortals, for that crime
Thou art adjudged to guard this joyless rock, 35
Erect, unslumbering, bending not the knee,
And many a cry and unavailing moan
To utter on the air. For Zeus is stern,
And new-made kings are cruel.
  Strength.   Be it so.
Why loiter in vain pity ? Why not hate 40
A god the gods hate ? — one, too, who betrayed
Thy glory unto men ?
  Hephaestus.   An awful thing
Is kinship joined to friendship.
  Strength.   Grant it be :
Is disobedience to the Father's word
A possible thing ? Dost quail not more for that ? 45
  Hephaestus. Thou, at least, art a stern one, ever bold.
  Strength. Why, if I wept, it were no remedy;
And do not *thou* spend labor on the air
To bootless uses.
  Hephaestus. Cursed handicraft!
I curse and hate thee, O my craft !
  Strength.   Why hate 50
Thy craft most plainly innocent of all
These pending ills ?

Hephaestus.   I would some other hand
Were here to work it!
   Strength.   All work hath its pain,
Except to rule the gods. There is none free
Except King Zeus.
   Hephaestus.   I know it very well;
I argue not against it.
   Strength.   Why not, then,
Make haste and lock the fetters over HIM,
Lest Zeus behold thee lagging?
   Hephaestus.   Here be chains.
Zeus may behold these.
   Strength.   Seize him; strike amain;
Strike with the hammer on each side his hands;
Rivet him to the rock.
   Hephaestus.   The work is done,
And thoroughly done.
   Strength.   Still faster grapple him;
Wedge him in deeper; leave no inch to stir.
He's terrible for finding a way out
From the irremediable.
   Hephaestus.   Here's an arm, at least,
Grappled past freeing.
   Strength.   Now, then, buckle me
The other securely. Let this wise one learn
He's duller than our Zeus.
   Hephaestus.   Oh, none but he
Accuse me justly.
   Strength.   Now, straight through the chest,
Take him and bite him with the clenching tooth
Of the adamantine wedge, and rivet him.
   Hephaestus. Alas, Prometheus, what thou sufferest
      here
I sorrow over.

Strength. Dost thou flinch again,
And breathe groans for the enemies of Zeus?
Beware lest thine own pity find thee out. 75
  Hephaestus. Thou dost behold a spectacle that turns
The sight o' the eyes to pity.
  Strength. I behold
A sinner suffer his sin's penalty.
But lash the thongs about his sides.
  Hephaestus. So much
I must do. Urge no farther than I must. 80
  Strength. Ay, but I *will* urge! and, with shout on shout,
Will hound thee at this quarry. Get thee down,
And ring amain the iron round his legs.
  Hephaestus. That work was not long doing.
  Strength. Heavily now
Let fall the strokes upon the perforant gyves; 85
For he who rates the work has a heavy hand.
  Hephaestus. Thy speech is savage as thy shape.
  Strength. Be thou
Gentle and tender, but revile not me
For the firm will and the untruckling hate.
  Hephaestus. Let us go. He is netted round with chains. [*Exit* HEPHAESTUS.
  Strength. Here, now, taunt on! and, having spoiled the gods 91
Of honors, crown withal thy mortal men
Who live a whole day out. Why, how could *they*
Draw off from thee one single of thy griefs?
Methinks the Daemons gave thee a wrong name, 95
Prometheus, which means Providence, because
Thou dost thyself need providence to see
Thy roll and ruin from the top of doom. [*Exit.*

[*Second Scene of Prologue.*]

PROMETHEUS (*alone*).

O holy Aether, and swift-wingèd Winds,
And River-wells, and Laughter innumerous 100
Of yon sea-waves! Earth, mother of us all,
And all-viewing cyclic Sun, I cry on you, —
Behold me a god, what I endure from gods!
    Behold, with throe on throe,
    How, wasted by this woe, 105
I wrestle down the myriad years of time!
    Behold how, fast around me,
The new King of the happy ones sublime
Has flung the chain he forged, has shamed and
    bound me!
Woe, woe! to-day's woe and the coming mor-
    row's 110
I cover with one groan. And where is found me
    A limit to these sorrows?
And yet what word do I say? I have foreknown
Clearly all things that should be; nothing done
Comes sudden to my soul; and I must bear 115
What is ordained with patience, being aware
Necessity doth front the universe
With an invincible gesture. Yet this curse
Which strikes me now I find it hard to brave
In silence or in speech. Because I gave 120
Honor to mortals, I have yoked my soul
To this compelling fate. Because I stole
The secret fount of fire, whose bubbles went
Over the ferule's brim, and manward sent
Art's mighty means and perfect rudiment, 125
That sin I expiate in this agony,
Hung here in fetters, 'neath the blanching sky.

Ah, ah me! what a sound!
What a fragrance sweeps up from a pinion unseen
Of a god, or a mortal, or nature between, 130
Sweeping up to this rock where the Earth has her
    bound,
To have sight of my pangs, or some guerdon obtain.
Lo, a god in the anguish, a god in the chain!
    The god Zeus hateth sore,
    And his gods hate again, 135
    As many as tread on his glorified floor,
Because I loved mortals too much evermore.
Alas me! what a murmur and motion I hear,
    As of birds flying near!
    And the air undersings 140
    The light stroke of their wings,
And all life that approaches I wait for in fear.

    [*Entrance of Chorus.*]
Chorus of Sea-nymphs. First strophe.

    Fear nothing! our troop
    Floats lovingly up
    With a quick-oaring stroke 145
    Of wings steered to the rock,
Having softened the soul of our father below.
For the gales of swift-bearing have sent me a sound,
And the clank of the iron, the malletted blow,
    Smote down the profound 150
    Of my caverns of old,
And struck the red light in a blush from my brow,
Till I sprang up unsandalled, in haste to behold,
And rushed forth on my chariot of wings manifold.

Prometheus. Alas me! alas me! 155
Ye offspring of Tethys, who bore at her breast

Many children, and eke of Oceanus, he,
Coiling still around earth with perpetual unrest!
 Behold me and see
  How transfixed with the fang
 Of a fetter I hang
On the high-jutting rocks of this fissure, and keep
An uncoveted watch o'er the world and the deep.

Chorus. First antistrophe.

I behold thee, Prometheus; yet now, yet now,
A terrible cloud whose rain is tears
Sweeps over mine eyes that witness how
 Thy body appears
Hung awaste on the rocks by infrangible chains;
For new is the hand, new the rudder, that steers
The ship of Olympus through surge and wind,
And of old things passed, no track is behind.[1]

Prometheus. Under earth, under Hades,
 Where the home of the shade is,
 All into the deep, deep Tartarus,
 I would he had hurled me adown.
I would he had plunged me, fastened thus
In the knotted chain, with the savage clang,
All into the dark, where there should be none,
Neither god nor another, to laugh and see.
 But now the winds sing through and shake
  The hurtling chains wherein I hang,
 And I in my naked sorrows make
  Much mirth for my enemy.

Chorus. Second strophe.

Nay! who of the gods hath a heart so stern
 As to use thy woe for a mock and mirth?

[1] The Greek means: "The mighty ones of old (i. e., the Titans) Zeus puts out of sight." This suggests the words of Prometheus that follow.

Who would not turn more mild to learn
   Thy sorrows? who of the heaven and earth
      Save Zeus? But he
        Right wrathfully
Bears on his sceptral soul unbent,
And rules thereby the heavenly seed,
Nor will he pause till he content
His thirsty heart in a finished deed,
Or till Another shall appear,
To win by fraud, to seize by fear,
The hard-to-be-captured government.

Prometheus. Yet even of *me* he shall have need,
That monarch of the blessed seed, —
Of me, of me who now am cursed
   By his fetters dire, —
To wring my secret out withal,
   And learn by whom his sceptre shall
Be filched from him, as was at first
     His heavenly fire.
But he never shall enchant me
   With his honey-lipped persuasion;
Never, never, shall he daunt me
With the oath and threat of passion,
Into speaking as they want me,
Till he loose this savage chain,
   And accept the expiation
Of my sorrow in his pain.

     Chorus.   *Second antistrophe.*

Thou art, sooth, a brave god,
   And, for all thou hast borne
From the stroke of the rod,
   Nought relaxest from scorn.

But thou speakest unto me
  Too free and unworn;
And a terror strikes through me
  And festers my soul,
    And I fear, in the roll 220
Of the storm, for thy fate
  In the ship far from shore;
Since the son of Saturnus [1] is hard in his hate,
And unmoved in his heart evermore.

[*First Scene of First Episode.*]

Prometheus. I know that Zeus is stern; 225
I know he metes his justice by his will;
And yet his soul shall learn
More softness when once broken by this ill;
And, curbing his unconquerable vaunt,
He shall rush on in fear to meet with me 230
Who rush to meet with him in agony,
To issues of harmonious covenant.

Chorus. Remove the veil from all things, and relate
The story to us, — of what crime accused,
Zeus smites thee with dishonorable pangs. 235
Speak, if to teach us do not grieve thyself.

Prometheus. The utterance of these things is torture to me,
But so, too, is their silence: each way lies
Woe strong as fate.
                When gods began with wrath,
And war rose up between their starry brows, 240
Some choosing to cast Cronos from his throne
That Zeus might king it there, and some in haste
With opposite oaths, that they would have no Zeus
To rule the gods forever, — I, who brought

---

[1] Elsewhere the translator generally uses the Greek name *Cronos*.

The counsel I thought meetest, could not move 245
The Titans, children of the Heaven and Earth,
What time, disdaining in their rugged souls
My subtle machinations, they assumed
It was an easy thing for force to take
The mastery of fate. My mother, then, 250
Who is called not only Themis, but Earth too,
(Her single beauty joys in many names)[1]
Did teach me with reiterant prophecy
What future should be, and how conquering gods
Should not prevail by strength and violence, 255
But by guile only. When I told them so,
They would not deign to contemplate the truth
On all sides round ; whereat I deemed it best
To lead my willing mother upwardly,
And set my Themis face to face with Zeus 260
As willing to receive her. Tartarus,
With its abysmal cloister of the Dark,
Because I gave that counsel, covers up
The antique Cronos and his siding hosts,
And, by that counsel helped, the king of gods 265
Hath recompensed me with these bitter pangs;
For kingship wears a cancer at the heart, —
Distrust in friendship. Do ye also ask
What crime it is for which he tortures me?
That shall be clear before you. When at first 270
He filled his father's throne, he instantly
Made various gifts of glory to the gods,
And dealt the empire out. Alone of men,
Of miserable men, he took no count,
But yearned to sweep their track off from the world, 275
And plant a newer race there. Not a god
Resisted such desire, except myself.

[1] More literally, "one form (i. e., one person) of many names."

AESCHYLUS

I dared it! *I* drew mortals back to light,
From meditated ruin deep as hell!
For which wrong I am bent down in these pangs   280
Dreadful to suffer, mournful to behold,
And I who pitied man am thought myself
Unworthy of pity; while I render out
Deep rhythms of anguish 'neath the harping hand
That strikes me thus, — a sight to shame your Zeus!   285

   Chorus. Hard as thy chains, and cold as all these
     rocks,
Is he, Prometheus, who withholds his heart
From joining in thy woe. I yearned before
To fly this sight; and, now I gaze on it,
I sicken inwards.

   Prometheus.   To my friends, indeed,   290
I must be a sad sight.

   Chorus.   And didst thou sin
No more than so?

   Prometheus.   I did restrain besides
My mortals from premeditating death.

   Chorus. How didst thou medicine the plague-fear
     of death?

   Prometheus. I set blind Hopes to inhabit in their
     house.   295

   Chorus. By that gift thou didst help thy mortals
     well.

   Prometheus. I gave them also fire.

   Chorus.   And have they now,
Those creatures of a day, the red-eyed fire?

   Prometheus. They have, and shall learn by it many
     arts.

   Chorus. And truly for such sins Zeus tortures thee,
And will remit no anguish? Is there set   301
No limit before thee to thine agony?

Prometheus. No other — only what seems good to
  HIM.
  Chorus. And how will it seem good? what hope
  remains?
Seest thou not that thou hast sinned? But that thou
  hast sinned 305
It glads me not to speak of, and grieves thee;
Then let it pass from both, and seek thyself
Some outlet from distress.
  Prometheus.   It is in truth
An easy thing to stand aloof from pain,
And lavish exhortation and advice 310
On one vexed sorely by it. I have known
All in prevision. By my choice, my choice,
I freely sinned, — I will confess my sin, —
And, helping mortals, found mine own despair.
I did not think indeed that I should pine 315
Beneath such pangs against such skyey rocks,
Doomed to this drear hill, and no neighboring
Of any life. But mourn not ye for griefs
I bear to-day: hear rather, dropping down
To the plain, how other woes creep on to me, 320
And learn the consummation of my doom.
Beseech you, nymphs, beseech you, grieve for me
Who now am grieving; for Grief walks the earth,
And sits down at the foot of each by turns.
  Chorus. We hear the deep clash of thy words, 325
    Prometheus, and obey.
  And I spring with a rapid foot away
  From the rushing car and the holy air,
    The track of birds;
  And I drop to the rugged ground, and there 330
    Await the tale of thy despair.

[*Second Scene of First Episode.*]

OCEANUS *enters.*

Oceanus. I reach the bourne of my weary road
Where I may see and answer thee,
Prometheus, in thine agony.
On the back of the quick-winged bird I glode,   335
And I bridled him in
With the will of a god.
Behold, thy sorrow aches in me
Constrained by the force of kin.
Nay, though that tie were all undone,   340
For the life of none beneath the sun
Would I seek a larger benison
Than I seek for thine.
And thou shalt learn my words are truth,
That no fair parlance of the mouth   345
Grows falsely out of mine.
Now give me a deed to prove my faith;
For no faster friend is named in breath
Than I, Oceanus, am thine.
  Prometheus. Ha! what has brought thee? Hast thou also come   350
To look upon my woe? How hast thou dared [1]
To leave the depths called after thee? the caves
Self-hewn, and self-roofed with spontaneous rock,
To visit Earth, the mother of my chain?
Hast come, indeed, to view my doom, and mourn   355
That I should sorrow thus? Gaze on, and see
How I, the fast friend of your Zeus, — how I
The erector of the empire in his hand,
Am bent beneath that hand in this despair.   359
  Oceanus. Prometheus, I behold; and I would fain

[1] Rather, "had the heart." Compare verse 765.

Exhort thee, though already subtle enough,
To a better wisdom. Titan, know thyself,
And take new softness to thy manners, since
A new king rules the gods. If words like these,
Harsh words and trenchant, thou wilt fling abroad, 365
Zeus haply, though he sit so far and high,
May hear thee do it, and so this wrath of his,
Which now affects thee fiercely, shall appear [1]
A mere child's sport at vengeance. Wretched god,
Rather dismiss the passion which thou hast, 370
And seek a change from grief. Perhaps I seem
To address thee with old saws and outworn sense;
Yet such a curse, Prometheus, surely waits
On lips that speak too proudly: thou, meantime,
Art none the meeker, nor dost yield a jot 375
To evil circumstance, preparing still
To swell the account of grief with other griefs
Than what are borne. Beseech thee, use me, then,
For counsel: [2] do not spurn against the pricks,
Seeing that who reigns, reigns by cruelty 380
Instead of right. And now I go from hence,
And will endeavor if a power of mine
Can break thy fetters through. For thee — be calm,
And smooth thy words from passion. Knowest thou
    not
Of perfect knowledge, thou who knowest too much, 385
That, where the tongue wags, ruin never lags?
    Prometheus. I gratulate thee who hast shared and
      dared
All things with me, except their penalty.
Enough so! leave these thoughts. It cannot be

---

[1] This prepares for the catastrophe of the play.

[2] Literally, "If you take me as a counsellor," — "If you take my advice, you will not kick against the pricks."

That thou shouldst move HIM. HE may *not* be moved; 390
And *thou*, beware of sorrow on this road.
   Oceanus. Ay! ever wiser for another's use
Than thine. The event, and not the prophecy,
Attests it to me. Yet, where now I rush,
Thy wisdom hath no power to drag me back, 395
Because I glory, glory, to go hence,
And win for thee deliverance from thy pangs,
As a free gift from Zeus.
   Prometheus. Why there, again,
I give thee gratulation and applause.
Thou lackest no good will. But, as for deeds, 400
Do nought! 't were all done vainly, helping nought,
Whatever thou wouldst do. Rather take rest,
And keep thyself from evil. If I grieve,
I do not therefore wish to multiply
The griefs of others. Verily, not so! 405
For still my brother's doom doth vex my soul, —
My brother Atlas, standing in the west,
Shouldering the column of the heaven and earth,
A difficult burden! I have also seen,
And pitied as I saw, the earth-born one, 410
The inhabitant of old Cilician caves,[1]
The great war-monster of the hundred heads
(All taken and bowed beneath the violent Hand),
Typhon the fierce, who did resist the gods,
And, hissing slaughter from his dreadful jaws, 415
Flash out ferocious glory from his eyes
As if to storm the throne of Zeus. Whereat,
The sleepless arrow of Zeus flew straight at him,
The headlong bolt of thunder breathing flame,
And struck him downward from his eminence 420
Of exultation; through the very soul

   [1] Compare Pindar's First Pythian Ode, page 75.

It struck him, and his strength was withered up
To ashes, thunder-blasted. Now he lies,
A helpless trunk, supinely, at full-length
Beside the strait of ocean,[1] spurred into 425
By roots of Aetna, high upon whose tops
Hephaestus sits, and strikes the flashing ore.
From thence the rivers of fire shall burst away [2]
Hereafter, and devour with savage jaws
The equal plains of fruitful Sicily, 430
Such passion he shall boil back in hot darts
Of an insatiate fury and sough of flame,
Fallen Typhon, howsoever struck and charred
By Zeus's bolted thunder. But for thee,
Thou art not so unlearned as to need 435
My teaching; let thy knowledge save thyself.
I quaff the full cup of a present doom,
And wait till Zeus hath quenched his will in wrath.

 Oceanus. Prometheus, art thou ignorant of this,
That words do medicine anger?
 Prometheus.   If the word 440
With seasonable softness touch the soul,
And, where the parts are ulcerous, sear them not
By any rudeness.
 Oceanus.   With a noble aim
To dare as nobly — is there harm in *that?*
Dost thou discern it? Teach me.
 Prometheus.   I discern 445
Vain aspiration, unresultive work.
 Oceanus. Then suffer me to bear the brunt of this,

---

[1] The Strait of Messina.

[2] The prediction of this eruption is an indication of Prometheus's prophetic power, and thus gives weight to his prediction of the overthrow of Zeus. The eruption took place in 478 B. C. Possibly this passage may have been introduced for a presentation of the play in Syracuse, within sight of Mt. Aetna.

Since it is profitable that one who is wise
Should seem not wise at all.
 Prometheus.   And such would seem
My very crime.
 Oceanus.   In truth thine argument   450
Sends me back home.
 Prometheus.   Lest any lament for me
Should cast thee down to hate.
 Oceanus.   The hate of him
Who sits a new king on the absolute throne?
 Prometheus. Beware of him, lest thine heart
  grieve by him.[1]
 Oceanus. Thy doom, Prometheus, be my teacher!
 Prometheus.   Go!   455
Depart! Beware! And keep the mind thou hast.
 Oceanus. Thy words drive after, as I rush before.
Lo, my four-footed bird sweeps smooth and wide
The flats of air with balanced pinions, glad
To bend his knee[2] at home in the ocean-stall.   460
     [OCEANUS *departs.*

  Chorus. First strophe.

I moan thy fate, I moan for thee,
 Prometheus! From my eyes too tender
Drop after drop incessantly
 The tears of my heart's pity render
My cheeks wet from their fountains free;   465
Because that Zeus, the stern and cold,
 Whose law is taken from his breast,
 Uplifts his sceptre manifest
  Over the gods of old.

   [1] Perhaps more literally, "lest his heart be offended."
   [2] I. e., rest. Compare verse 36.

PROMETHEUS BOUND

First antistrophe.

All the land is moaning 470
With a murmured plaint to-day;
All the mortal nations
Having habitations
In the holy Asia
Are a dirge entoning 475
For thine honor and thy brothers',
Once majestic beyond others
In the old belief, —
Now are groaning in the groaning
Of thy deep-voiced grief. 480

Second strophe.

Mourn the maids inhabitant
Of the Colchian land,[1]
Who with white, calm bosoms stand
In the battle's roar:
Mourn the Scythian tribes that haunt 485
The verge of earth, Mæotis' shore.

Second antistrophe.

Yea! Arabia's battle crown,
And dwellers in the beetling town
Mt. Caucasus sublimely nears —
An iron squadron, thundering down 490
With the sharp-prowed spears.[2]

But one other before have I seen to remain
By invincible pain,
Bound and vanquished, — one Titan! 't was Atlas,
who bears

[1] The Amazons.
[2] Apparently the Medes and Persians.

In a curse from the gods, by that strength of his
    own 495
  Which he evermore wears,
The weight of the heaven on his shoulder alone,
  While he sighs up the stars;
And the tides of the ocean wail, bursting their bars;
  Murmurs still the profound, 500
And black Hades roars up through the chasm of the
    ground,
And the fountains of pure-running rivers moan low
  In a pathos of woe.

[*Second Episode.*]

Prometheus. Beseech you, think not I am silent
    thus
Through pride or scorn. I only gnaw my heart 505
With meditation, seeing myself so wronged.
For see — their honors to these new-made gods,
What other gave but I, and dealt them out
With distribution? Ay! but here I am dumb;
For here I should repeat your knowledge to you, 510
If I spake aught. List rather to the deeds
I did for mortals; how, being fools before,
I made them wise and true in aim of soul.
And let me tell you, — not as taunting men,
But teaching you the intention of my gifts, — 515
How, first beholding, they beheld in vain,
And, hearing, heard not, but, like shapes in dreams,
Mixed all things wildly down the tedious time,
Nor knew to build a house against the sun
With wicketed sides, nor any woodcraft knew, 520
But lived, like silly ants, beneath the ground
In hollow caves unsunned. There came to them
No steadfast sign of winter, nor of spring

Flower-perfumed, nor of summer full of fruit,
But blindly and lawlessly they did all things, 525
Until I taught them how the stars do rise
And set in mystery, and devised for them
Number, the inducer of philosophies,
The synthesis of letters, and, beside,
The artificer of all things, memory, 530
That sweet muse-mother.   I was first to yoke
The servile beasts in couples, carrying
An heirdom of man's burdens on their backs.
I joined to chariots, steeds, that love the bit
They champ at, — the chief pomp of golden ease. 535
And none but I originated ships,
The seaman's chariots, wanderings on the brine
With linen wings. And I — O, miserable! —
Who did devise for mortals all these arts,
Have no device left now to save myself 540
From the woe I suffer.
  Chorus.   Most unseemly woe
Thou sufferest, and dost stagger from the sense
Bewildered! Like a bad leech falling sick.
Thou art faint at soul, and canst not find the drugs
Required to save thyself.
  Prometheus.   Hearken the rest, 545
And marvel further, what more arts and means
I did invent, — this, greatest: if a man
Fell sick, there was no cure, nor esculent
Not chrism nor liquid, but for lack of drugs
Men pined and wasted, till I showed them all 550
Those mixtures of emollient remedies
Whereby they might be rescued from disease.
I fixed the various rules of mantic art,
Discerned the vision from the common dream,
Instructed them in vocal auguries 555

Hard to interpret, and defined as plain
The wayside omens, — flights of crook-clawed
    birds, —
Showed which are by their nature fortunate,[1]
And which not so, and what the food of each,
And what the hates, affections, social needs   560
Of all to one another, — taught what sign
Of visceral lightness, colored to a shade,
May charm the genial gods, and what fair spots
Commend the lung and liver. Burning so
The limbs incased in fat, and the long chine,   565
I led my mortals on to an art abstruse,
And cleared their eyes to the image in the fire,
Erst filmed in dark. Enough said now of this.
For the other helps of man hid underground,
The iron and the brass, silver and gold,   570
Can any dare affirm he found them out
Before me? None, I know! unless he choose
To lie in his vaunt. In one word learn the whole, —
That all arts came to mortals from Prometheus.

   Chorus. Give mortals now no inexpedient help,   575
Neglecting thine own sorrow.[2] I have hope still
To see thee, breaking from the fetter here,
Stand up as strong as Zeus.
   Prometheus.   This ends not thus,
The oracular fate ordains. I must be bowed
By infinite woes and pangs to escape this chain.   580
Necessity is stronger than mine art.
   Chorus. Who holds the helm of that Necessity?
   Prometheus. The threefold Fates and the unfor-
    getting Furies.

---

[1] I. e., of good omen. See Aristophanes' *Birds*, p. 266.
[2] The Chorus hopes that if he will use his unbounded ingenuity in his own behalf, he will secure release and power.

Chorus. Is Zeus less absolute than these are?
Prometheus. Yea,
And therefore cannot fly what is ordained. 585
Chorus. What is ordained for Zeus, except to be
A king forever?
Prometheus. 'Tis too early yet
For thee to learn it: ask no more.
Chorus. Perhaps
Thy secret may be something holy?
Prometheus. Turn
To another matter: this, it is not time 590
To speak abroad, but utterly to veil
In silence. For by that same secret kept,
I 'scape this chain's dishonor, and its woe.

Chorus. First strophe.

    Never, oh never,
    May Zeus, the all-giver, 595
    Wrestle down from his throne
    In that might of his own
    To antagonize mine!
    Nor let me delay
    As I bend on my way 600
    Toward the gods of the shrine
    Where the altar is full
    Of the blood of the bull,
    Near the tossing brine
    Of Ocean my father. 605
May no sin be sped in the word that is said,
    But my vow be rather
        Consummated,
Nor evermore fail, nor evermore pine.[1]

---

[1] The prayer is suggested by the Titan's sufferings: —
"May I never offend in thought, word, or deed."

First antistrophe.

'T is sweet to have 610
  Life lengthened out
With hopes proved brave
  By the very doubt
Till the spirit infold
Those manifest joys which were foretold. 615
  But I thrill to behold
    Thee, victim doomed,
  By the countless cares
  And the drear despairs
    Forever consumed, — 620
And all because thou, who art fearless now
  Of Zeus above,
Didst overflow for mankind below
  With a free-souled, reverent love.

  Ah, friend, behold and see! 625
What's all the beauty of humanity?
  Can it be fair?
What's all the strength? Is it strong?
  And what hope can they bear,
These dying livers, living one day long? 630
  Ah, seest thou not, my friend,
    How feeble and slow,
    And like a dream, doth go
This poor blind manhood, drifted from its end?
  And how no mortal wranglings can confuse 635
    The harmony of Zeus?

Prometheus, I have learnt these things
  From the sorrow in thy face.
    Another song did fold its wings
  Upon my lips in other days, 640

When round the bath and round the bed
The hymeneal chant instead
   I sang for thee, and smiled,
And thou didst lead, with gifts and vows,
   Hesione, my father's child,   645
To be thy wedded spouse.[1]

        [*Third Episode.*]
          Io *enters.*

Io. What land is this? what people is here?
And who is he that writhes, I see,
   In the rock-hung chain?
Now what is the crime that hath brought thee to
   pain?   650
Now what is the land — make answer free —
Which I wander through in my wrong and fear,
   Ah, ah, ah me!
The gad-fly stingeth to agony!
O Earth, keep off that phantasm pale   655
Of earth-born Argus! — ah! I quail
   When my soul descries
That herdsman with the myriad eyes
Which seem, as he comes, one crafty eye.
Graves hide him not, though he should die;[2]   660
But he doggeth me in my misery
From the roots of death, on high, on high;
And along the sands of the siding deep,
All famine-worn, he follows me,
And his waxen reed doth undersound   665
   The waters round,
And giveth a measure that giveth sleep.

[1] I. e., How different is this song of the chorus from their joyous song at his marriage.

[2] More literally, "though he was slain (by Hermes), the Earth does not hide him." In her half frenzied state, Io considers the oestrus (gadfly) to be the ghost of Argus.

Woe, woe, woe!
Where shall my weary course be done?
What wouldst thou with me, Saturn's son? 670
And in what have I sinned, that I should go
Thus yoked to grief by thine hand forever?
   Ah, ah! dost vex me so
     That I madden and shiver
      Stung through with dread? 675
Flash the fire down to burn me!
Heave the earth up to cover me!
Plunge me in the deep, with the salt waves over me,
   That the sea-beasts may be fed!
    O king, do not spurn me 680
     In my prayer!
For this wandering ever longer, evermore,
   Hath overworn me,
   And I know not on what shore
   I may rest from my despair. 685
   Chorus. Hearest thou what the ox-horned maiden
     saith?[1]
   Prometheus. How could I choose but hearken what
     she saith,
The frenzied maiden? — Inachus's child? —
Who love-warms Zeus's heart, and now is lashed
By Heré's[2] hate along the unending ways? 690
   Io. Who taught thee to articulate that name, —
    My father's? Speak to his child
    By grief and shame defiled!
Who art thou, victim, thou who dost acclaim
Mine anguish in true words on the wide air; 695

---

[1] Io is represented as ox-horned. The ordinary myth said that she was turned into a heifer, but she could not be so represented in the theatre. This verse is better assigned to Io, — " Dost thou hear me?"

[2] The Roman Juno.

And callest, too, by name the curse that came
    From Heré unaware,
To waste and pierce me with its maddening goad?
    Ah, ah, I leap
With the pang of the hungry; I bound on the road;
    I am driven by my doom;   701
    I am overcome
By the wrath of an enemy strong and deep!
Are any of those who have tasted pain,
    Alas! as wretched as I?   705
Now tell me plain, doth aught remain
For my soul to endure beneath the sky?
Is there any help to be holpen by?
If knowledge be in thee, let it be said!
    Cry aloud — cry   710
To the wandering, woful maid.

    Prometheus. Whatever thou wouldst learn, I will declare;
No riddle upon my lips, but such straight words
As friends should use to each other when they talk.
Thou seest Prometheus, who gave mortals fire.   715

    Io. O common help of all men, known of all,
O miserable Prometheus, for what cause
Dost thou endure thus?

    Prometheus.   I have done with wail
For my own griefs but lately.

    Io.   Wilt thou not
Vouchsafe the boon to me?

    Prometheus.   Say what thou wilt,   720
For I vouchsafe all.

    Io.   Speak, then, and reveal
Who shut thee in this chasm.

    Prometheus.   The will of Zeus,
The hand of his Hephaestus.

Io. And what crime
Dost expiate so?
　Prometheus. Enough for thee I have told
In so much only.
　Io. Nay, but show besides 725
The limit of my wandering, and the time
Which yet is lacking to fulfil my grief.
　Prometheus. Why, not to know were better than
　　to know
For such as thou.
　Io. Beseech thee, blind me not
To that which I must suffer.
　Prometheus. If I do, 730
The reason is not that I grudge a boon.
　Io. What reason, then, prevents thy speaking out?
　Prometheus. No grudging, but a fear to break
　　thine heart.
　Io. Less care for me, I pray thee. Certainty
I count for advantage.
　Prometheus. Thou wilt have it so, 735
And therefore I must speak. Now hear —
　Chorus. Not yet.
Give half the guerdon my way. Let us learn
First what the curse is that befell the maid,
Her own voice telling her own wasting woes:
The sequence of that anguish shall await 740
The teaching of thy lips.
　Prometheus. It doth behoove
That thou, maid Io, shouldst vouchsafe to these
The grace they pray, — the more, because they are
　　called
Thy father's sisters; since to open out
And mourn out grief, where it is possible 745
To draw a tear from the audience, is a work
That pays its own price well.

PROMETHEUS BOUND

Io. I cannot choose
But trust you, nymphs, and tell you all ye ask,
In clear words, though I sob amid my speech
In speaking of the storm-curse sent from Zeus, 750
And of my beauty, from which height it took
Its swoop on me, poor wretch! left thus deformed
And monstrous to your eyes. For evermore
Around my virgin-chamber, wandering went
The nightly visions which entreated me 755
With syllabled smooth sweetness, — " Blessed maid,
Why lengthen out thy maiden hours, when fate
Permits the noblest spousal in the world?
When Zeus burns with the arrow of thy love,
And fain would touch thy beauty? — Maiden, thou
Despise not Zeus! depart to Lerné's mead 761
That's green around thy father's flocks and stalls,
Until the passion of the heavenly Eye
Be quenched in sight." Such dreams did all night long
Constrain me, — me, unhappy! — till I dared [1] 765
To tell my father how they trod the dark
With visionary steps. Whereat he sent
His frequent heralds to the Pythian fane,[2]
And also to Dodona,[3] and inquired
How best, by act or speech, to please the gods. 770
The same returning brought back oracles
Of doubtful sense, indefinite response,
Dark to interpret; but at last there came
To Inachus an answer that was clear,
Thrown straight as any bolt, and spoken out, — 775

---

[1] Rather, "took heart." She did not wish to tell her father such dreams. Compare verses 35, 351.
[2] Of Pythian Apollo, at Delphi.
[3] In Epirus; the oldest Hellenic shrine.

This: "He should drive me from my home and
    land,
And bid me wander to the extreme verge
Of all the earth; or, if he willed it not,
Should have a thunder with a fiery eye
Leap straight from Zeus to burn up all his race   780
To the last root of it." By which Loxian word
Subdued, he drove me forth, and shut me out,
He loath, me loath; but Zeus's violent bit
Compelled him to the deed: when instantly
My body and soul were changèd and distraught,   785
And, hornèd as ye see, and spurred along
By the fanged insect, with a maniac leap
I rushed on to Cenchrea's[1] limpid stream,
And Lerné's fountain-water. There, the earth-born,
The herdsman Argus, most immitigable   790
Of wrath, did find me out, and track me out
With countless eyes set staring at my steps;
And though an unexpected sudden doom
Drew him from life, I, curse-tormented still,
Am driven from land to land before the scourge   795
The gods hold o'er me. So thou hast heard the
    past;
And, if a better future thou canst tell,
Speak on. I charge thee, do not flatter me,
Through pity, with false words; for in my mind
Deceiving works more shame than torturing doth.   800

Chorus.

Ah, silence here!
Nevermore, nevermore,
Would I languish for
The stranger's word
To thrill in mine ear —   805

[1] Near Io's home at Argos.

Nevermore for the wrong and the woe and the fear
    So hard to behold,
    So cruel to bear,
Piercing my soul with a double-edged sword
    Of a sliding cold.   .   810
    Ah, Fate! ah, me!
    I shudder to see
This wandering maid in her agony.

Prometheus. Grief is too quick in thee, and fear too full:
Be patient till thou hast learnt the rest.
    Chorus.   Speak: teach.   815
To those who are sad already, it seems sweet,
By clear foreknowledge to make perfect, pain.
    Prometheus. The boon ye asked me first was lightly won;
For first ye asked the story of this maid's grief,
As her own lips might tell it. Now remains   820
To list what other sorrows she so young
Must bear from Heré. Inachus's child,
O thou! drop down thy soul my weighty words,
And measure out the landmarks which are set
To end thy wandering. Toward the orient sun   825
First turn thy face from mine, and journey on
Along the desert-flats till thou shalt come
Where Scythia's shepherd-peoples dwell aloft,
Perched in wheeled wagons under woven roofs,
And twang the rapid arrow past the bow.   830
Approach them not, but, siding in thy course
The rugged shore-rocks resonant to the sea,
Depart that country. On the left hand dwell
The iron-workers, called the Chalybès,
Of whom beware, for certes they are uncouth,   835

And nowise bland to strangers. Reaching so
The stream Hybristes (well the *scorner* called),[1]
Attempt no passage, — it is hard to pass, —
Or ere thou come to Caucasus itself,
That highest of mountains, where the river leaps 840
The precipice in his strength. Thou must toil up
Those mountain-tops that neighbor with the stars,
And tread the southway, and draw near, at last,
The Amazonian host that hateth man,
Inhabitants of Themiscyra, close 845
Upon Thermodon,[2] where the sea's rough jaw
Doth gnash at Salmydessa,[3] and provide
A cruel host to seamen, and to ships
A stepdame. They, with unreluctant hand,
Shall lead thee on and on till thou arrive 850
Just where the ocean-gates show narrowest
On the Cimmerian isthmus. Leaving which,
Behooves thee swim with fortitude of soul
The strait Maeotis. Ay, and evermore
That traverse shall be famous on men's lips, 855
That strait called Bosporus,[4] the horned one's road,
So named because of thee,[5] who so wilt pass
From Europe's plain to Asia's continent.
How think ye, nymphs? the king of gods appears
Impartial in ferocious deeds? Behold! 860
The god desirous of this mortal's love
Hath cursed her with these wanderings. Ah, fair child,
Thou hast met a bitter groom for bridal troth!

[1] No river is known of this name. Perhaps the Araxes is meant.
[2] Strictly, "on the banks of the Thermodon."
[3] More literally, "the Salmydessian Jaw (or promontory) of the sea." The *Jaw* is Salmydessus.
[4] The Cimmeric Bosporus, near the Crimea, not the Thracian Bosporus, near Constantinople.
[5] *Bosporus*, interpreted as *Ox-ford*.

For all thou yet hast heard can only prove
The incompleted prelude of thy doom. 865
 Io. Ah, ah!
 Prometheus. Is 't thy turn now to shriek and moan?
How wilt thou, when thou hast hearkened what remains?
 Chorus. Besides the grief thou hast told, can aught remain?
 Prometheus. A sea of foredoomed evil worked to storm.
 Io. What boots my life, then? why not cast myself 870
Down headlong from this miserable rock,
That, dashed against the flats, I may redeem
My soul from sorrow? Better once to die
Than day by day to suffer.
 Prometheus.   Verily,
It would be hard for thee to bear my woe 875
For whom it is appointed not to die.
Death frees from woe; but I before me see
In all my far prevision not a bound
To all I suffer, ere that Zeus shall fall
From being a king.
 Io.   And can it ever be 880
That Zeus shall fall from empire?
 Prometheus.   *Thou*, methinks
Would take some joy to see it.
 Io.   Could I choose?
I who endure such pangs now, by that god!
 Prometheus. Learn from me, therefore, that the event shall be.
 Io. By whom shall his imperial sceptred hand 885
Be emptied so?

Prometheus. Himself shall spoil himself,
Through his idiotic counsels.
　　Io.　　　　　　How? declare,
Unless the word bring evil.
　　Prometheus.　　　　He shall wed,
And in the marriage-bond be joined to grief.
　　Io. A heavenly bride, or human? Speak it out,
If it be utterable.
　　Prometheus. Why should I say which?　　891
It ought not to be uttered, verily.
　　Io.　　　　　　Then
It is his wife shall tear him from his throne?
　　Prometheus. It is his wife shall bear a son to him
More mighty than the father.
　　Io.　　　　　　From this doom　895
Hath he no refuge?
　　Prometheus.　　None: or ere that I
Loosed from these fetters —
　　Io.　　　　　Yea; but who shall loose
While Zeus is adverse?
　　Prometheus.　　One who is born of thee:
It is ordained so.
　　Io.　　What is this thou sayest?
A son of mine shall liberate thee from woe?　900
　　Prometheus. After ten generations count three more,
And find him in the third.
　　Io.　　　　　The oracle
Remains obscure.
　　Prometheus.　　And search it not to learn
Thine own griefs from it.[1]
　　Io.　　　　Point me not to a good
To leave me straight bereaved.

[1] Literally, "And do not seek either to learn thy own griefs."

Prometheus. I am prepared 905
To grant thee one of two things.
    Io. But which two?
Set them before me; grant me power to choose.
    Prometheus. I grant it; choose now! Shall I
        name aloud
What griefs remain to wound thee, or what hand
Shall save me out of mine?
    Chorus. Vouchsafe, O god, 910
The one grace of the twain to her who prays,
The next to me, and turn back neither prayer
Dishonored by denial. To herself
Recount the future wandering of her feet;
Then point me to the looser of thy chain, 915
Because I yearn to know him.
    Prometheus. Since ye will,
Of absolute will, this knowledge, I will set
No contrary against it, nor keep back
A word of all ye ask for. Io, first
To thee I must relate thy wandering course 920
Far winding. As I tell it, write it down
In thy soul's book of memories. When thou hast past
The refluent bound that parts two continents,[1]
Track on the footsteps of the orient sun
In his own fire across the roar of seas, — 925
Fly till thou hast reached the Gorgonaean flats
Beside Cisthené. There the Phorcides,
Three ancient maidens, live, with shape of swan,
One tooth between them, and one common eye,
On whom the sun doth never look at all 930
With all his rays, nor evermore the moon
When she looks through the night. Anear to whom
Are the Gorgon sisters three, enclothed with wings,

    [1] Return to the tale interrupted at verse 854.

With twisted snakes for ringlets, man-abhorred:
There is no mortal gazes in their face, 935
And gazing can breathe on. I speak of such
To guard thee from their horror. Ay, and list
Another tale of a dreadful sight: beware
The Griffins, those unbarking dogs of Zeus,
Those sharp-mouthed dogs!—and the Arimaspian
    host 940
Of one-eyed horsemen, habiting beside
The river of Pluto that runs bright with gold:
Approach them not, beseech thee. Presently
Thou 'lt come to a distant land, a dusky tribe
Of dwellers at the fountain of the Sun, 945
Whence flows the River Aethiops; wind along
Its banks, and turn off at the cataracts,[1]
Just as the Nile pours from the Bybline hills
His holy and sweet wave: his course shall guide
Thine own to that triangular Nile-ground [2] 950
Where, Io, is ordained for thee and thine
A lengthened exile. Have I said in this
Aught darkly or incompletely?—now repeat
The question, make the knowledge fuller! Lo,
I have more leisure than I covet here. 955
    Chorus. If thou canst tell us aught that 's left untold,
Or loosely told, of her most dreary flight,
Declare it straight; but, if thou hast uttered all,
Grant us that latter grace for which we prayed,
Remembering how we prayed it.
    Prometheus.   She has heard 960
The uttermost of her wandering. There it ends.
But, that she may be certain not to have heard

---

[1] Literally, "Until thou shalt come to the cataracts, where."
[2] The Delta of the Nile.

All vainly, I will speak what she endured
Ere coming hither, and invoke the past
To prove my prescience true.¹ And so — to leave
A multitude of words, and pass at once
To the subject of thy course — when thou hadst gone
To those Molossian plains which sweep around
Dodona shouldering Heaven, whereby the fane
Of Zeus Thesprotian keepeth oracle,
And, wonder past belief, where oaks do wave
Articulate adjurations — (ay, the same
Saluted thee in no perplexèd phrase,
But clear with glory, noble wife of Zeus
That shouldst be, there some sweetness took thy
 sense!)
Thou didst rush further onward, stung along
The ocean-shore, toward Rhea's mighty bay,²
And, tost back from it, wast tost to it again
In stormy evolution: and know well,
In coming time that hollow of the sea
Shall bear the name Ionian, and present
A monument of Io's passage through,³
Unto all mortals. Be these words the signs
Of my soul's power to look beyond the veil
Of visible things. The rest to you and her
I will declare in common audience,⁴ nymphs,
Returning thither where my speech brake off.⁵
There is a town, Canobus, built upon
The earth's fair margin, at the mouth of Nile,

---

¹ The Titan's knowledge of Io's course on her way to Scythia is an indication of his supernatural knowledge.

² The Ionian Sea, the Adriatic.

³ This etymology, like that of Bosporus, is fanciful.

⁴ Since Io had asked of her future wandering, and the Chorus of him who was to release Prometheus.

⁵ Return to the story broken off at verse 952.

And on the mound washed up by it : Io, there 990
Shall Zeus give back to thee thy perfect mind,
And only by the pressure and the touch
Of a hand not terrible ; and thou to Zeus
Shall bear a dusky son who shall be called
Thence Epaphus, *Touched.* That son shall pluck the fruit 995
Of all that land wide-watered by the flow
Of Nile ; but after him, when counting out
As far as the fifth full generation, then
Full fifty maidens,[1] a fair woman-race,
Shall back to Argos turn reluctantly, 1000
To fly the proffered nuptials of their kin,
Their father's brothers. These being passion-struck,
Like falcons bearing hard on flying doves,
Shall follow hunting at a quarry of love
They should not hunt ; till envious Heaven maintain 1005
A curse betwixt that beauty and their desire,[2]
And Greece receive them, to be overcome
In murtherous woman-war by fierce red hands
Kept savage by the night. For every wife
Shall slay a husband, dyeing deep in blood 1010
The sword of a double edge — (I wish indeed
As fair a marriage-joy to all my foes !)
One bride alone shall fail to smite to death
The head upon her pillow, touched with love,
Made impotent of purpose, and impelled 1015
To choose the lesser evil, — shame on her cheeks,[3]
Than blood-guilt on her hands ; which bride shall bear

[1] The Danaids.
[2] A better reading of the text makes Greece receive the maidens, while their cousins are slain.
[3] Literally, " to be called coward rather than murderess."

A royal race in Argos. Tedious speech
Were needed to relate particulars
Of these things; 't is enough that from her seed   1020
Shall spring the strong He,[1] famous with the bow,
Whose arms shall break my fetters off. Behold,
My mother Themis, that old Titaness,
Delivered to me such an oracle;
But how and when, I should be long to speak,   1025
And thou, in hearing, wouldst not gain at all.

Io. Eleleu, eleleu![2]
    How the spasm and the pain,
      And the fire on the brain,
        Strike, burning me through!   1030
How the sting of the curse, all aflame as it flew,
      Pricks me onward again!
How my heart in its terror is spurning my breast,
And my eyes like the wheels of a chariot roll round!
I am whirled from my course, to the east, to the west,
In the whirlwind of frenzy all madly inwound;   1035
And my mouth is unbridled for anguish and hate,
And my words beat in vain, in wild storms of unrest,
    On the sea of my desolate fate.   [Io *rushes out.*

      Chorus. Strophe.
    O, wise was he, O, wise was he,   1040
    Who first within his spirit knew,
    And with his tongue declared it true,
    That love comes best that comes unto
        The equal of degree!
    And that the poor and that the low   1045

---

[1] Heracles (Hercules).

[2] Greek war-cry. An attack of frenzy is needed as a motive to remove Io from the scene.

Should seek no love from those above,
Whose souls are fluttered with the flow
Of airs about their golden height,
Or proud because they see arow
    Ancestral crowns of light. 1050

Antistrophe.

Oh, never, never, may ye, Fates,
    Behold me with your awful eyes
    Lift mine too fondly up the skies
Where Zeus upon the purple waits!
    Nor let me step too near, too near,[1] 1055
To any suitor bright from heaven;
    Because I see, because I fear,
This loveless maiden vexed and laden
By this fell curse of Heré, driven
    On wanderings dread and drear. 1060

Epode.

Nay, grant an equal troth instead
    Of nuptial love, to bind me by!
It will not hurt, I shall not dread
    To meet it in reply.
But let not love from those above 1065
Revert and fix me, as I said,
    With that inevitable Eye!
I have no sword to fight that fight,
I have no strength to tread that path,
I know not if my nature hath 1070
The power to bear, I cannot see
Whither from Zeus's infinite
I have the power to flee.

[1] Literally, "Nor may I be visited by any suitor."

[*First Scene of Exodus.*]

Prometheus. Yet Zeus, albeit most absolute of will,
Shall turn to meekness, — such a marriage-rite   1075
He holds in preparation, which anon
Shall thrust him headlong from his gerent seat
Adown the abysmal void ; and so the curse
His father Cronos muttered in his fall,
As he fell from his ancient throne and cursed,[1]   1080
Shall be accomplished wholly. No escape
From all that ruin shall the filial Zeus
Find granted to him from any of his gods,
Unless I teach him. I the refuge know,
And I, the means. Now, therefore, let him sit   1085
And brave the imminent doom, and fix his faith
On his supernal noises, hurtling on
With restless hand the bolt that breathes out fire ;
For these things shall not help him, none of them,
Nor hinder his perdition when he falls   1090
To shame, and lower than patience : such a foe
He doth himself prepare against himself,
A wonder of unconquerable hate,
An organizer of sublimer fire
Than glares in lightnings, and of grander sound   1095
Than aught the thunder rolls, out-thundering it,
With power to shatter in Poseidon's fist [2]
The trident-spear, which, while it plagues the sea,

---

[1] I. e., that his son Zeus might be overthrown by a son, just as he had overthrown his father Cronus.

[2] The oracle of Themis ran, according to the myth, that Thetis should bear a son mightier than his father. Both Zeus and Poseidon (Neptune) desired her love. Wedded to Zeus she would bear a son who would find a missile mightier than the thunderbolt. If she were wedded to Poseidon her son would master the trident. See verse 894.

Doth shake the shores around it. Ay, and Zeus,
Precipitated thus, shall learn at length 1100
The difference betwixt rule and servitude.
> *Chorus.* Thou makest threats for Zeus of thy desires.
> *Prometheus.* I tell you all these things shall be fulfilled

Even so as I desire them.
> *Chorus.* Must we, then,

Look out for one shall come to master Zeus? 1105
> *Prometheus.* These chains weigh lighter than his sorrows shall.
> *Chorus.* How art thou not afraid to utter such words?
> *Prometheus.* What should *I* fear, who cannot die?
> *Chorus.* But *he*

Can visit thee with dreader woe than death's.
> *Prometheus.* Why, let him do it! I am here, prepared 1110

For all things and their pangs.
> *Chorus.* The wise are they

Who reverence Adrasteia.[1]
> *Prometheus.* Reverence thou,

Adore thou, flatter thou, whomever reigns,
Whenever reigning! But for me, your Zeus
Is less than nothing. Let him act and reign 1115
His brief hour out according to his will:
He will not, therefore, rule the gods too long.
But lo! I see that courier-god of Zeus,
That new-made menial of the new-crowned king:
He, doubtless, comes to announce to us something new. 1120

---

[1] Adrasteia (Nemesis) humbled the proud. Those reverence her who are humble.

[*Second Scene of Exodus.*]

HERMES *enters.*

Hermes. I speak to thee, the sophist, the talker-down
Of scorn by scorn, the sinner against gods,
The reverencer of men, the thief of fire,—
I speak to thee and adjure thee : Zeus requires
Thy declaration of what marriage-rite 1125
Thus moves thy vaunt, and shall hereafter cause
His fall from empire. Do not wrap thy speech
In riddles, but speak clearly. Never cast
Ambiguous paths, Prometheus, for my feet,[1]
Since Zeus, thou mayst perceive, is scarcely won 1130
To mercy by such means.

Prometheus. A speech well-mouthed
In the utterance, and full-minded in the sense,
As doth befit a servant of the gods!
New gods, ye newly reign, and think, forsooth,
Ye dwell in towers too high for any dart 1135
To carry a wound there! Have I not stood by
While two kings[2] fell from thence? and shall I not
Behold the third, the same who rules you now,
Fall, shamed to sudden ruin? Do I seem
To tremble and quail before your modern gods? 1140
Far be it from me! For thyself, depart;
Re-tread thy steps in haste. To all thou hast asked
I answer nothing.

Hermes. Such a wind of pride
Impelled thee of yore full sail upon these rocks.

---

[1] More plainly, "Do not impose on me a double journey," i. e., oblige me to return to learn details.

[2] Uranus and Cronus.

Prometheus. I would not barter — learn thou
    soothly that! — 1145
My suffering for thy service. I maintain
It is a nobler thing to serve these rocks
Than live a faithful slave to father Zeus.
Thus upon scorners I retort their scorn.
  Hermes. It seems that thou dost glory in thy despair.[1] 1150
  Prometheus. I glory? Would my foes did glory so,
And I stood by to see them! — naming whom,
Thou art not unremembered.
  Hermes.   Dost thou charge
Me also with the blame of thy mischance?
  Prometheus. I tell thee I loathe the universal gods,[2] 1155
Who, for the good I gave them, rendered back
The ill of their injustice.
  Hermes.   Thou art mad,
Thou art raving, Titan, at the fever-height.
  Prometheus. If it be madness to abhor my foes,
May I be mad!
  Hermes.   If thou wert prosperous, 1160
Thou wouldst be unendurable.
  Prometheus.   Alas!
  Hermes. Zeus knows not that word.
  Prometheus.   But maturing Time
Teaches all things.
  Hermes.   Howbeit, thou hast not learnt
The wisdom yet, thou needest.
  Prometheus.   If I had,
I should not talk thus with a slave like thee. 1165

---

[1] Better, "in thy sufferings."
[2] Better, "all the gods."

Hermes. No answer thou vouchsafest, I believe,
To the great Sire's requirement.
 Prometheus.   Verily
I owe him grateful service, and should pay it.
 Hermes. Why, thou dost mock me, Titan, as I stood
A child before thy face.
 Prometheus.   No child, forsooth,   1170
But yet more foolish than a foolish child,
If thou expect that I should answer aught
Thy Zeus can ask. No torture from his hand,
Nor any machination in the world,
Shall force mine utterance ere he loose, himself,   1175
These cankerous fetters from me. For the rest,
Let him now hurl his blanching lightnings down,
And with his white-winged snows, and mutterings deep
Of subterranean thunders, mix all things,
Confound them in disorder. None of this   1180
Shall bend my sturdy will, and make me speak
The name of his dethroner who shall come.
 Hermes. Can this avail thee? Look to it!
 Prometheus.   Long ago
It was looked forward to, precounselled of.
 Hermes. Vain god, take righteous courage! Dare for once   1185
To apprehend and front thine agonies
With a just prudence.
 Prometheus.   Vainly dost thou chafe
My soul with exhortation, as yonder sea
Goes beating on the rock. Oh! think no more
That I, fear-struck by Zeus to a woman's mind,
Will supplicate him, loathèd as he is,   1190
With feminine upliftings of my hands,
To break these chains. Far from me be the thought!

Hermes.   I have indeed, methinks, said much in vain,
For still thy heart beneath my showers of prayers 1195
Lies dry and hard, nay, leaps like a young horse
Who bites against the new bit in his teeth,
And tugs and struggles against the new-tried rein,
Still fiercest in the feeblest thing of all,
Which sophism is; since absolute will disjoined 1200
From perfect mind is worse than weak.   Behold,
Unless my words persuade thee, what a blast
And whirlwind of inevitable woe
Must sweep persuasion through thee!   For at first
The Father will split up this jut of rock 1205
With the great thunder and the bolted flame,
And hide thy body where a hinge of stone
Shall catch it like an arm ; and, when thou hast passed
A long black time within, thou shalt come out
To front the sun while Zeus's winged hound, 1210
The strong, carnivorous eagle, shall wheel down
To meet thee, self-called to a daily feast,
And set his fierce beak in thee, and tear off
The long rags of thy flesh, and batten deep
Upon thy dusky liver.[1]   Do not look 1215
For any end, moreover, to this curse,
Or ere some god appear to accept thy pangs
On his own head vicarious, and descend
With unreluctant step the darks of hell [2]
And gloomy abysses around Tartarus. 1220
Then ponder this, — this threat is not a growth

[1] I. e., the vulture will feed upon the liver until it is black. The liver was the seat of the affections, to the Greek mind, and thus is punished.

[2] The Centaur Chiron was to do this, being hopelessly wounded, and therefore resigning immortality, but such an event seemed improbable.

Of vain invention ; it is spoken and meant :
King Zeus's mouth is impotent to lie,
Consummating the utterance by the act.
So, look to it, thou ! take heed, and nevermore 1225
Forget good counsel to indulge self-will.
 Chorus. Our Hermes suits his reasons to the times,
At least I think so, since he bids thee drop
Self-will for prudent counsel. Yield to him !
When the wise err, their wisdom makes their shame.

    [*Third Scene of Exodus.*]
 Prometheus. Unto me the foreknower, this man-
  date of power 1231
   He cries, to reveal it.
What's strange in my fate, if I suffer from hate
   At the hour that I feel it ?
Let the locks of the lightning, all bristling and whiten-
  ing, 1235
   Flash, coiling me round,
While the aether goes surging 'neath thunder and
  scourging
   Of wild winds unbound !
Let the blast of the firmament whirl from its place
   The earth rooted below, 1240
And the brine of the ocean, in rapid emotion,
   Be driven in the face
Of the stars up in heaven, as they walk to and fro !
Let him hurl me anon into Tartarus — on —
   To the blackest degree, 1245
With Necessity's vortices strangling me down ;
But he cannot join death to a fate meant for *me !*
 Hermes. Why, the words that he speaks and the
  thoughts that he thinks
   Are maniacal ! — add,

If the Fate who hath bound him should loose not the
    links, 1250
    He were utterly mad.
  Then depart ye who groan with him,
  Leaving to moan with him;
Go in haste! lest the roar of the thunder anearing
Should blast you to idiocy, living and hearing. 1255
  Chorus. Change thy speech for another, thy thought
    for a new,
If to move me and teach me indeed be thy care;
For thy words swerve so far from the loyal and
    true
  That the thunder of Zeus seems more easy to
    bear.
How! couldst teach me to venture such vileness? be-
    hold! 1260
I *choose* with this victim this anguish foretold!
I recoil from the traitor in haste and disdain,
And I know that the curse of the treason is worse
    Than the pang of the chain.
  Hermes. Then remember, O nymphs, what I tell
    you before, 1265
  Nor, when pierced by the arrows that Até [1] will
    throw you,
Cast blame on your fate, and declare evermore
  That Zeus thrust you on anguish he did not fore-
    show you.
Nay, verily, nay! for ye perish anon
  For your deed, by your choice. By no blindness
    of doubt, 1270
No abruptness of doom, but by madness alone,
  In the great net of Até, whence none cometh out,
    Ye are wound and undone. [*Exit* HERMES.

[1] The goddess of blind infatuation and hence of ruin.

Prometheus. Ay! in act now, in word now no
    more,
        Earth is rocking in space.   1275
And the thunders crash up with a roar upon roar,
    And the eddying lightnings flash fire in my face,
And the whirlwinds are whirling the dust round and
    round,
    And the blasts of the winds universal leap free,
And blow each upon each with a passion of sound, 1280
    And aether goes mingling in storm with the sea.
Such a curse on my head, in a manifest dread,
    From the hand of your Zeus has been hurtled along.
O my mother's fair glory! O Aether, enringing
All eyes with the sweet common light of thy bring-
    ing!   1285
    Dost see how I suffer this wrong?[1]

[1] The first words of Prometheus in the play are an invocation of heaven and earth to look upon him. Here, he closes with the assurance that these see how unjustly he suffers. The last sentence is best taken as a statement, not as a question.

SOPHOCLES

> " Be his
> My special thanks, whose even-balanced soul,
> From first youth tested up to extreme old age,
> Business could not make dull, nor passion wild;
> Who saw life steadily, and saw it whole;
> The mellow glory of the Attic stage,
> Singer of sweet Colonus, and its child."
>
> MATTHEW ARNOLD.

SOPHOCLES was born about 495 B. C., in the village of Colonus, near Athens. Little is known of his early life, but he was chosen for his beauty to lead the chorus of boys in celebration of the victory at Salamis in 480 B. C. He took some part in public life, serving as a general with Pericles in the Samian war. Throughout his lifetime he was devoted to Athens, and died there at an advanced age in 406 B. C.

He won applause early in life by his acting, when the poet was also an actor, like Shakespeare, but we are told that on account of a weak voice he gave up taking part in plays and contented himself with writing them. His first literary competition was in 468 B. C., when he won the victory over Aeschylus, thirty years his senior. All through his career he was a favorite with the Athenians, winning eighteen victories at the Dionysiac festivals, and never falling below second place. His two important innovations in dramatic art were the introduction of a third actor and the use of painted scenery.

The difference in spirit between Aeschylus and Sophocles is shown in Browning's lines: —

> " Aeschylus enjoined us fear the gods,
> And Sophocles advised respect the kings."

The older poet shows how the fate of mortals is worked out by the inevitable laws of the gods. The younger, though acknowledging the inevitability of these laws, lays more stress on the motives of the individual, and is thus able to make his characters seem more human and to portray their development.

Of more than a hundred plays by Sophocles, we have only seven, all belonging to the period of his finished style. The subjects of all, as of Greek tragedy in general, are taken from legends of the heroes of Greece.

Three of the plays, *Oedipus the King*, *Oedipus at Colonus*, and *Antigone*, are based on one story, — the fate of the ruling house of Thebes, — and might seem to be a "trilogy," but that the dates of their production show that they were not written to form a sequence.

The *Antigone*, although written earliest (443 B. C.), forms the climax of the story given in these three tragedies. After the death at Colonus of Oedipus, former king of Thebes, his daughters Antigone and Ismene returned to Thebes, and lived in the king's house with their brother Eteocles. But Polyneices, their second brother, who had been unjustly driven forth, came against the city to capture it, with seven captains of Argos. The two brothers died at each other's hands, and Creon, their uncle, was made king. He decreed that Eteocles should be interred with due honors, but that Polyneices should lie unburied, since he had come as an enemy to the city and the temples of the gods. The offender of this decree should be put to death.

Here the play opens. The whole tragedy turns on the determination of Antigone to resist the king's decree, and follow out the divine law by burying her brother. This she does with a lofty unselfishness, "a purity of passion, a fixity of purpose, a sublime enthusiasm for duty," which make her, as Symonds called her, "the most perfect female character in Greek poetry."

The translation is by E. H. Plumptre.

ANTIGONE

PERSONS OF THE DRAMA

CREON, King of Thebes.　EURYDICE, wife of CREON.
HAEMON, son of CREON.　ANTIGONE, } daughters of OEDIPUS.
TEIRESIAS, a seer.　　　ISMENE,　 }
GUARD.　　　　　　　　(*Antigone is the betrothed of Haemon*)
MESSENGER.　　　　　CHORUS of Theban Elders.

SCENE. — Thebes, *in front of the Palace. Early morning. Hills in the distance on the left; on the right the city.*

Enter ANTIGONE *and* ISMENE.

Antigone. Ismene, mine own sister, darling one!
Is there, of ills that sprang from Oedipus,
One left that Zeus will fail to bring on us,
The two who yet remain? Nought is there sad,
Nought full of sorrow, steeped in sin or shame,　5
But I have seen it in thy woes and mine.
And now, what new decree is this they tell,
Our captain has enjoined on all the State?
Know'st thou? Hast heard? Or are they hid from thee,
The ills that come from foes upon our friends?　10
　Ismene. No tidings of our friends, Antigone,
Pleasant or painful, since that hour have come,
When we, two sisters, lost our brothers twain,
In one day dying by a twofold blow.
And since in this last night the Argive host　15
Has left the field, I nothing further know,
Nor brightening fortune, nor increasing gloom.
　Antigone. That knew I well, and therefore sent for thee
Beyond the gates, that thou mayst hear alone.
　Ismene. What meanest thou? It is but all too clear
Thou broodest darkly o'er some tale of woe.　21

Antigone. And does not Creon treat our brothers twain
One with the rights of burial, one with shame?
Eteocles, so say they, he interred
Fitly, with wonted rites, as one held meet
To pass with honor to the dead below.
But for the corpse of Polyneices, slain
So piteously, they say, he has proclaimed
To all the citizens, that none should give
His body burial, or bewail his fate,
But leave it still unwept, unsepulchred,[1]
A prize full rich for birds that scent afar
Their sweet repast. So Creon bids, they say,
Creon the good, commanding thee and me, —
Yes, me, I say, — and now is coming here,
To make it clear to those who know it not,
And counts the matter not a trivial thing;
But whoso does the things that he forbids,
For him there waits within the city's walls
The death of stoning. Thus, then, stands thy case;
And quickly thou wilt show, if thou art born
Of noble nature, or degenerate liv'st,
Base child of honored parents.
   Ismene.   How could I,
O daring in thy mood, in this our plight,
Or breaking law or keeping, aught avail?
   Antigone. Wilt thou with me share risk and toil?
Look to it.

---

[1] The horror with which the Greek mind thought of this prevention of burial rites is seen in the prayer of Polyneices (*Oed. Col.*, 1410), —

> "Give me honors meet,
> A seemly burial, decent funeral rites."

Compare the last request of Hector, p. 12.

Ismene. What risk is this? What purpose fills
    thy mind?
Antigone. Wilt thou help this my hand to lift the
    dead?
Ismene. Mean'st thou to bury him, when law for-
    bids?
Antigone. He is my brother; yes, and thine, though
    thou   50
Wouldst fain he were not. I desert him not.
    Ismene. O daring one, when Creon bids thee not?
    Antigone. He has no right to keep me from mine
    own.
    Ismene. Ah me! remember, sister, how our sire
Perished, with hate o'erwhelmed and infamy,   55
From evils that himself did bring to light,
With his own hand himself of eyes bereaving,
And how his wife and mother, both in one,
With twisted cordage, cast away her life;[1]
And thirdly, how our brothers in one day   60
In suicidal conflict wrought the doom,
Each of the other. And we twain are left;
And think, how much more wretchedly than all
We twain shall perish, if, against the law,
We brave our sovereign's edict and his power.   65
This first we need remember, we were born
Women; as such, not made to strive with men.
And next, that they who reign surpass in strength,

---

[1] Oedipus had been warned by an oracle that he would slay his father and marry his own mother. While trying to avoid this fate by leaving Corinth, the home of his supposed parents, he fulfils it by slaying Laius, King of Thebes, and wedding his queen Iocasta. Many years later the terrible truth is made known that these were his own parents, who had exposed him on a mountain to die when he was an infant. The queen Iocasta hangs herself at the awful news, and Oedipus puts out his own eyes.

And we must bow to this, and worse than this.
I then, entreating those that dwell below, 70
To judge me leniently, as forced to yield,
Will hearken to our rulers. Over-zeal
That still will meddle, little wisdom shows.
 Antigone. I will not ask thee, nor though thou shouldst wish
To do it, shouldst thou join with my consent. 75
Do what thou wilt, I go to bury him;
And good it were, in doing this, to die.
Loved I shall be with him whom I have loved,
Guilty of holiest crime. More time is mine
In which to share the favor of the dead, 80
Than that of those who live; for I shall rest
For ever there. But thou, if thus thou please,
Count as dishonored what the Gods approve.
 Ismene. I do them no dishonor, but I find
Myself too weak to war against the State. 85
 Antigone. Make what excuse thou wilt, I go to rear
A grave above the brother whom I love.
 Ismene. Ah, wretched me! how much I fear for thee!
 Antigone. Fear not for me. Thine own fate raise to safety.
 Ismene. At any rate, disclose this deed to none; 90
Keep it close hidden: I will hide it too.
 Antigone. Speak out! I bid thee. Silent, thou wilt be
More hateful to me, if thou fail to tell
My deed to all men.
 Ismene.   Fiery is thy mood,
Although thy deeds the very blood might chill. 95
 Antigone. I know I please the souls I ought to please.
 Ismene. Yes, if thou canst; thou seek'st the impossible.

Antigone. When strength shall fail me, then I 'll
  cease to strive.
Ismene. We should not hunt the impossible at all.
Antigone. If thou speak thus, my hatred wilt thou
  gain, 100
And rightly wilt be hated of the dead.
Leave me and my ill counsel to endure
This dreadful doom. I shall not suffer aught
So evil as a death dishonorable.
  Ismene. Go, then, if so thou wilt. Of this be sure, 105
Wild as thou art, thy friends must love thee still.

                                                    [*Exeunt.*

Enter CHORUS *of Theban Elders.*

STROPHE I.

Chorus. O light of yon bright sun,[1]
Fairest of all that ever shone on Thebes,
  Thebes with her seven high gates,
  Thou didst appear that day, 110
  Eye of the golden dawn,
  O'er Dircé's [2] streams advancing,
  Driving with quickened curb,
  In haste of headlong flight,
The warrior [3] who, in panoply of proof, 115
From Argos came, with shield of glittering white;
  Whom Polyneices brought,
  Roused by the strife of tongues
  Against our fatherland,
  As eagle shrieking shrill, 120

[1] The action of the drama begins at daybreak, and this hymn is therefore sung to the sun at its rising.

[2] A spring near Thebes.

[3] The "warrior" is used collectively for the whole Argive army under Adrastus that had come to invade Thebes and support the cause of Polyneices.

ANTIGONE

He hovered o'er our land,
With snow-white wing bedecked,
Begirt with myriad arms,
And flowing horsehair crests.

ANTISTROPHE I.

He stood above our towers, 125
Encircling, with his spears all blood-bestained,
The portals of our gates;
He went, before he filled
His jaws with blood of men,
Ere the pine-fed Hephaestus [1] 130
Had seized our crown of towers.
So loud the battle din
That Ares loves was raised around his rear,
A conflict hard e'en for his dragon foe.[2]
For breath of haughty speech 135
Zeus hateth evermore;
And seeing them advance,
With mighty rushing stream,
And clang of golden arms,
With brandished fire he hurls 140
One who rushed eagerly
From topmost battlement
To shout out, "Victory!"

STROPHE II.

Crashing to earth he fell,[3]
Down-smitten, with his torch, 145

---

[1] The god of fire is here used for the element itself.

[2] As the Argive army was compared to the eagle, so Thebes to the eagle's great enemy, the serpent. Here, probably, is a reference to the *mythos* of the descent of the Thebans from the dragon's teeth sown by Cadmus.

[3] The unnamed leader whose fall is thus singled out for special mention was Capaneus, who bore on his shield the figure of a naked man brandishing a torch and crying, "I will burn the city."

Who came, with madman's haste,
Drunken, with frenzied soul,
And swept o'er us with blasts,
The whirlwind blasts of hate.
Thus on one side they fare,   150
And Ares great, like war-horse in his strength,
Smiting now here, now there,
Brought each his several fate.
For seven chief warriors at the seven gates met,
Equals with equals matched,   155
To Zeus, the Lord of War,
Left tribute, arms of bronze;
All but the hateful ones,
Who, from one father and one mother sprung,
Stood wielding, hand to hand,   160
Their two victorious spears,
And had their doom of death as common lot.

ANTISTROPHE II.

But now, since Victory,
Of mightiest name, hath come
To Thebes, of chariots proud,   165
Joying and giving joy,
After these wars just past,
Learn ye forgetfulness,
And all night long, with dance and voice of hymns,
Let us go round in state   170
To all the shrines of Gods,
While Bacchus, making Thebes resound with dance,
Begins the strain of joy.
But, lo! our country's king,
Creon, Menoekeus' son,   175
New ruler, by new change,
And providence of God,

Comes to us, steering on some new device;
   For, lo! he hath convened,
   By herald's loud command,   180
This council of the elders of our land.

Enter CREON.

Creon. My friends, for what concerns our commonwealth,
The Gods who vexed it with the billowing storms
Have righted it again; and I have sent,
By special summons, calling you to come   185
Apart from all the others. This, in part,
As knowing ye did all along uphold
The might of Laius'[1] throne; in part again,
Because when Oedipus our country ruled,
And, when he perished, then towards his sons   190
Ye still were faithful in your steadfast mind.
And since they fell, as by a double death,
Both on the selfsame day with murderous blow,
Smiting and being smitten, now I hold
Their thrones and all their power of sov'reignty   195
By nearness of my kindred to the dead.[2]
And hard it is to learn what each man is,
In heart and mind and judgment, till he gain
Experience in princedom and in laws.
For me, whoe'er is called to guide a State,   200
And does not catch at counsels wise and good,
But holds his peace through any fear of man,
I deem him basest of all men that are,
And so have deemed long since; and whosoe'er
As worthier than his country counts his friend,   205

---

[1] The former king of Thebes, and father of Oedipus.
[2] Creon was son of Menoeceus and brother to Iocasta, the wife and mother of Oedipus.

I utterly despise him. I myself,
Zeus be my witness, who beholdeth all,
Would not keep silence, seeing danger come,
Instead of safety, to my subjects true.
Nor could I take as friend my country's foe ; 210
For this I know, that there our safety lies,
And sailing while the good ship holds her course,
We gather friends around us. By these rules
And such as these do I maintain the State.
And now I come, with edicts, close allied 215
To these in spirit, for my citizens,
Concerning those two sons of Oedipus ;
Eteocles, who died in deeds of might
Illustrious, fighting for our fatherland,
To honor him with sepulture, all rites 220
Duly performed that to the noblest dead
Of right belong. Not so his brother ; him
I speak of, Polyneices, who, returned
From exile, sought with fire to desolate
His father's city and the shrines of Gods, 225
Yea, sought to glut his rage with blood of men,
And lead them captives to the bondslave's doom ;
Him I decree that none shall dare entomb,
That none shall utter wail or loud lament,
But leave his corpse unburied, by the dogs 230
And vultures mangled, foul to look upon.
Such is my purpose. Ne'er, if I can help,
Shall the vile have more honor than the just ;
But whoso shows himself my country's friend,
Living or dead, from me shall honor gain. 235

Chorus. This is thy pleasure, O Menoekeus' son,
For him who hated, him who loved our State ;
And thou hast power to make what laws thou wilt,
Both for the dead and all of us who live.

Creon. Be ye then guardians of the things I
   speak. 240
Chorus. Commit this task to one of younger years.
Creon. Nay, watchmen are appointed for the corpse.
Chorus. What other task then dost thou lay on us?
Creon. Not to consent with those that disobey.
Chorus. None are so foolish as to seek for death. 245
Creon. Yet that shall be the doom; but love of
   gain
Hath oft with false hopes lured men to their death.

Enter GUARD.

Guard. I will not say, O king, that I have come
Panting with speed, and plying nimble feet,
For I had many halting-points of thought, 250
Backwards and forwards turning, round and round:
For now my mind would give me sage advice;
"Poor wretch, why go where thou must bear the blame?
Or wilt thou tarry, fool? Shall Creon know
These things from others? How wilt thou 'scape
   grief?" 255
Revolving thus, I came in haste, yet slow,
And thus a short way finds itself prolonged;
But, last of all, to come to thee prevailed.
And though I tell of nought, yet I will speak;
For this one hope I cling to, might and main, 260
That I shall suffer nought but destiny.
Creon. What is it then that causes such dismay?
Guard. First, for mine own share in it, this I say,
The deed I did not, do not know who did,
Nor should I rightly come to ill for it. 265
Creon. Thou feel'st thy way and fencest up thy deed
All round and round. 'T would seem thou hast some
   news.

Guard. Yea, news of fear engenders long delay.
Creon. Wilt thou not speak, and then depart in
  peace?
Guard. Well, speak I will. The corpse . . . Some
  one has been   270
But now and buried it, a little dust
O'er the skin scattering, with the wonted rites.[1]
  Creon. What say'st thou? What man dared this
    deed of guilt?
  Guard. I know not. Neither was there stroke of
    axe,
Nor earth cast up by mattock. All the soil   275
Was dry and hard, no track of chariot wheel;
But he who did it went and left no sign.
And when the first day-watchman showed it us,
The sight caused wonder and sore grief to all;
For he had disappeared: no tomb indeed   280
Was over him, but dust all lightly strown,
As by some hand that shunned defiling guilt;
And no sign was there of wild beast or dog
Having come and torn him. Evil words arose
Among us, guard to guard imputing blame,   285
Which might have come to blows, and none was there
To check its course, for each to each appeared
The man whose hand had done it. Yet not one
Had it brought home, but each disclaimed all know-
    ledge;
And we were ready in our hands to take   290
Bars of hot iron, and to walk through fire,
And call the Gods to witness none of us
Were privy to his schemes who planned the deed,
Nor his who wrought it. Then at last, when nought

---

[1] It was the rite of burial, not the actual interment, that was all-important to the Greek mind.

Was gained by all our searching, some one speaks,   295
Who made us bend our gaze upon the ground
In fear and trembling; for we neither saw
How to oppose it, nor, accepting it,
How we might prosper in it. And his speech
Was this, that all our tale should go to thee,   300
Not hushed up anywise. This gained the day;
And me, ill-starred, the lot condemns to win
This precious prize. So here I come to thee
Against my will; and surely do I trow
Thou dost not wish to see me. Still 'tis true   305
That no man loves the messenger of ill.
   Chorus. For me, my prince, my mind some time has thought
If this perchance has some divine intent.
   Creon. Cease then, before thou fillest me with wrath,
Lest thou be found, though full of years, a fool.   310
For what thou say'st is most intolerable,
That for this corpse the providence of Gods
Has any care. What! have they buried him,
As to their patron paying honors high,
Who came to waste their columned shrines with fire,   315
To desecrate their offerings and their lands,
And all their wonted customs? Dost thou see
The Gods approving men of evil deeds?
It is not so; but men of rebel mood,
Lifting their head in secret long ago,   320
Still murmured thus against me. Never yet
Had they their neck beneath the yoke, content
To bear it with submission. They, I know,
Have bribed these men to let the deed be done.
No thing in use by man, for power of ill,   325

Can equal money. This lays cities low,
This drives men forth from quiet dwelling-place,
This warps and changes minds of worthiest stamp,
To turn to deeds of baseness, teaching men
All shifts of cunning, and to know the guilt 330
Of every impious deed. But they who, hired,
Have wrought this crime, have laboured to their cost,
Or soon or late to pay the penalty.
But if Zeus still claims any awe from me,
Know this, and with an oath I tell it thee, 335
Unless ye find the very man whose hand
Has wrought this burial, and before mine eyes
Present him captive, death shall not suffice,
Till first, hung up still living, ye shall show
The story of this outrage, that henceforth, 340
Knowing what gain is lawful, ye may grasp
At that, and learn it is not meet to love
Gain from all quarters. By base profit won
You will see more destroyed than prospering.

Guard. May I then speak? Or shall I turn and go? 345

Creon. See'st not e'en yet how vexing are thy words?

Guard. Is it thine ears they trouble, or thy soul?

Creon. Why dost thou gauge my trouble where it is?

Guard. The doer grieves thy heart, but I thine ears.

Creon. Pshaw! what a babbler, born to prate art thou! 350

Guard. May be; yet I this deed, at least, did not.

Creon. Yes, and for money; selling e'en thy soul.

Guard. Ah me!
How dire it is, in thinking, false to think!

Creon. Prate about thinking: but unless ye show
To me the doers, ye shall say ere long 355
That scoundrel gains still work their punishment.
[*Exit.*
Guard. God send we find him! Should we find him not,
As well may be, (for this must chance decide,)
You will not see me coming here again;
For now, being safe beyond all hope of mine, 360
Beyond all thought, I owe the Gods much thanks.
[*Exit.*

STROPHE I.

Chorus. Many the forms of life,
   Wondrous and strange to see,
   But nought than man appears
   More wondrous and more strange. 365
   He, with the wintry gales,
   O'er the white foaming sea,
   'Mid wild waves surging round,
   Wendeth his way across:
Earth, of all Gods, from ancient days the first, 370
   Unworn and undecayed.
He, with his ploughs that travel o'er and o'er,
   Furrowing with horse and mule,
   Wears ever year by year.

ANTISTROPHE I.

   The thoughtless tribe of birds, 375
   The beasts that roam the fields,
   The brood in sea-depths born,
   He takes them all in nets
   Knotted in snaring mesh,
   Man, wonderful in skill. 380
   And by his subtle arts
   He holds in sway the beasts

That roam the fields, or tread the mountain's
    height;
  And brings the binding yoke
Upon the neck of horse with shaggy mane,   385
    Or bull on mountain crest,
    Untamable in strength.

Strophe II.

And speech, and thought as swift as wind,
And tempered mood for higher life of states,
    These he has learnt, and how to flee   390
    Or the clear cold of frost unkind,
    Or darts of storm and shower,
Man all-providing. Unprovided, he
Meeteth no chance the coming days may bring;
    Only from Hades, still   395
    He fails to find escape,
Though skill of art may teach him how to flee
From depths of fell disease incurable.

Antistrophe II.

  So, gifted with a wondrous might,
Above all fancy's dreams, with skill to plan, 400
    Now unto evil, now to good,
    He turns. While holding fast the laws,
    His country's sacred rights,
That rest upon the oath of Gods on high,
High in the State: an outlaw from the State,   405
    When loving, in his pride,
    The thing that is not good;
Ne'er may he share my hearth, nor yet my thoughts,
Who worketh deeds of evil like to this.

Enter GUARDS *bringing in* ANTIGONE.

As to this portent which the Gods have sent,   410

I stand in doubt. Can I, who know her, say
That this is not the maid Antigone?
O wretched one of wretched father born,
Thou child of Oedipus,
What means this? Surely 't is not that they bring 415
Thee as a rebel 'gainst the king's decree,
And taken in the folly of thine act?
   Guard. Yes! She it was by whom the deed was
     done.
We found her burying. Where is Creon, pray? 419
   Chorus. Back from his palace comes he just in time.
          Enter CREON.
   Creon. What chance is this, with which my coming
     fits?
   Guard. Men, O my king, should pledge themselves
     to nought;
For cool reflection makes their purpose void.
I surely thought I should be slow to come here,
Cowed by thy threats, which then fell thick on me; 425
But now persuaded by the sweet delight
Which comes unlooked for, and beyond our hopes,
I come, although I swore the contrary,
Bringing this maiden, whom in act we found
Decking the grave. No need for lots was now; 430
The prize was mine, and not another man's.
And now, O king, take her, and as thou wilt,
Judge and convict her. I can claim a right
To wash my hands of all this troublous coil.
   Creon. How and where was it that ye seized and
     brought her? 435
   Guard. She was in act of burying. Thou knowest
     all.
   Creon. Dost know and rightly speak the tale thou
     tell'st?

Guard. I saw her burying that self-same corpse
Thou bad'st us not to bury. Speak I clear? 439
  Creon. How was she seen, and taken in the act?
  Guard. The matter passed as follows : — When we came,
With all those dreadful threats of thine upon us,
Sweeping away the dust which, lightly spread,
Covered the corpse, and laying stript and bare
The tainted carcase, on the hill we sat 445
To windward, shunning the infected air,
Each stirring up his fellow with strong words,
If any shirked his duty. This went on
Some time, until the glowing orb of day
Stood in mid-heaven, and the scorching heat 450
Fell on us. Then a sudden whirlwind rose,
A scourge from heaven, raising squalls on earth,
And filled the plain, the leafage stripping bare
Of all the forest, and the air's vast space
Was thick and troubled, and we closed our eyes, 455
Until the plague the Gods had sent was past;
And when it ceased, a weary time being gone,
The girl is seen, and with a bitter cry,
Shrill as a bird's, when it beholds its nest
All emptied of its infant brood, she wails; 460
Thus she, when she beholds the corpse all stript,
Groaned loud with many moanings, and she called
Fierce curses down on those who did the deed.
And in her hand she brings some fine, dry dust,
And from a vase of bronze, well wrought, upraised,
She pours the three libations o'er the dead.[1] 466
And we, beholding, give her chase forthwith,

---

[1] The three libations were sometimes separately of wine, milk, and honey. Here the narrative implies that Antigone had only one urn, but adhered to the sacred number in her act of pouring.

And run her down, nought terrified at us.
And then we charged her with the former deed,
As well as this. And nothing she denied.
But this to me both bitter is and sweet,
For to escape one's self from ill is sweet,
But to bring friends to trouble, this is hard
And painful. Yet my nature bids me count
Above all these things safety for myself.
  Creon. [*To* ANTIGONE.] Thou, then — yes, thou,
    who bend'st thy face to earth —
Confessest thou, or dost deny the deed?
  Antigone. I own I did it, and will not deny.
  Creon. [*To* GUARD.] Go thou thy way, where'er thy
    will may choose,
Freed from a weighty charge. [*Exit* GUARD.
  [*To* ANTIGONE.] And now for thee.
Say in few words, not lengthening out thy speech,
Knew'st thou the edicts which forbade these things?
  Antigone. I knew them. Could I fail? Full clear
    were they.
  Creon. And thou didst dare to disobey these laws?
  Antigone. Yes, for it was not Zeus who gave them
    forth,
Nor Justice, dwelling with the Gods below,
Who traced these laws for all the sons of men;
Nor did I deem thy edicts strong enough,
That thou, a mortal man, shouldst overpass
The unwritten laws of God that know not change.
They are not of to-day nor yesterday,
But live forever, nor can man assign
When first they sprang to being. Not through fear
Of any man's resolve was I prepared
Before the Gods to bear the penalty
Of sinning against these. That I should die

I knew (how should I not?), though thy decree
Had never spoken. And, before my time
If I shall die, I reckon this a gain ;
For whoso lives, as I, in many woes, 500
How can it be but he shall gain by death ?
And so for me to bear this doom of thine
Has nothing painful. But, if I had left
My mother's son unburied on his death,
In that I should have suffered ; but in this 505
I suffer not. And should I seem to thee
To do a foolish deed, 't is simply this, —
I bear the charge of folly from a fool.

Chorus. The maiden's stubborn will, of stubborn sire
The offspring shows itself. She knows not yet 510
To yield to evils.

Creon. Know then, minds too stiff
Most often stumble, and the rigid steel
Baked in the furnace, made exceeding hard,
Thou seest most often split and shivered lie ;
And I have known the steeds of fiery mood 515
With a small curb subdued. It is not meet
That one who lives in bondage to his neighbors
Should think too proudly. Wanton outrage then
This girl first learnt, transgressing these my laws ;
But this, when she has done it, is again 520
A second outrage, over it to boast,
And laugh as having done it. Surely, then,
She is the man, not I, if, all unscathed,
Such deeds of might are hers. But be she child
Of mine own sister, or of one more near 525
Than all the kith and kin of Household Zeus,
She and her sister shall not 'scape a doom
Most foul and shameful ; for I charge her, too,
With having planned this deed of sepulture.

Go ye and call her. 'T was but now within 530
I saw her raving, losing self-command.
And still the mind of those who in the dark
Plan deeds of evil is the first to fail,
And so convicts itself of secret guilt.
But most I hate when one found out in guilt 535
Will seek to gloze and brave it to the end.
    Antigone. And dost thou seek aught else beyond my death?
    Creon. Nought else for me. That gaining, I gain all.
    Antigone. Why then delay? Of all thy words not one
Pleases me now (and may it never please!), 540
And so all mine must grate upon thine ears.
And yet how could I higher glory gain
Than placing my true brother in his tomb?
There is not one of these but would confess
It pleases them, did fear not seal their lips. 545
The tyrant's might in much besides excels,
And it may do and say whate'er it will.
    Creon. Of all the race of Cadmus thou alone
Look'st thus upon the deed.
    Antigone.   They see it too
As I do, but their tongue is tied for thee. 550
    Creon. Art not ashamed against their thoughts to think?
    Antigone. There is nought base in honoring our own blood.
    Creon. And was he not thy kin who fought against him?
    Antigone. Yea, brother, of one father and one mother.
    Creon. Why then give honor which dishonors him? 555

Antigone. The dead below will not repeat thy words.
Creon. Yes, if thou give like honor to the godless.
Antigone. It was his brother, not his slave that died.
Creon. Wasting this land, while *he* died fighting for it.
Antigone. Yet Hades still craves equal rites for all.
Creon. The good craves not the portion of the bad. 561
Antigone. Who knows if this be holy deemed below?
Creon. Not even when he dies can foe be friend.
Antigone. My nature leads to sharing love, not hate.
Creon. Go then below; and if thou must have love, 565
Love them. While I live, women shall not rule.

Enter ISMENE, *led in by* Attendants.

Chorus. And, lo! Ismene at the gate
Comes shedding tears of sisterly regard,
And o'er her brow a gathering cloud
    Mars the deep roseate blush, 570
    Bedewing her fair cheek.
Creon. [*To* ISMENE.] And thou who, creeping as a viper creeps,
Didst drain my life in secret, and I knew not
That I was rearing two accursèd ones,
Subverters of my throne, — come, tell me, then, 575
Wilt thou confess thou took'st thy part in this,
Or wilt thou swear thou didst not know of it?
Ismene. I did the deed, if she did, go with her,
Yea, share the guilt, and bear an equal blame.
Antigone. Nay, justice will not suffer this, for thou
Didst not consent, nor did I let thee join. 581
Ismene. Nay, in thy troubles, I am not ashamed
In the same boat with thee to share thy fate.

Antigone. Who did it, Hades knows, and those below:
I do not love a friend who loves in words. 585
Ismene. Do not, my sister, put me to such shame,
As not to let me join in death with thee,
And so to pay due reverence to the dead.
Antigone. Share not my death, nor make thine own this deed
Thou hadst no hand in. My death shall suffice. 590
Ismene. What life to me is sweet, bereaved of thee?
Antigone. Ask Creon there, since thou o'er him dost watch.
Ismene. Why vex me so, in nothing bettered by it?
Antigone. 'T is pain indeed, to laugh my laugh at thee. 594
Ismene. But now, at least, how may I profit thee?
Antigone. Save thou thyself. I grudge not thy escape.
Ismene. Ah, woe is me! and must I miss thy fate?
Antigone. Thou mad'st thy choice to live, and I to die.
Ismene. 'T was not because I failed to speak my thoughts.
Antigone. To these didst thou, to those did I seem wise. 600
Ismene. And yet the offence is equal in us both.
Antigone. Take courage. Thou dost live. My soul long since
Hath died to render service to the dead.
Creon. Of these two girls the one goes mad but now,
The other ever since her life began. 605
Ismene. E'en so, O king; no mind that ever lived
Stands firm in evil days, but goes astray.
Creon. Thine did, when, with the vile, vile deeds thou chosest.

Ismene. How could I live without her presence
    here?
Creon. Speak not of presence. She is here no
    more.   610
Ismene. And wilt thou slay thy son's betrothèd
    bride?
Creon. Full many a field there is which he may
    plough.
Ismene. None like that plighted troth 'twixt him
    and her.
Creon. Wives that are vile I love not for my sons.
Ismene. Ah, dearest Haemon, how thy father
    shames thee!   615
Creon. Thou with that marriage dost but vex my
    soul.
Chorus. And wilt thou rob thy son of her he loved?
Creon. 'T is Death, not I, shall break the marriage
    off.
Chorus. Her doom is fixed, it seems, then. She
    must die.
Creon. Fixed, yes, by me and thee. No more
    delay,   620
Lead them within, ye slaves. These must be kept
Henceforth as women, suffered not to roam;
For even boldest natures shrink in fear
When they see Hades overshadowing life.
    [*Exeunt* GUARDS *with* ANTIGONE *and* ISMENE.

STROPHE I.

Chorus. Blessed are those whose life no woe doth
    taste!   625
    For unto those whose house
The Gods have shaken, nothing fails of curse
Or woe, that creeps to generations far.

E'en thus a wave, (when spreads,
With blasts from Thracian coasts,   630
The darkness of the deep,)
Up from the sea's abyss
Hither and thither rolls the black sand on,
And every jutting peak,
Swept by the storm-wind's strength,   635
Lashed by the fierce wild waves,
Re-echoes with the far-resounding roar.

ANTISTROPHE I.

I see the woes that smote, in ancient days,
The seed of Labdacus,
Who perished long ago, with grief on grief   640
Still falling, nor does this age rescue that;
Some God still smites it down,
Nor have they any end:
For now there rose a gleam,
Over the last weak shoots,   645
That sprang from out the race of Oedipus;
Yet this the blood-stained scythe
Of those that reign below
Cuts off relentlessly,   649
And maddened speech, and frenzied rage of heart.

STROPHE II.

Thy power, O Zeus, what haughtiness of man,
Yea, what can hold in check?
Which neither sleep, that maketh all things old,
Nor the long months of Gods that never fail,
Can for a moment seize.   655
But still as Lord supreme,
Waxing not old with time,
Thou dwellest in Thy sheen of radiancy
On far Olympus' height.

Through future near or far as through the past, 660
　　One law holds ever good,
Nought comes to life of man unscathed throughout by
　　woe.

Antistrophe II.

For hope to many comes in wanderings wild,
　　A solace and support ;
To many as a cheat of fond desires, 665
And creepeth still on him who knows it not,
　　Until he burn his foot
　　Within the scorching flame.
　　Full well spake one of old,
That evil ever seems to be as good 670
　　To those whose thoughts of heart
　　God leadeth unto woe,
And without woe, he spends but shortest space of
　　time.

And here comes Haemon, last of all thy sons:
　　Comes he bewailing sore 675
The fate of her who should have been his bride,
　　The maid Antigone,
　　Grieving o'er vanished joys?

Enter HAEMON.

Creon. Soon we shall know much more than seers
　　can tell.
Surely thou dost not come, my son, to rage 680
Against thy father, hearing his decree,
Fixing her doom who should have been thy bride ;
Or dost thou love us still, whate'er we do?
　　Haemon. My father, I am thine ; and thou dost
　　　　guide
With thy wise counsels, which I gladly follow. 685

No marriage weighs one moment in the scales
With me, while thou dost guide my steps aright.
   Creon. This thought, my son, should dwell within
      thy breast,
That all things stand below a father's will;
For so men pray that they may rear and keep   690
Obedient offspring by their hearths and homes,
That they may both requite their father's foes,
And pay with him like honors to his friend.
But he who reareth sons that profit not,
What could one say of him but this, that he   695
Breeds his own sorrow, laughter to his foes?
Lose not thy reason, then, my son, o'ercome
By pleasure, for a woman's sake, but know,
A cold embrace is that to have at home
A worthless wife, the partner of thy bed.   700
What ulcerous sore is worse than one we love
Who proves all worthless? No! with loathing scorn,
As hateful to thee, let that girl go wed
A spouse in Hades. Taken in the act
I found her, her alone of all the State,   705
Rebellious. And I will not make myself
False to the State. She dies. So let her call
On Zeus, the lord of kindred. If I rear
Of mine own stock things foul and orderless,
I shall have work enough with those without.   710
For he who in the life of home is good
Will still be seen as just in things of state;
I should be sure that man would govern well,
And know well to be governed, and would stand
In war's wild storm, on his appointed post,   715
A just and good defender. But the man
Who by transgressions violates the laws,
Or thinks to bid the powers that be obey,

He must not hope to gather praise from me.
No! we must follow whom the State appoints, 720
In things or just and trivial, or, may be,
The opposite of these. For anarchy
Is our worst evil, brings our commonwealth
To utter ruin, lays whole houses low,
In battle strife hurls firm allies in flight; 725
But they who yield to guidance, — these shall find
Obedience saves most men. Thus health should come
To what our rulers order; least of all
Ought men to bow before a woman's sway.
Far better, if it must be so, to fall 730
By a man's hand, than thus to bear reproach,
By woman conquered.
   Chorus.   Unto us, O king,
Unless our years have robbed us of our wit,
Thou seemest to say wisely what thou say'st.
   Haemon. The Gods, my father, have bestowed on man 735
His reason, noblest of all earthly gifts;
And that thou speakest wrongly these thy words
I cannot say (God grant I ne'er know how
Such things to utter!), yet another's thoughts
May have some reason. 'Tis my lot to watch 740
What each man says or does, or blames in thee,
For dread thy face to one of low estate,
Who speaks what thou wilt not rejoice to hear.
But I can hear the things in darkness said,
How the whole city wails this maiden's fate, 745
As one "who of all women most unjustly,
For noblest deed must die the foulest death,
Who her own brother, fallen in the fray,
Would neither leave unburied, nor expose
To carrion dogs, or any bird of prey, 750

May she not claim the meed of golden praise?"
Such is the whisper that in secret runs
All darkling. And for me, my father, nought
Is dearer than thy welfare. What can be
A nobler prize of honor for the son
Than a sire's glory, or for sire than son's?
I pray thee, then, wear not one mood alone,
That what thou say'st is right, and nought but that;
For he who thinks that he alone is wise,
His mind and speech above what others have,
Such men when searched are mostly empty found.
But for a man to learn, though he be wise,
Yea, to learn much, and know the time to yield,
Brings no disgrace. When winter floods the streams,
Thou see'st the trees that bend before the storm,
Save their last twigs, while those that will not yield
Perish with root and branch. And when one hauls
Too tight the mainsail rope, and will not slack,
He has to end his voyage with deck o'erturned.
Do thou then yield; permit thyself to change.
Young though I be, if any prudent thought
Be with me, I at least will dare assert
The higher worth of one, who, come what will,
Is full of knowledge. If that may not be,[1]
(For nature is not wont to take that bent,)
'T is good to learn from those who counsel well.

   Chorus. My king, 't is fit that thou shouldst learn from him,
If he speaks words in season; and, in turn,
That thou [*to* HAEMON] shouldst learn of him, for both
    speak well.

   Creon. Shall we at our age stoop to learn from him,
Young as he is, the lesson to be wise?

---

[1] I. e., if he is not wise, he should accept advice.

Haemon. Learn nought thou shouldst not learn. And if I'm young,
Thou shouldst my deeds and not my years consider.
Creon. Is that thy deed to reverence rebel souls?
Haemon. I would bid none waste reverence on the base. ₇₈₅
Creon. Has not that girl been seized with that disease?
Haemon. The men of Thebes with one accord say, "No."
Creon. And will my subjects tell us how to rule?
Haemon. Dost thou not see thou speakest like a boy?
Creon. Must I then rule for others than myself?
Haemon. That is no State which hangs on one man's will. ₇₉₁
Creon. Is not the State deemed his who governs it?
Haemon. Brave rule! Alone, and o'er an empty land!
Creon. This boy, it seems, will be his bride's ally.
Haemon. If thou art she, for thou art all my care.
Creon. Basest of base, against thy father pleading! ₇₉₆
Haemon. Yea, for I see thee sin a grievous sin.
Creon. And do I sin revering mine own sway?
Haemon. Thou show'st no reverence, trampling on God's laws. ₇₉₉
Creon. O guilty soul, by woman's craft beguiled!
Haemon. Thou wilt not find me slave unto the base.
Creon. Thy every word is still on her behalf.
Haemon. Yea, and on thine and mine, and Theirs below.
Creon. Be sure thou shalt not wed her while she lives.

Haemon. Then she must die, and, dying, others
 slay.
Creon. And dost thou dare to come to me with
 threats?
Haemon. Is it a threat against vain thoughts to
 speak?
Creon. Thou to thy cost shalt teach me wisdom's
 ways,
Thyself in wisdom wanting.
 Haemon. I would say
Thou wast unwise, if thou wert not my father.
 Creon. Thou woman's slave, I say, prate on no
 more.
Haemon. Wilt thou then speak, and, speaking,
 listen not?
Creon. Nay, by Olympos! Thou shalt not go free
To flout me with reproaches. Lead her out
Whom my soul hates, that she may die forthwith
Before mine eyes, and near her bridegroom here.
 Haemon. No! Think it not! Near me she shall
 not die,
And thou shalt never see my face alive,
That thou mayst storm at those who like to yield.
 [*Exit.*
Chorus. The man has gone, O king, in hasty
 mood.
A mind distressed in youth is hard to bear.
 Creon. Let him do what he will, and bear himself
As more than man, he shall not save those girls.
 Chorus. What! Dost thou mean to slay them
 both alike?
Creon. Not her who touched it not; there thou
 say'st well.
Chorus. What form of death mean'st thou to slay
 her with?

Creon. Leading her on to where the desert path
Is loneliest, there alive, in rocky cave
Will I immure her, just so much of food
Before her set as may avert pollution,[1]   830
And save the city from the guilt of blood ;
And there, invoking Hades, whom alone
Of all the Gods she worships, she, perchance,
Shall gain escape from death, or then shall know   834
That Hades-worship is but labor lost.   [*Exit.*

STROPHE.

Chorus. O Love, in every battle victor owned ;
    Love, rushing on thy prey,
Now on a maiden's soft and blooming cheek,
    In secret ambush hid ;
Now o'er the broad sea wandering at will,   840
    And now in shepherd's folds ;
Of all the Undying Ones none 'scape from thee,
    Nor yet of mortal men
Whose lives are measured as a fleeting day ;
And who has thee is frenzied in his soul.   845

ANTISTROPHE.

Thou makest vile the purpose of the just,
    To his own fatal harm ;
Thou hast stirred up this fierce and deadly strife,
    Of men of nearest kin ;
The charm of eyes of bride beloved and fair   850
    Is crowned with victory,
And dwells on high among the powers that rule,
    Equal with holiest laws ;

---

[1] " Creon's words point to the popular feeling that if some food, however little, were given to those thus buried alive, the guilt of starving them to death was averted."

ANTIGONE

For Aphrodite, she whom none subdues,
Sports in her might and majesty divine. 855

    I, even I, am borne
    Beyond the appointed laws;
    I look on this, and cannot stay
    The fountain of my tears.
    For, lo! I see her, see Antigone 860
    Wend her sad, lonely way
To that bride-chamber where we all must lie.

Enter ANTIGONE.

Antigone. Behold, O men of this my fatherland,
    I wend my last lone way,
Seeing the last sunbeam, now and nevermore; 865
    He leads me yet alive,
    Hades that welcomes all,
    To Acheron's dark shore,
    With neither part nor lot
    In marriage festival, 870
    Nor hath the marriage hymn
    Been sung for me as bride,
But I shall be the bride of Acheron.
    Chorus. And hast thou not all honor, worthiest praise,
Who goest to the home that hides the dead, 875
Not smitten by the sickness that decays,
    Nor by the sharp sword's meed,
But of thine own free will, in fullest life,
    Alone of mortals, thus
    To Hades tak'st thy way? 880
    Antigone. I heard of old her pitiable end,[1]

---

[1] "The thoughts of Antigone go back to the story of one of her own race, whose fate was in some measure like her own. Niobe,

On Sipylos' high crag,
The Phrygian stranger from a far land come,
   Whom Tantalos begat;
   Whom growth of rugged rock,
   Clinging as ivy clings,
   Subdued, and made its own:
   And now, so runs the tale,
   There, as she melts in shower,
   The snow abideth aye,
And still bedews yon cliffs that lie below
   Those brows that ever weep.
With fate like hers God brings me to my rest.
   Chorus. A Goddess she, and of the high Gods
      born;[1]
And we are mortals, born of mortal seed.
And lo! for one who liveth but to die,
To gain like doom with those of heavenly race,
   Is great and strange to hear.
   Antigone. Ye mock me then. Alas! Why wait
      ye not,
By all our fathers' Gods, I ask of you,
   Till I have passed away,
   But flout me while I live?
   O city that I love,
   O men that claim as yours
   That city stored with wealth,
   O Dirkè, fairest fount,
O grove of Thebes, that boasts her chariot host,
   I bid you witness all,
   How, with no friends to weep,
   By what stern laws condemned,

daughter of Tantalus, became the wife of Amphion, and then, boasting of her children as more and more goodly than those of Leto, provoked the wrath of Apollo and Artemis, who slew her children. She, going to Sipylus, in Phrygia, was there turned into a rock."

[1] Tantalus, the father of Niobe, was himself a son of Zeus.

I go to that strong dungeon of the tomb,
    For burial strange, ah me!
Nor dwelling with the living, nor the dead.
  Chorus. Forward and forward still to farthest verge
    Of daring hast thou gone,   915
And now, O child, thou hast rushed violently
    Where Right erects her throne ;
Surely thou payest to the uttermost
    Thy father's debt of guilt.
  Antigone. Ah! thou hast touched the quick of all
    my grief,   920
The thrice-told tale of all my father's woe,
    The fate which dogs us all,
The old Labdakid race of ancient fame.
    Woe for the curses dire
    Of that defilèd bed,   925
    With foulest incest stained,
    My mother's with my sire,
Whence I myself have sprung, most miserable.
    And now, I go to them,
    To sojourn in the grave,   930
    Accursèd, and unwed ;
    Ah, brother, thou didst find
    Thy marriage fraught with ill,
And thou, though dead, hast smitten down my life.
  Chorus. Acts reverent and devout   935
    May claim devotion's name,
But power, in one to whom power comes as trust,
    May never be defied ;
    And thee, thy stubborn mood,
    Self-chosen, layeth low.   940
  Antigone. Unwept, without a friend,
    Unwed, and whelmed in woe,
I journey on this road that open lies.

No more shall it be mine (O misery!)
To look upon yon daylight's holy eye; 945
　　And yet, of all my friends,
　　Not one bewails my fate,
　　No kindly tear is shed.

　　　　Enter CREON.

Creon. And know ye not, if men have leave to speak
Their songs and wailings thus to stave off death, 950
That they will never stop? Lead, lead her on,
Without delay, and, as I said, immure
In yon cavernous tomb, and then depart.
Leave her to choose, or drear and lonely death,
Or, living, in the tomb to find her home. 955
Our hands are clean in all that touches her;
But she no more shall dwell on earth with us.
　　Antigone. [*Turning towards the cavern.*] O tomb,
　　　my bridal chamber, vaulted home,
Guarded right well for ever, where I go
To join mine own, of whom the greater part 960
Among the dead doth Persephassa [1] hold;
And I, of all the last and saddest, wend
My way below, life's little span unfilled.
And yet I go, and feed myself with hopes
That I shall meet them, by my father loved, 965
Dear to my mother, well-beloved of thee,
Thou darling brother: I, with these my hands,
Washed each dear corpse, arrayed you, poured libations,
In rites of burial; and in care for thee,
Thy body, Polyneices, honoring, 970
I gain this recompense. [And yet in sight

[1] Persephone, or Proserpina, queen among the dead.

Of all that rightly judge, the deed was good;
I had not done it had I come to be
A mother with her children, — had not dared,
Though 't were a husband dead that mouldered there,
Against my country's will to bear this toil. 975
And am I asked what law constrained me thus?
I answer, had I lost a husband dear,
I might have had another; other sons
By other spouse, if one were lost to me: 980
But when my father and my mother sleep
In Hades, then no brother more can come.
And therefore, giving thee the foremost place,
I seemed in Creon's eyes, O brother dear,
To sin in boldest daring. Therefore now 985
He leads me, having taken me by force,
Cut off from marriage bed and marriage song, —
Untasting wife's true joy, or mother's bliss,
With infant at her breast, — but all forlorn,
Bereaved of friends, in utter misery, 990
Alive, I tread the chambers of the dead.]
What law of Heaven have I transgressed against?
What use for me, ill-starred one, still to look
To any God for succor, or to call
On any friend for aid? For holiest deed 995
I bear this charge of rank unholiness.
If acts like these the Gods on high approve,
We, taught by pain, shall own that we have sinned;
But if these sin [*looking at* CREON], I pray they suffer
    not
Worse evils than the wrongs they do to me. 1000
  Chorus. Still do the same wild blasts
    Vex her who standeth there.
  Creon. Therefore shall these her guards
    Weep sore for this delay.

Chorus. Ah me! this word of thine
  Tells of death drawing nigh.
Creon. I cannot bid thee hope
  For other end than this.
Antigone. O citadel of Thebes, my native land,
  Ye Gods of ancient days,
  I go, and linger not.
Behold me, O ye senators of Thebes,
The last, lone scion of the kingly race,
What things I suffer, and from whom they come,
Revering still the laws of reverence.
        [*Guards lead* ANTIGONE *away.*

STROPHE I.

Chorus. So did the form of Danaë bear of old,[1]
  In brazen palace hid,
  To lose the light of heaven,
And in her tomb-like chamber was enclosed:
Yet she, O child, was noble in her race,
And well she stored the golden shower of Zeus.
But great and dread the might of Destiny:
  Nor kingly wealth, nor war,
  Nor tower, nor dark-hulled ships
  Beaten by waves, escape.

ANTISTROPHE I.

So too was shut, enclosed in dungeon cave,
  Bitter and fierce in mood,
  The son of Dryas,[2] king

---

[1] Danaë, though shut up by her father Acrisius, received the golden shower of Zeus, and became the mother of Perseus. See page 70.

[2] The son of Dryas was Lycurgus, who appears in the Iliad, vi. 130, as having, like Pentheus, opposed the worship of Dionysus; he has thus fallen under the wrath of Zeus, who deprived him of sight, and entombed him in a cavern. The Muses are here mentioned as the companions and nurses of Dionysus.

Of yon Edonian tribes, for vile reproach,
By Dionysos' hands, and so his strength   1030
And soul o'ermad wastes drop by drop away,
And so he learnt that he, against the God,
   Spake his mad words of scorn;
   For he the Maenad throng
   And bright fire fain had stopped,   1035
   And roused the Muses' wrath.

STROPHE II.

And by the double sea [1] of those Dark Rocks [2]
   Are shores of Bosporos,
And Thracian isle, as Salmydessos [3] known,
   Where Ares, whom they serve,   1040
   God of the region round,
   Saw the dire, blinding wound,
   That smote the twin-born sons
Of Phineus by relentless step-dame's hand, —
   Dark wound, on dark-doomed eyes,   1045
   Not with the stroke of sword,
But blood-stained hands, and point of spindle sharp.

ANTISTROPHE II.

And they in misery, miserable fate,
   Wasting away, wept sore,
Born of a mother wedded with a curse.   1050

---

[1] The last instance is taken from the early legends of Attica. Boreas, it was said, carried off Oreithyia, daughter of Erechtheus, and by her had two sons and a daughter, Cleopatra. The latter became the wife of Phineus, king of Salmydessus, and bore two sons to him, Plexippus and Pandion. Phineus then divorced her, married another wife, Idaea, and then, at her instigation, deprived his two sons by the former marriage of their sight, and confined Cleopatra in a dungeon. She too, like Danaë and Niobe, was "a child of Gods," and the Erechtheion on the Acropolis was consecrated to the joint worship of her grandfather and of Poseidon.

[2] See Pindar, page 82.   [3] See Aeschylus, page 118, line 847.

   And she who claimed descent
   From men of ancient fame,
   The old Erechtheid race,
   Amid her father's winds,
 Daughter of Boreas, in far distant caves   1055
   Was reared, a child of Gods,
   Swift moving as the steed
   O'er lofty crag, and yet
 The ever-living Fates bore hard on her.

   Enter TEIRESIAS, *guided by a Boy.*

Teiresias. Princes of Thebes, we come as travellers joined,   1060
One seeing for both, for still the blind must use
A guide's assistance to direct his steps.
 Creon. And what new thing, Teiresias, brings thee here?
 Teiresias. I'll tell thee, and do thou the seer obey.
 Creon. Of old I was not wont to slight thy thoughts.   1065
 Teiresias. So didst thou steer our city's course full well.
 Creon. I bear my witness from good profit gained.
 Teiresias. Know, then, thou walk'st on fortune's razor-edge.
 Creon. What means this? How I shudder at thy speech!
 Teiresias. Soon shalt thou know, as thou dost hear the signs   1070
Of my dread art. For sitting, as of old,
Upon my ancient seat of augury,
Where every bird finds haven, lo! I hear
Strange cry of wingèd creatures, shouting shrill,
With inarticulate passion, and I knew   1075

That they were tearing each the other's flesh
With bloody talons, for their whirring wings
Made that quite clear: and straightway I, in fear,
Made trial of the sacrifice that lay
On fiery altar. And Hephaestos' flame 1080
Shone not from out the offering; but there oozed
Upon the ashes, trickling from the bones,
A moisture, and it smouldered, and it spat,
And, lo! the gall was scattered to the air,
And forth from out the fat that wrapped them round
The thigh bones fell. Such omens of decay 1086
From holy sacrifice I learnt from him,
This boy, who now stands here, for he is still
A guide to me, as I to others am.
And all this evil falls upon the State, 1090
From out thy counsels; for our altars all,
Our sacred hearths are full of food for dogs
And birds unclean, the flesh of that poor wretch
Who fell, the son of Oedipus. And so
The Gods no more hear prayers of sacrifice, 1095
Nor own the flame that burns the victim's limbs;
Nor do the birds give cry of omen good,
But feed on carrion of a slaughtered corpse.
Think thou on this, my son: to err, indeed,
Is common unto all, but having erred, 1100
He is no longer reckless or unblest,
Who, having fallen into evil, seeks
For healing, nor continues still unmoved.
Self-will must bear the charge of stubbornness:
Yield to the dead, and outrage not a corpse. 1105
What prowess is it fallen foes to slay?
Good counsel give I, planning good for thee,
And of all joys the sweetest is to learn
From one who speaketh well, should that bring gain.

Creon. Old man, as archers aiming at their mark,
So ye shoot forth your venomed darts at me ; 1111
I know your augur's tricks, and by your tribe
Long since am tricked and sold. Yes, gain your gains,
Get Sardis' amber metal, Indian gold ;
That corpse ye shall not hide in any tomb. 1115
Not though the eagles, birds of Zeus, should bear
Their carrion morsels to the throne of God,
Not even fearing this pollution dire,
Will I consent to burial. Well I know
That man is powerless to pollute the Gods. 1120
But many fall, Teiresias, dotard old,
A shameful fall, who gloze their shameful words
For lucre's sake, with surface show of good.

 Teiresias. Ah me! Does no man know, does none consider . . .

 Creon. Consider what? What trite poor saw comes now? 1125

 Teiresias. How far good counsel is of all things best?

 Creon. So far, I trow, as folly is worst ill.

 Teiresias. Of that disease thy soul, alas! is full.

 Creon. I will not meet a seer with evil words.

 Teiresias. Thou dost so, saying I divine with lies.

 Creon. The race of seers is ever fond of gold. 1131

 Teiresias. And that of tyrants still loves lucre foul.

 Creon. Dost know thou speak'st thy words of those that rule?

 Teiresias. I know. Through me thou rul'st a city saved.

 Creon. Wise seer art thou, yet given o'ermuch to wrong. 1135

 Teiresias. Thou 'lt stir me to speak out my soul's dread secrets.

Creon. Out with them; only speak them not for
    gain.
Teiresias. So is 't, I trow, in all that touches thee.
Creon. Know that thou shalt not bargain with my
    will.
Teiresias. Know, then, and know it well, that thou
    shalt see   1140
Not many winding circuits of the sun,
Before thou giv'st as quittance for the dead,
A corpse by thee begotten;[1] for that thou
Hast to the ground cast one that walked on earth,
And foully placed within a sepulchre   1145
A living soul; and now thou keep'st from them,
The Gods below, the corpse of one unblest,
Unwept, unhallowed, and in these things thou
Canst claim no part, nor yet the Gods above;
But they by thee are outraged; and they wait,   1150
The sure though slow avengers of the grave,
The dread Erinnyes of the mighty Gods,[2]
For thee in these same evils to be snared.
Search well if I say this as one who sells
His soul for money. Yet a little while,   1155
And in thy house the wail of men and women
Shall make it plain. And every city stirs
Itself in arms against thee, owning those
Whose limbs the dogs have buried, or fierce wolves,
Or wingèd birds have brought the accursèd taint   1160
To region consecrate. Doom like to this,
Sure darting as an arrow to its mark,
I launch at thee, (for thou dost vex me sore,)
An archer aiming at the very heart,

---

[1] This of course foretells the death of Haemon.

[2] These goddesses are the avengers of all violations of filial duty or the claims of kinship.

And thou shalt not escape its fiery sting.　　　1165
And now, O boy, lead thou me home again,
That he may vent his spleen on younger men,
And learn to keep his tongue more orderly,
With better thoughts than this his present mood. [*Exit.*

　Chorus. The man has gone, O king, predicting woe,
And well we know, since first our raven hair　　　1171
Was mixed with gray, that never yet his words
Were uttered to our State and failed of truth.

　Creon. I know it too, 't is that that troubles me.
To yield is hard, but, holding out, to smite　　　1175
One's soul with sorrow, this is harder still.

　Chorus. We need wise counsel, O Menoekeus' son.

　Creon. What shall I do? Speak thou, and I'll obey.

　Chorus. Go then, and free the maiden from her tomb,[1]
And give a grave to him who lies exposed.　　　1180

　Creon. Is this thy counsel? Dost thou bid me yield?

　Chorus. Without delay, O king, for lo! they come,
The Gods' swift-footed ministers of ill,
And in an instant lay the self-willed low.　　　1184

　Creon. Ah me! 't is hard; and yet I bend my will
To do thy bidding. With necessity
We must not fight at such o'erwhelming odds.

　Chorus. Go then and act! Commit it not to others.

　Creon. E'en as I am I'll go. Come, come, my men,
Present or absent, come, and in your hands　　　1190
Bring axes: come to yonder eminence.
And I, since now my judgment leans that way,
Who myself bound her, now myself will loose,
Too much I fear lest it should wisest prove
Maintaining ancient laws to end my life.　　　[*Exit.*

　　　[1] The cave in which Antigone had been immured alive.

Strophe I.

Chorus. O Thou of many names,[1] 1196
   Of that Cadmeian maid [2]
   The glory and the joy,
   Whom Zeus as offspring owns,
   Zeus, thundering deep and loud, 1200
Who watchest over famed Italia,[3]
And reign'st o'er all the bays that Deo [4] claims
   On fair Eleusis' coast.
Bacchos, who dwell'st in Thebes, the mother-town
   Of all thy Bacchant train, 1205
   Along Ismenus' stream,
   And with the dragon's brood;[5]

Antistrophe I.

   Thee, o'er the double peak
   Of yonder height the blaze
   Of flashing fire beholds, 1210
   Where nymphs of Corycos [6]

[1] The exulting hopes of the Chorus, rising out of Creon's repentance, seem purposely brought into contrast with the tragedy which is passing while they are in the very act of chanting their hymns. This hymn is addressed to Dionysus.

[2] Semele, the bride of Zeus, who perished when the God revealed himself as the Thunderer. In dying she gave birth to Dionysus.

[3] Southern Italy, the Magna Graecia of the old geographers, is named as famous both for its wines and its *cultus* of Bacchus. A better reading here is Icaria, a rural district of Attica,—the home of Thespis, the legendary founder of the Greek drama, in the sixth century before our era. Excavations were conducted there in 1888 by the American School at Athens.

[4] The goddess Demeter, who with Bacchus (or Iacchus) was worshipped at Eleusis with secret rites.

[5] The people descended from the serpent's teeth sown by Cadmus.

[6] From Italia and Eleusis the Chorus passes to Parnassus, as the centre of the Bacchic *cultus*. On the twin peaks above Delphi flames were said to have been seen, telling of the presence of the God. The Corycian Cave is high up on the mountain.

Go forth in Bacchic dance,
And by the flowery stream of Castaly,
And Thee, the ivied slopes of Nysa's hills,[1]
  And vine-clad promontory, 1215
(While words of more than mortal melody
  Shout out the well-known name,)
  Send forth, the guardian lord
  Of the wide streets of Thebes.

Strophe II.

Above all cities Thou, 1220
With her, thy mother whom the thunder slew,
  Dost look on it with love;
And now, since all the city bendeth low
  Beneath the sullen plague,
  Come Thou with cleansing tread 1225
  O'er the Parnassian slopes,
  Or o'er the moaning straits.[2]

Antistrophe II.

O Thou, who lead'st the band,
The choral band of stars still breathing fire,[3]
  Lord of the hymns of night, 1230
The child of highest Zeus; appear, O king,
  With Thyian maidens wild,
  Who all night long in dance,
  With frenzied chorus sing
  Thy praise, their lord, Iacchos. 1235

---

[1] The "ivied slopes" are those of the Euboean Nysa.

[2] The "moaning straits" of the Euripus, if the God is thought of as coming from Nysa; the "slopes," if he comes from Parnassus.

[3] The imagery of the Bacchic *thiasos*, with its torch-bearers moving in rhythmic order, is transferred to the heavens, and the stars themselves are thought of as a choral band led by the Lord of life and joy.

Enter **Messenger.**

Messenger. Ye men of Cadmus and Amphion's house,[1]
I know no life of mortal man which I
Would either praise or blame. 'T is Fortune's chance
That raiseth up, and Fortune bringeth low,
The man who lives in good or evil plight; 1240
And prophet of men's future there is none.
For Creon, so I deemed, deserved to be
At once admired and envied, having saved
This land of Cadmus from the hands of foes;
And, having ruled with fullest sovereignty, 1245
He lived and prospered, joyous in a race
Of goodly offspring. Now, all this is gone;
For when men lose the joys that sweeten life,
I cannot deem they live, but rather count
As if a breathing corpse. His heaped-up stores 1250
Of wealth are large, so be it, and he lives
With all a sovereign's state; and yet, if joy
Be absent, all the rest I count as nought,
And would not weigh them against pleasure's charm,
More than a vapor's shadow.
   Chorus. What is this? 1255
What new disaster tell'st thou of our chiefs?
   Messenger. Dead are they, and the living cause their death.
   Chorus. Who slays, and who is slaughtered? Tell thy tale.
   Messenger. Haemon is dead, slain, weltering in his blood.
   Chorus. By his own act, or by his father's hand?

---

[1] In the myths of the foundation of Thebes, Amphion was said to have built its walls by the mere power of his minstrelsy, the stones moving, as he played, each into its appointed place.

Messenger. His own, in wrath against his father's
  crime.   1261
Chorus. O prophet! true, most true, those words of
  thine.
Messenger. Since things stand thus, we well may
  counsel take.
Chorus. Lo! Creon's wife comes, sad Eurydice.
She from the house approaches, hearing speech   1265
About her son, or else by accident.

Enter EURYDICE.

Eurydice. I on my way, my friends, as suppliant
  bound,
To pay my vows at Pallas' shrine, have heard
Your words, and so I chanced to draw the bolt
Of the half-opened door, when lo! a sound   1270
Falls on my ears, of evil striking home,
And terror-struck I fall in deadly swoon
Back in my handmaids' arms; yet tell it me,
Tell the tale once again, for I shall hear,
By long experience disciplined to grief.   1275
Messenger. Dear lady, I will tell thee: I was by,
And will not leave one word of truth untold.
Why should we smooth and gloze, where all too soon
We should be found as liars? Truth is still
The only safety. Lo! I went with him,   1280
Thy husband, in attendance, to the edge
Of yonder plain, where still all ruthlessly
The corpse of Polyneices lay exposed,
Mangled by dogs. And, having prayed to her,
The Goddess of all pathways,[1] and to Pluto,   1285

---

[1] Hecate, here apparently identified with Persephone, and named also as the Goddess who, being the guardian of highways, was wroth with Thebes for the pollution caused by the unburied corpse of Polyneices.

To temper wrath with pity, him they washed
With holy washing; and what yet was left
We burnt in branches freshly cut, and heaped
A high-raised grave from out his native soil,
And then we entered on the stone-paved home, 1290
Death's marriage-chamber for the ill-starred maid.
And some one hears, while standing yet afar,
Shrill voice of wailing near the bridal bower,
By funeral rites unhallowed, and he comes
And tells my master, Creon. On his ears, 1295
Advancing nearer, falls a shriek confused
Of bitter sorrow, and with groaning loud,
He utters one sad cry, "Me miserable!
And am I then a prophet? Do I wend
This day the dreariest way of all my life? 1300
My son's voice greets me. Go, my servants, go,
Quickly draw near, and standing by the tomb,
Search ye and see; and where the stone torn out
Shall make an opening, look ye in, and say
If I hear Haemon's voice, or if my soul 1305
Is cheated by the Gods." And then we searched,
As he, our master, in his frenzy bade us;
And, in the furthest corner of the vault,
We saw her hanging by her neck, with cord
Of linen threads entwined, and him we found 1310
Clasping her form in passionate embrace,
And mourning o'er the doom that robbed him of her,
His father's deed, and that his marriage bed,
So full of woe. When Creon saw him there,
Groaning aloud in bitterness of heart, 1315
He goes to him, and calls in wailing voice,
"Poor boy! what hast thou done? Hast thou then lost
Thy reason? In what evil sinkest thou?

Come forth, my child, on bended knee I ask thee."
And then the boy, with fierce, wild-gleaming eyes, 1320
Glared at him, spat upon his face, and draws,
Still answering nought, the sharp two-handled sword.
Missing his aim, (his father from the blow
Turning aside,) in anger with himself,
The poor ill-doomed one, even as he was, 1325
Fell on his sword, and drove it through his breast,
Full half its length, and clasping, yet alive,
The maiden's arm, still soft, he there breathes out
In broken gasps, upon her fair white cheek,
Swift stream of bloody shower. So they lie, 1330
Dead bridegroom with dead bride, and he has gained,
Poor boy, his marriage rites in Hades' home,
And left to all men witness terrible,
That man's worst ill is want of counsel wise.
[*Exit* EURYDICE.

Chorus. What dost thou make of this? She turn-
  eth back, 1335
Before one word, or good or ill, she speaks.

Messenger. I too am full of wonder. Yet with hopes
I feed myself, she will not think it meet,
Hearing her son's woes, openly to wail
Out in the town, but to her handmaids [1] there 1340
Will give command to wail her woe at home.
Too trained a judgment has she so to err.

Chorus. I know not. To my mind, or silence hard,
Or vain wild cries, are signs of bitter woe.

Messenger. Soon we shall know, within the house
  advancing, 1345
If, in the passion of her heart, she hides
A secret purpose. Truly dost thou speak;
There is a terror in that silence hard.

[1] Compare the wailing of women for Hector, page 19.

Seeing CREON *approaching with the corpse of* HAEMON *in his arms.*

Chorus. And lo! the king himself is drawing nigh,
And in his hands he bears a record clear,   1350
No woe (if I may speak) by others caused,
  Himself the great offender.

Enter CREON, *bearing* HAEMON'S *body.*

Creon. Woe! for the sins of souls of evil mood,
  Stern, mighty to destroy!
O ye who look on those of kindred race,   1355
  The slayers and the slain,
Woe for mine own rash plans that prosper not!
Woe for thee, son; but new in life's career,
  And by a new fate dying!
    Woe! woe!   1360
  Thou diest, thou art gone,
Not by thine evil counsel, but by mine.
  Chorus. Ah me! Too late thou seem'st to see the right.
  Creon.   Ah me!
I learn the grievous lesson. On my head,
God, pressing sore, hath smitten me and vexed,   1365
In ways most rough and terrible (ah me!),
Shattering my joy, as trampled under foot.
Woe! woe! Man's labors are but labor lost.

Enter Second Messenger.

Second Messenger. My master! thou, as one who hast full store,
One source of sorrow bearest in thine arms,   1370
And others in thy house, too soon, it seems,
Thou need'st must come and see.
  Creon.   And what remains
Worse evil than the evils that we bear?

Second Messenger. Thy wife is dead, that corpse's
    mother true,
Ill starred one, smitten with a blow just dealt.   1375
    Creon. O agony!
Haven of Death, that none may pacify,
    Why dost thou thus destroy me?
             Turning to MESSENGER.
O thou who comest, bringing in thy train
    Woes horrible to tell,   1380
Thou tramplest on a man already slain.
What say'st thou? What new tidings bring'st to me?
    Ah me! ah me!
Is it that now there waits in store for me
My own wife's death to crown my misery?   1385
    Chorus. Full clearly thou mayst see. No longer now
Does yon recess conceal her.
    The gates open and show the dead body of EURYDICE.
    Creon.   Woe is me!
This second ill I gaze on, miserable,
What fate, yea, what still lies in wait for me?
Here in my arms I bear what was my son;   1390
And there, O misery! look upon the dead.
Ah, wretched mother! ah, my son! my son!
    Second Messenger. In frenzy wild she round the
    altar clung,
And closed her darkening eyelids, and bewailed
The noble fate of Megareus,[1] who died   1395
Long since, and then again that corpse thou hast;
And last of all she cried a bitter cry
Against thy deeds, the murderer of thy sons.
    Creon. Woe! woe! alas!
I shudder in my fear. Will no one strike   1400

---

[1] In the legend which Sophocles here follows, Megarus, a son of Creon and Eurydice, had offered himself as a sacrifice to save the state from its dangers.

A deadly blow with sharp two-edgèd sword?
  Fearful my fate, alas!
And with a fearful woe full sore beset.
  Second Messenger. She in her death charged thee
    with being the cause
Of all their sorrows, these and those of old.
  Creon. And in what way struck she the murderous
    blow?
  Second Messenger. With her own hand below her
    heart she stabbed,
Hearing her son's most pitiable fate.
  Creon. Ah me! The fault is mine. On no one
    else,
Of all that live, the fearful guilt can come;
I, even I, did slay thee, woe is me!
I, yes, I speak the truth. Lead me, ye guards,
Lead me forth quickly; lead me out of sight,
More crushed to nothing than is nothing's self.
  Chorus. Thou counsellest gain, if gain there be in
    ills,
For present ills when shortest then are best.
  Creon. O, come thou then, come thou,
The last of all my dooms, that brings to me
Best boon, my life's last day. Come then, O come,
That never more I look upon the light.
  Chorus. These things are in the future. What is
    near,
That we must do. O'er what is yet to come
They watch, to Whom that work of right belongs.
  Creon. I did but pray for what I most desire.
  Chorus. Pray thou for nothing then: for mortal
    man
There is no issue from a doom decreed.
  Creon [*looking at the two corpses*]. Lead me
    then forth, vain shadow that I am,

Who slew thee, O my son, unwillingly,
And thee too — (O my sorrow!) — and I know not
Which way to look or turn. All near at hand   1430
Is turned to evil; and upon my head
There falls a doom far worse than I can bear.
   Chorus. Man's highest blessedness,
     In wisdom chiefly stands;
And in the things that touch upon the Gods,   1435
     'T is best in word or deed,
     To shun unholy pride;
Great words of boasting bring great punishments,
     And so to gray-haired age
     Teach wisdom at the last.   1440

EURIPIDES

EURIPIDES, the last of the "tragic triad of immortal fames," was born on the island of Salamis in 480 B. C., the year of the famous battle there. Whether he was born, as tradition says, on the very day of the battle, is uncertain, but the story at least gives us a chain with which to bind together the three poets: Aeschylus fought at Marathon in 490 and at Salamis in 480 B. C., Sophocles led the paean of thanksgiving for the battle of Salamis, and in the year of that battle Euripides was born.

Unlike the other two, Euripides took no part in public affairs, but spent his life in seclusion and study. He died in 406 B. C. (the same year as Sophocles), in Macedonia, where he had lived some years at the court of King Archelaus.

"Euripides is the mediator between ancient and modern drama." During the fifth century a change had come over the spirit of the Athenian people which made natural a change in the dramas presented to them. Their faith in their national religion, which was the foundation of all their dramatic art, was undermined, and their interest in mythical stories thereby lessened. The heroes of the old tales no longer excited interest of themselves, and could be made to do it only by being endowed with more realism, having their joys and sorrows and human passions portrayed more vividly than ever before. Euripides saw this need, and supplied it by drawing men not as they should be, as Sophocles said he himself had done, but as they actually were. For this innovation, necessary and right as it was, he was severely criticised by the conservative among his contemporaries, notably by the poet Aristophanes, who believed that the tragedies of Aeschylus and Sophocles were the only right models.

The popularity of Euripides with the masses is undoubted, and is attested by the well-known story that many of the Athenian prisoners taken by the Syracusans in 415 B. C. received their liberty in return for their recitations of parts of his plays. His tragedies were played or read with interest well into the Christian era, and had a marked influence upon the Roman drama, and the classical tragedy in France. He appeals to the reader of to-day perhaps more than the other Greek tragedians, because he is more "modern" in his treatment of the same human interests that are alive for us to-day. Mrs. Browning has described him in these well-known lines: —

> "Our Euripides the Human
> With his droppings of warm tears,
> And his touches of things common
> Till they rose to touch the spheres."

The story of the *Heracles* (*Hercules*) may be briefly told. The last of the twelve labors which Heracles had to perform for his cousin Eurystheus was to fetch the three-headed dog, Cerberus, from the lower world. He departed on this mission, leaving his father Amphitryon, his wife Megara, and his sons under the protection of his wife's father, Creon, the aged king of Thebes. During his absence, Lycus, after slaying Creon, assumes the throne, and determines to put to death the family of Heracles, lest they should avenge the murder of the king. Heracles returns from Hades just in time to save them, and in his turn kills Lycus. As he is offering an expiatory sacrifice after the deed, he is struck with madness sent by his arch-enemy, the goddess Hera, and in his frenzy slays his own wife and children, believing them to be those of the hated Eurystheus. In his agony when he awakens and discovers the truth, he is about to kill himself, but is persuaded by Theseus to come to Athens and there seek pardon from the gods.

The following portions of the play are from the translation of Robert Browning, which is included in his poem *Aristophanes' Apology*.[1]

THE FATE OF HERACLES

This ode is sung by the Chorus of Thebans in honor of Heracles, who they fear may have perished on his mission to Hades. They give an account of his former labors, wrought for Eurystheus, and lament that he is not at hand to deliver his father, his wife, and his children, who are even now to be slain by Lycus, the usurping king.

EVEN a dirge, can Phoibos suit 386
In song to music jubilant
For all its sorrow: making shoot
His golden plectron o'er the lute,
Melodious ministrant. 390
And I, too, am of mind to raise,
Despite the imminence of doom,
A song of joy, outpour my praise
To him — what is it rumor says? —
Whether — now buried in the ghostly gloom 395
Below ground — he was child of Zeus indeed,
Or mere Amphitruon's mortal seed —
To him I weave the wreath of song, his labor's meed.
For, is my hero perished in the feat?

[1] Mr. Browning preferred to transliterate Greek proper names instead of using the Latin forms, which are more familiar to English readers. Thus *Phoibos* is for Phoebus Apollo; *Peneios* for Peneus, the chief river of Thessaly; *Haides* for Hades, the place of departed spirits; *Kentaur* for Centaur, a fabulous race of beings, half horse and half man; *Mukenai* for Mycenae, the chief fortress and palace in Argolis; *Kuknos* for Cycnus; *Kuklops* for Cyclops, one of the race which was said to have built the "Cyclopean walls" of Tiryns; *Herakles* for Hercules; *Eurustheus* for Eurystheus, king of Tiryns, who was allowed by the gods to impose twelve tasks or "labors" on his mightier kinsman Hercules; *Asklepios* for Aesculapius; *Plouton* for Pluto; *Amphitruon* for Amphitryo.

The virtues of brave toils, in death complete, 400
These save the dead in song, — their glory-garland
    meet!

First, then, he made the wood
Of Zeus a solitude,
Slaying its lion-tenant; and he spread
The tawniness behind — his yellow head 405
Enmuffled by the brute's, backed by that grin of dread.[1]
The mountain-roving savage Kentaur-race
He strewed with deadly bow about their place,
Slaying with winged shafts: Peneios knew,
Beauteously-eddying, and the long tracts too 410
Of pasture trampled fruitless, and as well
Those desolated haunts Mount Pelion under,
And, grassy up to Homolé, each dell
Whence, having filled their hands with pine-tree
    plunder,
Horse-like was wont to prance from, and subdue 415
The land of Thessaly, that bestial crew.
The golden-headed spot-backed stag he slew,
That robber of the rustics: glorified
Therewith the goddess who in hunter's pride
Slaughters the game along Oinoé's side.[2] 420
And, yoked abreast, he brought the chariot-breed
To pace submissive to the bit, each steed
That in the bloody cribs of Diomede
Champed and, unbridled, hurried down that gore
For grain, exultant the dread feast before — 425
Of man's flesh:[3] hideous feeders they of yore!
All as he crossed the Hebros' silver-flow

---

[1] Heracles killed the Nemean lion by strangling it, and clothed himself in its impenetrable hide, the jaws covering his head.

[2] The golden-horned hind was dedicated to Artemis.

[3] Diomed, a king in Thrace, fed his mares on the strangers coming

Accomplished he such labor, toiling so
For Mukenaian tyrant; ay, and more —
He crossed the Melian shore 430
And, by the sources of Amauros, shot
To death that strangers'-pest
Kuknos, who dwelt in Amphanaia: not
Of fame for good to guest!

And next, to the melodious maids he came, 435
Inside the Hesperian court-yard : hand must aim
At plucking gold fruit from the appled leaves,
Now he had killed the dragon, backed like flame,
Who guards the unapproachable he weaves
Himself all round, one spire about the same. 440
And into those sea-troughs of ocean dived
The hero, and for mortals calm contrived,
Whatever oars should follow in his wake.
And under heaven's mid-seat his hands thrust he,
At home with Atlas: and, for valor's sake, 445
Held the gods up their star-faced mansionry.[1]
Also, the rider-host of Amazons
About Maiotis many-streamed, he went
To conquer through the billowy Euxine once,
Having collected what an armament 450
Of friends from Hellas, all on conquest bent
Of that gold-garnished cloak, dread girdle-chase ! [2]
So Hellas gained the girl's barbarian grace
And at Mukenai saves the trophy still —
Go wonder there, who will ! 455

to his country. Heracles overcame the king, and took the horses to Mycenae. See the Alcestis, page 221, line 736.

[1] While Atlas went to get the apples of the Hesperides for Heracles that hero undertook the giant's task of holding the heavens on his shoulders.

[2] Eurystheus required Heracles to bring home the girdle of Hippolyta, queen of the Amazons.

And the ten thousand headed hound
Of many a murder, the Lernaian snake
He burned out, head by head, and cast around
His darts a poison thence,¹ — darts soon to slake
Their rage in that three-bodied herdsman's gore   460
Of Erutheia.² Many a running more
He made for triumph and felicity,
And, last of toils, to Haides, never dry
Of tears, he sailed : and there he, luckless, ends
His life completely, nor returns again.   465
The house and home are desolate of friends,
And where the children's life-path leads them, plain
I see, — no step retraceable, no god
Availing, and no law to help the lost!
The oar of Charon marks their period,³   470
Waits to end all. Thy hands, these roofs accost! —
To thee, though absent, look their uttermost!

But if in youth and strength I flourished still,
Still shook the spear in fight, did power match will
In these Kadmeian co-mates of my age,   475
They would, — and I, — when warfare was to wage,
Stand by these children; but I am bereft
Of youth now, lone of that good genius left!

But hist, desist! for here come these, —
Draped as the dead go, under and over, —   480

---

¹ The Lernaean Hydra had nine heads, one of which was immortal. Whenever one was cut off two others appeared in its place. Heracles burned off the heads one by one, and buried the ninth, which was immortal, under a rock. He dipped his arrow-points in the poisonous gore of the monster.

² Geryon, a three-bodied monster, whose oxen Heracles captured for Eurystheus.

³ Charon was the ferryman of the souls of the dead over the river Styx in the lower world. See the Alcestis, page 211, line 375, and page 219, line 637.

Children long since — now hard to discover —
Of the once so potent Herakles!
And the loved wife dragging, in one tether
About her feet, the boys together;
And the hero's aged sire comes last! 485
Unhappy that I am! Of tears which rise, —
How am I all unable to hold fast,
Longer, the aged fountains of these eyes!

. . . .

THE MADNESS OF HERACLES

Heracles returned from the lower world just in time to save his family from death by himself slaying Lycus. While he is offering sacrifice to cleanse him from this murder, the frenzy comes upon him. Since it was against the Greek spirit to put such a scene as the following before the eyes of the audience, it is narrated to the Chorus by a messenger.

The victims were before the hearth of Zeus,
A household-expiation: since the king
O' the country, Herakles had killed and cast
From out the dwelling; and a beauteous choir 985
Of boys stood by, his sire, too, and his wife.
And now the basket had been carried round
The altar in a circle, and we used
The consecrated speech. Alkmené's son, —
Just as he was about, in his right hand, 990
To bear the torch, that he might dip into
The cleansing-water, — came to a stand-still;
And, as their father yet delayed, his boys
Had their eyes on him. But he was himself
No longer: lost in rollings of the eyes; 995
Out-thrusting eyes — their very roots — like blood!
Froth he dropped down his bushy-bearded cheek,
And said, — together with a madman's laugh —

"Father! why sacrifice, before I slay
Eurustheus? why have twice the lustral fire, 1000
And double pains, when 't is permitted me
To end, with one good hand-sweep, matters here?
Then, — when I hither bring Eurusthens' head, —
Then for these just slain, wash hands once for all!
Now, — cast drink-offerings forth, throw baskets
 down! 1005
Who gives me bow and arrows, who my club?
I go to that Mukenai! One must match
Crowbars and mattocks, so that — those sunk stones
The Kuklops squared with picks and plumb-line
 red [1] —
I, with my bent steel, may o'ertumble town!" 1010
Which said, he goes and — with no car to have —
Affirms he has one! mounts the chariot-board,
And strikes, as having really goad in hand!
And two ways laughed the servants — laugh with
 awe;
And one said, as each met the other's stare, 1015
"Playing us boys' tricks? or is master mad?"
But up he climbs, and down along the roof,
And, dropping into the men's place, maintains
He 's come to Nisos city,[2] when he 's come
Only inside his own house! then reclines 1020
On floor, for couch, and, as arrived indeed,
Makes himself supper; goes through some brief stay,
Then says he 's traversing the forest-flats
Of Isthmos;[3] thereupon lays body bare
Of bucklings, and begins a contest with 1025

---

[1] The mighty Cyclopean walls at Mycenae are still to be seen.

[2] Megara, on the route to Mycenae.

[3] Corinth, the seat of the Isthmian Games, in which Heracles fancies himself to engage.

— No one! and is proclaimed the conqueror —
He by himself — having called out to hear
— Nobody! Then, if you will take his word,
Blaring against Eurustheus horribly,
He's at Mukenai. But his father laid 1030
Hold of the strong hand and addressed him thus:
"O son, what ails thee? Of what sort is this
Extravagance? Has not some murder-craze,
Bred of those corpses thou didst just despatch,
Dancèd thee drunk?" But he, — taking him to crouch, 1035
Eurustheus' sire, that apprehensive touched
His hand, a suppliant, — pushes him aside,
Gets ready quiver, and bends bow against
His children — thinking them Eurustheus' boys
He means to slay. They, horrified with fear, 1040
Rushed here and there, — this child, into the robes
O' the wretched mother, — this, beneath the shade
O' the column, — and this other, like a bird,
Cowered at the altar-foot. The mother shrieks
"Parent — what dost thou? — kill thy children?" So
Shriek the old sire and crowd of servitors. 1045
But he, outwinding him, as round about
The column ran the boy, — a horrid whirl
O' the lathe his foot described! — stands opposite,
Strikes through the liver![1] and supine the boy 1050
Bedews the stone shafts, breathing out his life.
But "Victory!" he shouted, boasted thus:
"Well, this one nestling of Eurustheus — dead —
Falls by me, pays back the paternal hate!"
Then bends bow on another who was crouched 1055
At base of altar — overlooked, he thought —

[1] For the liver, used much like the English *heart*, see Prometheus, page 132, line 1215.

And now prevents [1] him, falls at father's knee,
Throwing up hand to beard and cheek above.
"O dearest!" cries he, "father, kill me not!
Yours, I am — your boy: not Eurustheus' boy   1060
You kill now!" But he, rolling the wild eye
Of Gorgon, — as the boy stood all too close
For deadly bowshot, — mimicry of smith
Who batters red-hot iron, — hand o'er head
Heaving his club, on the boy's yellow hair   1065
Hurls it and breaks the bone. This second caught, —
He goes, would slay the third, one sacrifice
He and the couple; but, beforehand here,
The miserable mother catches up,
Carries him inside house and bars the gate.   1070
Then he, as he were at those Kuklops' work,[2]
Digs at, heaves doors up, wrenches doorposts out,
Lays wife and child low with the selfsame shaft.
And this done, at the old man's death he drives;
But there came, as it seemed to us who saw,   1075
A statue — Pallas with the crested head,
Swinging her spear — and threw a stone which smote
Herakles' breast and stayed his slaughter-rage,
And sent him safe to sleep. He falls to ground —
Striking against the column with his back —   1080
Column which, with the falling of the roof,
Broken in two, lay by the altar-base.
And we, foot-free now from our several flights,
Along with the old man, we fastened bonds
Of rope-noose to the column, so that he,   1085
Ceasing from sleep, might not go adding deeds
To deeds done. And he sleeps a sleep, poor wretch,
No gift of any god! since he has slain
Children and wife. For me, I do not know
What mortal has more misery to bear.   1090

[1] In original sense, *anticipates*.   [2] Cf. p. 198, line 1009.

ALCESTIS

Admetus, a king of Thessaly, was doomed to die, but the god Apollo, who had once, as a punishment for an offence to Zeus, served him for a year, and so become attached to the family, begged the Fates to release him from this necessity. They agreed to spare Admetus if some one else would die in his stead. This his wife Alcestis, alone, was willing to do. But after her death, Heracles, the strongest of the heroes, passing through Thessaly on his way to Thrace to perform his eighth labor, learned of the calamity, and going to her tomb wrestled with Death and compelled the release of Alcestis and restored her to Admetus. The play opens on the day appointed for Alcestis' death. The situation is stated by Apollo in the prologue.

The *Alcestis* is the earliest of the extant plays of Euripides, being presented in 438 B.C. It is not a tragedy in the strict sense of the term, but took the place of the so-called Satyrdrama, at the close of the presentation of three tragedies (a *trilogy*).

The translation of the *Alcestis* here given is Robert Browning's, included in the poem *Balaustion's Adventure*, written in 1871. The italicized lines are by Browning, not by Euripides, but serve well as an interpretation of the rest, which for the most part is a literal translation from the Greek.[1]

There slept a silent palace in the sun,
With plains adjacent and Thessalian peace —
Pherai, where King Admetos ruled the land.

Out from the portico there gleamed a God,
Apollon: for the bow was in his hand. 5
The quiver at his shoulder, all his shape
One dreadful beauty. And he hailed the house
As if he knew it well and loved it much:
" O Admeteian domes, where I endured,
Even the God I am, to drudge awhile, 10
Do righteous penance for a reckless deed,

[1] For Mr. Browning's transliteration of Greek names see p. 193.

Accepting the slaves' table thankfully!"
Then told¹ how Zeus had been the cause of all,
Raising the wrath in him which took revenge
And slew those forgers of the thunderbolt 15
Wherewith Zeus blazed the life from out the breast
Of Phoibos' son Asklepios (I surmise,
Because he brought the dead to life again)
And so, for punishment, must needs go slave,
God as he was, with a mere mortal lord: 20
— Told how he came to King Admetos' land,
And played the ministrant, was herdsman there,
Warding all harm away from him and his
Till now; "For, holy as I am," *said he,*
"The lord I chanced upon was holy too: 25
Whence I deceived the Moirai,² drew from death
My master, this same son of Pheres, — ay,
The Goddesses conceded him escape
From Hades, when the fated day should fall,
Could he exchange lives, find some friendly one 30
Ready, for his sake, to content the grave.
But trying all in turn, the friendly list,
Why, he found no one, none who loved so much,
Nor father, nor the aged mother's self
That bore him, no, not any save his wife, 35
Willing to die instead of him and watch
Never a sunrise nor a sunset more:
And she is even now within the house,
Upborne by pitying hands, the feeble frame
Gasping its last of life out; since to-day 40
Destiny is accomplished, and she dies,
And I, lest here pollution light on me,
Leave, as ye witness, all my wonted joy
In this dear dwelling. Ay, — for here comes Death

¹ The Fates.   ² Verses 13-23 are a paraphrase.

Close on us of a sudden! who, pale priest 45
Of the mute people, means to bear his prey
To the house of Hades. The symmetric step!
How he treads true to time and place and thing,
Dogging day, hour and minute, for death's-due!"

And we observed another Deity, 50
Half in, half out the portal, — watch and ward, —
Eyeing his fellow: formidably fixed,
Yet faltering too at who affronted him, 53

. . . .
So, each antagonist
Silently faced his fellow and forbore. 71
Till Death shrilled, hard and quick, in spite and fear:

"Ha ha, and what may'st thou do at the domes,[1]
Why hauntest here, thou Phoibos? Here again
At the old injustice, limiting our rights, 75
Balking of honor due us Gods o' the grave?
Was 't not enough for thee to have delayed
Death from Admetos, — with thy crafty art
Cheating the very Fates, — but thou must arm
The bow-hand and take station, press 'twixt me 80
And Pelias' daughter,[2] who then saved her spouse, —
Did just that, now thou comest to undo, —
Taking his place to die, Alkestis here?"

But the God sighed, "Have courage! All my arms,
This time, are simple justice and fair words." 85

Then each plied each with rapid interchange:

"What need of bow, were justice arms enough?"
"Ever it is my wont to bear the bow."

[1] I. e., at this house. Cf. lines 9, 421.   [2] Alcestis.

"Ay, and with bow, not justice, help this house!"
"I help it, since a friend's woe weighs me too." 90
"And now, — wilt force from me this second corpse?"
"By force I took no corpse at first from thee."
"How then is he above ground, not beneath?"
"He gave his wife instead of him, thy prey."
"And prey, this time at least, I bear below!" 95
"Go take her! — for I doubt persuading thee . . ."
"To kill the doomed one? What my function else?"
"No! Rather, to despatch the true mature."
"Truly I take thy meaning, see thy drift!"
"Is there a way then she may reach old age?" 100
"No way! I glad me in my honors too!"
"But, young or old, thou tak'st one life, no more!"
"Younger they die, greater my praise redounds!"
"If she die old, — the sumptuous funeral!"
"Thou layest down a law the rich would like." 105
"How so? Did wit lurk there and 'scape thy sense?"
"Who could buy substitutes would die old men."
"It seems thou wilt not grant me, then, this grace?"
"This grace I will not grant: thou know'st my ways."
"Ways harsh to men, hateful to Gods, at least!" 110
"All things thou canst not have: my rights for me!"

And then Apollon prophesied, — I think,
More to himself than to impatient Death,
Who did not hear or would not heed the while, —
For he went on to say " Yet even so, 115

Cruel above the measure, thou shalt clutch
No life here! Such a man do I perceive
Advancing to the house of Pheres now,
Sent by Eurustheus[1] to bring out of Thrace,
The winter world, a chariot with its steeds! 120
He indeed, when Admetos proves the host,
And he the guest, at the house here, — he it is
Shall bring to bear such force, and from thy hands
Rescue this woman. Grace no whit to me
Will that prove, since thou dost thy deed the same, 125
And earnest too my hate, and all for nought!"

But how should Death or stay or understand?
Doubtless, he only felt the hour was come,
And the sword free; for he but flung some taunt —
"Having talked much, thou wilt not gain the more! 130
This woman, then, descends to Hades' hall
Now that I rush on her, begin the rites
O' the sword; for sacred, to us Gods below,
That head whose hair this sword shall sanctify!" [2]

And, in the fire-flash of the appalling sword, 135
The uprush and the outburst, the onslaught
Of Death's portentous passage through the door,
Apollon stood a pitying moment-space:
I caught one last gold gaze upon the night
Nearing the world now: and the God was gone, 140
And mortals left to deal with misery,
As in came stealing slow, now this, now that
Old sojourner throughout the country-side,[3]
Servants grown friends to those unhappy here:

---

[1] King of Tiryns, who imposed on Heracles the twelve "labors."
Cf. p. 192 f. The next line refers to the eighth labor. Cf. line 736.
[2] A lock of hair was cut from the victim before sacrifice.
[3] This marks the entrance of the chorus.

And, cloudlike in their increase, all these griefs 145
Broke and began the over-brimming wail,
Out of a common impulse, word by word.

" What now may mean the silence at the door?
Why is Admetos' mansion stricken dumb?
Not one friend near, to say if we should mourn 150
Our mistress dead, or if Alkestis lives
And sees the light still, Pelias' child — to me,
To all, conspicuously the best of wives
That ever was toward husband in this world!
Hears any one or wail beneath the roof, 155
Or hands that strike each other, or the groan
Announcing all is done and nought to dread?
Still not a servant stationed at the gates!
O Paian,[1] that thou wouldst dispart the wave
O' the woe, be present! Yet, had woe o'erwhelmed
The housemates, they were hardly silent thus: 161
It cannot be, the dead is forth and gone.
Whence comes thy gleam of hope?[2] I dare not hope:
What is the circumstance that heartens thee?
How could Admetos have dismissed a wife 165
So worthy, unescorted to the grave?
Before the gates I see no hallowed vase
Of fountain-water, such as suits death's door;
Nor any clipt locks strew the vestibule,[3]
Though surely these drop when we grieve the dead, 170
Nor hand sounds smitten against youthful hand,
The women's way. And yet — the appointed time —
How speak the word? — this day is even the day
Ordained her for departing from its light.
O touch calamitous to heart and soul! 175

---

[1] God of healing, often identified with Apollo.
[2] These questions are addressed by one of the chorus to another.
[3] The hair was cut as a sign of mourning for near friends.

ALCESTIS 207

Needs must one, when the good are tortured so,
Sorrow, — one reckoned faithful from the first."

*Then their souls rose together, and one sigh
Went up in cadence from the common mouth:
How* "Vainly — anywhither in the world   180
Directing or land-labor or sea-search —
To Lukia or the sand-waste, Ammon's seat [1] —
Might you set free their hapless lady's soul
From the abrupt Fate's footstep instant now.
Not a sheep-sacrificer at the hearths   185
Of Gods had they to go to: one there was
Who, if his eyes saw light still, — Phoibos' son,[2]—
Had wrought so she might leave the shadowy place
And Hades' portal; for he propped up Death's
Subdued ones till the Zeus-flung thunder-flame   190
Struck him; and now what hope of life were hailed
With open arms? For, all the king could do
Is done already, — not one God whereof
The altar fails to reek with sacrifice:
And for assuagement of these evils — nought!"   195

*But here they broke off, for a matron moved
Forth from the house: and, as her tears flowed fast,
They gathered round.* "What fortune shall we hear?
For mourning thus, if aught affect thy lord,
We pardon thee: but lives the lady yet   200
Or has she perished? — that we fain would know!"

"Call her dead, call her living, each style serves,"

---

[1] In Egypt, where was a temple to Zeus Ammon.
[2] Asclepius (Aesculapius), the god of healing, who once restored a dead man to life, and for his presumption was smitten by Zeus' thunderbolt. See page 202, line 18.

The matron said: " though grave-ward bowed, she breathed ;
Nor knew her husband what the misery meant
Before he felt it: hope of life was none :   205
The appointed day pressed hard; the funeral pomp
He had prepared too."
                        When the friends broke out:
" Let her in dying know herself at least
Sole wife, of all the wives 'neath the sun wide,
For glory and for goodness!" — "Ah, how else   210
Than best? who controverts the claim?" *quoth she:*
" What kind of creature should the woman prove
That has surpassed Alkestis? — surelier shown
Preference for her husband to herself
Than by determining to die for him?   215
But so much all our city knows indeed:
Hear what she did indoors and wonder then!
For, when she felt the crowning day was come,
She washed with river-waters her white skin,
And, taking from the cedar closets forth   220
Vesture and ornament, bedecked herself
Nobly, and stood before the hearth, and prayed:
' Mistress,[1] because I now depart the world,
Falling before thee the last time, I ask —
Be mother to my orphans! wed the one   225
To a kind wife, and make the other's mate
Some princely person : nor, as I who bore
My children perish, suffer that they too
Die all untimely, but live, happy pair,
Their full glad life out in the fatherland!' 230
And every altar through Admetos' house
She visited and crowned and prayed before,
Stripping the myrtle-foliage from the boughs,

[1] Perhaps addressed to Persephone, goddess of the dead.

Without a tear, without a groan, — no change
At all to that skin's nature, fair to see, 235
Caused by the imminent evil. But this done —
Reaching her chamber, falling on her bed,
There, truly, burst she into tears and spoke:
' O bride-bed, where I loosened from my life
Virginity for that same husband's sake 240
Because of whom I die now — fare thee well!
Since nowise do I hate thee: me alone
Hast thou destroyed; for, shrinking to betray
Thee and my spouse, I die: but thee, O bed,
Some other woman shall possess as wife — 245
Truer, no! but of better fortune, say!'
— So falls on, kisses it till all the couch
Is moistened with the eyes' sad overflow.
But, when of many tears she had her fill,
She flings from off the couch, goes headlong forth, 250
Yet — forth the chamber — still keeps turning back
And casts her on the couch again once more.
Her children, clinging to their mother's robe,
Wept meanwhile: but she took them in her arms,
And, as a dying woman might, embraced 255
Now one and now the other: 'neath the roof,
All of the household servants wept as well,
Moved to compassion for their mistress; she
Extended her right hand to all and each,
And there was no one of such low degree 260
She spoke not to nor had an answer from.
Such are the evils in Admetos' house.
Dying, — why, he had died; but, living, gains
Such grief as this he never will forget!"

And when they questioned of Admetos, "Well — 265
Holding his dear wife in his hands, he weeps;

Entreats her not to give him up, and seeks
The impossible, in fine : for there she wastes
And withers by disease, abandoned now,
A mere dead weight upon her husband's arm.   270
Yet, none the less, although she breathe so faint,
Her will is to behold the beams o' the sun :
Since never more again, but this last once,
Shall she see sun, its circlet or its ray.
But I will go, announce your presence, — friends   275
Indeed; since 't is not all so love their lords
As seek them in misfortune, kind the same :
But you are the old friends I recognize."

And at the word she turned again to go
The while they waited, taking up the plaint   280
To Zeus again : " What passage from this strait ?
What loosing of the heavy fortune fast
About the palace ? Will such help appear,
Or must we clip the locks and cast around
Each form already the black peplos' fold ?   285
Clearly the black robe, clearly ! All the same,
Pray to the Gods ! — like Gods' no power so great !
O thou king Paian, find some way to save !
Reveal it, yea, reveal it ! Since of old
Thou found'st a cure, why, now again become   290
Releaser from the bonds of Death, we beg,
And give the sanguinary Hades pause ! "
So the song dwindled into a mere moan,
How dear the wife, and what her husband's woe ;
When suddenly —
     " Behold, behold ! " *breaks forth :*
" Here is she coming from the house indeed !   296
Her husband comes, too ! Cry aloud, lament,
Pheraian land, this best of women, bound —
So is she withered by disease away —

For realms below and their infernal king! 300
Never will we affirm there's more of joy
Than grief in marriage; making estimate
Both from old sorrows anciently observed,
And this misfortune of the king we see —
Admetos who, of bravest spouse bereaved, 305
Will live life's remnant out, no life at all!"

So wailed they, while a sad procession wound
Slow from the innermost o' the palace, stopped
At the extreme verge of the platform-front:
There opened, and disclosed Alkestis' self, 310
The consecrated lady, borne to look
Her last — and let the living look their last —
She at the sun, we at Alkestis. 313

. . . .

"Sun, and thou light of day, and heavenly dance 360
O' the fleet cloud-figure!" (*so her passion paused,*
While the awe-stricken husband made his moan,
Muttered now this now that ineptitude:)
"Sun that sees thee and me, a suffering pair,
Who did the Gods no wrong whence thou should'st
       die!" 365
Then, as if caught up, carried in their course,
Fleeting and free as cloud and sunbeam are,
She missed no happiness that lay beneath:
"O thou wide earth, from these my palace roofs,
To distant nuptial chambers once my own 370
In that Iolkos of my ancestry!" —
There the flight failed her. "Raise thee, wretched one!
Give us not up! Pray pity from the Gods!"

Vainly Admetos: for "I see it — see
The two-oared boat! The ferryer of the dead, 375

Charon, hand hard upon the boatman's-pole,
Calls me — even now calls — ' Why delayest thou ?
Quick ! Thou obstructest all made ready here
For prompt departure : quick, then ! ' "
                              " Woe is me !
A bitter voyage this to undergo,   380
Even i' the telling ! Adverse Powers above,
How do ye plague us ! "
                Then a shiver ran :
" He has me — seest not ? — hales me, — who is it ? —
To the hall o' the Dead — ah, who but Hades' self,[1]
He, with the wings there, glares at me, one gaze   385
All that blue brilliance, under the eyebrow !
What wilt thou do ? Unhand me ! Such a way
I have to traverse, all unhappy one ! "

" Way — piteous to thy friends, but, most of all,
Me and thy children : ours assuredly   390
A common partnership in grief like this ! "

Whereat they closed about her ; but " Let be !
Leave, let me lie now ! Strength forsakes my feet.
Hades is here, and shadowy on my eyes
Comes the night creeping. Children — children, now
Indeed, a mother is no more for you !   395
Farewell, O children, long enjoy the light ! "

" Ah me, the melancholy word I hear,
Oppressive beyond every kind of death !
No, by the Deities, take heart nor dare   400
To give me up — no, by our children too
Made orphans of ! But rise, be resolute,

---

[1] Here, as in Homer, Hades is a person, not a place, — the lord of the lower world.

Since, thou departed, I no more remain!
For in thee are we bound up, to exist
Or cease to be — so we adore thy love!" 405

— *Which brought out truth to judgment. At this
  word*
*And protestation, all the truth in her
Claimed to assert itself: she waved away
The blue-eyed black-wing'd phantom, held in check
The advancing pageantry of Hades there,* 410
*And, with no change in her own countenance,
She fixed her eyes on the protesting man,
And let her lips unlock their sentence, — so!*

"Admetos, — how things go with me thou seest, —
I wish to tell thee, ere I die, what things 415
I will should follow. I — to honor thee,
Secure for thee, by my own soul's exchange,
Continued looking on the daylight here —
Die for thee — yet, if so I pleased, might live,
Nay, wed what man of Thessaly I would, 420
And dwell i' the dome with pomp and queenliness.
I would not, — would not live bereft of thee,
With children orphaned, neither shrank at all,
Though having gifts of youth wherein I joyed.
Yet, who begot thee and who gave thee birth, 425
Both of these gave thee up; no less, a term
Of life was reached when death became them well,
Ay, well — to save their child and glorious die:
Since thou wast all they had, nor hope remained
Of having other children in thy place. 430
So, I and thou had lived out our full time,
Nor thou, left lonely of thy wife, wouldst groan
With children reared in orphanage: but thus

Some God disposed things, willed they so should be.
Be they so! Now do thou remember this, 435
Do me in turn a favor — favor, since
Certainly I shall never claim my due,
For nothing is more precious than a life;
But a fit favor, as thyself wilt say,
Loving our children here no less than I, 440
If head and heart be sound in thee at least:
Uphold them, make them masters of my house,
Nor wed and give a step-dame to the pair,
Who, being a worse wife than I, through spite
Will raise her hand against both thine and mine. 445
Never do this at least, I pray to thee!
For hostile the new-comer, the step-dame,
To the old brood — a very viper she
For gentleness! Here stand they, boy and girl;
The boy has got a father, a defence 450
Tower-like, he speaks to and has answer from:
But thou, my girl, how will thy virginhood
Conclude itself in marriage fittingly?
Upon what sort of sire-found yoke-fellow
Art thou to chance? with all to apprehend — 455
Lest, casting on thee some unkind report,
She blast thy nuptials in the bloom of youth.
For neither shall thy mother watch thee wed,
Nor hearten thee in childbirth, standing by
Just when a mother's presence helps the most! 460
No, for I have to die: and this my ill
Comes to me, nor to-morrow, no, nor yet
The third day of the month, but now, even now,
I shall be reckoned among those no more.
Farewell, be happy! And to thee, indeed, 465
Husband, the boast remains permissible
Thou hadst a wife was worthy! and to you,
Children: as good a mother gave you birth."

"Have courage!" *interposed the friends.* "For him
I have no scruple to declare — all this   470
Will he perform, except he fail of sense."

"All this shall be — shall be!" *Admetos sobbed:*
"Fear not! And, since I had thee living, dead
Alone wilt thou be called my wife: no fear
That some Thessalian ever styles herself   475
Bride, hails this man for husband in thy place!
No woman, be she of such lofty line
Or such surpassing beauty otherwise!
Enough of children: gain from these I have,
Such only may the Gods grant! since in thee   480
Absolute is our loss, where all was gain.
And I shall bear for thee no year-long grief,
But grief that lasts while my own days last, love!
Love! For my hate is she who bore me, now:
And him I hate, my father: loving-ones   485
Truly, in word not deed! But thou didst pay
All dearest to thee down, and buy my life,
Saving me so! Is there not cause enough
That I who part with such companionship
In thee, should make my moan? I moan, and more:
For I will end the feastings — social flow   491
O' the wine friends flock for, garlands and the Muse
That graced my dwelling. Never now for me
To touch the lyre, to lift my soul in song
At summons of the Lydian flute; since thou   495
From out my life hast emptied all the joy!
And this thy body, in thy likeness wrought
By some wise hand of the artificers,
Shall lie disposed within my marriage-bed:
This I will fall on, this enfold about,   500
Call by thy name, — my dear wife in my arms

216 *EURIPIDES*

Even though I have not, I shall seem to have —
A cold delight, indeed, but all the same
So should I lighten of its weight my soul!
And, wandering my way in dreams perchance, 505
Thyself wilt bless me: for, come when they will,
Even by night our loves are sweet to see.
But were the tongue and tune of Orpheus [1] mine,
So that to Koré [2] crying, or her lord,
In hymns, from Hades I might rescue thee — 510
Down would I go, and neither Plouton's dog
Nor Charon, he whose oar sends souls across,
Should stay me till again I made thee stand
Living, within the light! But, failing this,
There, where thou art, await me when I die, 515
Make ready our abode, my house-mate still!
For in the self-same cedar, me with thee
Will I provide that these our friends shall place,
My side lay close by thy side! Never, corpse
Although I be, would I division bear 520
From thee, my faithful one of all the world!"

. . . .

. . . All she seemed to notice in his speech 548
Was what concerned her children.

. . . .

So, bending to her children all her love, 553
She fastened on their father's only word
To purpose now, and followed it with this:
" O children, now yourselves have heard these things —
Your father saying he will never wed
Another woman to be over you,
Nor yet dishonor me!"

[1] The greatest of mythical musicians, who rescued his wife Eurydice from Hades, but lost her before reaching the upper world.
[2] Cora or the *Maiden*, applied to Persephone, goddess of the dead.

                    " And now at least
I say it, and I will accomplish too ! "

" Then, for such promise of accomplishment,
Take from my hand these children ! "
                              " Thus I take —
Dear gift from the dear hand ! "
                        " Do thou become
Mother, now, to these children in my place ! "

" Great the necessity I should be so,
At least, to these bereaved of thee ! "
                              " Child — child !
Just when I needed most to live, below
Am I departing from you both ! "
                              " Ah me !
And what shall I do, then, left lonely thus ? "
" Time will appease thee : who is dead is naught."
" Take me with thee — take, by the Gods below ! "
" We are sufficient, we who die for thee."
" O Powers, ye widow me of what a wife ! "
" And truly the dimmed eye draws earthward now ! "
" Wife, if thou leav'st me, I am lost indeed ! "
" She once was — now is nothing, thou mayst say."
" Raise thy face, nor forsake thy children thus ! "
" Ah, willingly indeed I leave them not !
But — fare ye well, my children ! "
                              " Look on them —
Look ! "
            " I am nothingness."
                        " What dost thou ? Leav'st . . ."
" Farewell ! "

    And in the breath she passed away.
" Undone — me miserable ! " *moaned the king,*   582
While friends released the long-suspended sigh,
" Gone is she: no wife for Admetos more ! "

Such was the signal : how the woe broke forth,   585
Why tell ? — or how the children's tears ran fast
Bidding their father note the eyelids' stare,
Hands' droop, each dreadful circumstance of death.

" Ay, she hears not, she sees not : I and you,
'T is plain, are stricken hard and have to bear ! "   590
Was all Admetos answered.
 · · · · · · · · ·
So, friends came round him, took him by the hand,   606
Bade him remember our mortality,
Its due, its doom : how neither was he first,
Nor would be last, to thus deplore the loved.

" I understand," *slow the words came at last.*   610
" Nor of a sudden did the evil here
Fly on me : I have known it long ago,
Ay, and essayed myself in misery ;
Nothing is new. You have to stay, you friends,
Because the next need is to carry forth   615
The corpse here : you must stay and do your part,
Chant proper paean to the God below ;
Drink-sacrifice he likes not. I decree
That all Thessalians over whom I rule
Hold grief in common with me ; let them shear   620
Their locks, and be the peplos black they show !
And you who to the chariot yoke your steeds,
Or manage steeds one-frontleted, — I charge,
Clip from each neck with steel the mane away !

And through my city, nor of flute nor lyre 625
Be there a sound till twelve full moons succeed.
For I shall never bury any corpse
Dearer than this to me, nor better friend:
One worthy of all honor from me, since
Me she has died for, she and she alone." 630

With that, he sought the inmost of the house,
He and his dead, to get grave's garniture,
While the friends sang the paean that should peal.
" Daughter of Pelias with farewell from me,
I' the house of Hades have thy unsunned home! 635
Let Hades know, the dark-haired deity, —
And he who sits to row and steer alike,
Old corpse-conductor, let him know he bears
Over the Acherontian lake, this time,
I' the two-oared boat, the best — oh, best by far 640
Of womankind! For thee, Alkestis Queen!
Many a time those haunters of the Muse
Shall sing thee to the seven-stringed mountain-shell,[1]
And glorify in hymns that need no harp,
At Sparta when the cycle comes about, 645
And that Karneian month [2] wherein the moon
Rises and never sets the whole night through:
So too at splendid and magnificent
Athenai.[3] Such the spread of thy renown,
And such the lay that, dying, thou hast left 650
Singer and sayer. O that I availed
Of my own might to send thee once again
From Hades' hall, Kokutos' stream,[4] by help
O' the oar that dips the river, back to day!"

---

[1] The Greek lyre, made in early times with a tortoise-shell as sounding board.   [2] August–September.
[3] Athens.   [4] Cocytus, a river of Hades.

So, the song sank to prattle in her praise: 655
"Light, from above thee, lady, fall the earth,
Thou only one of womankind to die,
Wife for her husband! If Admetos take
Anything to him like a second spouse —
Hate from his offspring and from us shall be 660
His portion, let the king assure himself!
No mind his mother had to hide in earth
Her body for her son's sake, nor his sire
Had heart to save whom he begot, — not they,
The white-haired wretches! only thou it was, 665
I' the bloom of youth, didst save him and so die!
Might it be mine to chance on such a mate
And partner! For there's penury in life
Of such allowance: were she mine at least,
So wonderful a wife, assuredly 670
She would companion me throughout my days
And never once bring sorrow!"
                          A great voice —
"My hosts here!"
              Oh, the thrill that ran through us! 673

. . . .

Sudden into the midst of sorrow, leapt 688
Along with the gay cheer of that great voice,
Hope, joy, salvation: Herakles was here! 690
Himself, o' the threshold, sent his voice on first
To herald all that human and divine
I' the weary happy face of him, — half God,
Half man, which made the god-part God the more.

"Hosts mine," *he broke upon the sorrow with,*
"Inhabitants of this Pheraian soil,
Chance I upon Admetos inside here?" 697

. . . .

ALCESTIS

"He is in the house," *they answered. After all,* 722
They might have told the story, talked their best
About the inevitable sorrow here. 724

. . . .

"Yea, Pheres' son is in-doors, Herakles. 728
But say, what sends thee to Thessalian soil,
Brought by what business to this Pherai town?" 730

"A certain labor that I have to do
Eurustheus the Tirunthian," *laughed the God.*

"And whither wendest — on what wandering
Bound now?"   (*They had an instinct, guessed what meant
Wanderings, labors, in the God's light mouth.*) 735

"After the Thrakian Diomedes' car
With the four horses." [1]

"Ah, but canst thou that?
Art inexperienced in thy host to be?"

"All-inexperienced: I have never gone
As yet to the land o' the Bistones." [2]

"Then, look
By no means to be master of the steeds 741
Without a battle!"

"Battle there may be:
I must refuse no labor, all the same."

"Certainly, either having slain a foe
Wilt thou return to us, or, slain thyself, 745
Stay there!"

"And, even if the game be so,
The risk in it were not the first I run."

[1] Referring to the eighth labor of Heracles. Cf. p. 195.
[2] A tribe of Thracians.

"But, say thou overpower the lord o' the place,
What more advantage dost expect thereby?"

"I shall drive off his horses to the king." 750

"No easy handling them to bit the jaw!"

"Easy enough; except, at least, they breathe
Fire from their nostrils!"
                    "But they mince up men
With those quick jaws!"
                    "You talk of provender
For mountain-beasts, and not mere horses' food!" 755

"Thou mayst behold their mangers caked with gore!"

"And of what sire does he who bred them boast
Himself the son?"
                    "Of Ares, king o' the targe —
Thrakian, of gold throughout."
                            Another laugh.
"Why, just the labor, just the lot for me 760
Dost thou describe in what I recognize!
Since hard and harder, high and higher yet,
Truly this lot of mine is like to go
If I must needs join battle with the brood
Of Ares: ay, I fought Lukaon first, 765
And again, Kuknos:[1] now engage in strife
This third time, with such horses and such lord.
But there is nobody shall ever see
Alkmené's son shrink foemen's hand before!"

. . . .

They gladly stopped the dialogue, 775
Shifted the burthen to new shoulder straight,

[1] Referring to two notable contests of Heracles: with Lycaon, king
of Arcadia, and Cycnus (see page 195, line 433), a son of Ares.

ALCESTIS

As, "Look where comes the lord o' the land, himself,
Admetos, from the palace!" *they outbroke
In some surprise, as well as much relief.
What had induced the king to waive his right* 780
And luxury of woe in loneliness?

*Out he came quietly; the hair was clipt,
And the garb sable; else no outward sign
Of sorrow as he came and faced his friend.* 784

. . . .

"Hail, child of Zeus, and sprung from Perseus[1] too!"
The salutation ran without a fault. 787
"And thou, Admetos, King of Thessaly!"
"Would, as thou wishest me, the grace might fall!
But my good-wisher, that thou art, I know." 790
"What's here? these shorn locks, this sad show of thee?"
"I must inter a certain corpse to-day."
"Now, from thy children God avert mischance!"
"They live, my children; all are in the house!"
"Thy father — if 't is he departs indeed, 795
His age was ripe at least."
                                "My father lives,
And she who bore me lives too, Herakles."
"It cannot be thy wife Alkestis gone?"
"Two-fold the tale is, I can tell of her."
"Dead dost thou speak of her, or living yet?" 800
"She is — and is not: hence the pain to me!"

[1] Alcmene, the mother of Heracles, was the granddaughter of Perseus.

"I learn no whit the more, so dark thy speech!"
"Know'st thou not on what fate she needs must fall?"
"I know she is resigned to die for thee."
"How lives she still, then, if submitting so?" 805
"Eh, weep her not beforehand! wait till then!"
"Who is to die is dead; doing is done."
"To be and not to be are thought diverse."
"Thou judgest this — I, that way, Herakles!"

"Well, but declare what causes thy complaint! 810
Who is the man has died from out thy friends?"

"No man: I had a woman in my mind."
"Alien, or some one born akin to thee?"
"Alien: but still related to my house."
"How did it happen then that here she died?" 815
"Her father dying left his orphan here."
"Alas, Admetos — would we found thee gay,
Not grieving!"
   "What as if about to do
Subjoinest thou that comment?"
     "I shall seek
Another hearth, proceed to other hosts." 820
"Never, O king, shall that be! No such ill
Betide me!"
   "Nay, to mourners should there come
A guest, he proves importunate!"
     "The dead —
Dead are they: but go thou within my house!"
"'T is base carousing beside friends who mourn." 825

"The guest-rooms, whither we shall lead thee, lie
Apart from ours."
                    "Nay, let me go my way!
Ten thousandfold the favor I shall thank!"

"It may not be thou goest to the hearth
Of any man but me!" *so made an end*   830
Admetos, softly and decisively,
Of the altercation. Herakles forbore:
And the king bade a servant lead the way,
Open the guest-rooms ranged remote from view
O' the main hall; tell the functionaries, next,   835
They had to furnish forth a plenteous feast,
And then shut close the doors o' the hall, midway,
"Because it is not proper friends who feast
Should hear a groaning or be grieved," *quoth he.*

. . . .

The king, too, watched great Herakles go off   860
All faith, love, and obedience to a friend.

And when they questioned him, the simple ones,
"What dost thou? Such calamity to face,
Lies full before thee — and thou art so bold
As play the host, Admetos? Hast thy wits?"   865
He replied calmly to each chiding tongue:
"But if from house and home I forced away
A coming guest, wouldst thou have praised me more?
No, truly! since calamity were mine,
Nowise diminished; while I showed myself   870
Unhappy and inhospitable too:
So adding to my ills this other ill,
That mine were styled a stranger-hating house.
Myself have ever found this man the best
Of entertainers when I went his way   875
To parched and thirsty Argos."

"If so be —
Why didst thou hide what destiny was here,
When one came that was kindly, as thou say'st?"

"He never would have willed to cross my door
Had he known aught of my calamities.   880
And probably to some of you I seem
Unwise enough in doing what I do;
Such will scarce praise me: but these halls of mine
Know not to drive off and dishonor guests."

And so, the duty done, he turned once more   885
To go and busy him about his dead.
As for the sympathizers left to muse,
There was a change, a new light thrown on things,
Contagion from the magnanimity
O' the man whose life lay on his hand so light,   890
As up he stepped, pursuing duty still
" Higher and harder," as he laughed and said.
Somehow they found no folly now in the act
They blamed erewhile: Admetos' private grief
Shrank to a somewhat pettier obstacle   895
I' the way o' the world: they saw good days had
    been,
And good days, peradventure, still might be,
Now that they overlooked the present cloud
Heavy upon the palace opposite.
And soon the thought took words and music thus.   900

"Harbor of many a stranger, free to friend,
Ever and always, O thou house o' the man
We mourn for! Thee, Apollon's very self,
The lyric Puthian, deigned inhabit once,
Become a shepherd here in thy domains,[1]   905

[1] See page 201, line 5.

ALCESTIS

And pipe, adown the winding hill-side paths,
Pastoral marriage-poems to thy flocks
At feed: while with them fed in fellowship,
Through joy i' the music, spot-skin lynxes; ay,
And lions too, the bloody company,   910
Came, leaving Othrus' dell;[1] and round thy lyre,
Phoibos, there danced the speckle-coated fawn,
Pacing on lightsome fetlock past the pines
Tress-topped, the creature's natural boundary,
Into the open everywhere; such heart   915
Had she within her, beating joyous beats,
At the sweet reassurance of thy song!
Therefore the lot o' the master is, to live
In a home multitudinous with herds,
Along by the fair-flowing Boibian lake,[2]   920
Limited, that ploughed land and pasture-plain,
Only where stand the sun's steeds, stabled west
I' the cloud, by that mid-air which makes the clime
Of those Molossoi:[3] and he rules as well
O'er the Aigaian,[4] up to Pelion's shore, —   925
Sea-stretch without a port! Such lord have we:
And here he opens house now, as of old,
Takes to the heart of it a guest again:
Though moist the eyelid of the master, still
Mourning his dear wife's body, dead but now!"   930

  .   .   .   .

They ended, for Admetos entered now;   940
Having disposed all duteously indoors. . . .
He would have bidden the kind presence there   950
Observe that, — since the corpse was coming out,
Cared for in all things that befit the case,
Carried aloft, in decency and state,

---

[1] In Thessaly.   [2] In Thessaly.
[3] A people of Epirus, near to Thessaly.   [4] The Aegean Sea.

228   *EURIPIDES*

To the last burial place and burning pile,[1] —
'Twere proper friends addressed, as custom prompts,
Alkestis bound on her last journeying.   956

. . . .

"Unhappy in thy daring! Noble dame,   1238
Best of the good, farewell! With favoring face
May Hermes the infernal,[2] Hades too,   1240
Receive thee! And if there, — ay, there, — some touch
Of further dignity await the good,
Sharing with them, mayst thou sit throned by her
The Bride of Hades,[3] in companionship!"

Wherewith, the sad procession wound away,   1245
Made slowly for the suburb sepulchre.
            . . . We faced about,   1256
Fronted the palace where the mid-hall-gate
Opened, . . .
[Saw] a certain ancient servitor: . . .   1266
This functionary was the trusted one
We saw deputed by Admetos late   1275
To lead in Herakles. . . .

. . . .

"Many the guests" — so he soliloquized   1283
In musings burdensome to breast before,
When it seemed not too prudent tongue should wag —
"Many, and from all quarters of this world,
The guests I now have known frequent our house,
For whom I spread the banquet; but than this,
Never a worse one did I yet receive
At the hearth here! One who seeing, first of all,   1390
The master's sorrow, entered gate the same,
And had the hardihood to house himself.

[1] But if the body had been burned, Heracles could not have recovered Alcestis from Death.
[2] Hermes was the escort of the dead to the lower world.
[3] Persephone.

Did things stop there! But, modest by no means,
He took what entertainment lay to hand,
Knowing of our misfortune, — did we fail   1295
In aught of the fit service, urged us serve
Just as a guest expects! And in his hands
Taking the ivied goblet, drinks and drinks
The unmixed product of black mother-earth,
Until the blaze o' the wine went round about   1300
And warmed him : then he crowns with myrtle sprigs
His head, and howls discordance — twofold lay
Was thereupon for us to listen to —
This fellow singing, namely, nor restrained
A jot by sympathy with sorrows here —   1305
While we o' the household mourned our mistress —
    mourned,
That is to say, in silence — never showed
The eyes, which we kept wetting, to the guest —
For there Admetos was imperative.
And so, here am I helping make at home   1310
A guest, some fellow ripe for wickedness,
Robber or pirate, while she goes her way
Out of our house: and neither was it mine
To follow in procession, nor stretch forth
Hand, wave my lady dear a last farewell,   1315
Lamenting who to me and all of us
Domestics was a mother: myriad harms
She used to ward away from every one,
And mollify her husband's ireful mood.
I ask then, do I justly hate or no   1320
This guest, this interloper on our grief?"

    .   .   .   .

So, he stood petting up his puny hate,   1395
Parent-wise, proud of the ill-favored babe.
Not long! A great hand, careful lest it crush,

Startled him on the shoulder: up he stared,
And over him, who stood but Herakles!

. . . .

"Thou, there!" *hailed*
This grand benevolence the ungracious one — 1422
" Why look'st so solemn and so thought-absorbed?
To guests a servant should not sour-faced be,
But do the honors with a mind urbane. 1425
While thou, contráriwise, beholding here
Arrive thy master's comrade, hast for him
A churlish visage, all one beetle-brow —
Having regard to grief that's out-of-door!
Come hither, and so get to grow more wise! 1430
Things mortal — know'st the nature that they have?
No, I imagine! whence could knowledge spring?
Give ear to me, then! For all flesh to die,
Is nature's due; nor is there any one
Of mortals with assurance he shall last 1435
The coming morrow: for, what's born of chance
Invisibly proceeds the way it will,
Not to be learned, no fortune-teller's prize.
This, therefore, having heard and known through me,
Gladden thyself! Drink! Count the day-by-day 1440
Existence thine, and all the other — chance!
Ay, and pay homage also to by far
The sweetest of divinities for man,
Kupris![1] Benignant Goddess will she prove!
But as for aught else, leave and let things be! 1445
And trust my counsel, if I seem to speak
To purpose — as I do, apparently.
Wilt not thou, then, — discarding overmuch
Mournfulness, do away with this shut door,
Come drink along with me, be-garlanded 1450
This fashion? Do so, and — I well know what —

[1] A by-name of Aphrodite, goddess of love, worshipped on Cyprus.

From this stern mood, this shrunk-up state of mind,
The pit-pat fall o' the flagon-juice down throat
Soon will dislodge thee from bad harborage!
Men being mortal should think mortal-like: 1455
Since to your solemn, brow-contracting sort,
All of them, — so I lay down law at least, —
Life is not truly life but misery."

Whereto the man with softened surliness:
" We know as much: but deal with matters, now, 1460
Hardly befitting mirth and revelry."
" No intimate, this woman that is dead:
Mourn not too much! For, those o' the house itself,
Thy masters live, remember!"
                         " Live indeed?
Ah, thou know'st nought o' the woe within these walls!"
" I do — unless thy master spoke me false 1466
Somehow!"
           " Ay, ay, too much he loves a guest,
"Too much, that master mine!" *so muttered he.*
" Was it improper he should treat me well,
Because an alien corpse was in the way?" 1470
" No alien, but most intimate indeed!"
" Can it be, some woe was, he told me not?"
" Farewell and go thy way! Thy cares for thee —
To us, our master's sorrow is a care."
" This word begins no tale of alien woe!" 1475
" Had it been other woe than intimate,
I could have seen thee feast, nor felt amiss."
" What! have I suffered strangely from my host?"
" Thou cam'st not at a fit reception-time:
With sorrow here beforehand: and thou seest 1480
Shorn hair, black robes."

"But who is it that's dead?
Some child gone? or the aged sire perhaps?"
"Admetos' wife, then! she has perished, guest!"
"How sayest? And did ye house me, all the same?"
"Ay: for he had thee in that reverence 1485
He dared not turn thee from his door away!"
"O hapless and bereft of what a mate!"
"All of us now are dead, not she alone!"
"But I divined it! seeing, as I did,
His eye that ran with tears, his close-clipt hair, 1490
His countenance! Though he persuaded me,
Saying it was a stranger's funeral
He went with to the grave: against my wish,
He forced on me that I should enter doors,
Drink in the hall o' the hospitable man 1495
Circumstanced so! And do I revel yet
With wreath on head? But — thou to hold thy peace
Nor tell me what a woe oppressed my friend!
Where is he gone to bury her? Where am I
To go and find her?"
      "By the road that leads 1500
Straight to Larissa, thou wilt see the tomb,
Out of the suburb, a carved sepulchre."

*So said he, and therewith dismissed himself
Inside to his lamenting.* 1504
. . . .
[HERAKLES.]
"O much-enduring heart and hand of mine! 1524
Now show what sort of son she bore to Zeus,
That daughter of Elektruon, Tiruns' child,[1]
Alkmené! for that son must needs save now

[1] Tiryns, in Argolis, was the home of Alcmene.

The just-dead lady: ay, establish here
I' the house again Alkestis, bring about
Comfort and succor to Admetos so! 1530
I will go lie in wait for Death, black-stoled
King of the corpses! I shall find him, sure,
Drinking, beside the tomb, o' the sacrifice:
And if I lie in ambuscade, and leap
Out of my lair, and seize — encircle him 1535
Till one hand join the other round about —
There lives not who shall pull him out from me,
Rib-mauled, before he let the woman go!
But even say I miss the booty, — say,
Death comes not to the boltered blood, — why then,
Down go I, to the unsunned dwelling-place 1541
Of Koré and the king there, — make demand,
Confident I shall bring Alkestis back,
So as to put her in the hands of him
My host, that housed me, never drove me off: 1545
Though stricken with sore sorrow, hid the stroke,
Being a noble heart and honoring me!
Who of Thessalians, more than this man, loves
The stranger?[1] Who, that now inhabits Greece?
Wherefore he shall not say the man was vile 1550
Whom he befriended, — native noble heart!"

So, one look upward, as if Zeus might laugh
Approval of his human progeny, —
One summons of the whole magnific frame,
Each sinew to its service, — up he caught, 1555
And over shoulder cast, the lion-shag,
Let the club go, —for had he not those hands?
And so went striding off, on that straight way
Leads to Larissa and the suburb tomb.

. . . .

[1] Hospitality was a cardinal virtue of the Greeks.

So, to the struggle off strode Herakles. 1573
*   . . . And presently* 1577
In came the mourners from the funeral,
One after one, until we hoped the last
Would be Alkestis and so end our dream. 1580
Could they have really left Alkestis lone
I' the wayside sepulchre! Home, all save she!
And when Admetos felt that it was so,
By the stand-still: when he lifted head and face
From the two hiding hands and peplos' fold, 1585
And looked forth, knew the palace, knew the hills,
Knew the plains, knew the friendly frequence there,
And no Alkestis any more again,
Why, the whole woe billow-like broke on him.

"O hateful entry, hateful countenance 1590
O' the widowed halls!" — *he moaned.* "What was
   to be?
Go there? Stay here? Speak, not speak? All was
   now
Mad and impossible alike; one way
And only one was sane and safe — to die:
Now he was made aware how dear is death, 1595
How lovable the dead are, how the heart
Yearns in us to go hide where they repose,
When we find sunbeams do no good to see,
Nor earth rests rightly where our footsteps fall.
His wife had been to him the very pledge, 1600
Sun should be sun, earth — earth; the pledge was
   robbed,
Pact broken, and the world was left no world."
He stared at the impossible mad life:
Stood, while they urged "Advance — advance! Go
   deep

ALCESTIS

Into the utter dark, thy palace-core!" 1605
They tried what they called comfort, " touched the quick
Of the ulceration in his soul," *he said,*
With memories, — " once thy joy was thus and thus!"
True comfort were to let him fling himself [1]
Into the hollow grave o' the tomb, and so 1610
Let him lie dead along with all he loved.

One bade him note that his own family
Boasted a certain father whose sole son,
Worthy bewailment, died: and yet the sire
Bore stoutly up against the blow and lived; 1615
For all that he was childless now, and prone
Already to gray hairs, far on in life.
Could such a good example miss effect?
Why fix foot, stand so, staring at the house,
Why not go in, as that wise kinsman would? 1620

" Oh that arrangement of the house I know!
How can I enter, how inhabit thee
Now that one cast of fortune changes all?
Oh me, for much divides the then from now!
Then — with those pine-tree torches, Pelian pomp 1625
And marriage-hymns, I entered, holding high
The hand of my dear wife; while many-voiced
The revelry that followed me and her
That's dead now, — friends felicitating both,
As who were lofty-lineaged, each of us 1630
Born of the best, two wedded and made one;
Now — wail is wedding-chant's antagonist,
And, for white peplos, stoles in sable state
Herald my way to the deserted couch!"

[1] Verses 1609–1619 are a paraphrase.

The one word more they ventured was "This grief
Befell thee witless of what sorrow means,   1636
Close after prosperous fortune: but, reflect!
Thou hast saved soul and body. Dead, thy wife —
Living, the love she left. What's novel here?
Many the man, from whom Death long ago   1640
Loosed the life-partner!"
                            *Then Admetos spoke:
Turned on the comfort, with no tears, this time.*

And as the voice of him grew, gathered strength,   1648
And groaned on, and persisted to the end,
We felt how deep had been descent in grief,   1650
And with what change he came up now to light,
And left behind such littleness as tears.

"Friends, I account the fortune of my wife
Happier than mine, though it seem otherwise:
For, her indeed no grief will ever touch,   1655
And she from many a labor pauses now,
Renowned one! Whereas I, who ought not live,
But do live, by evading destiny,
Sad life am I to lead, I learn at last!
For how shall I bear going in-doors here?   1660
Accosting whom? By whom saluted back,
Shall I have joyous entry? Whither turn?
Inside, the solitude will drive me forth,
When I behold the empty bed — my wife's —
The seat she used to sit upon, the floor   1665
Unsprinkled as when dwellers loved the cool,
The children that will clasp my knees about,
Cry for their mother back: these servants too
Moaning for what a guardian they have lost!
Inside my house such circumstance awaits.   1670

Outside, — Thessalian people's marriage-feasts
And gatherings for talk will harass me,
With overflow of women everywhere;
It is impossible I look on them —
Familiars of my wife and just her age! 1675
And then, whoever is a foe of mine,
And lights on me — why, this will be his word —
'See there! alive ignobly, there he skulks
That played the dastard when it came to die,
And, giving her he wedded, in exchange, 1680
Kept himself out of Hades safe and sound,
The coward! Do you call that creature — man?
He hates his parents for declining death,
Just as if he himself would gladly die!'
This sort of reputation shall I have, 1685
Beside the other ills enough in store.
Ill-famed, ill-faring, — what advantage, friends,
Do you perceive I gain by life for death?"

That was the truth. . . . 1689
The grief was getting to be infinite — 1696
Grief, friends fell back before. Their office shrank
To that old solace of humanity —
"Being born mortal, bear grief! Why born else?"
And they could only meditate anew. 1700

"They, too, upborne by airy help of song,
And haply science, which can find the stars,
Had searched the heights: had sounded depths as well
By catching much at books where logic lurked,
Yet nowhere found they aught could overcome 1705
Necessity: not any medicine served,
Which Thrakian tablets treasure,[1] Orphic voice

[1] Magical incantations ascribed to Orpheus the bard, whose home was in Thrace.

Wrote itself down upon: nor remedy
Which Phoibos gave to the Asklepiadai;[1]
Cutting the roots of many a virtuous herb   1710
To solace overburdened mortals. None!
Of this sole goddess, never may we go
To altar nor to image: sacrifice
She hears not. All to pray for is — 'Approach!
But, oh, no harder on me, awful one,   1715
Than heretofore! Let life endure thee still!
For, whatsoe'er Zeus' nod decree, that same
In concert with thee hath accomplishment.
Iron, the very stuff o' the Chaluboi,[2]
Thou, by sheer strength, dost conquer and subdue; 1720
Nor, of that harsh abrupt resolve of thine,
Any relenting is there!'
                      "O my king!
Thee also, in the shackles of those hands,
Not to be shunned, the Goddess grasped! Yet, bear!
Since never wilt thou lead from underground   1725
The dead ones, wail thy worst! If mortals die, —
The very children of immortals, too,
Dropped 'mid our darkness, these decay as sure!
Dear indeed was she while among us: dear,
Now she is dead, must she forever be: 1730
Thy portion was to clasp, within thy couch,
The noblest of all women as a wife.
Nor be the tomb of her supposed some heap
That hides mortality: but like the Gods
Honored, a veneration to a world   1735
Of wanderers! Oft the wanderer, struck thereby,
Who else had sailed past in his merchant-ship,
Ay, he shall leave ship, land, long wind his way

[1] Sons, that is, followers, of Aesculapius, the god of healing.
[2] See Prometheus, page 117, line 834.

Up to the mountain-summit, till there break
Speech forth: 'So, this was she, then, died of
  old   1740
To save her husband! now, a deity
She bends above us. Hail, benignant one!
Give good!' Such voices so will supplicate.
But — can it be? Alkmené's offspring comes,
Admetos! — to thy house advances here!"   1745

. . . .

Ay, he it was advancing! In he strode,   1757
And took his stand before Admetos, — turned
Now by despair to such a quietude,
He neither raised his face nor spoke, this time, 1760
The while his friend surveyed him steadily.

. . . .

Under the great guard of one arm, there leant   1771
A shrouded something, live and woman-like,
Propped by the heart-beats 'neath the lion-coat.
When he had finished his survey, it seemed,
The heavings of the heart began subside,   1775
The helpful breath returned, and last the smile
Shone out, all Herakles was back again,
As the words followed the saluting hand.

"To friendly man, behoves we freely speak,
Admetos! — nor keep buried, deep in breast,   1780
Blame we leave silent. I assuredly
Judged myself proper, if I should approach
By accident calamities of thine,
To be demonstrably thy friend: but thou
Told'st me not of the corpse then claiming care,   1785
That was thy wife's, but didst install me guest
I' the house here, as though busied with a grief
Indeed, but then, mere grief beyond thy gate:

And so, I crowned my head, and to the Gods
Poured my libations in thy dwelling-place,   1790
With such misfortune round me. And I blame —
Certainly blame thee, having suffered thus!
But still I would not pain thee, pained enough:
So let it pass! Wherefore I seek thee now,
Having turned back again though onward bound,   1795
That I will tell thee. Take and keep for me
This woman, till I come thy way again,
Driving before me, having killed the king
O' the Bistones, that drove of Thrakian steeds:
In such case, give the woman back to me!   1800
But should I fare, — as fare I fain would not,
Seeing I hope to prosper and return, —
Then, I bequeath her as thy household slave.
She came into my hands with good hard toil!
For, what find I, when started on my course,   1805
But certain people, a whole country-side,
Holding a wrestling-bout? as good to me
As a new labor: whence I took, and here
Come keeping with me, this, the victor's prize.
For, such as conquered in the easy work,   1810
Gained horses which they drove away: and such
As conquered in the harder, — those who boxed
And wrestled, — cattle; and, to crown the prize,
A woman followed.[1] Chancing as I did,
Base were it to forego this fame and gain!   1815
Well, as I said, I trust her to thy care:
No woman I have kidnapped, understand!
But good hard toil has done it: here I come!
Some day, who knows? even thou wilt praise the
    feat!'"

[1] So in the funeral games in honor of Patroclus, described by Homer, a slave-woman is the first prize in the chief contest.

Admetos raised his face and eyed the pair: 1820
Then, hollowly and with submission, spoke,
And spoke again, and spoke time after time,
When he perceived the silence of his friend
Would not be broken by consenting word.
As a tired slave goes adding stone to stone 1825
Until he stop some current that molests,
So poor Admetos piled up argument
Vainly against the purpose all too plain
In that great brow acquainted with command.

"Nowise dishonoring, nor amid my foes 1830
Ranking thee, did I hide my wife's ill fate;
But it were grief superimposed on grief,
Shouldst thou have hastened to another home.
My own woe was enough for me to weep!
But, for this woman, — if it so may be, — 1835
Bid some Thessalian, — I entreat thee, king! —
Keep her, — who has not suffered like myself!
Many of the Pheraioi [1] welcome thee.
Be no reminder to me of my ills!
I could not, if I saw her come to live, 1840
Restrain the tear! Inflict on me diseased
No new disease: woe bends me down enough!
Then, where could she be sheltered in my house,
Female and young too? For that she is young,
The vesture and adornment prove. Reflect! 1845
Should such an one inhabit the same roof
With men? And how, mixed up, a girl, with youths,
Shall she keep pure, in that case? No light task
To curb the May-day youngster, Herakles!
I only speak because of care for thee. 1850
Or must I, in avoidance of such harm,

[1] People of Pherae.

Make her to enter, lead her life within
The chamber of the dead one, all apart?
How shall I introduce this other, couch
This where Alkestis lay? A double blame   1855
I apprehend: first, from the citizens —
Lest some tongue of them taunt that I betray
My benefactress, fall into the snare
Of a new fresh face: then, the dead one's self, —
Will she not blame me likewise? Worthy, sure,   1860
Of worship from me! circumspect my ways,
And jealous of a fault, are bound to be.
But thou, — O woman, whosoe'er thou art,
Know, thou hast all the form, art like as like
Alkestis, in the bodily shape! Ah me!   1865
Take, — by the Gods, — this woman from my sight,
Lest thou undo me, the undone before!
Since I seem — seeing her — as if I saw
My own wife! And confusions cloud my heart,
And from my eyes the springs break forth! Ah
 me   1870
Unhappy — how I taste for the first time
My misery in all its bitterness!"

Whereat the friends conferred: "The chance, in
 truth,
Was an untoward one — none said otherwise.
Still, what a God comes giving, good or bad,   1875
That, one should take and bear with. Take her,
 then!"

*Herakles, — not unfastening his hold
On that same misery, beyond mistake
Hoarse in the words, convulsive in the face, —*
"I would that I had such a power," *said he*,   1880

" As to lead up into the light again
Thy very wife, and grant thee such a grace."

" Well do I know thou wouldst: but where the hope?
There is no bringing back the dead to light."

" Be not extravagant in grief, no less!
Bear it, by augury of better things!"

" 'T is easier to advise ' bear up,' than bear!"

" But how carve way i' the life that lies before,
If bent on groaning ever for the past?"

" I myself know that: but a certain love
Allures me to the choice I shall not change."

" Ay, but, still loving dead ones, still makes weep."

" And let it be so! She has ruined me,
And still more than I say: that answers all."

" Oh, thou hast lost a brave wife: who disputes?"

" So brave a one — that he whom thou behold'st
Will never more enjoy his life again!"

" Time will assuage! The evil yet is young!"

" Time, thou mayst say, will; if time mean — to die."

" A wife — the longing for new marriage-joys
Will stop thy sorrow!"
"Hush, friend, — hold thy peace!
What hast thou said! I could not credit ear!"

" How then? Thou wilt not marry, then, but keep
A widowed couch?"
"There is not any one
Of womankind shall couch with whom thou seest!"

"Dost think to profit thus in any way   1906
The dead one?"
                "Her, wherever she abide,
My duty is to honor."
                        "And I praise—
Indeed I praise thee! Still, thou hast to pay
The price of it, in being held a fool!"   1910

"Fool call me—only one name call me not!
Bridegroom!"
                "No: it was praise, I portioned thee,
Of being good true husband to thy wife!"

"When I betray her, though she is no more,
May I die!"
                And the thing he said was true: 1915
For out of Herakles a great glow broke.

. . . .

"Then, since thou canst be faithful to the death,   1926
Take, deep into thy house, my dame!" smiled he.

"Not so!—I pray, by thy Progenitor!"

"Thou wilt mistake in disobeying me!"

"Obeying thee, I have to break my heart!"   1930

"Obey me! Who knows but the favor done
May fall into its place as duty too?"

So, he was humble, would decline no more
Bearing a burden: he just sighed "Alas!
Wouldst thou hadst never brought this prize from
        game!"   1935

"Yet, when I conquered there, thou conquered'st!"

"All excellently urged! Yet—spite of all,
Bear with me! let the woman go away!"

"She shall go, if needs must: but ere she go,
See if there *is* need!"
                    "Need there is! At least,
Except I make thee angry with me, so!"   1941
"But I persist, because I have my spice
Of intuition likewise: take the dame!"
"Be thou the victor, then! But certainly
Thou dost thy friend no pleasure in the act!"   1945
"Oh, time will come when thou shalt praise me!
    Now —
Only obey!"
              "Then, servants, since my house
Must needs receive this woman, take her there!"
"I shall not trust this woman to the care
Of servants."
                "Why, conduct her in, thyself,   1950
If that seem preferable!"
                    "I prefer,
With thy good leave, to place her in thy hands!"
"I would not touch her! Entry to the house —
That, I concede thee."
                "To thy sole right hand,
I mean to trust her!"
                "King! Thou wrenchest this
Out of me by main force, if I submit!"   1956
"Courage, friend! Come, stretch hand forth! Good!
    Now touch
The stranger-woman!"
                "There! A hand I stretch —
As though it meant to cut off Gorgon's head!"

"Hast hold of her?"
    "Fast hold."
        "Why, then, hold fast
And have her! and, one day, asseverate   1961
Thou wilt, I think, thy friend, the son of Zeus,
He was the gentle guest to entertain!
Look at her! See if she, in any way,
Present thee with resemblance of thy wife!"   1965

Ah, but the tears come, find the words at fault!
There is no telling how the hero twitched
The veil off: and there stood, with such fixed eyes
And such slow smile, Alkestis' silent self!
It was the crowning grace of that great heart,   1970
To keep back joy : procrastinate the truth
Until the wife, who had made proof and found
The husband wanting, might essay once more,
Hear, see, and feel him renovated now —
Able to do, now, all herself had done,   1975
Risen to the height of her : so, hand in hand,
The two might go together, live and die.

Beside, when he found speech, you guess the speech.
He could not think he saw his wife again :
It was some mocking God that used the bliss   1980
To make him mad! Till Herakles must help :
Assure him that no spectre mocked at all ;
He was embracing whom he buried once.
Still, — did he touch, might he address the true, —
True eye, true body of the true live wife?   1985

And Herakles said, smiling, "All was truth.
Spectre? Admetos had not made his guest
One who played ghost-invoker, or such cheat!

ALCESTIS 247

O, he might speak and have response, in time!
All heart could wish was gained now — life for death:
Only, the rapture must not grow immense: 1991
Take care, nor wake the envy of the Gods!"[1]

"O thou, of greatest Zeus true son," — *so spoke
Admetos when the closing word must come,*
"Go ever in a glory of success,   1995
And save, that sire, his offspring to the end!
For thou hast — only thou — raised me and mine
Up again to this light and life!" Then asked[2]
Tremblingly, how was trod the perilous path
Out of the dark into the light and life: 2000
How it had happened with Alkestis there.

And Herakles said little, but enough —
How he engaged in combat with that king
O' the daemons: how the field of contest lay   2004
By the tomb's self: how he sprang from ambuscade,
Captured Death, caught him in that pair of hands.

*But all the time, Alkestis moved not once
Out of the set gaze and the silent smile ;
And a cold fear ran through Admetos' frame :*
"Why does she stand and front me, silent thus?"[3]   2010

Herakles solemnly replied "Not yet
Is it allowable thou hear the things
She has to tell thee; let evanish quite
That consecration to the lower Gods,

---

[1] A proud heart called down the vengeance of Nemesis.
[2] Verses 1998–2006 are a paraphrase.
[3] The poet gives an explanation of the silence of Alcestis, which was necessary, since the actor who had taken this part was otherwise occupied.

And on our upper world the third day rise! 2015
Lead her in, meanwhile; good and true thou art,
Good, true, remain thou! Practise piety
To stranger-guests the old way! So, farewell!
Since forth I fare, fulfil my urgent task
Set by the king, the son of Sthenelos." [1] 2020

Fain would Admetos keep that splendid smile
Ever to light him. " Stay with us, thou heart!
Remain our house-friend!"
                              " At some other day!
Now, of necessity, I haste!" *smiled he.*
" But mayst thou prosper, go forth on a foot 2025
Sure to return! Through all the tetrarchy
Command my subjects that they institute
Thanksgiving-dances for the glad event,
And bid each altar smoke with sacrifice!
For we are minded to begin a fresh 2030
Existence, better than the life before;
Seeing I own myself supremely blest."

Whereupon all the friendly moralists
Drew this conclusion: chirped, each beard to each:
" Manifold are thy shapings, Providence! 2035
Many a hopeless matter Gods arrange.
What we expected never came to pass:
What we did not expect, Gods brought to bear;
So have things gone, this whole experience through!"

[1] Eurystheus.

ARISTOPHANES

ALTHOUGH Comedy originated about the same time as Tragedy, the middle of the sixth century before Christ, it was not recognized by the Athenian State until after the Persian Wars, when it was admitted to the official programme of the City Dionysia. The subject of the comic performances was far less restricted than that of the tragic, — mythology, the basis of tragedy, being here treated only in parody, — and the chorus was often used as the mouthpiece of the poet to speak directly to the audience. The essence of the Old Comedy, says Sir Richard Jebb, "was a satirical censorship, unsparing in personalities, of public and of private life — of morality, of statesmanship, of education, of literature, of social usage — in a word, of everything which had an interest for the city or which could amuse the citizens. Preserving all the freedom of banter and of riotous fun to which its origin gave it an historical right, it aimed at associating with this a strong practical purpose — the expression of a democratic public opinion in such a form that no misconduct or folly could altogether disregard it. . . . At Athens the poet of the Old Comedy had an influence analogous, perhaps, rather to that of a journalist than to that of the modern dramatist."

The eleven Greek comedies which have come down to us are all from the hand of one author — fortunately for us by far the greatest of the comedians — Aristophanes. Little is known of his life beyond the fact that he brought out his first play in 427 B. C., when "almost a boy." His birth was probably in or about the year 448 B. C., and his death about 385 B. C. He was an "Athenian of the Athenians." He belonged to the conservative party, and seemed opposed to every sign of democracy or innovation.

It was on this ground that he was so bitter an enemy of the poet Euripides, who had deviated from the established path of tragedy. The *Frogs*, presented to the public in 405 B. C. shortly after the death of both Sophocles and Euripides, is the culmination of the attack upon the latter. In this play Dionysus goes down to Hades to bring back a poet, since all the great poets of Athens were now dead, and his festivals, at which all plays were presented, were left without fitting celebration. Aeschylus and Euripides contend in the lower world for the palm of tragedy, which Sophocles yields without a contest to the former, and it is at length awarded to Aeschylus.

In the *Birds*, an earlier play of 414 B. C., *Peithetaerus* (*Plausible*) and *Euelpides* (*Hopeful*), two enterprising Athenians, who are weary of the unending lawsuits in their own town, persuade the birds under the leadership of *King Hoopoe* to build a city — *Cloud-cuckooborough*[1] — in midair. This cuts off the gods from men, and causes the gods so much inconvenience that they send envoys to treat with the birds. Finally *Peithetaerus* marries *Basileia* (*Princess*), the daughter of Zeus. The play was probably intended in part to ridicule the ambition of the Athenians in making the disastrous expedition which went the year before against Syracuse under Alcibiades and Nicias; but it is as fanciful as the "Midsummer Night's Dream."

The following translations are by John Hookham Frere. Often they are free paraphrases, strongly contrasted with Mr. Browning's literalness.

[1] *Nephelococcugia.* See page 267.

THE BIRDS

THE PLANS FOR THE CITY.

PEISTHETAIRUS.[1] EUELPIDES. HOOPOE.

SCENE. — *A wild desolate country with a bare open prospect on one side, and some upright rocks covered with shrubs and brushwood in the centre of the stage.* PEISTHETAIRUS *and* EUELPIDES *appear as a couple of worn-out pedestrian travellers, the one with a raven and the other with a jackdaw on his hand. They appear to be seeking for a direction, from the motions and signals made to them by the Birds.*

Euelpides [*speaking to his jackdaw*]. Right on, do ye say? to the tree there in the distance?
Peisthetairus [*speaking first to his raven, and then to his companion*]. Plague take ye! Why this creature calls us back!
Euelpides. What use can it answer tramping up and down?
We're lost, I tell ye: our journey's come to nothing.
Peisthetairus. To think of me travelling a thousand stadia   5
With a raven for my adviser!
Euelpides.   Think of me too,
Going at the instigation of a jackdaw,
To wear my toes and my toe-nails to pieces!
Peisthetairus. I don't know even the country where we've got to.
Euelpides. And yet you expect to find a country here,   10
A country for yourself!
Peisthetairus.   Truly not I;

---

[1] *Peithetaerus* is the better form, but the translator's spelling has been preserved.

Not even Execestides[1] could do it,
That finds himself a native everywhere.
    Euelpides. Oh dear! We're come to ruin, utter ruin!
    Peisthetairus. Then go that way, can't ye: "the Road to Ruin!" 15
    Euelpides. He has brought us to a fine pass, that crazy fellow,
Philocrates the poulterer; he pretended
To enable us to find where Tereus lives;[2]
The king that was, the Hoopoe that is now;
Persuading us to buy these creatures of him, 20
That raven there for threepence, — and this other,
This little Tharrelides[3] of a jackdaw,
He charged a penny for: but neither of 'em
Are fit for anything but to bite and scratch.
    [*Speaking to his jackdaw.*]
Well, what are ye after now? — gaping and poking!
You've brought us straight to the rock. Where would you take us? 26
There's no road here!
    Peisthetairus. No, none, not even a path.
    Euelpides. Nor don't your raven tell us anything?
    Peisthetairus. She's altered somehow — she croaks differently.
    Euelpides. But which way does she point? What does she say? 30
    Peisthetairus. Say? Why, she says she'll bite my fingers off.

---

[1] He is attacked again in this play, as a foreign barbarian arrogating to himself the privileges of a true-born Athenian.

[2] See page 257, line 119, page 261, note 2.

[3] Tharrelides was nicknamed Jackdaw, and Euelpides *in contempt of his jackdaw* calls it a Tharrelides! The raven and the jackdaw are characteristic. Peisthetairus is the bearer of the sagacious bird, his companion is equipped with a jackdaw.

Euelpides. Well, truly it's hard upon us, hard indeed,
To go with our own carcases to the crows,[1]
And not be able to find 'em after all.
Turning to the audience.[2]
For our design, most excellent spectators,   35
(Our passion, our disease, or what you will)
Is the reverse of that which Sacas[3] feels;
For he, though not a native, strives perforce
To make himself a citizen: whilst we,
Known and acknowledged as Athenians born   40
(Not hustled off, nor otherwise compelled),
Have deemed it fitting to betake ourselves
To these our legs, and make our person scarce.

Not through disgust or hatred or disdain
Of our illustrious birthplace, which we deem   45
Glorious and free; with equal laws ordained
For fine and forfeiture and confiscation,
With taxes universally diffused;
And suits and pleas abounding in the Courts.

For grasshoppers sit only for a month   50
Chirping upon the twigs; but our Athenians
Sit chirping and discussing all the year,
Perched upon points of evidence and law.

---

[1] "Go to the crows" was a common expression, meaning, "Go to the devil."

[2] Peisthetairus, it will be seen, allows his companion to put himself forward, with the newly discovered natives; remaining himself in the background as the person of authority, making use of the other as his herald; he allows him also to address the audiences, not choosing to compromise himself by unnecessary communications.

The full and complete account of their motives and design is, moreover, much better suited to the careless gossiping character of Euelpides.

[3] Acestor, a tragical poet, not being a genuine Athenian, was called Sacas, from the name of a Scythian tribe.

Therefore we trudge upon our present travels,
With these our sacrificial implements,
To seek some easier unlitigious place;
Meaning to settle there and colonize.
Our present errand is in search of Tereus
(The Hoopoe that is now), to learn from him
If in his expeditions, flights, and journeys,
He ever chanced to light on such a spot.

Peisthetairus. Holloh!
Euelpides. What's that?
Peisthetairus. My raven here points upwards. Decidedly!
Euelpides. Ay, and here's my jackdaw too,
Gaping as if she saw something above.
Yes, — I'll be bound for it; this must be the place:
We'll make a noise, and know the truth of it.
Peisthetairus. Then "kick against the rock."[1]
Euelpides. Knock you your head
Against the rock! — and make it a double knock!
Peisthetairus. Then fling a stone at it!
Euelpides. With all my heart, Holloh there!
Peisthetairus. What do you mean with your Holloh?
You should cry Hoop for a Hoopoe.
Euelpides. Well then, Hoop!
Hoop and holloh, there! — Hoopoe, Hoopoe, I say!
Trochilus, the Hoopoe's servant. What's here?
Who's bawling there? Who wants my master?

[*The door is opened, and both parties start at seeing each other.*

Euelpides. Oh mercy, mighty Apollo! what a beak!

---

[1] "To kick against the rock" was proverbial.

Trochilus. Out! out upon it! a brace of bird-
    catchers! 75
Euelpides. No, no; don't be disturbed; think
    better of us.
Trochilus. You'll both be put to death.
Euelpides.   But we're not men.
Trochilus. Not men! what are ye? what do ye
    call yourselves?
Euelpides. The fright has turned me into a yel-
    low-hammer. 79
Trochilus. Poh! Stuff and nonsense!
Euelpides.   I can prove it to ye.
Search!
Trochilus. But your comrade here; what bird is he?
Peisthetairus. I'm changed to a golden pheasant
    just at present.
Euelpides. Now tell me, in heaven's name, what
    creature are ye?
Trochilus. I'm a slave bird.
Euelpides.   A slave? how did it happen?
Were you made prisoner by a fighting cock? 85
Trochilus. No. When my master made himself a
    Hoopoe,
He begged me to turn bird to attend upon him.
Euelpides. Do birds then want attendance?
Trochilus.   Yes, of course,
In his case, having been a man before,
He longs occasionally for human diet, 90
His old Athenian fare: pilchards, for instance.
Then I must fetch the pilchards; sometimes por-
    ridge;
He calls for porridge, and I mix it for him.
Euelpides. Well, you're a dapper waiter, a di-
    dapper;

But didapper, I say, do step within there, 95
And call your master out.
  Trochilus.   But just at present
He's taking a little rest after his luncheon,
Some myrtle berries and a dish of worms.
  Euelpides. No matter, call him here. We wish to
   speak to him.
  Trochilus. He'll not be pleased, I'm sure; but
   notwithstanding, 100
Since you desire it, I'll make bold to call him. [*Exit.*
  Peisthetairus [*looking after him*]. Confound ye,
I say, you've frightened me to death.
  Euelpides. He has scared away my jackdaw; it's
   flown away.
  Peisthetairus. You let it go yourself, you coward.
  Euelpides.   Tell me,
Have not you let your raven go?
  Peisthetairus.   Not I. 105
  Euelpides. Where is it then?
  Peisthetairus.   Flown off of its own accord.
  Euelpides. You did not let it go! you're a brave
   fellow!

     The HOOPOE *from within.*

Hoopoe. Open the door, I say; let me go forth.
 The royal HOOPOE *appears with a tremendous beak and crest.*

  Euelpides. O Hercules, what a creature! What a
   plumage!
And a triple tier of crests; what can it be! 110
  Hoopoe. Who called? who wanted me?
  Euelpides.   May the heavenly powers . . . .
. . . . Confound ye, I say [*aside*].
  Hoopoe.   You mock at me perhaps,
Seeing these plumes. But, stranger, you must know—

That once I was a man.
 Euelpides.   We did not laugh
At you, sir.
 Hoopoe. What, then, were you laughing at?   115
 Euelpides. Only that beak of yours seemed rather
  odd.
 Hoopoe. It was your poet Sophocles[1] that reduced
  me
To this condition with his tragedies.
 Euelpides. What are you, Tereus? Are you a
  bird, or what?   119
 Hoopoe. A bird.
 Euelpides.   Then where are all your feathers?
 Hoopoe.   Gone.
 Euelpides. In cousequence of an illness?
 Hoopoe.   No, the birds
At this time of the year leave off their feathers.
But you! What are ye? Tell me.
 Euelpides.   Mortal men.
 Hoopoe. What countrymen?
 Euelpides.   Of the country of the Triremes.[2]
 Hoopoe. Jurymen, I suppose?
 Euelpides.   Quite the reverse,
We're anti-jurymen.
 Hoopoe.   Does that breed still   126
Continue amongst you?
 Euelpides.   Some few specimens[3]
You'll meet with, here and there, in country places.

---

[1] In his tragedy of *Tereus*, Sophocles had represented him as transformed (probably only in the last scenes) with the head and beak of a bird.

[2] Galleys with three banks of oars. The Athenians were at that time undisputed masters of the sea.

[3] The love of litigation and the passion for sitting on juries seems

Hoopoe. And what has brought you here? What
    was your object?
Euelpides. We wished to advise with you.
Hoopoe.   With me! For what?
Euelpides. Because you were a man: the same as
    us;   131
And found yourself in debt: the same as us;
And did not like to pay: the same as us;
And after that, you changed into a bird;
And ever since have flown and wandered far   135
Over the lands and seas, and have acquired
All knowledge that a bird or man can learn.
    Therefore we come as suppliants, to beseech
Your favor and advice to point us out
Some comfortable country, close and snug,   140
A country like a blanket or a rug,
Where we might fairly fold ourselves to rest.
    Hoopoe. Do you wish then for a greater State than
        Athens?
    Euelpides. Not greater; but more suitable for us.

. . . .

    Peisthetairus. Ha! What a power is here! What
        opportunities!   170
If I could only advise you. I see it all!
The means for an infinite empire and command!
    Hoopoe. And what would you have us do? What's
        your advice?
    Peisthetairus. Do? What would I have ye do?
        Why first of all
Don't flutter and hurry about all open-mouthed,   175
In that undignified way. With us, for instance,
At home, we should cry out "What creature's that?"

to have infected the whole Athenian community with the exception
of a few who retained their old agricultural habits.

And Teleas would be the first to answer,
"A mere poor creature, a weak restless animal,
A silly bird, that's neither here nor there." [1]   180
   Hoopoe. Yes, Teleas might say so. *It would be like him.*
But tell me, what would you have us do?
   Peisthetairus [*emphatically*].   Concentrate!
Bring all your birds together. Build a city.
   Hoopoe. The birds! How could we build a city? Where?
   Peisthetairus. Nonsense. You can't be serious. What a question!   185
Look down.
   Hoopoe. I do.
   Peisthetairus.   Look up now.
   Hoopoe.   So I do.
   Peisthetairus. Now turn your neck round.
   Hoopoe.   I should sprain it though.
   Peisthetairus. Come, what d' ye see?
   Hoopoe.   The clouds and sky; that's all.
   Peisthetairus. Well, that we call the pole and the atmosphere;
And would it not serve you birds for a metropole?   190
   Hoopoe. Pole? Is it called a pole?
   Peisthetairus.   Yes, that's the name.
Philosophers of late call it the pole;
Because it wheels and rolls itself about,
As it were, in a kind of a roly-poly way.[2]
Well, there then, you may build and fortify,   195

---

[1] The lines between inverted commas may be understood either as the words of Teleas or as a description of him; the ambiguity exists in the original and is evidently intentional. It is continued in the next line of the Hoopoe's answer.

[2] The comic poets ridiculed the new prevailing passion for astronomical and physical science.

And call it your Metropolis — your Acropolis.
From that position you'll command mankind,
And keep them in utter, thorough subjugation:
Just as you do the grasshoppers and locusts.
And if the gods offend you, you'll blockade 'em, 200
And starve 'em to a surrender.
    Hoopoe.   In what way?
    Peisthetairus. Why, thus. Your atmosphere is placed, you see,
In a middle point, just betwixt earth and heaven.
    A case of the same kind occurs with us.
Our people in Athens, if they send to Delphi [1]   205
With deputations, offerings, or what not,
Are forced to obtain a pass from the Boeotians:
Thus when mankind on earth are sacrificing,
If you should find the Gods grown mutinous
And insubordinate, you could intercept   210
All their supplies of sacrificial smoke.
    Hoopoe. By the earth and all its springs! springes and nooses![2]
Odds, nets and snares! This is the cleverest notion:
And I could find it in my heart to venture,
If the other birds agree to the proposal.   215
    Peisthetairus. But who must state it to them?
    Hoopoe.   You yourself,
They'll understand ye, I found them mere barbarians,
But living here a length of time amongst them,
I have taught them to converse and speak correctly.[3]

---

[1] The most famous oracle of Apollo was at Delphi.

[2] The Hoopoe's exclamation and oath are in the original, as they are here represented, exactly in the style of Bob Acres.

[3] The characteristic impertinence of a predominant people, considering their own language as that which ought to be universally spoken.

Peisthetairus. How will you summon them?
Hoopoe. That's easy enough;
I'll just step into the thicket here hard by,
And call my nightingale.[1] She'll summon them.
And when they hear her voice, I promise you
You'll see them all come running here pell-mell.
Peisthetairus. My dearest, best of birds! don't
    lose a moment,
I beg, but go directly into the thicket;
Nay, don't stand here, go call your nightingale.
[*Exit* HOOPOE.

Song from behind the scene, supposed to be sung by the HOOPOE.

> Awake! awake!
> Sleep no more, my gentle mate!
>   With your tiny tawny bill,
>   Wake the tuneful echo shrill,
>   On vale or hill;
>   Or in her airy, rocky seat,
>   Let her listen and repeat
>   The tender ditty that you tell,
>   The sad lament,
>   The dire event,
>   To luckless Itys[2] that befell.
>   Thence the strain
>   Shall rise again,
>   And soar amain,

---

[1] A female performer on the flute, a great favorite of the public and with the poet, after a long absence from Athens engaged to perform in this play, which was exhibited with an unusual recklessness of expense.

[2] Itys was killed by his mother Procne and served up to his father Tereus to eat, as revenge for wrong done her. The gods, in indignation, changed Tereus into a hoopoe, and Procne into a nightingale, in which form she ever bewails her lost son.

Up to the lofty palace gate,
Where mighty Apollo sits in state;
In Jove's abode, with his ivory lyre,
Hymning aloud to the heavenly choir. 245
  While all the gods shall join with thee
  In a celestial symphony.
A solo on the flute, supposed to be the nightingale's call
Peisthetairus. O Jupiter! the dear, delicious bird!
With what a lovely tone she swells and falls,
Sweetening the wilderness with delicate air. 250
  Euelpides. Hist!
  Peisthetairus.   What?
  Euelpides.   Be quiet, can't ye?
  Peisthetairus.   What's the matter?
  Euelpides. The Hoopoe is just preparing for a song.
  Hoopoe. Hoop! hoop!
      Come in a troop,
        Come at a call, 255
        One and all,
      Birds of a feather,
      All together.
    Birds of a humble, gentle bill,
    Smooth and shrill, 260
      Dieted on seeds and grain,
      Rioting on the furrowed plain,
        Pecking, hopping,
        Picking, popping,
    Among the barley newly sown. 265
    Birds of bolder, louder tone,
      Lodging in the shrubs and bushes,
      Mavises and thrushes,
    On the summer berries browsing,
    On the garden fruits carousing, 270
    All the grubs and vermin smousing.

You that in a humbler station,
With an active occupation,
Haunt the lowly watery mead,
Warring against the native breed, 275
 The gnats and flies, your enemies;
In the level marshy plain
Of Marathon, pursued and slain.

You that in a squadron driving
From the seas are seen arriving, 280
With the cormorants and mews
Haste to land and hear the news!
 All the feathered airy nation,
 Birds of every size and station,
 Are convened in convocation. 285
 For an envoy, queer and shrewd,
 Means to address the multitude,
And submit to their decision
A surprising proposition,
For the welfare of the State. 290
 Come in a flurry,
 With a hurry-scurry,
Hurry to the meeting and attend to the debate.
. . . .

Address of the Chorus to the Audience (The so-called Parabasis).

Ye Children of Man! whose life is a span,
Protracted with sorrow from day to day,
Naked and featherless, feeble and querulous,
Sickly, calamitous, creatures of clay!
Attend to the words of the Sovereign Birds 5
(Immortal, illustrious, lords of the air),
Who survey from on high, with a merciful eye,

Your struggles of misery, labor, and care.
Whence you may learn and clearly discern
Such truths as attract your inquisitive turn ; 10
Which is busied of late, with a mighty debate,
A profound speculation about the creation,
And organical life, and chaotical strife,
With various notions of heavenly motions,
And rivers and oceans, and valleys and mountains, 15
And sources of fountains, and meteors on high,
And stars in the sky. We propose by-and-by
(If you'll listen and hear) to make it all clear.
And Prodicus[1] henceforth shall pass for a dunce,
When his doubts are explained and expounded at
    once. 20

  Before the creation of Aether and Light,
Chaos and Night together were plight,
In the dungeon of Erebus foully bedight.
Nor Ocean, or Air, or substance was there,
Or solid or rare, or figure or form, 25
But horrible Tartarus ruled in the storm :
  At length, in the dreary chaotical closet
Of Erebus old, was a privy deposit,
By Night the primaeval in secrecy laid ;
A Mystical Egg, that in silence and shade 30
Was brooded and hatched ; till time came about :
And Love, the delightful, in glory flew out,
In rapture and light, exulting and bright,
Sparkling and florid, with stars in his forehead,
His forehead and hair, and a flutter and flare, 35
As he rose in the air, triumphantly furnished
To range his dominions, on glittering pinions,
All golden and azure, and blooming and burnished :

---

[1] A Sophist of Ceos, contemporary with Socrates.

He soon, in the murky Tartarean recesses,
With a hurricane's might, in his fiery caresses
Impregnated Chaos; and hastily snatched
To being and life, begotten and hatched,
The primitive Birds: but the Deities all,
The celestial Lights, the terrestrial Ball,
Were later of birth, with the dwellers on earth,
More tamely combined, of a temperate kind;
When chaotical mixture approached to a fixture.

Our antiquity proved, it remains to be shown,
That Love is our author, and master alone;
Like him, we can ramble, and gambol and fly
O'er ocean and earth, and aloft to the sky:
And all the world over we're friends to the lover,
And when other means fail, we are found to prevail,
When a peacock or pheasant is sent as a present.

All lessons of primary daily concern,
You have learnt from the Birds, and continue to learn,
Your best benefactors and early instructors;
We give you the warning of seasons returning.

When the cranes are arranged, and muster afloat
In the middle air, with a creaking note,
Steering away to the Lybian [1] sands;
Then careful farmers sow their lands;
The crazy vessel is hauled ashore,
The sail, the ropes, the rudder and oar
Are all unshipped, and housed in store.

The shepherd is warned, by the kite reappearing,
To muster his flock, and be ready for shearing.

You quit your old cloak, at the swallow's behest,
In assurance of summer, and purchase a vest.

---

[1] The cranes went to Africa to spend the winter.

For Delphi, for Ammon, Dodona,[1] in fine, 70
For every oracular temple and shrine,
The Birds are a substitute equal and fair,
For on us you depend, and to us you repair
For counsel and aid, when a marriage is made,
A purchase, a bargain, a venture in trade : 75
Unlucky or lucky, whatever has struck ye,
An ox or an ass, that may happen to pass,
A voice in the street, or a slave that you meet,
A name or a word by chance overheard,
If you deem it an omen, you call it a *Bird ;*[2] 80
And if birds are your omens, it clearly will follow,
That birds are a proper prophetic Apollo.

    Then take us as gods, and you 'll soon find the odds,[3]
We 'll serve for all uses, as Prophets and Muses ;
We 'll give ye fine weather, we 'll live here together ; 85
We 'll not keep away, scornful and proud, a-top of a cloud,
(In Jupiter's way) ; but attend every day,
To prosper and bless, all you possess,
And all your affairs, for yourselves and your heirs.
And as long as you live, we shall give 90
You wealth and health, and pleasure and treasure,
In ample measure ;
And never bilk you of pigeon's milk,
Or potable gold ; you shall live to grow old,

[1] Ammon was an oracle of Zeus in Libya. For Dodona, see the *Prometheus of Aeschylus*, page 115, line 769.

[2] The Greek word for bird came to be used for *omen*, since omens were so frequently taken from the flight of birds. See the *Prometheus of Aeschylus*, p. 108, line 557.

[3] The series of short lines at the end of a Parabasis was to be repeated with the utmost volubility and rapidity, as if in a single breath. A comic effect is sometimes produced in this way on our own stage.

In laughter and mirth, on the face of the earth, 95
Laughing, quaffing, carousing, bousing,
  Your only distress, shall be the excess
Of ease and abundance and happiness.
. . . .

Men come to enjoy the New City's privileges.

Poet. " For the festive, happy day,
    Muse prepare an early lay,
    To Nephelococcugia."

Peisthetairus. What's here to do? What are you? Where do you come from?

Poet. An humble menial of the Muses' train, 5
As Homer expresses it.

Peisthetairus.   A menial, are you?
With your long hair?[1] A menial?

Poet.   'T is not that,
No! but professors of the poetical art
Are simply styled the " Menials of the Muses,"
As Homer expresses it.

Peisthetairus.   Aye, the Muse has given you
A ragged livery. Well, but friend, I say — 11
Friend! — Poet! — What the plague has brought you here?

Poet. I've made an ode upon your new-built city,
And a charming composition for a chorus,
And another, in Simonides's manner. 15

Peisthetairus. When were they made? What time? How long ago?

Poet. From early date, I celebrate in song,
The noble Nephelococcugian State.

Peisthetairus. That's strange, when I'm just sacrificing here,
For the first time, to give the town a name. 20

    [1] Slaves were forbidden to wear long hair.

Poet. Intimations, swift as air,
　　To the Muses' ear, are carried,
　Swifter than the speed and force
　　Of the fiery-footed horse;
　　　Hence, the tidings never tarried.　　25
　Father, patron, mighty lord,[1]
　　Founder of the rising State,
　What thy bounty can afford,
　　Be it little, be it great,
　　With a quick resolve, incline　　30
　　To bestow on me and mine.
Peisthetairus. This fellow will breed a bustle, and
　　make mischief,
If we don't give him a trifle, and get rid of him.
You there,[2] you've a spare waistcoat; pull it off!
And give it this same clever, ingenious poet —　　35
There, take the waistcoat, friend! Ye seem to want it!
　Poet. Freely, with a thankful heart,
　　What a bounteous hand bestows,
　Is received in friendly part;
　　But amid the Thracian snows,　　40
　Or the chilly Scythian plain,
　　He the wanderer, cold and lonely,
　　With an under-waistcoat only,
　Must a further wish retain;
　　Which, the Muse averse to mention,　　45
　　To your gentle comprehension,
　Trusts her enigmatic strain.
Peisthetairus. I comprehend it enough; you want
　　a jerkin;

---

[1] The Scholiast informs us that these lines are in ridicule of certain mendicatory passages in the poems of Pindar; one in particular, addressed to Hiero on the foundation of a new city.

[2] This was said to the priest who was conducting a sacrifice.

Here, give him yours; one ought to encourage genius.
There, take it, and good-by to ye!

Poet.[1]　　　　　　　　　Well, I'm going;
And as soon as I get to the town, I'll set to work;
And finish something, in this kind of way.

　　"Seated on your golden throne,
　　　Muse, prepare a solemn ditty,
　　　　To the mighty,
　　　　To the flighty,
　　　To the cloudy, quivering, shivering,
　　　To the lofty-seated city."

Peisthetairus. Well, I should have thought that jerkin might have cured him
Of his "quiverings and shiverings." How the plague.
Did the fellow find us out? I should not have thought it.
Come, once again, go round with the basin and ewer.
Peace! Silence! Silence![2]

Enter a Soothsayer with a great air of arrogance and self-importance. He comes on the authority of a book of Oracles (which he pretends to possess, but which he never produces), in virtue of which he lays claim to certain sacrificial perquisites and fees. Peisthetairus encounters him with a different version composed upon the spot; in virtue of which he dismisses the Soothsayer with a good lashing.

Soothsayer.　　　　　　　Stop the sacrifice!
Peisthetairus. What are you?
Soothsayer.　　A Soothsayer, that's what I am.

---

[1] The Poet withdraws, gradually turning round and reciting. Peisthetairus does not appear to take notice, but watches till he is fairly gone.

[2] Sacrifices were to be performed in silence in order to avoid the chance of words of ill-omen.

Peisthetairus. The worse luck for ye.
Soothsayer. Friend, are you in your senses?
Don't trifle absurdly with religious matters.
Here's a prophecy of Bakis, which expressly
Alludes to Nephelococcugia.
Peisthetairus. How came it, then, you never prophesied
Your prophecies before the town was built?
Soothsayer. The spirit withheld me.
Peisthetairus. And is it allowable now,
To give us a communication of them?
Soothsayer. Hem!
"Moreover, when the crows and daws unite,
To build and settle, in the midway right,
Between tall Corinth and fair Sicyon's height,
Then to Pandora, let a milk white goat
Be slain, and offered, and a comely coat
Given to the Soothsayer, and shoes a pair;
When he to you this Oracle shall bear."
Peisthetairus. Are the shoes mentioned?
Soothsayer [*pretending to feel for his papers*].
Look at the book, and see!
"And let him have the entrails [1] for his share."
Peisthetairus. Are the entrails mentioned?
Soothsayer [*as before*]. Look at the book, and see!
"If you, predestined youth, shall do these things,
Then you shall soar aloft, on eagle's wings;
But, if you do not, you shall never be
An eagle, nor a hawk, nor bird of high degree."
Peisthetairus. Is all this, there?
Soothsayer [*as before*]. Look at the book, and see!
Peisthetairus. This Oracle differs most remarkably,
From that which *I* transcribed in Apollo's temple.

[1] The heart, liver, and lungs.

> "If at the sacrifice . . . ¹ which you prepare,   90
> An uninvited vagabond . . . should dare
> To interrupt you, and demand a share,
> Let cuffs and buffets . . . be the varlet's lot.
> Smite him between the ribs . . . and spare
>   him not."

Soothsayer. Nonsense you 're talking!

Peisthetairus [*with the same action as the* SOOTH-
SAYER, *as if he were feeling for papers*]. Look at
the book, and see!   95

> "Thou shalt in no wise heed them, or forbear
> To lash and smite those eagles of the air,
> Neither regard their names, for it is written,
> Lampon and Diopithes shall be smitten."

Soothsayer. Is all this there?

Peisthetairus [*producing a horsewhip*]. Look at
the book and see!   100
Get out! with a plague and a vengeance.

Soothsayer.   O dear! oh!

Peisthetairus. Go soothsay somewhere else, you
rascal, run!   [*Exit* SOOTHSAYER.

The Completion of the New City.

Enter a MESSENGER, *quite out of breath; and speaking in short
snatches.*

Messenger. Where is he? Where? Where is he?
Where? Where is he?

The president Peisthetairus?

Peisthetairus [*coolly*].   Here am I.

Messenger [*in a gasp of breath*]. Your fortifica-
tion 's finished.

---

¹ The breaks in the text may serve to indicate what was more distinctly expressed by the actor, namely, that Peisthetairus's Oracle is
an extempore production.

Peisthetairus. Well, that's well.
Messenger. A most amazing, astonishing work it is!
So, that Theagenes and Proxenides[1]
Might flourish and gasconade and prance away,
Quite at their ease, both of them four-in-hand,
Driving abreast upon the breadth of the wall,
Each in his own new chariot.
Peisthetairus. You surprise me.
Messenger. And the height (for I made the measurement myself)
Is exactly a hundred fathoms.
Peisthetairus. Heaven and earth!
How could it be? such a mass! who could have built it?
Messenger. The Birds; no creature else, no foreigners,
Egyptian bricklayers, workmen or masons,
But, they themselves, alone, by their own efforts
(Even to my surprise, as an eye-witness), —
The Birds, I say, completed everything:
There came a body of thirty thousand cranes
(I won't be positive, there might be more)
With stones from Africa, in their craws and gizzards,
Which the stone-curlews and stone-chatterers
Worked into shape and finished. The sand-martens
And mud-larks, too, were busy in their department,
Mixing the mortar, while the water birds,
As fast as it was wanted, brought the water
To temper, and work it.
Peisthetairus [*in a fidget*]. But, who served the masons?
Who did you get to carry it?

---

[1] Pretenders to great wealth and affecting extraordinary expense and display.

Messenger.   To carry it?
Of course, the carrion crows, and carrying pigeons.
   Peisthetairus [*in a fuss, which he endeavors to
      conceal*]. Yes! yes! But after all, to load
      your hods,
How did you manage that?
   Messenger.   Oh capitally,   30
I promise you. There were the geese, all barefoot
Trampling the mortar, and, when all was ready,
They handed it into the hods, so cleverly,
With their flat feet!
   Peisthetairus. [*A bad joke, as a vent for irrita-
      tion.*[1]]   They *footed* it, you mean —
Come; it was handily done though, I confess.   35
   Messenger. Indeed, I assure you, it was a sight to
      see them;
And trains of ducks, there were, clambering the lad-
      ders,
With their duck legs, like bricklayer's 'prentices,
All dapper and handy, with their little trowels.
   Peisthetairus.[2] In fact, then, it's no use engaging
      -foreigners,   40
Mere folly and waste, we've all within ourselves.
  Ah, well now, come! But about the woodwork?
     Heh!
Who were the carpenters? Answer me that!
   Messenger. The woodpeckers, of course: and there
      they were,
Laboring upon the gates, driving and banging,   45

---

[1] Like Falstaff, when he is annoyed and perplexed, joking perforce.

[2] Peisthetairus is at a loss; unable to think of a new objection, he maintains his importance by a wise observation. As soon as an objection occurs, he states it with great eagerness; but with no better success than before.

With their hard hatchet beaks, and such a din,
Such a clatter, as they made, hammering and hack-
    ing,
In a perpetual peal, pelting away
Like shipwrights, hard at work in the arsenal.
And now their work is finished, gates and all,   50
Staples and bolts, and bars and everything;
The sentries at their posts; patrols appointed;
The watchmen in the barbican; the beacons
Ready prepared for lighting; all their signals
Arranged — but I 'll step out, just for a moment,   55
To wash my hands. You 'll settle all the rest.

The Visit of Prometheus.

PROMETHEUS. PEISTHETAIRUS. CHORUS.

    Prometheus [*enters muffled up, peeping about him
    with a look of anxiety and suspicion*]. O dear!
If Jupiter should chance to see me!
Where 's Peisthetairus? Where?
    Peisthetairus.   Why, what 's all this?
This fellow muffled up?
    Prometheus.   Do look behind me;
Is anybody watching? any gods
Following and spying after me?
    Peisthetairus.   No, none,   5
None that I can see, there 's nobody. But you!
What are ye?
    Prometheus. Tell me, what 's the time of day?
    Peisthetairus. Why, noon, past noon; but tell me,
    who are ye? Speak.
    Prometheus. Much past, — how much?
    Peisthetairus [*aside*]. Confound the fool, I say.
The insufferable blockhead!

Prometheus.   How's the sky?   10
Open or overcast?   Are there any clouds?
   Peisthetairus [*aloud and angrily*].   Be hanged!
   Prometheus.   Then I'll disguise myself no longer.
   Peisthetairus.   My dear Prometheus!
   Prometheus.   Hold your tongue, I beg;
Don't mention my name!   If Jupiter should see me,
Or overhear ye, I'm ruined and undone.[1]   15
But now, to give you a full complete account
Of everything that's passing, there in heaven —
The present state of things. . . . But first I'll trouble you
To take the umbrella, and hold it overhead,
Lest they should overlook us.
   Peisthetairus.   What a thought!   20
Just like yourself!   A true Promethean thought!
Stand under it, here!   Speak boldly; never fear.
   Prometheus. D' ye mind me?
   Peisthetairus.   Yes, I mind ye.   Speak away.
   Prometheus [*emphatically*].   Jupiter's ruined.
   Peisthetairus.   Ruined!   How?   Since when?
   Prometheus. From the first hour you fortified and
          planted   25
Your atmospheric settlements.   Ever since,
There's not a mortal offers anything
In the shape of sacrifice.   No smoke of victims!
No fumes of incense!   Absolutely nothing!
We're keeping a strict fast — fasting perforce,   30
From day to day — the whole community.
   And the inland barbarous gods in the upper country
Are broken out, quite mutinous and savage,
With hunger and anger; threatening to come down

---

[1] See the *Prometheus* of Aeschylus, page 101, line 364.

With all their force ; if Jupiter refuses 35
To open the ports, and allow them a free traffic
For their entrails and intestines,¹ as before.
  Peisthetairus [*a little annoyed at being obliged to
    ask the question*]. What — are there other
    barbarous gods, besides,
In the upper country?
  Prometheus.   Barbarous? — to be sure!
They 're all of Execestides's kindred.² 40
  Peisthetairus [*as before hesitating, but with a
    sort of affected ease*]. Well — but — the
    name now. The same barbarous deities —
What name do you call 'em ?
  Prometheus. [*surprised at* PEISTHETAIRUS'S *igno-
    rance*].   Call them ! The Triballi !³
  Peisthetairus [*giving vent to his irritation by a
    forced joke*]. Ah ! well then, that accounts
    for our old saying : —
Confound the *Tribe* of them !
  Prometheus [*annoyed and drily*]. Precisely so.
But, now to business. Thus much, I can tell ye ; 45
That envoys will arrive immediately
From Jupiter and those upland wild Triballi,
To treat for a peace. But, you must not consent
To ratify or conclude,⁴ till Jupiter
Acknowledges the sovereignty of the birds ; 50
Surrendering up to you the sovereign queen,
Whom you must marry.
  Peisthetairus.   Why, what queen is that ?

---

¹ Of the sacrifices. Compare page 270, line 81.
² Noted elsewhere in this play as having no just claim to the rights of a citizen.
³ A barbarous people of Thrace. See page 419.
⁴ Allusions to the *Prometheus* of Aeschylus, pages 95, 127.

Prometheus. What queen? A most delightful charming girl,
Jove's housekeeper, that manages his matters,
Serves out his thunderbolts, arranges everything; 55
The constitutional laws and liberties,
Morals and manners, the marine department,
Freedom of speech, and threepence for the juries.
    Peisthetairus. Why, that seems all in all.
    Prometheus. Yes, everything,
I tell ye, in having her, you 've everything: 60
I came down hastily, to say thus much;
I 'm hearty, ye know; I stick to principle.
Steady to the human interest — always was.[1]
    Peisthetairus. Yes! we 're obliged to you for our roast victuals.
    Prometheus. And I hate these present gods, you know, most thoroughly. 65
I need not tell you that.
    Peisthetairus [2] [*with a sort of half sneer*]. No, no, you need not,
You 're known of old, for an enemy to the gods.
    Prometheus. Yes, yes, like Timon, I 'm a perfect Timon;[3]
Just such another. But I must be going;
Give me the umbrella; if Jupiter should see me, 70
He 'll think that I 'm attending a procession.[4]

---

[1] Prometheus had incurred the wrath of Jupiter by his kindness to mankind in having bestowed on them the gift of fire.

[2] Peisthetairus, who has learned all that he wanted to know, does not care to lose his time in listening to professions of zeal and attachment. He contrives, however, to conclude civilly with a piece of obliging attention.

[3] Timon of Athens (see p. 445) hated gods as well as men.

[4] The Canephoroi were followed by a person bearing an umbrella and a folding chair.

278   *ARISTOPHANES*

Peisthetairus. That's well, but don't forget the
 folding chair,
For a part of your disguise. Here, take it with you.

  The Gods and the Birds make a Truce.
  NEPTUNE. *The* TRIBALLIAN ENVOY. HERCULES.

Neptune. There's Nephelococcugia, that's the town,
The point we're bound to, with our embassy.
   Turning to the TRIBALLIAN.
But you! What a figure have ye made yourself!
What a way to wear a mantle! slouching off
From the left shoulder! hitch it round, I tell ye, 5
On the right side. For shame — come — so; that's
 better,
These folds, too, bundled up. There, throw them
 round
Even and easy — so. Why, you're a savage,
A natural born savage. Oh! democracy!
What will it bring us to? When such a ruffian 10
Is voted into an embassy!
 Triballian [*to* NEPTUNE, *who is pulling his dress
  about*]. Come, hands off! Hands off!
 Neptune. Keep quiet, I tell ye, and hold your
  tongue,
For a very beast: in all my life in heaven,
I never saw such another. — Hercules, 14
I say, what shall we do? What should you think?
 Hercules. What would I do? What do I think?
  I've told you
Already . . . I think to throttle him — the fellow,
Whoever he is, that's keeping us blockaded.[1]
 Neptune. Yes, my good friend; but we were sent,
  you know,
To treat for a peace. Our embassy is for peace. 20

---

[1] Hercules's instinctive impulse is to use force.

Hercules. That makes no difference; or if it does,
It makes me long to throttle him the more.
  Peisthetairus [*very busy, affecting not to see them.*]
    Give me the Silphium spice. Where's the
      cheese-grater?
  Bring cheese here, somebody! Mend the charcoal
      fire.
    Hercules. Mortal, we greet you and hail you!
      Three of us —   25
  Three deities.
    Peisthetairus [*without looking up*]. But I'm en-
      gaged at present;
  A little busy, you see, mixing my sauce.
    Hercules. Why sure! How can it be? what dish
      is this?
  Birds seemingly![1]
    Peisthetairus [*without looking up*]. Some indi-
      vidual birds,
  Opposed to the popular democratic birds,   30
  Rendered themselves obnoxious.
    Hercules.   So, you've plucked them,
  And put them into sauce, *provisionally?*
    Peisthetairus [*looking up*]. Oh! bless me, Her-
      cules, I'm quite glad to see you.
  What brings you here?
    Hercules.   We're come upon an embassy
  From heaven, to put an end to this same war. . . . 35
    Servant [*to* PEISTHETAIRUS]. The cruet's empty,
      our oil is out.
    Peisthetairus.   No matter,
  Fetch more, fetch plenty, I tell ye. We shall want it.
    Hercules. For, in fact, it brings no benefit to us,

---

[1] Hercules was proverbially a gourmand. It is through this weakness that Peisthetairus wins him over to his side.

The continuance of the war prolonging it;
And you yourselves, by being on good terms
Of harmony with the gods . . . why, for the future,
You'd never need to know the want of rain,
For water in your tanks; and we could serve ye
With reasonable, seasonable weather,
According as you wished it, wet or dry.
And this is our commission coming here,
As envoys, with authority to treat.
  Peisthetairus. Well, the dispute, you know, from
    the beginning,
Did not originate with us. The war
(If we could hope in any way to bring you
To reasonable terms) might be concluded.
Our wishes, I declare it, are for peace.
If the same wish prevails upon your part,
The arrangement in itself is obvious.
A retrocession on the part of Jupiter.
The birds, again to be reintegrated
In their estate of sovereignty. This seems
The fair result; and if we can conclude,
I shall hope to see the ambassadors to supper.
  Hercules. Well, this seems satisfactory; I consent.
  Neptune [*to* HERCULES]. What's come to ye?
    What do ye mean? Are ye gone mad?
You glutton; would you ruin your own father,[1]
Depriving him of his ancient sovereignty?
  Peisthetairus[2] [*to* NEPTUNE]. Indeed! And would
    not it be a better method
For all you deities, and confirm your power,
To leave the birds to manage things below?
You sit there, muffled in your clouds above,

[1] Jupiter (Zeus).
[2] With the civil, good-humored sneer of a superior understanding.

While all mankind are shifting, skulking, lurking,
And perjuring themselves here out of sight. 70
Whereas, if you would form a steady strict
Alliance with the Birds, when any man
(Using the common old familiar oath —
" By Jupiter and the crow ") forswore himself,
The crow would pick his eyes out, for his pains. 75
> *Neptune.* Well, that seems plausible — that's fairly put.
> *Hercules.* I think so, too.
> *Peisthetairus* [*to the* TRIBALLIAN]. Well, what say you?
> *Triballian.*   Say true.[1]
> *Peisthetairus.*[2] Yes. He consents, you see! But I'll explain now

The services and good offices we could do you. 80
Suppose a mortal made a vow, for instance,
To any of you; then he delays and shuffles,
And says, "the gods are easy creditors."
In such a case, we could assist ye, I say,
To levy a fine.
> *Neptune* [*open to conviction, but anxious to proceed on sure ground*]. How would you do it? Tell me. 85
> *Peisthetairus.* Why, for example, when he's counting money,

Or sitting in the bath, we give the warrant
To a pursuivant of ours, a kite or magpie;
And they pounce down immediately, and distrain
Cash or apparel, money or money's worth, 90
To twice the amount of your demand upon him.

---

[1] The Triballian speaks very imperfect Greek, but seems to mean that he favors breaking off the negotiations and returning to Olympus. So the interpretation which Peisthetairus puts upon his words is comic.

[2] Very volubly — quite at his ease.

Hercules. Well, I 'm for giving up the sovereignty,
For my part.
Neptune [*convinced, but wishing to avoid responsibility, by voting last*]. The Triballian, what says he?
Hercules [*aside to the* TRIBALLIAN, *showing his fist*]. You, sir; do you want to be well banged or not?
Mind, how you vote! Take care how you provoke me. 95
Triballian. Yaw, yaw. Goot, goot.
Hercules. He 's of the same opinion.
Neptune. Then, since you 're both agreed, I must agree.
Hercules [*shouting to* PEISTHETAIRUS, *the negotiators having withdrawn to consult at the extremity of the stage*]. Well, you! we 've settled this concern, you see,
About the sovereignty; we 're all agreed.
Peisthetairus. O, faith there 's one thing more, I recollect, 100
Before we part; a point that I must mention.
As for dame Juno, we 'll not speak of her;
I 've no pretensions, Jupiter may keep her;
But, for that other queen, his manager,
The sovereign goddess, her surrender to me 105
Is quite an article indispensable.
Neptune.[1] Your views, I find, are not disposed for peace:
We must turn homewards.
Peisthetairus. As you please, so be it.
Cook, mind what you 're about there with the sauce;
Let 's have it rich and savory, thicken it up! 110

---
[1] With gravity and dignity.

Hercules. How now, man? Neptune! are you flying off?
Must we remain at war, here, for a woman?
Neptune. But what are we to do?
Hercules. Do? Why, make peace.
Neptune.[1] I pity you really! I feel quite ashamed
And sorry to see you ruining yourself! 115
If anything should happen to your father,
After surrendering the sovereignty,
What's to become of you? When you yourself
Have voted away your whole inheritance:
At his decease, you must remain a beggar. 120
    Peisthetairus [*aside to* HERCULES]. Ah there! I
        thought so; he's coming over ye;
Step here a moment! Let me speak to ye!
Your uncle's chousing you, my poor dear friend;
You've not a farthing's worth of expectation,
From what your father leaves. Ye can't inherit 125
By law : ye 're illegitimate, ye know.
    Hercules. Heigh-day! Why, what do you mean?
    Peisthetairus. I mean the fact!
Your mother was a foreigner;[2] Minerva
Is counted an heiress, everybody knows;
How could that be, supposing her own father 130
To have had a lawful heir?
    Hercules. But, if my father
Should choose to leave the property to me,
In his last will.
    Peisthetairus. The law would cancel it!
And Neptune, he that's using all his influence
To work upon ye, he'd be the very first 135

[1] In great wrath like an uncle scolding a great fool of a nephew.
[2] Marriages between Athenians and foreigners were not legal.

To oppose ye, and oust ye, as the testator's brother.
I'll tell ye what the law says, Solon's law :

> " A foreign heir shall not succeed,
> Where there are children of the lawful breed:
> But, if no native heir there be, 140
> The kinsman nearest in degree
> Shall enter on the property."

Hercules. Does nothing come to me, then ? Nothing at all,
Of all my father leaves ?
Peisthetairus. Nothing at all,
I should conceive. But you perhaps can tell me. 145
Did he, your father, ever take ye with him,
To get ye enrolled upon the register ?[1]
Hercules. No, truly I . . . thought it strange, . . .
he . . . never did.
Peisthetairus. Well, but don't think things strange.
Don't stand there, stammering, 150
Puzzling and gaping. Trust yourself to me,
'T is I must make your fortune after all!
If you 'll reside and settle amongst us here,
I 'll make you chief commander among the birds,
Captain, and Autocrat and everything. 155
Here you shall domineer and rule the roast,
With splendor and opulence and pigeon's milk.
Hercules [*in a more audible voice, and in a formal decided tone* [2]]. I agreed with you before :
I think your argument
Unanswerable. I shall vote for the surrender.

[1] Viz. of the citizens.
[2] They had withdrawn apart, and their previous conversation was supposed not to have been audible to Neptune and the Triballian, whose by-play might have consisted in Neptune's formal attempts to soothe and gain the Triballian, who would only shrug his shoulders.

Peisthetairus [*to* NEPTUNE]. And what say you?
Neptune [*firmly and vehemently*]. Decidedly I dissent. 161
Peisthetairus. Then it depends upon our other friend,
It rests with the Triballian; what say you?
Triballian. Me tell you; pretty girl, grand beautiful queen,
Give him to birds.
Hercules. Aye, give her up, you mean. 165
Neptune. Mean! He knows nothing about it. He means nothing
But chattering like a magpie.
Peisthetairus.[1] Well, "the magpies."
He means the magpies or the birds in general.
The republic of the birds — their government —
That the surrender should be made to them. 170
Neptune [*in great wrath*]. Well, settle it yourselves; amongst yourselves;
In your own style: I've nothing more to say.
Hercules [*to Peisthetairus*]. Come, we're agreed in fact, to grant your terms;
But you must come, to accompany us to the sky;
To take back this same queen, and the other matters. 175
Peisthetairus [*very quietly*]. It happens lucky enough, with this provision
For a marriage feast. It seems prepared on purpose.
Hercules. Indeed, and it does. Suppose in the meanwhile,
I superintend the cookery, and turn the roast,
While you go back together.

---

[1] Peisthetairus, being sure of his point, amuses himself with arguing nonsensically to provoke Neptune.

Neptune [*with a start of surprise and disgust*].
    Turn the roast! 180
A pretty employment! Won't you go with us?
  Hercules. No, thank ye; I'm mighty comfortable here.
  Peisthetairus. Come, give me a marriage robe; I must be going.

THE FROGS

The Crossing of the Styx.

Bacchus, accompanied by his slave Xanthias, has come down to the lower world to get a tragic poet to carry back to Athens. Charon, the old ferryman, is ready at the bank of the Styx to carry him across to Hades.

CHARON. BACCHUS. XANTHIAS.

  Charon. Hoy! Bear a hand, there. — Heave ashore.
  Bacchus.   What's this?
  Xanthias. The lake it is, the place he told us of.
By Jove! and there's the boat, and here's old Charon.
  Bacchus. Well, Charon! Welcome, Charon! Welcome kindly!
  Charon. Who wants the ferryman? Anybody waiting 5
To remove from the sorrows of life? A passage anybody
To Lethe's wharf? — to Cerberus's Reach?
To Tartarus? — to Taenarus?[1] — to Perdition?
  Bacchus. Yes, I.
  Charon.   Get in then.
  Bacchus (*hesitatingly*). Tell me, where are you going?
To Perdition really — ?

---

[1] Cape Matapan, the most southerly point of Greece and of Europe, where was a cavern which was said to lead to Hades.

*Charon (not sarcastically, but civilly, in the way
of business).* Yes, to oblige you, I will
With all my heart — Step in there.
  Bacchus. Have a care!
Take care, good Charon! Charon, have a care!

        BACCHUS *gets into the boat.*

Come, Xanthias, come!
  Charon. I take no slaves aboard
Except they 've volunteer'd for the naval victory.[1]
  Xanthias. I could not: — I was suffering with sore
    eyes.
  Charon. You must trudge away then, round by the
    end of the lake there.
  Xanthias. And whereabouts shall I wait?
  Charon. At the Stone of Repentance,
By the Slough of Despond beyond the Tribula-
    tions;
You understand me?
  Xanthias. Yes, I understand you;
A lucky, promising direction, truly.
  Charon (to Bacchus). Sit down at the oar.
Come quick, if there's more coming!
  (*To Bacchus again*) Holloh! what's that you 're
    doing?

    [BACCHUS *is seated in a buffoonish attitude on the side of
    the boat where the oar was fastened.*

  Bacchus. What you told me.
I 'm sitting at the oar.
  Charon. Sit *there*, I tell you,
You Fatguts; that's your place.
  Bacchus (changes his place). Well, so I do.

---

[1] The Athenians were in such straits for lack of soldiers that they offered freedom to any slave who volunteered.

Charon. Now ply your hands and arms.
Bacchus (*makes a silly motion with his arms*).
    Well, so I do.   25
Charon. You 'd best leave off your fooling.   Take
    to the oar,
And pull away.
    Bacchus.   But how shall I contrive?
I 've never served on board.— I 'm only a landsman;
I 'm quite unused to it. —
    Charon.   We can manage it.
As soon as you begin you shall have some music   30
That will teach you to keep time.
    Bacchus.   What music 's that?
    Charon. A chorus of Frogs — uncommon musical
        Frogs.
    Bacchus. Well, give me the word and the time.
    Charon.   Whooh up, up; whooh up, up.

CHORUS.[1]

Brekeke-kesh, koash, koash,
Shall the Choral Quiristers of the Marsh   35
Be censured and rejected as hoarse and harsh;
    And their Chromatic essays
    Deprived of praise?
No, let us raise afresh
Our obstreperous Brekeke-kesh;   40
The customary croak and cry
    Of the creatures
    At the theatres,[2]
In their yearly revelry.
Brekeke-kesh, koash, koash.   45

---

[1] The Chorus in this play was made up of men dressed to represent frogs.
[2] The region near the theatre was marshy.

Bacchus (*rowing in great misery*).
    How I 'm maul'd,
    How I 'm gall'd ;
    Worn and mangled to a mash —
    There they go! "*Koash, koash!*"
Frogs.   Brekeke-kesh, koash, koash.   50
Bacchus. Oh, beshrew,
    All your crew ;
  You don't consider how I smart.
Frogs.   Now for a sample of the Art !
  Brekeke-kesh, koash, koash.   55
Bacchus. I wish you hang'd, with all my heart.
  Have you nothing else to say ?
  "*Brekeke-kesh, koash*" all day !
Frogs.   We 've a right, we 've a right ;
    And we croak at ye for spite.   60
    We 've a right, we 've a right ;
    Day and night, day and night ;
    Night and day,
    Still to creak and croak away.
Phoebus and every Grace   65
Admire and approve of the croaking race ;
And the egregious guttural notes
That are gargled and warbled in their lyrical throats.
    In reproof of your scorn
    Mighty Pan nods his horn ;   70
    Beating time to the rhyme
    With his hoof, with his hoof.
    Persisting in our plan
    We proceed as we began,
    Breke-kesh, breke-kesh, koash, koash.
Bacchus. Oh, the Frogs, consume and rot 'em,   76
    I 've a blister on my bottom.
    Hold your tongues, you tuneful creatures.

Frogs.   Cease with your profane entreaties
         All in vain for ever striving:
           Silence is against our natures.
         With the vernal heat reviving,
           Our aquatic crew repair
         From their periodic sleep,
         In the dark and chilly deep,
         To the cheerful upper air;
         Then we frolic here and there
         All amidst the meadows fair;
         Shady plants of asphodel
         Are the lodges where we dwell;
         Chanting in the leafy bowers
         All the livelong summer hours,
         Till the sudden gusty showers
         Send us headlong, helter-skelter,
         To the pool to seek for shelter;
         Meagre, eager, leaping, lunging,
         From the sedgy wharfage plunging
         To the tranquil depth below,
         There we muster all a-row;
         Where, secure from toil and trouble,
         With a tuneful bubble-bubble,
         Our symphonious accents flow.
         Brekeke-kesh, koash, koash.
Bacchus. I forbid you to proceed.
Frogs.   That would be severe indeed;
         Arbitrary, bold, and rash —
         Brekeke-kesh, koash, koash.
Bacchus. I command you to desist —
        — Oh, my back, there! oh, my wrist!
          What a twist!
          What a sprain!
Frogs.   Once again —

THE FROGS

           We renew the tuneful strain.
           Brekeke-kesh, koash, koash.
Bacchus. I disdain — (Hang the pain!)   115
           All your nonsense, noise, and trash.
           O, my blister! O, my sprain!
Frogs. Brekeke-kesh, koash, koash.
           Friends and Frogs, we must display
           All our powers of voice to-day;   120
           Suffer not this stranger here,
           With fastidious foreign ear,
           To confound us and abash.
           Brekeke-kesh, koash, koash.
Bacchus. Well, my spirit is not broke,   125
           If it's only for the joke,
           I'll outdo you with a croak.
           Here it goes, (*very loud*) "Koash, koash."
Frogs. Now for a glorious croaking crash,
               (*Still louder*).
           Brekeke-kesh, koash, koash.   130
Bacchus [*splashing with his oar*].
           I'll disperse you with a splash.
Frogs. Brekeke-kesh, koash, koash.
Bacchus. I'll subdue
           Your rebellious, noisy crew —
           Have amongst you there, slap-dash.   135
                      [*Strikes at them.*
Frogs. Brekeke-kesh, koash, koash.
           We defy your oar and you.
Charon. Hold! We're ashore just — shift your oar. Get out.
— Now pay for your fare.
    Bacchus.   There — there it is — the twopence.[1]

---

[1] A small coin was pnt into the mouth of the corpse as a fee for Charon.

HERODOTUS

HERODOTUS, the Father of History, as he has been called since Cicero's time, was born about 484 B. C. He was a native not of Greece proper but of Halicarnassus, a city of Asia Minor, founded by the Dorians but at the time of his birth subject to the Persians. When he was a little over thirty years of age he was obliged to leave his native city on account of political dissensions there, and traveled for more than ten years, traversing Asia Minor and European Greece in all directions, and making a long visit to Egypt. He was a great admirer of Athens, where on one occasion he is said to have received a gift of ten talents ($10,000) from the people for a recitation from his works, which glorify that city as the savior of Greece in the contests with Persia. Finally he became a citizen of Thurii, a new Athenian colony in southern Italy, where he died about 425 B. C.

The History, Herodotus's one great work, has come down to us in its entirety. The subject was the conflict between the Greeks and the Barbarians (Asiatics) which culminated in the Persian wars of invasion. The first six of the nine books deal with the earlier history of the two nations, and form a magnificent introduction to the description of the final conflict in the last three books.

Before Herodotus, the writing of history had been confined to two classes of people, — the Epic Poets, who aimed at the picturesque rather than the accurate, and the Logographers, who stated unconnected facts without regard to form. He was the first to describe historical events with attention to literary style, unity of theme, and fidelity to facts. As a writer, he has been universally praised by both ancients and moderns. "O that I were in a condition," says Lucian, "to resemble Herodotus, if only in some measure! I by no means say in all his gifts, but only in some single point; as for instance, the beauty of his language, or its harmony, or the natural and peculiar grace of the Ionic dialect, or his fulness of thought, or by whatever name those thousand beauties are called which, to the despair of his imitator, are united in him."

His trustworthiness has many times been called into question by those who urge that his credulity, his love of effect, and his partisanship for Athens unfitted him for the historian's office. But it seems clear at least that he was not willfully deceitful, and that the picture he paints of the world of his time is the world as it appeared to him.

Canon Rawlinson's translation is used in the following passages.

THE TAKING OF BABYLON

HAVING, however, thus wreaked his vengeance on the Gyndes by dispersing it through three hundred and sixty channels, Cyrus, with the first approach of the ensuing spring, marched forward against Babylon. The Babylonians, encamped without their walls, awaited his coming. A battle was fought at a short distance from the city, in which the Babylonians were defeated by the Persian king, whereupon they withdrew within their defences. Here they shut themselves up, and made light of his siege, having laid in a store of provisions for many years in preparation against this attack; for when they saw Cyrus conquering nation after nation, they were convinced that he would never stop, and that their turn would come at last.

Cyrus was now reduced to great perplexity, as time went on and he made no progress against the place. In this distress either some one made the suggestion to him, or he bethought himself of a plan, which he proceeded to put in execution. He placed a portion of his army at the point where the river enters the city, and another body at the back of the place where it issues forth, with orders to march into the town by the bed of the stream, as soon as the water became shallow enough: he then himself drew off with the unwarlike portion of his host, and made for the place where Nitocris dug the basin for the river, where he did exactly what she had done formerly: he turned the Euphrates by a canal into the basin, which was then a marsh, on which the river sank to such an extent that the natural bed of the stream became fordable. Hereupon the Persians, who had been left for the purpose at Babylon by the river-side, entered the stream, which had now sunk so as to reach about midway up a man's thigh, and thus got into the town. Had the Babylonians been apprised of what Cyrus was about, or had they noticed their danger, they would not have allowed the entrance of the Persians within the city, which was what ruined them utterly, but would have made fast all the street-gates which gave upon the river, and mounting upon the walls along both sides of the stream, would so have caught the enemy as it were in a trap. But, as it was, the Persians came upon them by surprise and so took the city. Owing to the vast size of the place, the inhabitants of the central parts (as the residents at Babylon declare) long after the outer portions of the town were taken, knew nothing of what had chanced, but as they were engaged in a festival, continued dancing and revelling until they learnt the capture but too certainly. Such, then, were the circumstances of the first taking of Babylon. (*Book I., Chapters 190, 191.*)

PERSIAN CUSTOMS

THE customs which I know the Persians to observe are the following. They have no images of the gods, no temples nor altars, and consider the use of them a sign of folly. This comes, I think, from their not believing the gods to have the same nature with men, as the Greeks imagine. Their wont, however, is to ascend the summits of the loftiest mountains, and there to offer sacrifice to Jupiter, which is the name they give to the whole circuit of the firmament. They likewise offer to the sun and moon, to the earth, to fire, to water, and to the winds. These are the only gods whose worship has come down to them from ancient times. At a later period they began the worship of Urania, which they borrowed from the Arabians and Assyrians. Mylitta is the name by which the Assyrians know this goddess, whom the Arabians call Alilat, and the Persians Mitra.

To these gods the Persians offer sacrifice in the following manner: they raise no altar, light no fire, pour no libations; there is no sound of the flute, no putting on of chaplets, no consecrated barley-cake; but the man who wishes to sacrifice brings his victim to a spot of ground which is pure from pollution, and there calls upon the name of the god to whom he intends to offer. It is usual to have the turban encircled with a wreath, most commonly of myrtle. The sacrificer is not allowed to pray for blessings on himself alone, but he prays for the welfare of the kind, and of the whole Persian people, among whom he is of necessity included. He cuts the victim in pieces, and having boiled the flesh, he lays it out upon the tenderest herbage that he can find, trefoil especially. When all is ready, one of the Magi comes forward and chants a hymn, which they say recounts the origin of the gods. It is not lawful to offer sacrifice unless there is a Magus present. After waiting a short time the sacrificer carries the flesh of the victim away with him, and makes whatever use of it he may please.

Of all the days in the year, the one which they celebrate most is their birthday. It is customary to have the board furnished on that day with an ampler supply than common. The richer Persians cause an ox, a horse, a camel, and an ass to be baked whole and so served up to them; the poorer classes use instead the smaller kinds of cattle. They eat little solid food, but abundance of dessert, which is set on the table a few dishes at a time: this it is which makes them say that "the Greeks, when they eat, leave off hungry, having nothing worth mention served up to them after the meats; whereas, if they had more put before them, they would not stop eating." They are very fond of wine, and drink it in large quantities. Such are their customs in these matters.

It is also their general practice to deliberate upon affairs of weight when they are drunk; and then on the morrow, when they are sober, the decision to which they came the night before is put before them by the master of the house in which it was made; and if it is then approved of, they act on it; if not, they set it aside. Sometimes, however, they are sober at their first deliberation, but in this case they always reconsider the matter under the influence of wine. (*Book I., Chapters 131–133.*)

THE NILE

Now the Nile, when it overflows, floods not only the Delta, but also the tracts of country on both sides the stream which are thought to belong to Libya and Arabia, in some places reaching to the extent of two days' journey from its banks, in some even exceeding that distance, but in others falling short of it.

Concerning the nature of the river, I was not able to gain any information either from the priests or from others. I was particularly anxious to learn from them why the Nile, at the commencement of the summer solstice, begins to rise, and continues to increase for a hundred days; and why, as soon as that number is past, it forthwith retires and contracts its stream, continuing low during the whole of the winter until the summer solstice comes round again. On none of these points could I obtain any explanation from the inhabitants, though I made every inquiry, wishing to know what was commonly reported, — they could neither tell me what special virtue the Nile has which makes it so opposite in its nature to all other streams, nor why, unlike every other river, it gives forth no breezes from its surface.

Some of the Greeks, however, wishing to get a reputation for cleverness, have offered explanations of the phenomena of the river, for which they have accounted in three different ways. Two of these I do not think it worth while to speak of, further than simply to mention what they are. One pretends that the Etesian winds cause the rise of the river by preventing the Nile-water from running off into the sea. But in the first place it has often happened, that when the Etesian winds did not blow, the Nile has risen according to its usual wont; and further, if the Etesian winds produced the effect, the other rivers which flow in a direction opposite to those winds ought to present the same phenomena as the Nile, and the more so as they are all smaller streams, and have a weaker current. But these rivers, of which there are many both in Syria and Libya, are entirely unlike the Nile in this respect.

The second opinion is even more unscientific than the one just mentioned, and also, if I may so say, more marvellous. It is that the Nile acts so strangely because it flows from the ocean, and that the ocean flows all round the earth.

The third explanation, which is very much more plausible than either of the others, is positively the furthest from the truth; for there is really nothing in what it says, any more than in the other theories. It is, that the inundation of the Nile is caused by the melting of snows. Now, as the Nile flows out of Libya, through Ethiopia, into Egypt, how is it possible that it can be formed of melted snow, running, as it does, from the hottest regions of the world into cooler countries? Many are the proofs whereby any one capable of reasoning on the subject may be convinced that it is most unlikely this should be the case. The first and strongest argument is furnished by the winds, which always blow hot from these regions. The second is, that rain and frost are unknown there. Now, whenever snow falls, it must of necessity rain within five days; so that, if there were snow, there must be rain also in those parts. Thirdly, it is certain that the natives of the country are black with the heat, that the kites and the swallows remain there the whole year, and that the cranes, when they fly from the rigors of a Scythian winter, flock thither to pass the cold season. If then, in the country whence the Nile has its source, or in that through which it flows, there fell ever so little snow, it is absolutely impossible that any of these circumstances could take place.

As for the writer who attributes the phenomenon to the ocean, his account is involved in such obscurity that it is impossible to disprove it by argument. For my part I know of no river called Ocean, and I think that Homer, or one of the earlier poets, invented the name, and introduced it into his poetry.

Perhaps, after censuring all the opinions that have been put forward on this obscure subject, one ought to propose some theory of one's own. I will therefore proceed to explain what I think to be the reason of the Nile's swelling in the summer-time. During the winter, the sun is driven out of his usual course by the storms, and removes to the upper parts of Libya. This is the whole secret in the fewest possible words; for it stands to reason that the country to which the Sun-god approaches the nearest, and which he passes most directly over, will be scantest of water, and that there the streams which feed the rivers will shrink the most.

To explain, however, more at length, the case is this. The sun, in his passage across the upper parts of Libya, affects them in the following way. As the air in those regions is constantly clear, and the country warm through the absence of cold winds, the sun in his passage across them acts upon them exactly as he is wont to act elsewhere in summer, when his path is in the middle of heaven — that is, he attracts the water. After attracting it, he again repels it into the upper regions, where the winds lay hold of it, scatter it, and reduce it to a vapor, whence it naturally enough comes to pass that the winds which blow from this quarter — the south and southwest — are of all winds the most rainy. And my own opinion is that the sun does not get rid of all the water which he draws year by year from the Nile, but retains some about him. When the winter begins to soften, the sun goes back again to his old place in the middle of the heaven, and proceeds to attract water equally from all countries. Till then the other rivers run big, from the quantity of rain-water which they bring down from countries where so much moisture falls that all the land is cut into gullies; but in summer, when the showers fail, and the sun attracts their water, they become low. The Nile, on the contrary, not deriving any of its bulk from rains, and being in winter subject to the attraction of the sun, naturally runs at that season, unlike all other streams, with a less burthen of water than in the summer-time. For in summer it is exposed to attraction equally with all other rivers, but in winter it suffers alone. The sun, therefore, I regard as the sole cause of the phenomenon.

It is the sun also in my opinion which, by heating the space through which it passes, makes the air in Egypt so dry. There is thus perpetual summer in the upper parts of Libya. Were the position of the heavenly regions reversed, so that the place where now the north wind and the winter have their dwelling became the station of the south wind and of the noonday, while, on the other hand, the station of the south wind became that of the north, the consequence would be that the sun, driven from the mid-heaven by the winter and the northern gales, would betake himself to the upper parts of Europe, as he now does to those of Libya, and then I believe his passage across Europe would affect the Ister exactly as the Nile is affected at the present day.

And with respect to the fact that no breeze blows from the Nile, I am of opinion that no wind is likely to arise in very hot countries, for breezes love to blow from some cold quarter.

Let us leave these things, however, to their natural course, to continue as they are and have been from the beginning. With regard to the *sources* of the Nile, I have found no one among all those with whom I have conversed, whether Egyptians, Libyans, or Greeks, who professed to have any knowledge, except a single person. He was the scribe who kept the register of the sacred treasures of Minerva in the city of Sais, and he did not seem to me to be in earnest when he said that he knew them perfectly well. His story was as follows: "Between Syêné, a city of the Thebais, and Elephantiné, there are" (he said) "two hills with sharp conical tops; the name of the one is Crophi, of the other, Mophi. Midway between them are the fountains of the Nile, fountains which it is impossible to fathom. Half the water runs northward into Egypt, half to the south towards Ethiopia." The fountains were known to be unfathomable, he declared, because Psammetichus, an Egyptian king, had made trial of them. He had caused a rope to be made, many thousand fathoms in length, and had sounded the fountain with it, but could find no bottom. By this the scribe gave me to understand, if there was any truth at all in what he said, that in this fountain there are certain strong eddies, and a regurgitation, owing to the force wherewith the water dashes against the mountains, and hence a sounding-line cannot be got to reach the bottom of the spring.

No other information on this head could I obtain from any quarter. All that I succeeded in learning further of the more distant portions of the Nile, by ascending myself as high as Elephantiné, and making inquiries concerning the parts beyond, was the following: As one advances beyond Elephantiné, the land rises. Hence it is necessary in this part of the river to attach a rope to the boat on each side, as men harness an ox, and so proceed on the journey. If the rope snaps, the vessel is borne away down-stream by the force of the current. The navigation continues the same for four days, the river winding greatly, like the Maeander, and the distance traversed amounting to twelve schoenoi.[1] Here you come upon a smooth and level plain, where the Nile flows in two branches, round an island called Tachompso. The country above Elephantiné is inhabited by the Ethiopians, who possess one half of this island, the Egyptians occupying the other. Above the island there is a great lake, the shores of which are inhabited by Ethiopian nomads; after passing it, you come again to the stream of the Nile, which runs into the lake. Here you land, and travel for forty days along the banks of the river, since it is impossible to proceed further in a boat on account of the sharp peaks which jut out from the water, and the sunken rocks which abound in that part of the stream. When you have passed this portion of the river in the space of forty days, you go on board another boat, and proceed by water for twelve days more, at the end of which time you reach a great city called Meroë, which is said to

[1] About twenty-four leagues, or seventy-two miles.

be the capital of the other Ethiopians. The only gods worshipped by the inhabitants are Jupiter and Bacchus; to whom great honors are paid. There is an oracle of Jupiter in the city, which directs the warlike expeditions of the Ethiopians; when it commands, they go to war, and in whatever direction it bids them march, thither straightway they carry their arms.

On leaving this city, and again mounting the stream, in the same space of time which it took you to reach the capital from Elephantiné, you come to the Deserters, who bear the name of Asmach. This word, translated into our language, means "the men who stand on the left hand of the king." These Deserters are Egyptians of the warrior caste, who, to the number of two hundred and forty thousand, went over to the Ethiopians in the reign of King Psammetichus. The cause of their desertion was the following: Three garrisons were maintained in Egypt at that time, one in the city of Elephantiné, against the Ethiopians, another in the Pelusiac Daphnae, against the Syrians and Arabians, and a third, against the Libyans, in Marea. (The very same posts are to this day occupied by the Persians, whose forces are in garrison both in Daphnae and in Elephantiné.) Now it happened that on one occasion the garrisons were not relieved during the space of three years; the soldiers, therefore, at the end of that time, consulted together, and having determined by common consent to revolt, marched away towards Ethiopia. Psammetichus, informed of the movement, set out in pursuit, and coming up with them, besought them with many words not to desert the gods of their country, nor abandon their wives and children. "Nay, but," said one of the deserters with an unseemly gesture, "wherever we go, we are sure enough of finding wives and children." Arrived in Ethiopia, they placed themselves at the disposal of the king. In return, he made them a present of a tract of land which belonged to certain Ethiopians with whom he was at feud, bidding them expel the inhabitants and take possession of their territory. From the time that this settlement was formed, their acquaintance with Egyptian manners has tended to civilize the Ethiopians.

Thus the course of the Nile is known, not only throughout Egypt, but to the extent of four months' journey either by land or water above the Egyptian boundary; for on calculation it will be found that it takes that length of time to travel from Elephantiné to the country of the Deserters. There the direction of the river is from west to east. Beyond, no one has any certain knowledge of its course, since the country is uninhabited by reason of the excessive heat. (*Book II., Chapters 19–31.*)

EGYPTIAN CUSTOMS

CONCERNING Egypt itself I shall extend my remarks to a great length, because there is no country that possesses so many wonders, nor any that has such a number of works which defy description. Not only is the climate different from that of the rest of the world, and the rivers unlike any other rivers, but the people also, in most of their manners and customs, exactly reverse the common practice of mankind. The women attend the markets and trade, while the men sit at home at the loom; and here, while the rest of the world works the woof up the warp, the Egyptians work it down; the women likewise carry burthens

EGYPTIAN CUSTOMS

upon their shoulders, while the men carry them upon their heads. They eat their food out of doors in the streets. A woman cannot serve the priestly office, either for god or goddess, but men are priests to both; sons need not support their parents unless they choose, but daughters must, whether they choose or no.

In other countries the priests have long hair, in Egypt their heads are shaven; elsewhere it is customary, in mourning, for near relations to cut their hair close; the Egyptians, who wear no hair at any other time, when they lose a relative, let their beards and the hair of their heads grow long. All other men pass their lives separate from animals; the Egyptians have animals always living with them: others make barley and wheat their food; it is a disgrace to do so in Egypt, where the grain they live on is spelt, which some call *zea*. Dough they knead with their feet, but they mix mud, and even take up dirt, with their hands. Their men wear two garments apiece, their women but one. They put on the rings and fasten the ropes to sails inside, others put them outside. When they write or calculate, instead of going, like the Greeks, from left to right, they move their hand from right to left; and they insist, notwithstanding, that it is they who go to the right, and the Greeks who go to the left. They have two quite different kinds of writing, one of which is called sacred, the other common.

They are religious to excess, far beyond any other race of men, and use the following ceremonies: They drink out of brazen cups, which they scour every day: there is no exception to this practice. They wear linen garments, which they are specially careful to have always fresh washed. Their dress is entirely of linen, and their shoes of the papyrus plant:

it is not lawful for them to wear either dress or shoes of any other material. They bathe twice every day in cold water, and twice each night. Besides which they observe, so to speak, thousands of ceremonies. (*Book II., 35-37.*)

CROCODILES AND THE HIPPOPOTAMUS

The following are the peculiarities of the crocodile: During the four winter months they eat nothing; they are four-footed, and live indifferently on land or in the water. The female lays and hatches her eggs ashore, passing the greater portion of the day on dry land, but at night retiring to the river, the water of which is warmer than the night-air and the dew. Of all known animals this is the one which from the smallest size grows to be the greatest: for the egg of the crocodile is but little bigger than that of the goose, and the young crocodile is in proportion to the egg; yet when it is full grown, the animal measures frequently seventeen cubits, and even more. It has the eyes of a pig, teeth large and tusk-like, of a size proportioned to its frame; unlike any other animal, it is without a tongue; it cannot move its under jaw, and in this respect too it is singular, being the only animal in the world which moves the upper jaw, but not the under. It has strong claws and a scaly skin, impenetrable upon the back. In the water it is blind, but on land it is very keen of sight. As it lives chiefly in the river, it has the inside of its mouth constantly covered with leeches; hence it happens that, while all the other birds and beasts avoid it, with the trochilus it lives at peace, since it owes much to that bird: for the crocodile, when he leaves the water and comes out upon the land, is in the habit of lying with his mouth wide open, facing the western breeze: at such times the trochilus goes into his mouth and devours the leeches. This benefits the crocodile, who is pleased, and takes care not to hurt the trochilus.

The crocodile is esteemed sacred by some of the Egyptians, by others he is treated as an enemy. Those who live near Thebes, and those who dwell around Lake Moeris, regard them with especial veneration. In each of these places they keep one crocodile in particular, who is taught to be tame and tractable. They adorn his ears with ear-rings of molten stone or gold, and put bracelets on his forepaws, giving him daily a set portion of bread, with a certain number of victims; and, after having thus treated him with the greatest possible attention while alive, they embalm him when he dies and bury him in a sacred repository. The people of Elephantiné, on the other hand, are so far from considering these animals as sacred that they even eat their flesh. In the Egyptian language they are not called crocodiles, but *champsae*. The name of crocodiles was given them by the Ionians, who remarked their resemblance to the lizards, which in Ionia live in the walls, and are called crocodiles.

The modes of catching the crocodile are many and various. I shall only describe the one which seems to me most worthy of mention. They bait a hook with a chine of pork and let the meat be carried out into the middle of the stream, while the hunter upon the bank holds a living pig, which he belabors. The crocodile hears its cries and, making for the sound, encounters the pork, which he instantly swallows down. The men on the shore haul, and when they have got him to land, the first thing the hunter does is to plaster his eyes with mud. This once accomplished, the animal is dispatched with ease, otherwise he gives great trouble.

The hippopotamus, in the canton of Paprêmis, is a sacred animal, but not in any other part of Egypt. It may be thus described: It is a quadruped, cloven-footed, with hoofs like an ox, and a flat nose. It has the mane and tail of a horse, huge tusks which are very conspicuous, and a voice like a horse's neigh. In size it equals the biggest oxen, and its skin is so tough that when dried it is made into javelins. (*Book II., 69-71.*)

SESOSTRIS

PASSING over [Mis, Nitocris, and Moeris] I shall speak of the king who reigned next, whose name was Sesostris. He, the priests said, first of all proceeded in a fleet of ships of war from the Arabian Gulf along the shores of the Erythraean Sea, subduing the nations as he went, until he finally reached a sea which could not be navigated by reason of the shoals. Hence he returned to Egypt, where, they told me, he collected a vast armament, and made a progress by land across the continent, conquering every people which fell in his way. In the countries where the natives withstood his attack, and fought gallantly for their liberties, he erected pillars on which he inscribed his own name and country, and how that he had here reduced the inhabitants to subjection by the might of his arms; where, on the contrary, they submitted readily and without a struggle, he inscribed on the pillars, in addition to these particulars, an emblem to mark that they were a nation of women, that is, unwarlike and effeminate.

In this way he traversed the whole continent of

Asia, whence he passed on into Europe, and made himself master of Scythia and of Thrace, beyond which countries I do not think that his army extended its march. For thus far the pillars which he erected are still visible, but in the remoter regions they are no longer found. Returning to Egypt from Thrace, he came on his way to the banks of the river Phasis. Here I cannot say with any certainty what took place. Either he of his own accord detached a body of troops from his main army and left them to colonize the country, or else a certain number of his soldiers, wearied with their long wanderings, deserted, and established themselves on the banks of this stream.

There can be no doubt that the Colchians are an Egyptian race. Before I heard any mention of the fact from others, I had remarked it myself. After the thought had struck me, I made inquiries on the subject both in Colchis and in Egypt, and I found that the Colchians had a more distinct recollection of the Egyptians than the Egyptians had of them. Still the Egyptians said that they believed the Colchians to be descended from the army of Sesostris. . . . I will add a further proof of the identity of the Egyptians and the Colchians. These two nations weave their linen in exactly the same way, and this is a way entirely unknown to the rest of the world; they also in their whole mode of life and in their language resemble one another. The Colchian linen is called by the Greeks Sardinian, while that which comes from Egypt is known as Egyptian.

The pillars which Sesostris erected in the conquered countries have for the most part disappeared, but in the part of Syria called Palestine, I myself saw them still standing, with the writing above mentioned, and the emblem distinctly visible. In Ionia also, there are two representations of this prince engraved upon rocks, one on the road from Ephesus to Phocaea, the other between Sardis and Smyrna. In each case the figure is that of a man, four cubits and a span high, with a spear in his right hand and a bow in his left, the rest of his costume being likewise half Egyptian, half Ethiopian. There is an inscription across the breast from shoulder to shoulder in the sacred character of Egypt, which says, " With my own shoulders I conquered this land." The conqueror does not tell who he is, or whence he comes, though elsewhere Sesostris records these facts. Hence it has been imagined by some of those who have seen these forms that they are figures of Memnon; but such as think so err very widely from the truth.

This Sesostris, the priests went on to say, upon his return home accompanied by vast multitudes of people whose countries he had subdued, was received by his brother, whom he had made viceroy of Egypt on his departure, at Daphnae near Pelusium, and invited by him to a banquet, which he attended, together with his sons. Then his brother piled a quantity of wood all round the building, and having so done set it alight. Sesostris, discovering what had happened, took counsel instantly with his wife, who had accompanied him to the feast, and was advised by her to lay two of their six sons upon the fire, and so make a bridge across the flames, whereby the rest might effect their escape. Sesostris did as she recommended, and thus, while two of his sons were burnt to death, he himself and his other children were saved.

The king then returned to his own land and took vengeance upon his brother, after which he proceeded to make use of the multitudes whom he had brought with him from the conquered countries, partly to drag the huge masses of stone which were moved in the course of his reign to the temple of Vulcan, partly to dig the numerous canals with which the whole of Egypt is intersected. By these forced labors the entire face of the country was changed; for whereas Egypt had formerly been a region suited both for horses and carriages, henceforth it became entirely unfit for either. Though a flat country throughout its whole extent, it is now unfit for either horse or carriage, being cut up by the canals, which are extremely numerous and run in all directions. The king's object was to supply Nile water to the inhabitants of the towns situated in the mid-country, and not lying upon the river; for previously they had been obliged, after the subsidence of the floods, to drink a brackish water which they obtained from wells.

Sesostris also, they declared, made a division of the soil of Egypt among the inhabitants, assigning square plots of ground of equal size to all, and obtaining his chief revenue from the rent which the holders were required to pay him every year. If the river carried away any portion of a man's lot, he appeared before the king, and related what had happened; upon which the king sent persons to examine and determine by measurement the exact extent of the loss; and thenceforth only such a rent was demanded of him as was proportionate to the reduced size of his land. From this practice, I think, geometry first came to be known in Egypt, whence it passed into Greece. The sun-dial, however, and the gnomon, with the division of the day into twelve parts, were received by the Greeks from the Babylonians. (*Book II., Chapters 102-109*).

THE PYRAMID OF CHEOPS

TILL the death of Rhampsinitus, the priests said, Egypt was excellently governed, and flourished greatly; but after him Cheops succeeded to the throne, and plunged into all manner of wickedness. He closed the temples, and forbade the Egyptians to offer sacrifice, compelling them instead to labor, one and all, in his service. Some were required to drag blocks of stone down to the Nile from the quarries in the Arabian range of hills; others received the blocks after they had been conveyed in boats across the river, and drew them to the range of hills called the Libyan. A hundred thousand men labored constantly, and were relieved every three months by a fresh lot. It took ten years' oppression of the people to make the causeway for the conveyance of the stones, a work not much inferior, in my judgment, to the pyramid itself. This causeway is five furlongs in length, ten fathoms wide, and in height, at the highest part, eight fathoms. It is built of polished stone, and is covered with carvings of animals. To make it took ten years, as I said — or rather to make the causeway, the works on the mound where the pyramid stands, and the underground chambers, which Cheops intended as vaults for his own use; these last were built on a sort of island, surrounded by water introduced from the Nile by a canal. The pyramid itself was twenty years in building. It is a square, eight hundred feet each way, and the height the same, built entirely of polished stone, fitted together with the utmost care. The stones of which it is composed are none of them less than thirty feet in length.

The pyramid was built in steps, battlement-wise, as

THE PYRAMID OF CHEOPS 313

it is called, or, according to other, altar-wise. After laying the stone for the base, they raised the remaining stones to their places by means of machines formed of short wooden planks. The first machine raised them from the ground to the top of the first step. On this there was another machine, which received the stone upon its arrival and conveyed it to the second step, whence a third machine advanced it still higher. Either they had as many machines as there were steps in the pyramid, or possibly they had but a single machine, which, being easily moved, was transferred from tier to tier as the stone rose — both accounts are given, and therefore I mention both. The upper portion of the pyramid was finished first, then the middle, and finally the part which was lowest and nearest the ground. There is an inscription in Egyptian characters on the pyramid which records the quantity of radishes, onions, and garlic consumed by the laborers who constructed it; and I perfectly well remember that the interpreter who read the writing to me said that the money expended in this way was 1600 talents[1] of silver. If this, then, is a true record, what a vast sum must have been spent on the iron tools used in the work and on the feeding and clothing of the laborers, considering the length of time the work lasted, which has already been stated, and the additional time — no small space, I imagine — which must have been occupied by the quarrying of the stones, their conveyance, and the formation of the underground apartments. (*Book II., Chapters 124, 125.*)

[1] $1,600,000.

THE BATTLE OF MARATHON[1]

The Athenians were drawn up in order of battle in a sacred close belonging to Hercules, when they were joined by the Plataeans, who came in full force to their aid. . . .

The Athenian generals were divided in their opinions; and some advised not to risk a battle, because they were too few to engage such a host as that of the Medes; while others were for fighting at once, and among these last was Miltiades. He therefore, seeing that opinions were thus divided, and that the less worthy counsel appeared likely to prevail, resolved to go to the polemarch, and have a conference with him. For the man on whom the lot fell to be polemarch at Athens was entitled to give his vote with the ten generals, since anciently the Athenians allowed him an equal right of voting with them. The polemarch at this juncture was Callimachus of Aphidnae; to him therefore Miltiades went, and said : —

"With thee it rests, Callimachus, either to bring Athens to slavery, or, by securing her freedom, to leave behind thee to all future generations a memory beyond even Harmodius and Aristogeiton.[2] For never since the time that Athenians became a people were they in so great a danger as now. If they bow their necks beneath the yoke of the Medes, the woes which they will have to suffer when given into the power of Hippias[2] are already determined on ; if, on the other hand, they fight and overcome, Athens may rise to be

---

[1] 490 B. C.   [2] See page 50.
[3] After his expulsion from Athens in 510 B. C. the tyrant Hippias retired to the court of Darius in Asia Minor. He conducted this second Persian expedition against the Greeks.

the very first city in Greece. How it comes to pass
that these things are likely to happen, and how the
determining of them in some sort rests with thee, I
will now proceed to make clear. We generals are
teń in number, and our votes are divided : half of us
wish to engage, half to avoid a combat. Now, if we
do not fight, I look to see a great disturbance at
Athens which will shake men's resolutions, and then
I fear they will submit themselves ; but if we fight
the battle before any unsoundness show itself among
our citizens, let the gods but give us fair play, and we
are well able to overcome the enemy. On thee therefore we depend in this matter, which lies wholly in
thine own power. Thou hast only to add thy vote to
my side and thy country will be free, and not free
only, but the first state in Greece. Or, if thou pre-
ferrest to give thy vote to them who would decline the
combat, then the reverse will follow."

Miltiades by these words gained Callimachus; and
the addition of the polemarch's vote caused the decision to be in favor of fighting. Hereupon all those
generals who had been desirous of hazarding a battle,
when their turn came to command the army gave up
their right to Miltiades. He, however, though he accepted their offers, nevertheless waited, and would not
fight, until his own day of command arrived in due
course.

Then at length, when his own turn was come, the
Athenian battle was set in array, and this was the
order of it. Callimachus the polemarch led the right
wing, for it was at that time a rule with the Athenians to give the right wing to the polemarch. After
this followed the tribes, according as they were numbered, in an unbroken line ; while last of all came

the Plataeans, forming the left wing. And ever since that day it has been a custom with the Athenians, in the sacrifices and assemblies held each fifth year at Athens, for the Athenian herald to implore the blessing of the gods on the Plataeans conjointly with the Athenians. Now as they marshalled the host upon the field of Marathon, in order that the Athenian front might be of equal length with the Median,[1] the ranks of the centre were diminished, and it became the weakest part of the line, while the wings were both made strong with a depth of many ranks.

So when the battle was set in array, and the victims showed themselves favorable, instantly the Athenians, so soon as they were let go, charged the barbarians at a run. Now the distance between the two armies was little short of eight furlongs. The Persians, therefore, when they saw the Greeks coming on at speed, made ready to receive them, although it seemed to them that the Athenians were bereft of their senses, and bent upon their own destruction; for they saw a mere handful of men coming on at a run without either horsemen or archers. Such was the opinion of the barbarians; but the Athenians in close array fell upon them, and fought in a manner worthy of being recorded. They were the first of the Greeks, so far as I know, who introduced the custom of charging the enemy at a run, and they were likewise the first who dared to look upon the Median garb, and to face men clad in that fashion. Until this time the very name of the Medes had been a terror to the Greeks to hear.

The two armies fought together on the plain of Marathon for a length of time; and in the mid battle,

[1] Median and Persian were synonymous terms.

where the Persians themselves and the Sacae [1] had their place, the barbarians were victorious, and broke and pursued the Greeks into the inner country; but on the two wings the Athenians and the Plataeans defeated the enemy. Having so done, they suffered the routed barbarians to fly at their ease, and joining the two wings in one, fell upon those who had broken their own centre, and fought and conquered them. These likewise fled, and now the Athenians hung upon the runaways and cut them down, chasing them all the way to the shore, on reaching which they laid hold of the ships and called aloud for fire.

It was in the struggle here that Callimachus the polemarch, after greatly distinguishing himself, lost his life; Stesilaus too, the son of Thrasilaus, one of the generals, was slain; and Cynegirus,[2] the son of Euphorion, having seized on a vessel of the enemy's by the ornament at the stern, had his hand cut off by the blow of an axe, and so perished; as likewise did many other Athenians of note and name.

Nevertheless the Athenians secured in this way seven of the vessels, while with the remainder the barbarians pushed off, and taking aboard their Eretrian prisoners from the island where they had left them, doubled Cape Sunium, hoping to reach Athens before the return of the Athenians. The Alcmaeonidae were accused by their countrymen of suggesting this course to them; they had, it was said, an understanding with the Persians, and made a signal to them, by raising a shield, after they were embarked in their ships.

The Persians accordingly sailed round Sunium. But the Athenians with all possible speed marched

---

[1] See page 253, note 3. [2] A brother of the poet Aeschylus.

away to the defence of their city, and succeeded in reaching Athens before the appearance of the barbarians; and as their camp at Marathon had been pitched in a precinct of Hercules, so now they encamped in another precinct of the same god at Cynosarges. The barbarian fleet arrived, and lay to off Phalerum,[1] which was at that time the haven of Athens; but after resting awhile upon their oars,[2] they departed and sailed away to Asia.

There fell in this battle of Marathon, on the side of the barbarians, about six thousand and four hundred men; on that of the Athenians, one hundred and ninety-two. Such was the number of the slain on the one side and the other. A strange prodigy likewise happened at this fight. Epizelus, the son of Cuphagoras, an Athenian, was in the thick of the fray, and behaving himself as a brave man should, when suddenly he was stricken with blindness, without blow of sword or dart, and this blindness continued thenceforth during the whole of his after life. The following is the account which he himself, as I have heard, gave of the matter: he said that a gigantic warrior, with a huge beard, which shaded all his shield, stood over against him, but the ghostly semblance passed him by, and slew the man at his side. Such, as I understand, was the tale which Epizelus told.

[1] The bay of Phalerum is nearer Athens than the Piraeus, but is not so well sheltered nor so deep.

[2] Better, perhaps, "lying at anchor off Phalērum for a while."

THUCYDIDES

"THUCYDIDES," says Sir Richard Jebb, "was the greatest historian of antiquity, and, if not the greatest that ever lived, as some have deemed him, at least the historian whose work is the most wonderful, when it is viewed relatively to the age in which he did it."

He was born in Athens not earlier than 470 B. C., and possibly not before 455. By family ties he was brought into connection with Cimon, the son of Miltiades, and other men who were shaping the events of his time, — the brilliant period of the Periclean age. The turning point of his life came in 424 B. C., when he was one of the Athenian generals in the Peloponnesian war. While he was in command of the fleet off the Thracian coast, the Spartan general Brasidas surprised and captured Amphipolis, the stronghold of the Athenian possessions in northern Greece. Thucydides arrived with the fleet just too late to save the city. Whether his delay was excusable or not is uncertain, but at any rate he was held responsible for the disaster, and was deprived of his command. For twenty years, until the close of the war in 403 B. C., he lived in exile, spending much of his time in travel. He visited the homes of the Peloponnesian allies, and was thus enabled to view the war from the Spartan as well as the Athenian standpoint. He himself speaks of the increased leisure for studying events which his banishment secured to him, and the opportunity it offered for gathering materials for his history from combatants in both armies. In 403 B. C. he returned to Athens for a short time, but soon retired to his property in Thrace, where he worked at his history until his death, not far from 398 B. C.

At the very outset of the Peloponnesian War, Thucydides foresaw that the struggle would be of great importance, and he planned to give a complete account of it from its beginning in 431 B. C. to the end. At his death, however, his history had reached only the twenty-first year of the war. His aim was "to preserve an accurate record of the war not only in view of the intrinsic interest and importance of the facts, but also in order that these facts might be permanent sources of political teaching to posterity." He hoped, as he himself tells us, that his history would be of profit to "those who desire an exact knowledge of the past as a key to the future, which in all probability will repeat or resemble the past. The work is meant to be a possession forever, not the rhetorical triumph of an hour."

The following passages are from Jowett's translation.

THE PLAGUE AT ATHENS

The prosperity of Athens during the age of Pericles increased the jealousy of her sister states, and from this arose the long struggle known as the Peloponnesian War. The immediate cause of conflict was the help given by Athens to Corcyra in a war against Corinth. Corinth enlisted Megara and Sparta on her side and declared war against Athens in 431 B. C.

As soon as summer returned,[1] the Peloponnesian army, comprising as before two thirds of the force of each confederate state, under the command of the Lacedaemonian king Archidamus, the son of Zeuxidamus, invaded Attica, where they established themselves and ravaged the country. They had not been there many days when the plague broke out at Athens for the first time. A similar disorder is said to have previously smitten many places, particularly Lemnos,

[1] This was in 430 B. C.

but there is no record of such a pestilence occurring elsewhere, or of so great a destruction of human life. For a while physicians, in ignorance of the nature of the disease, sought to apply remedies; but it was in vain, and they themselves were among the first victims, because they oftenest came into contact with it. No human art was of any avail, and as to supplications in temples, inquiries of oracles, and the like, they were utterly useless, and at last men were overpowered by the calamity and gave them all up.

The disease is said to have begun south of Egypt in Aethiopia; thence it descended into Egypt and Libya, and after spreading over the greater part of the Persian empire, suddenly fell upon Athens. It first attacked the inhabitants of the Piraeus, and it was supposed that the Peloponnesians had poisoned the cisterns, no conduits having as yet been made there. It afterwards reached the upper city, and then the mortality became far greater. As to its probable origin or the causes which might or could have produced such a disturbance of nature, every man, whether a physician or not, will give his own opinion. But I shall describe its actual course, and the symptoms by which any one who knows them beforehand may recognize the disorder should it ever reappear. For I was myself attacked, and witnessed the sufferings of others.

The season was admitted to have been remarkably free from ordinary sickness; and if anybody was already ill of any other disease, it was absorbed in this. Many who were in perfect health, all in a moment, and without any apparent reason, were seized with violent heats in the head and with redness and inflammation of the eyes. Internally the throat and the tongue were quickly suffused with blood, and the breath became unnatural and fetid. There followed sneezing and hoarseness; in a short time the disorder, accompanied by a violent cough, reached the chest; then fastening lower down, it would move the stomach and bring on all the vomits of bile to which physicians have ever given names; and they were very distressing. An ineffectual retching, producing violent convulsions, attacked most of the sufferers; some as soon as the previous symptoms had abated, others not until long afterwards. The body externally was not so very hot to the touch, nor yet pale; it was of a livid color inclining to red, and breaking out in pustules and ulcers. But the internal fever was intense; the sufferers could not bear to have on them even the finest linen garment; they insisted on being naked, and there was nothing which they longed for more eagerly than to throw themselves into cold water. And many of those who had no one to look after them actually plunged into the cisterns, for they were tormented by unceasing thirst, which was not in the least assuaged whether they drank little or much. They could not sleep; a restlessness which was intolerable never left them. While the disease was at its height the body, instead of wasting away, held out amid these sufferings in a marvellous manner, and either they died on the seventh or ninth day, not of weakness, for their strength was not exhausted, but of internal fever, which was the end of most; or, if they survived, then the disease descended into the bowels and there produced violent ulceration; severe diarrhœa at the same time set in, and at a later stage caused exhaustion, which finally, with few exceptions, carried them off. For the disorder which had originally settled in the head passed gradually through the whole body, and, if a person got over the worst, would often seize the extremities and leave its mark, attacking the fingers and the toes; and some escaped with the loss of these, some with the loss of their eyes. Some again had no sooner recovered than they were seized with forgetfulness of all things and knew neither themselves nor their friends.

The malady took a form not to be described, and the fury with which it fastened upon each sufferer was too much for human nature to endure. There was one circumstance in particular which distinguished it from ordinary diseases. The birds and animals which feed on human flesh, although so many bodies were lying unburied, either never came near them, or died if they touched them. This was proved by a remarkable disappearance of the birds of prey, who were not to be seen either about the bodies or anywhere else; while in the case of the dogs the fact was even more obvious, because they live with man.

Such was the general nature of the disease: I omit many strange peculiarities which characterized individual cases. None of the ordinary sicknesses attacked any one while it lasted, or, if they did, they ended in the plague. Some of the sufferers died from want of care, others equally who were receiving the greatest attention. No single remedy could be deemed a specific; for that which did good to one did harm to another. No constitution was of itself strong enough to resist or weak enough to escape the attacks; the disease carried off all alike, and defied every mode of treatment. Most appalling was the despondency which seized upon any one who felt himself sickening; for he instantly abandoned his mind to despair, and, instead of holding out, absolutely threw away his chance of life. Appalling too was the rapidity with which men caught the infection; dying like sheep if they attended on one another; and this was the principal cause of mortality. When they were afraid to visit one another, the sufferers died in their solitude, so that many houses were empty because there had been no one left to take care of the sick; or if they ventured they perished, especially those who aspired to heroism. For they went to see their friends without thought of themselves and were ashamed to leave them, even at a time when the very relations of the dying were at last growing weary and ceased to make lamentations, overwhelmed by the vastness of the calamity. But whatever instances there may have been of such devotion, more often the sick and the dying were tended by the pitying care of those who had recovered, because they knew the course of the disease and were themselves free from apprehension. For no one was ever attacked a second time, or not with a fatal result. All men congratulated them, and they themselves, in the excess of their joy at the moment, had an innocent fancy that they could not die of any other sickness.

The crowding of the people out of the country into the city aggravated the misery, and the newly arrived suffered most. For, having no houses of their own, but inhabiting in the height of summer stifling huts, the mortality among them was dreadful, and they perished in wild disorder. The dead lay as they had died, one upon another, while others hardly alive wallowed in the streets and crawled about every fountain craving for water. The temples in which they lodged were full of corpses of those who died in them; for the violence of the calamity was such that men, not knowing where to turn, grew reckless of all law, human and divine. The customs which had hitherto been observed at funerals were universally violated, and they buried their dead each one as best he could. Many, having no proper appliances, because the deaths in their household had been so frequent, made no scruple of using the burial-place of others. When one man had raised a funeral pile, others would come, and throwing on their dead first, set fire to it; or when some other corpse was already burning, before they could be stopped would throw their own dead upon it, and depart.

There were other and worse forms of lawlessness which the plague introduced at Athens. Men who had hitherto concealed their indulgence in pleasure now grew bolder. For, seeing the sudden change, — how the rich died in a moment, and those who had nothing immediately inherited their property, — they reflected that life and riches were alike transitory, and they resolved to enjoy themselves while they could, and to think only of pleasure. Who would be willing to sacrifice himself to the law of honor when he knew not whether he would ever live to be held in honor? The pleasure of the moment and any sort of thing which conduced to it took the place both of honor and of expediency. No fear of God or law of man deterred a criminal. Those who saw all perishing alike, thought that the worship or neglect of the Gods made no difference. For offences against human law no punishment was to be feared; no one would live long enough to be called to account. Already a far heavier sentence had been passed and was hanging over a man's head; before that fell, why should he not take a little pleasure?

Such was the grievous calamity which now afflicted the Athenians; within the walls their people were dying, and without, their country was being ravaged. In their troubles they naturally called to mind a verse which the elder men among them declared to have been current long ago: —

"A Dorian war will come and a plague with it."

There was a dispute about the precise expression; some saying that *limos*, a famine, and not *loimos*, a plague, was the original word. Nevertheless, as might have been expected, for men's memories reflected their sufferings, the argument in favor of *loimos* prevailed at the time. But if ever in future years another Dorian war arises which happens to be accompanied by a famine, they will probably repeat the verse in the other form. The answer of the oracle to the Lacedaemonians when the God was asked "whether they should go to war or not," and he replied, "that if they fought with all their might, they would conquer, and that he himself would take their part," was not forgotten by those who had heard of it, and they quite imagined that they were witnessing the fulfilment of his words. The disease certainly did set in immediately after the invasion of the Peloponnesians, and did not spread into Peloponnesus in any degree worth speaking of, while Athens felt its ravages most severely, and next to Athens the places which were most populous. Such was the history of the plague. (*Book II., Chapters 47–54.*)

PUBLIC FUNERAL AT ATHENS [1]

DURING the same winter, in accordance with an old national custom, the funeral of those who first fell in this war was celebrated by the Athenians at the public charge. The ceremony is as follows : Three days before the celebration they erect a tent in which the bones of the dead are laid out, and every one brings to his own dead any offering which he pleases. At the time of the funeral the bones are placed in chests of cypress wood, which are conveyed on hearses; there is one chest for each tribe. They also carry a single empty litter decked with a pall for all whose bodies are missing, and cannot be recovered after the battle. The procession is accompanied by any one who chooses, whether citizen or stranger, and the female relatives of the deceased are present at the place of interment and make lamentation. The public sepulchre is situated in the most beautiful spot outside the walls ; there they always bury those who fall in war; only after the battle of Marathon the dead, in recognition of their preëminent valor, were interred on the field. When the remains have been laid in the earth, some man of known ability and high reputation, chosen by the city, delivers a suitable oration over them; after which the people depart. Such is the manner of interment ; and the ceremony was repeated from time to time throughout the war. Over those who were the first buried Pericles was chosen to speak. At the fitting moment he advanced from the sepulchre to a lofty stage, which had been erected in order that he might be heard as far as possible by the multitude, and spoke as follows : — . . .

[1] In the winter of 431–430 B. C.

"I will speak first of our ancestors, for it is right and becoming that now, when we are lamenting the dead, a tribute should be paid to their memory. There has never been a time when they did not inhabit this land, which by their valor they have handed down from generation to generation, and we have received from them a free state. But if they were worthy of praise, still more were our fathers, who added to their inheritance, and after many a struggle transmitted to us, their sons, this great empire. And we ourselves, assembled here to-day, who are still most of us in the vigor of life, have chiefly done the work of improvement, and have richly endowed our city with all things, so that she is sufficient for herself both in peace and war. Of the military exploits by which our various possessions were acquired, or of the energy with which we or our fathers drove back the tide of war, Hellenic or Barbarian, I will not speak, for the tale would be long and is familiar to you. But before I praise the dead, I should like to point out by what principles of action we rose to power, and under what institutions and through what manner of life our empire became great. For I conceive that such thoughts are not unsuited to the occasion, and that this numerous assembly of citizens and strangers may profitably listen to them.

"Our form of government does not enter into rivalry with the institutions of others. We do not copy our neighbors, but are an example to them. It is true that we are called a democracy, for the administration is in the hands of the many and not of the few. But while the law secures equal justice to all alike in their private disputes, the claim of excellence is also recognized; and when a citizen is in any way distinguished, he is preferred to the public service, not as a matter of privilege, but as the reward of merit. Neither is poverty a bar, but a man may benefit his country whatever be the obscurity of his condition. There is no exclusiveness in our public life, and in our private intercourse we are not suspicious of one another, nor angry with our neighbor if he does what he likes; we do not put on sour looks at him which, though harmless, are not pleasant. While we are thus unconstrained in our private intercourse, a spirit of reverence pervades our public acts; we are prevented from doing wrong by respect for authority and for the laws, having an especial regard to those which are ordained for the protection of the injured as well as to those unwritten laws which bring upon the transgressor of them the reprobation of the general sentiment.

"And we have not forgotten to provide for our weary spirits many relaxations from toil; we have regular games and sacrifices throughout the year; at home the style of our life is refined; and the delight which we daily feel in all these things helps to banish melancholy. Because of the greatness of our city the fruits of the whole earth flow in upon us; so that we enjoy the goods of other countries as freely as of our own.

"Then, again, our military training is in many respects superior to that of our adversaries. Our city is thrown open to the world, and we never expel a foreigner or prevent him from seeing or learning anything of which the secret if revealed to an enemy might profit him. We rely not upon management or trickery, but upon our own hearts and hands. And in the matter of education, whereas they from early youth are always undergoing laborious exercises which are to make them brave, we live at ease, and yet are equally ready to face the perils which they face. And here is the proof. The Lacedaemonians come into Attica not by themselves, but with their whole confederacy following; we go alone into a neighbor's country; and although our opponents are fighting for their homes and we on a foreign soil, we have seldom any difficulty in overcoming them. Our enemies have never yet felt our united strength; the care of a navy divides our attention, and on land we are obliged to send our own citizens everywhere. But they, if they meet and defeat a part of our army, are as proud as if they had routed us all, and when defeated they pretend to have been vanquished by us all.

"If then we prefer to meet danger with a light heart, but without laborious training, and with a courage which is gained by habit and enforced by law, are we not greatly the gainers? Since we do not anticipate the pain, although when the hour comes we can be as brave as those who never allow themselves to rest; and thus too our city is equally admirable in peace and in war. For we are lovers of the beautiful, yet simple in our tastes, and we cultivate the mind without loss of manliness. Wealth we employ, not for talk and ostentation, but when there is a real use for it. To avow poverty with us is no disgrace; the true disgrace is in doing nothing to avoid it. An Athenian citizen does not neglect the state because he takes care of his own household; and even those of us who are engaged in business have a very fair idea of politics. We alone regard a man who takes no interest in public affairs, not as a harmless, but as a useless character; and if few of us are originators, we are all sound judges of a policy. The great impediment to action is, in our opinion, not discussion, but the want of that knowledge which is gained by discussion preparatory to action. For we have a peculiar power of thinking before we act and of acting too, whereas other men are courageous from ignorance, but hesitate upon reflection. And they are surely to be esteemed the bravest spirits who, having the clearest sense both of the pains and pleasures of life, do not on that account shrink from danger. In doing good, again, we are unlike others — we make our friends by conferring, not by receiving favors. Now he who confers a favor is the firmer friend, because he would fain by kindness keep alive the memory of an obligation; but the recipient is colder in his feelings, because he knows that in requiting another's generosity he will not be winning gratitude, but only paying a debt. We alone do good to our neighbors not upon a calculation of interest, but in the confidence of freedom and in a frank and fearless spirit. To sum up: I say that Athens is the school of Hellas, and that the individual Athenian in his own person seems to have the power of adapting himself to the most varied forms of action with the utmost versatility and grace. This is no passing and idle word, but truth and fact; and the assertion is verified by the position to which these qualities have raised the state. For in the hour of trial, Athens alone among her contemporaries is superior to the report of her. No enemy who comes against her is indignant at the reverses which he sustains at the hands of such a city; no subject complains that his masters are unworthy of him. And we shall assuredly not be without witnesses; there are mighty monuments of our power which will make us the wonder of this and of succeeding ages; we shall not need the praises of Homer or of any other panegyrist whose poetry may please for the moment, although his representation of the facts will not bear the light of day. For we have compelled every land and every sea to open a path for our valor, and have everywhere planted eternal memorials of our friendship and of our enmity. Such is the city for whose sake these men nobly fought and died; they could not bear the thought that she might be taken from them; and every one of us who survive should gladly toil on her behalf." (*Book II., Chapters 34-41.*)

THE SIEGE OF PLATAEA

DURING the same winter the Plataeans, who were still besieged by the Peloponnesians and Boeotians, began to suffer from the failure of provisions. They had no hope of assistance from Athens and no other chance of deliverance. So they and the Athenians who were shut up with them contrived a plan of forcing their way over the enemy's walls. The idea was suggested by Theaenetus, the son of Tolmides, a diviner, and Eumolpides, the son of Daïmachus, one of their generals. At first they were all desirous of joining, but afterwards half of them somehow lost heart, thinking the danger too great, and only two hundred and twenty agreed to persevere. They first made ladders equal in length to the height of the enemy's wall, which they calculated by help of the layers of bricks on the side facing the town, at a place where the wall had accidentally not been plastered. A great many counted at once, and, although some might make mistakes, the

THE SIEGE OF PLATAEA

calculation would be oftener right than wrong; for they repeated the process again and again, and, the distance not being great, they could see the wall distinctly enough for their purpose. In this manner they ascertained the proper length of the ladders, taking as a measure the thickness of the bricks.

The Peloponnesian wall was double, and consisted of an inner circle looking towards Plataea, and an outer intended to guard against an attack from Athens; they were at a distance of about sixteen feet from one another. This interval of sixteen feet was partitioned off into lodgings for the soldiers, by which the two walls were joined together, so that they appeared to form one thick wall with battlements on both sides. At every tenth battlement there were large towers, filling up the space between the walls, and extending both to the inner and outer face; there was no way at the side of the towers, but only through the middle of them. During the night, whenever there was storm and rain, the soldiers left the battlements and kept guard from the towers, which were not far from each other and were covered overhead. Such was the plan of the wall with which Plataea was invested.

When the Plataeans had completed their preparations they took advantage of a night on which there was a storm of wind and rain and no moon, and sallied forth. They were led by the authors of the attempt. First of all they crossed the ditch which surrounded the town; then they went forward to the wall of the enemy. The guard did not discover them, for the night was so dark that they could not be seen, while the clatter of the storm drowned the noise of their approach. They marched a good way apart from each other, that the clashing of their arms might not betray them; and they were lightly equipped, having the right foot bare that they might be less liable to slip in the mud. They now set about scaling the battlements, which they knew to be deserted, choosing a space between two of the towers. Those who carried the ladders went first, and placed them against the wall; they were followed by twelve others, armed only with sword and breastplate, under the command of Ammeas, the son of Coroebus: he was the first to mount; after him came the twelve, six ascending each of the two towers on the right and left. To these succeeded more men lightly armed with short spears, others following who bore their shields, that they might have less difficulty in mounting the wall; the shields were to be handed to them as soon as they were near the enemy. A considerable number had now ascended, when they were discovered by the guards. One of the Plataeans, taking hold of the battlements, threw down a tile which made noise in falling: immediately a shout was raised and the enemy rushed out upon the wall; for in the dark and stormy night they did not know what the alarm meant. At the same time, in order to distract their attention, the Plataeans who were left in the city made a sally against the Peloponnesian wall on the side opposite to the place at which their friends were getting over. The besiegers were in great excitement, but every one remained at his own post, and dared not stir to give assistance, being at a loss to imagine what was happening. The three hundred who were appointed to act in any sudden emergency marched along outside the walls towards the spot from which the cry proceeded, and fire-signals indicating danger were raised towards Thebes. But the Plataeans in the city had numerous counter signals ready on the wall, which they now lighted and held up, thereby hoping to render the signals of the enemy unintelligible, that so the Thebans, misunderstanding the true state of affairs, might not arrive until the men had escaped and were in safety.

Meanwhile the Plataeans were scaling the walls. The first party had mounted, and, killing the sentinels, had gained possession of the towers on either side. Their followers now began to occupy the passages, lest the enemy should come through and fall upon them. Some of them placed ladders upon the wall against the towers, and got up more men. A shower of missiles proceeding both from the upper and lower parts of the towers kept off all assailants. Meanwhile the main body of the Plataeans, who were still below, applied to the wall many ladders at once, and, pushing down the battlements, made their way over through the space between the towers. As each man got to the other side he halted upon the edge of the ditch, whence then he shot darts and arrows at any one who came along under the wall and attempted to impede their passage. When they had all passed over, those who had occupied the towers came down, the last of them not without great difficulty, and proceeded towards the ditch. By this time the three hundred were upon them; they had lights, and the Plataeans, standing on the edge of the ditch, saw them all the better out of the darkness, and shot arrows and threw darts at them where their bodies were exposed; they themselves were concealed by the darkness, while the enemy were dazed by their own lights. And so the Plataeans, down to the last man of them all, got safely over the ditch, though with great exertion and only after a hard struggle; for the ice in it was not frozen hard enough to bear, but was half water, as is commonly the case when the wind is from the east and not from the north. And the snow which the east wind brought in the night had greatly swollen the water, so that they could scarcely accomplish the passage. It was the violence of the storm, however, which enabled them to escape at all.

From the ditch the Plataeans, leaving on the right hand the shrine of Androcrates, ran all together along the road to Thebes. They made sure that no one would ever suspect them of having fled in the direction of their enemies. On their way they saw the Peloponnesians pursuing them with torches on the road which leads to Athens by Cithaeron and Dryoscephalae. For nearly a mile the Plataeans continued on the Theban road; they then turned off and went by the way of the mountain leading to Erythrae and Hysiae, and so, getting to the hills, they escaped to Athens. Their number was two hundred and twelve, though they had been originally more, for some of them went back to the city and never got over the wall; one who was an archer was taken at the outer ditch. The Peloponnesians at length gave up the pursuit and returned to their lines. But the Plataeans in the city, knowing nothing of what had happened, for those who had turned back had informed them that not one was left alive, sent out a herald at daybreak, wanting to make a truce for the burial of the dead; they then discovered the truth and returned. Thus the Plataeans scaled the wall and escaped. (*Book III., Chapters 20-24*).

THE RETREAT FROM SYRACUSE

In 415 B. C., Alcibiades persuaded Athens to undertake the great Sicilian expedition against the Dorian city of Syracuse. He purposed through this to gain control of all Sicily, and to make that island the base of operations against Africa and Italy. The expedition consisted of forty thousand men under Alcibiades, Nicias, Demosthenes, and Lamachus. Immediately on their arrival at Sicily Alcibiades was summoned back to Athens to answer a charge of sacrilege. He escaped to Sparta and revealed the plans of Athens to her enemies. A small Spartan fleet was sent to Syracuse under an able commander, Gylippus, which destroyed the Athenian fleet. Thucydides here describes the destruction of the land force, early in September, 413 B. C.

On the third day after the sea-fight, when Nicias and Demosthenes thought that their preparations were complete, the army began to move. They were in a dreadful condition; not only was there the great fact that they had lost their whole fleet, and instead of their expected triumph had brought the utmost peril upon Athens as well as upon themselves, but also the sights which presented themselves as they quitted the camp were painful to every eye and mind. The dead were unburied, and when any one saw the body of a friend lying on the ground he was smitten with sorrow and dread, while the sick or wounded who still survived, but had to be left, were even a greater trial to the living, and more to be pitied than those who were gone. Their prayers and lamentations drove their companions to distraction; they would beg that they might be taken with them, and call by name any friend or relation whom they saw passing; they would hang upon their departing comrades and follow as far as they could, and when their limbs and strength failed them and they dropped behind, many were the imprecations and cries which they uttered. So that the whole army was in tears, and such was their despair that they could hardly make up their minds to stir, although they were leaving an enemy's country, having suffered calamities too great for tears already, and dreading miseries yet greater in the unknown future. There was also a general feeling of shame and self-reproach, — indeed they seemed, not like an army, but like the fugitive population of a city captured after a siege; and of a great city too. For the whole multitude who were marching together numbered not less than forty thousand. Each of them took with him anything he could carry which was likely to be of use. Even the heavy-armed and cavalry, contrary to their practice when under arms, conveyed about their persons their own food, some because they had no attendants, others because they could not trust them; for they had long been deserting, and most of them had gone off all at once. Nor was the food which they carried sufficient; for the supplies of the camp had failed. Their disgrace and the universality of the misery, although there might be some consolation in the very community of suffering, was nevertheless at that moment hard to bear, especially when they remembered from what pomp and splendor they had fallen into their present low estate. Never had an Hellenic army experienced such a reverse. They had come intending to enslave others, and they were going away in fear that they would be themselves enslaved. Instead of the prayers and hymns with which they had put to sea, they were now departing amid appeals to heaven of another sort. They were no longer sailors, but landsmen, depending, not upon their fleet, but upon their infantry. Yet in face of the great danger which still threatened them all these things appeared endurable.

Nicias, seeing the army disheartened at their terrible fall, went along the ranks and encouraged and consoled them as well as he could. In his fervor he raised his voice as he passed from one to another, and spoke louder and louder, desiring that the benefit of his words might reach as far as possible.

"Even now, Athenians and allies, we must hope: men have been delivered out of worse straits than these, and I would not have you judge yourselves too severely on account either of the reverses which you have sustained or of your present undeserved miseries. I too am as weak as any of you; for I am quite prostrated by my disease, as you see. And although there was a time when I might have been thought equal to the best of you in the happiness of my private and public life, I am now in as great danger and as much at the mercy of fortune as the meanest. Yet my days have been passed in the performance of many a religious duty, and of many a just and blameless action. Therefore my hope of the future remains unshaken, and our calamities do not appal me as they might. Who knows that they may not be lightened? For our enemies have had their full share of success, and if our expedition provoked the jealousy of any God, by this time we have been punished enough. Others ere now have attacked their neighbors; they have done as men will do, and suffered what men can bear. We may therefore begin to hope that the Gods will be more merciful to us; for we now invite their pity rather than their jealousy. And look at your own well-armed ranks; see how many brave soldiers you are, marching in solid array, and do not be dismayed; bear in mind that wherever you plant yourselves you are a city already, and that no city of Sicily will find it easy to resist your attack, or can dislodge you if you choose to settle. Provide for the safety and good order of your own march, and remember every one of you that on whatever spot a man is compelled to fight, there if he conquer he may find a home and a fortress. We must press forward day and night, for our supplies are but scanty. The Sicels through fear of the Syracusans still adhere to us, and if we can only reach any part of their territory we shall be among friends, and you may consider yourselves secure. We have sent to them, and they have been told to meet us and bring food. In a word, soldiers, let me tell you that you must be brave; there is no place near to which a coward can fly. And if you now escape your enemies, those of you who are not Athenians may see once more the home for which they long, while you Athenians will again rear aloft the fallen greatness of Athens. For men, and not walls or ships in which are no men, constitute a state."

Thus exhorting his troops Nicias passed through the army, and wherever he saw gaps in the ranks or the men dropping out of line, he brought them back to their proper place. Demosthenes did the same for the troops under his command, and gave them similar exhortations. The army marched disposed in a hollow oblong: the division of Nicias leading, and that of Demosthenes following; the hoplites enclosed within their ranks the baggage-bearers and the rest of the army. When they arrived at the ford of the river Anapus they found a force of the Syracusans and of their allies drawn up to meet them; these they

THE RETREAT FROM SYRACUSE 341

put to flight, and getting command of the ford, proceeded on their march. The Syracusans continually harassed them, the cavalry riding alongside, and the light-armed troops hurling darts at them. On this day the Athenians proceeded about four and a half miles and encamped at a hill. On the next day they started early, and, having advanced more than two miles, descended into a level plain and encamped. The country was inhabited, and they were desirous of obtaining food from the houses, and also water which they might carry with them, as there was little to be had for many miles in the country which lay before them. Meanwhile the Syracusans had gone on before them, and at a point where the road ascends a steep hill called the Acraean height, and there is a precipitous ravine on either side, were blocking up the pass by a wall. On the next day the Athenians advanced, although again impeded by the numbers of the enemy's cavalry who rode alongside, and of their javelin-men who threw darts at them. For a long time the Athenians maintained the struggle, but at last retired to their own encampment. Their supplies were now cut off, because the horsemen circumscribed their movements.

In the morning they started early and resumed their march. They pressed onwards to the hill where the way was barred, and found in front of them the Syracusan infantry drawn up to defend the wall, in deep array, for the pass was narrow. Whereupon the Athenians advanced and assaulted the barrier, but the enemy, who were numerous and had the advantage of position, threw missiles upon them from the hill, which was steep, and so, not being able to force their way, they again retired and rested. During the conflict, as is often the case in the fall of the year, there came on a storm of rain and thunder, whereby the Athenians were yet more disheartened, for they thought that everything was conspiring to their destruction. While they were resting, Gylippus and the Syracusans despatched a division of their army to raise a wall behind them across the road by which they had come; but the Athenians sent some of their own troops and frustrated their intention. They then retired with their whole army in the direction of the plain and passed the night. On the following day they again advanced. The Syracusans now surrounded and attacked them on every side, and wounded many of them. If the Athenians advanced they retreated, but charged them when they retired, falling especially upon the hindermost of them, in the hope that, if they could put to flight a few at a time, they might strike a panic into the whole army. In this fashion the Athenians struggled on for a long time, and having advanced about three quarters of a mile rested in the plain. The Syracusans then left them and returned to their own encampment.

The army was now in a miserable plight, being in want of every necessary; and by the continual assaults of the enemy great numbers of the soldiers had been wounded. Nicias and Demosthenes, perceiving their condition, resolved during the night to light as many watch-fires as possible, and lead off their forces. They intended to take another route and march towards the sea in the direction opposite to that from which the Syracusans were watching them. Now their whole line of march lay, not towards Catana, but towards the other side of Sicily, in the direction of Camarina and Gela, and the cities, Hellenic or Barbarian, of

THE RETREAT FROM SYRACUSE 343

that region. So they lighted numerous fires and departed in the night. And then, as constantly happens in armies, especially in very great ones, and as might be expected when they were marching by night in an enemy's country, and with the enemy from whom they were flying not far off, there arose a panic among them, and they fell into confusion. The army of Nicias, which led the way, kept together, and was considerably in advance, but that of Demosthenes, which was the larger half, got severed from the other division, and marched in less order. At daybreak they succeeded in reaching the sea, and striking into the Helorine road marched along it, intending as soon as they arrived at the river Cacyparis to follow up the stream through the interior of the island. They were expecting that the Sicels for whom they had sent would meet them on this road. When they had reached the river they found there also a guard of the Syracusans cutting off the passage by a wall and palisade. They forced their way through, and crossing the river, passed on towards another river which is called the Erineus, this being the direction in which their guides led them.

When daylight broke and the Syracusans and their allies saw that the Athenians had departed, most of them thought that Gylippus had let them go on purpose, and were very angry with him. They easily found the line of their retreat, and quickly following, came up with them about the time of the midday meal. The troops of Demosthenes were last; they were marching slowly and in disorder, not having recovered from the panic of the previous night, when they were overtaken by the Syracusans, who immediately fell upon them and fought. Separated as they were from the others, they were easily hemmed in by the Syracusan cavalry and driven into a narrow space. The division of Nicias was as much as six miles in advance, for he marched faster, thinking that their safety depended at such a time, not in remaining and fighting, if they could avoid it, but in retreating as quickly as they could, and resisting only when they were positively compelled. Demosthenes, on the other hand, who had been more incessantly harassed throughout the retreat, because marching last he was first attacked by the enemy, now, when he saw the Syracusans pursuing him, instead of pressing onward, had ranged his army in order of battle. Thus lingering he was surrounded, and he and the Athenians under his command were in the greatest danger and confusion. For they were crushed into a walled enclosure, having a road on both sides and planted thickly with olive-trees, and missiles were hurled at them from all points. The Syracusans naturally preferred this mode of attack to a regular engagement. For to risk themselves against desperate men would have been only playing into the hands of the Athenians. Moreover, every one was sparing of his life; their good fortune was already assured, and they did not want to fall in the hour of victory. Even by this irregular mode of fighting they thought that they could overpower and capture the Athenians.

And so when they had gone on all day assailing them with missiles from every quarter, and saw that they were quite worn out with their wounds and all their other sufferings, Gylippus and the Syracusans made a proclamation, first of all to the islanders, that any of them who pleased might come over to them and have their freedom. But only a few cities ac-

THE RETREAT FROM SYRACUSE 345

cepted the offer. At length an agreement was made for the entire force under Demosthenes. Their arms were to be surrendered, but no one was to suffer death, either from violence or from imprisonment, or from want of the bare means of life. So they all surrendered, being in number six thousand, and gave up what money they had. This they threw into the hollows of shields and filled four. The captives were at once taken to the city. On the same day Nicias and his division reached the river Erineus, which he crossed, and halted his army on a rising ground.

On the following day he was overtaken by the Syracusans, who told him that Demosthenes had surrendered, and bade him do the same. He, not believing them, procured a truce while he sent a horseman to go and see. Upon the return of the horseman bringing assurance of the fact, he sent a herald to Gylippus and the Syracusans, saying that he would agree, on behalf of the Athenian state, to pay the expenses which the Syracusans had incurred in the war, on condition that they should let his army go; until the money was paid he would give Athenian citizens as hostages, a man for a talent. Gylippus and the Syracusans would not accept these proposals, but attacked and surrounded this division of the army as well as the other, and hurled missiles at them from every side until the evening. They too were grievously in want of food and necessaries. Nevertheless they meant to wait for the dead of the night and then to proceed. They were just resuming their arms, when the Syracusans discovered them and raised the Paean. The Athenians, perceiving that they were detected, laid down their arms again, with the exception of about three hundred men who broke through the enemy's guard, and made their escape in the darkness as best they could.

When the day dawned Nicias led forward his army, and the Syracusans and the allies again assailed them on every side, hurling javelins and other missiles at them. The Athenians hurried on to the river Assinarus. They hoped to gain a little relief if they forded the river, for the mass of horsemen and other troops overwhelmed and crushed them; and they were worn out by fatigue and thirst. But no sooner did they reach the water than they lost all order and rushed in; every man was trying to cross first, and, the enemy pressing upon them at the same time, the passage of the river became hopeless. Being compelled to keep close together they fell one upon another, and trampled each other under foot: some at once perished, pierced by their own spears; others got entangled in the baggage and were carried down the stream. The Syracusans stood upon the further bank of the river, which was steep, and hurled missiles from above on the Athenians, who were huddled together in the deep bed of the stream and for the most part were drinking greedily. The Peloponnesians came down the bank and slaughtered them, falling chiefly upon those who were in the river. Whereupon the water at once became foul, but was drunk all the same, although muddy and dyed with blood, and the crowd fought for it.

At last, when the dead bodies were lying in heaps upon one another in the water and the army was utterly undone, some perishing in the river, and any who escaped being cut off by the cavalry, Nicias surrendered to Gylippus, in whom he had more confidence than in the Syracusans. He entreated him and the

Lacedaemonians to do what they pleased with himself, but not to go on killing the men. So Gylippus gave the word to make prisoners. Thereupon the survivors, not including, however, a large number whom the soldiers concealed, were brought in alive. As for the three hundred who had broken through the guard in the night, the Syracusans sent in pursuit and seized them. The total of the public prisoners when collected was not great; for many were appropriated by the soldiers, and the whole of Sicily was full of them, they not having capitulated like the troops under Demosthenes. A large number also perished; the slaughter at the river being very great, quite as great as any which took place in the Sicilian war; and not a few had fallen in the frequent attacks which were made upon the Athenians during their march. Still many escaped, some at the time, others ran away after an interval of slavery, and all these found refuge at Catana.

The Syracusans and their allies collected their forces and returned with the spoil, and as many prisoners as they could take with them, into the city. The captive Athenians and allies they deposited in the quarries, which they thought would be the safest place of confinement. Nicias and Demosthenes they put to the sword, although against the will of Gylippus. For Gylippus thought that to carry home with him to Lacedaemon the generals of the enemy, over and above all his other successes, would be a brilliant triumph. One of them, Demosthenes, happened to be the greatest foe, and the other the greatest friend of the Lacedaemonians, both in the same matter of Pylos and Sphacteria. For Nicias had taken up their cause, and had persuaded the Athenians to make the peace which set at liberty the prisoners taken in the island. The Lacedaemonians were grateful to him for the service, and this was the main reason why he trusted Gylippus and surrendered himself to him. But certain Syracusans, who had been in communication with him, were afraid (such was the report) that on some suspicion of their guilt he might be put to the torture and bring trouble on them in the hour of their prosperity. Others, and especially the Corinthians, feared that, being rich, he might by bribery escape and do them further mischief. So the Syracusans gained the consent of the allies and had him executed. For these or the like reasons he suffered death. No one of the Hellenes in my time was less deserving of so miserable an end; for he lived in the practice of every virtue.

Those who were imprisoned in the quarries were at the beginning of their captivity harshly treated by the Syracusans. There were great numbers of them, and they were crowded in a deep and narrow place. At first the sun by day was still scorching and suffocating, for they had no roof over their heads, while the autumn nights were cold, and the extremes of temperature engendered violent disorders. Being cramped for room they had to do everything on the same spot. The corpses of those who died from their wounds, exposure to the weather, and the like, lay heaped one upon another. The smells were intolerable, and they were at the same time afflicted by hunger and thirst. During eight months they were allowed only about half a pint of water and a pint of food a day. Every kind of misery which could befall man in such a place befell them. This was the condition of all the captives for about ten weeks. At

THE RETREAT FROM SYRACUSE 349

length the Syracusans sold them, with the exception of the Athenians and of any Sicilian or Italian Greeks who had sided with them in the war. The whole number of the public prisoners is not accurately known, but they were not less than seven thousand.

Of all the Hellenic actions which took place in this war, or indeed of all Hellenic actions which are on record, this was the greatest — the most glorious to the victors, the most ruinous to the vanquished; for they were utterly and at all points defeated, and their sufferings were prodigious. Fleet and army perished from the face of the earth; nothing was saved, and of the many who went forth few returned home.

Thus ended the Sicilian expedition. (*Book VIII., Chapters 75-87.*)

XENOPHON

XENOPHON, the only other Greek historian besides Herodotus and Thucydides, of the so-called classical period, whose works are extant, was born near Athens about 430 B. C. Early in life he came under the influence of Socrates, for whom he felt the warmest admiration and affection, and whose character he vindicates from charges made against him by anecdotes illustrating his daily mode of life and conversation, in the *Memorabilia,* or *Recollections of Socrates.*

After the close of the Peloponnesian War in 403 B. C., Xenophon received an invitation to join the expedition of Cyrus the Younger, a Persian prince who was gathering a force of Greek mercenaries with the hope of wresting the throne from his brother, the Persian king Artaxerxes. Xenophon consulted Socrates and the Delphic oracle, and joined the campaign, neither as officer nor as soldier, but out of a spirit of adventure. When Cyrus was killed in the battle of Cunaxa, 401 B. C., and the chief Greek officers were assassinated, Xenophon became the leading spirit of the army, and directed its retreat through the country of the enemy to the Black Sea, and thence to the Hellespont. He describes this entire expedition in the *Anabasis,* or *March to Babylon,* — a title which belongs strictly only to the first of the seven "books" of the work. On his return, he served under the Spartan king Agesilaus, and perhaps even fought with him against Athens at the battle of Coronea in 394 B. C. Before or after this event, he was formally banished from Athens, but he was presented by the Lacedaemonians with an estate in Elis, where he made his home and wrote most of his books in the quiet of a country life. The decree of banishment from Athens was revoked, and one of his sons died in battle fighting for that city, but he seems not to have cared to live again in his former home, and died in Corinth about 355 B. C.

The chief historical work of Xenophon, besides the *Anabasis*, is the *Hellenica*, in which he continues the history of Greece from the point at which Thucydides left it to the battle of Mantinea in 362 B. C., in which his son Gryllus fell. This history, although valuable for the facts it gives, is told uninterestingly, and from a prejudiced point of view.

Besides these works and the *Cyropaedia*, — which is a historical romance, having Cyrus the Great as its hero, and intended to set forth the author's ideal of a state and a military leader, — Xenophon composed several political essays, an essay on hunting, on horsemanship, etc., — the earliest specimens of this branch of literature.

The following passages from the translation by H. G. Dakyns are used by permission of the Macmillan Company.

SOCRATES AND ARISTODEMUS

From the Memorabilia, Book 1. iv. §§ 7-19.

Socrates. Well, and doubtless you feel to have a spark of wisdom yourself?

Aristodemus. Put your questions, and I will answer.

Socrates. And yet you imagine that elsewhere no spark of wisdom is to be found? And that, too, when you know that you have in your body a tiny fragment only of the mighty earth, a little drop of the great waters, and of the other elements, vast in their extent, you got, I presume, a particle of each towards the compacting of your bodily frame? Mind alone, it would seem, which is nowhere to be found, you had the lucky chance to snatch up and make off with, you cannot tell how. And these things around and about us, enormous in size, infinite in number, owe their orderly arrangement, as you suppose, to some vacuity of wit?

Aristodemus. It may be, for my eyes fail to see the master agents of these, as one sees the fabricators of things produced on earth.

Socrates. No more do you see your own soul, which is the master agent of your body; so that, as far as that goes, you may maintain, if you like, that you do nothing with intelligence, but everything by chance.

At this point Aristodemus: I assure you, Socrates, that I do not disdain the Divine power. On the contrary, my belief is that the Divinity is too grand to need any service which I could render.

Socrates. But the grander that power is, which deigns to tend and wait upon you, the more you are called upon to honor it.

Aristodemus. Be well assured, if I could believe the gods take thought at all for men, I would not neglect them.

Socrates. How can you suppose that they do not so take thought? Who, in the first place, gave to man alone of living creatures his erect posture, enabling him to see farther in front of him and to contemplate more freely the height above, and to be less subject to distress than other creatures endowed like himself with eyes and ears and mouth. Consider next how they gave to the beast of the field feet as a means of progression only, but to man they gave in addition hands — those hands which have achieved so much to raise us in the scale of happiness above all animals. Did they not make the tongue also? which belongs indeed alike to man and beast, but in man they fashioned it so as to play on different parts of the mouth at different times, whereby we can produce articulate speech, and have a code of signals to express our every want to one another. Nor did it content the Godhead merely to watch over the interests of man's body. What is of far higher import, He implanted in man the noblest and most excellent type of soul. For what other creature, to begin with, has a soul to appreciate the existence of the Gods who have arranged this grand and beauteous universe? What other tribe of animals save man can render service to the gods? How apt is the spirit of man to take precautions against hunger and thirst, cold and heat, to alleviate disease and foster strength! how suited to labor with a view to learning! how capable of garnering in the storehouse of his memory all that he has heard or seen or understood! Is it not most evident to you that by the side of other animals men live and move a race of gods — by nature excellent, in beauty of body and of soul supreme? For, mark you, had a creature of man's wit been encased in the body of an ox, he would have been powerless to carry out his wishes, just as the possession of hands divorced from human wit is profitless. And then you come, you who have obtained these two most precious attributes, and give it as your opinion that the gods take no thought or care for you. Why, what will you have them to do, that you may believe and be persuaded that you too are in their thoughts?

Aristodemus. When they treat me as you tell us they treat you, and send me counsellors to warn me what I am to do and what abstain from doing, I will believe.

Socrates. Send you counsellors! Come now, what when the people of Athens make inquiry by oracle, and the Gods' answer comes? Are you not an Athenian? Think you not that to you also the answer is given? What when they send portents to forewarn the states of Hellas? or to all mankind? Are you not a man? a Hellene? Are not these intended for you also? Can it be that you alone are excepted as a single instance of Divine neglect? Again, do you suppose that the Gods could have implanted in the heart of man the belief in their capacity to work him weal or woe had they not the power? Would not men have discovered the imposture in all this lapse of time? Do you not perceive that the wisest and most perdurable of human institutions — be they cities or tribes of men — are ever the most God-fearing; and in the individual man the riper his age and judgment, the deeper his religiousness? Ah, my good sir (he broke forth), lay to heart and understand that even as your own mind within you can turn and dispose of your body as it lists, so ought we to think that the wisdom which abides within the universal frame does so dispose of all things as it finds agreeable to itself; for hardly may it be that your eye is able to range over many a league, but that the eye of God is powerless to embrace all things at a glance; or that to your soul it is given to dwell in thought on matters here, or far away in Egypt, or in Sicily, but that the wisdom and thought of God is not sufficient to include all things at one instant under His care. If only you would copy your own behavior where human beings are concerned! It is by acts of service and of kindness that you discover which of your fellows are willing to requite you in kind. It is by taking another into your counsel that you arrive at the secret of his wisdom. If, on like principle, you will but make trial of the gods by acts of service, whether they will choose to give you counsel in matters obscure to mortal vision, you shall discover the nature and the greatness of Godhead to be such that they are able at once to see all things, and to hear all things, and to be present everywhere, nor does the least thing escape their watchful care.

To my mind the effect of words like these was to cause those about him to hold aloof from unholiness, baseness, and injustice, not only whilst they were seen of men, but even in the solitary place, since they must believe that no part of their conduct could escape the eye of Heaven.

THE CHOICE OF HERACLES

A STORY OF PRODICUS OF CEOS

From the Memorabilia, Book II. i. §§ 22-34.

" WHEN Heracles was emerging from boyhood into the bloom of youth, having reached that season in which the young man, now standing upon the verge of independence, shows plainly whether he will enter upon the path of virtue or of vice, he went forth into a quiet place, and sat debating with himself which of those two paths he should pursue; and as he sat there musing, there appeared to him two women of great stature, which drew nigh to him. The one was fair to look upon, frank and free by gift of nature, her limbs adorned with purity and her eyes with bashfulness; sobriety set the rhythm of her gait, and she was clad in white apparel. The other was of a different type; the fleshy softness of her limbs betrayed her nurture, while the complexion of her skin was embellished, that she might appear whiter and rosier than she really was, and her figure, that she might seem taller than nature made her; she stared with wide-open eyes, and the raiment wherewith she was clad served but to reveal the ripeness of her bloom. With frequent glances she surveyed her person, or looked to see if others noticed her; while ever and anon she fixed her gaze upon the shadow of herself intently.

"Now when these two had drawn nearer to Heracles, she who was first named advanced at an even pace toward him, but the other, in her eagerness to outstrip her, ran forward to the youth, exclaiming, 'I see you, Heracles, in doubt and difficulty what path of life to choose; make me your friend, and I will lead you to the pleasantest road and easiest. This I promise you: you shall taste all of life's sweets and escape all bitters. In the first place, you shall not trouble your brain with war or business; other topics shall engage your mind; your only speculation, what meat or drink you shall find agreeable to your palate; what delight of ear or eye; what pleasure of smell or touch; how you shall pillow your limbs in softest slumber; how cull each individual pleasure without alloy of pain; and if ever the suspicion steal upon you that the stream of joys will one day dwindle, trust me I will not lead you where you shall replenish the store by toil of body and trouble of soul. No! others shall labor, but you shall reap the fruit of their labors; you shall withhold your hand from nought which shall bring you gain. For to all my followers I give authority and power to help themselves freely from every side.'

"Heracles, hearing these words, made answer: 'What, O lady, is the name you bear?' To which she: 'Know that my friends call me Happiness, but they that hate me have their own nicknames for me, Vice and Naughtiness.'

"But just then the other of those fair women approached, and spoke: 'Heracles, I too am come to you, seeing that your parents are well known to me, and in your nurture I have gauged your nature; wherefore I entertain good hope that if you choose the path which leads to me, you shall greatly bestir yourself to be the doer of many a doughty deed of noble emprise; and that I too shall be held in even higher honor for your sake, lit with the lustre shed by valorous deeds. I will not cheat you with preludings of pleasure, but I will relate to you the things that are according to the ordinances of God in very truth. Know then that among things that are lovely and of good report, not one have the Gods bestowed upon mortal man apart from toil and pains. Would you obtain the favor of the gods, then must you pay these same gods service; would you be loved by your friends, you must benefit these friends; do you desire to be honored by the state, you must give the state your aid; do you claim admiration for your virtue from all Hellas, you must strive to do some good to Hellas; do you wish earth to yield her fruits to you abundantly, to earth must you pay your court; do you seek to amass riches from your flocks and herds, on them must you bestow your labor; or is it your ambition to be potent as a warrior, able to save your friends and to subdue your foes, then must you learn the arts of war from those who have the knowledge, and practice their application in the field when learned;

or would you e'en be powerful of limb and body, then must you habituate limbs and body to obey the mind, and exercise yourself with toil and sweat.'

"At this point (as Prodicus relates), Vice broke in, exclaiming: 'See you, Heracles, how hard and long the road is by which yonder woman would escort you to her festal joys. But I will guide you by a short and easy road to happiness.'

"Then spoke Virtue: 'Nay, wretched one, what good thing hast thou? or what sweet thing art thou acquainted with — that wilt stir neither hand nor foot to gain it? Thou, that mayest not even await the desire of pleasure, but, or ever that desire springs up, art already satiated: eating before thou hungerest, and drinking before thou thirstest; who to eke out an appetite must invent an army of cooks and confectioners; and to whet thy thirst must lay down costliest wines, and run up and down in search of ice in summer-time; to help thy slumbers soft coverlets suffice not, but couches and feather-beds must be prepared thee, and rockers to rock thee to rest; since desire for sleep in thy case springs not from toil, but from vacuity and nothing in the world to do. Thus thou educatest thy friends: with insult in the night season, and drowse of slumber during the precious hours of the day. Immortal, thou art cast forth from the company of gods, and by good men art dishonored; that sweetest sound of all, the voice of praise, has never thrilled thine ears; and the fairest of all fair visions is hidden from thine eyes that have never beheld one bounteous deed wrought by thine own hand. If thou openest thy lips in speech, who will believe thy words? If thou hast need of aught, none shall satisfy thee. What sane man will venture to join

THE CHOICE OF HERACLES

thy rabble rout? Ill indeed are thy revellers to look upon, young men impotent in body, and old men witless in mind: in the heyday of life they batten in sleek idleness, and wearily do they drag through an age of wrinkled wretchedness: and why? they blush with shame at the thought of deeds done in the past, and groan for weariness at what is left to do. During their youth they ran riot through their sweet things, and laid up for themselves large store of bitterness against the time of eld. But my companionship is with the gods; and with the good among men my conversation; no bounteous deed, divine or human, is wrought without my aid. Therefore am I honored in Heaven preëminently, and upon earth among men whose right it is to honor me; as a beloved fellow-worker of all craftsmen; a faithful guardian of house and lands, whom the owners bless; a kindly helpmeet of servants; a brave assistant in the labors of peace; an unflinching ally in the deeds of war; a sharer in all friendships indispensable. To my friends is given an enjoyment of meats and drinks, which is sweet in itself and devoid of trouble, in that they can endure until desire ripens, and sleep more delicious visits them than those who toil not. Yet they are not pained to part with it; nor for the sake of slumber do they let slip the performance of their duties. Among my followers the youth delights in the praises of his elders, and the old man glories in the honor of the young; with joy they call to memory their deeds of old, and in to-day's well-doing are well pleased. For my sake are they dear in the sight of God, beloved of their friends and honored by the country of their birth. When the appointed goal is reached they lie not down in oblivion with dishonor, but bloom afresh — their praise resounded on the lips of men forever. Toils like these, O son of noble parents, Heracles, it is yours to meet with, and having endured, to enter into the heritage assured you of transcendent happiness.'"

SOCRATES AND CHAERECRATES

From the Memorabilia, Book II. iii. §§ 1-19.

AT another time the differences between two brothers named Chaerephon and Chaerecrates, both well known to him, had drawn his attention; and on seeing the younger of the two he thus addressed him : —

Socrates. Tell me, Chaerecrates, you are not, I take it, one of those strange people who believe that goods are better and more precious than a brother; and that, too, although the former are but senseless chattels which need protection, the latter a sensitive and sensible being who can afford it; and what is more, he is himself alone, whilst as for them their name is legion. And here again is a marvellous thing: that a man should count his brother a loss, because the goods of his brother are not his; but he does not count his fellow-citizens loss, and yet their possessions are not his; only it seems in their case he has wits to see that to dwell securely with many and have enough is better than to own the whole wealth of a community and to live in dangerous isolation; but this same doctrine as applied to brothers they ignore. Again, if a man have the means, he will purchase domestic slaves, because he wants assistants in his work; he will acquire friends, because he needs their support; but this brother of his — who cares about brothers? It seems a friend may be discovered in an ordinary citizen, but not in a blood relation who is also a brother. And yet it is a great vantage-ground toward friendship to have sprung from the same loins and to have been suckled at the same breasts, since even among beasts a certain natural craving and sympathy springs up between creatures reared together. Added to which, a man who has brothers commands more respect from the rest of the world than the man who has none, and who must fight his own battles.

Chaerecrates. I dare say, Socrates, where the differences are not profound, reason would a man should bear with his brother, and not avoid him for some mere trifle's sake, for a brother of the right sort is, as you say, a blessing; but if he be the very antithesis of that, why should a man lay to his hand to achieve the impossible?

Socrates. Well now, tell me, is there nobody whom Chaerephon can please any more than he can please yourself; or do some people find him agreeable enough?

Chaerecrates. Nay, there you hit it. That is just why I have a right to detest him. He can be pleasing enough to others, but to me, whenever he appears on the scene, he is not a blessing — no! but by every manner of means the reverse.

Socrates. May it not happen that just as a horse is no gain to the inexpert rider who essays to handle him, so in like manner, if a man tries to deal with his brother after an ignorant fashion, this same brother will kick?

Chaerecrates. But is it likely now? How should I be ignorant of the art of dealing with my brother if I know the art of repaying kind words and good deeds in kind? But a man who tries all he can to annoy me by word and deed, I can neither bless nor benefit, and, what is more, I will not try.

Socrates. Well, now, that is a marvellous statement, Chaerecrates. Your dog, the serviceable guardian of your flocks, who will fawn and lick the hand of your shepherd, when you come near him can only growl and show his teeth. Well, you take no notice of the dog's ill-temper, you try to propitiate him by kindness; but your brother? If your brother were what he ought to be, he would be a great blessing to you — that you admit; and, as you further confess, you know the secret of kind acts and words, yet you will not set yourself to apply means to make him your best of friends?

Chaerecrates. I am afraid, Socrates, that I have no wisdom or cunning to make Chaerephon bear himself towards me as he should.

Socrates. Yet there is no need to apply any recondite or novel machinery. Only bait your hook in the way best known to yourself, and you will capture him, whereupon he will become your devoted friend.

Chaerecrates. If you are aware that I know some love-charm, Socrates, of which I am the happy but unconscious possessor, pray make haste and enlighten me.

Socrates. Answer me, then. Suppose you wanted to get some acquaintance to invite you to dinner when he next keeps holy day, what steps would you take?

Chaerecrates. No doubt I should set him a good example by inviting him myself on a like occasion.

Socrates. And if you wanted to induce some friend to look after your affairs during your absence abroad, how would you achieve your purpose?

Chaerecrates. No doubt I should present a precedent in undertaking to look after his in like circumstance.

Socrates. And if you wished to get some foreign friend to take you under his roof while visiting his country, what would you do?

Chaerecrates. No doubt I should begin by offering him the shelter of my own roof when he came to Athens, in order to enlist his zeal in furthering the objects of my visit; it is plain I should first show my readiness to do as much for him in a like case.

Socrates. Why, it seems you are an adept after all in all the philtres known to man, only you chose to conceal your knowledge all the while; or is it that you shrink from taking the first step because of the scandal you will cause by kindly advances to your brother? And yet it is commonly held to redound to a man's praise to have outstripped an enemy in mischief or a friend in kindness. Now if it seemed to me that Chaerephon were better fitted to lead the way towards this friendship, I should have tried to persuade him to take the first step in winning your affection, but now I am persuaded the first move belongs to you, and to you the final victory.

Chaerecrates. A startling announcement, Socrates, from your lips, and most unlike you, to bid me the younger take precedence of my elder brother. Why, it is contrary to the universal custom of mankind, who look to the elder to take the lead in everything, whether as a speaker or an actor.

Socrates. How so? Is it not the custom everywhere for the younger to step aside when he meets his elder in the street, and to give him place? Is he not expected to get up and offer him his seat, to pay him the honor of a soft couch, to yield him precedence in argument?

My good fellow, do not stand shilly-shallying, but put out your hand caressingly, and you will see the worthy soul will respond with alacrity. Do you not note your brother's character, proud and frank and sensitive to honor? He is not a mean and sorry rascal to be caught by a bribe — no better way indeed for such riff-raff. No! gentle natures need a finer treatment. You can best hope to work on them by affection.

Chaerecrates. But suppose I do, and suppose that, for all my attempts, he shows no change for the better?

Socrates. At the worst you will have shown yourself to be a good, honest, brotherly man, and he will appear as a sorry creature on whom kindness is wasted. But nothing of the sort is going to happen, as I conjecture. My belief is that as soon as he hears your challenge he will embrace the contest; pricked on by emulous pride, he will insist upon getting the better of you in kindness of word and deed.

At present you two are in the condition of two hands formed by God to help each other, but which have let go their business, and have turned to hindering one another all they can. You are a pair of feet fashioned on the Divine plan to work together, but which have neglected this in order to trammel each other's gait. Now is it not insensate stupidity to use for injury what was meant for advantage? And yet in fashioning two brothers God intends them, methinks, to be of more benefit to one another than either two hands or two feet or two eyes, or any other of those pairs which belong to man from his birth.

Consider how powerless these hands of ours if called
upon to combine their action at two points more than
a single fathom's length apart; and these feet could
not stretch asunder even a bare fathom; and these
eyes, for all the wide-reaching range we claim for
them, are incapable of seeing simultaneously the back
and front of an object at even closer quarters. But
a pair of brothers, linked in bonds of amity, can work
each for the other's good, though seas divide them.

THE BATTLE OF CUNAXA

From the Anabasis, Book I. viii. §§ 14-29.

AT this time the barbarian army was evenly advancing, and the Hellenic division was still riveted to the
spot, completing its formation as the various contin-
gents came up. Cyrus, riding past at some distance
from the lines, glanced his eye first in one direction
and then in the other, so as to take a complete survey
of friends and foes; when Xenophon the Athenian,
seeing him, rode up from the Hellenic quarter to
meet him, asking whether he had any orders to give.
Cyrus, pulling up his horse, begged him to make
the announcement generally known that the omens
from the victims, internal and external, were good.
While he was still speaking he heard a confused murmur passing through the ranks, and asked what it
meant. The other replied that it was the watchword
being passed down for the second time. Cyrus won-
dered who had given the order, and asked what the
watchword was. On being told it was "Zeus our
Saviour and Victory," he replied, "I accept it; so
let it be," and with that remark rode away to his own

position. And now the two battle lines were no more than three or four furlongs apart, when the Hellenes began chanting the paean, and at the same time advanced against the enemy.

But with the forward movement a certain portion of the line curved onwards in advance, with wave-like sinuosity, and the portion left behind quickened to a run; and simultaneously a thrilling cry burst from all lips, like that in honor of the war-god — eleleu! eleleu! and the running became general. Some say they clashed their shields and spears, thereby causing terror to the horses; and before they had got within arrowshot the barbarians swerved and took to flight. And now the Hellenes gave chase with might and main, checked only by shouts to one another not to race, but to keep their ranks. The enemy's chariots, reft of their charioteers, swept onwards, some through the enemy themselves, others past the Hellenes. They, as they saw them coming, opened a gap and let them pass. One fellow, like some dumfounded mortal on a race-course, was caught by the heels, but even he, they said, received no hurt; nor indeed, with the single exception of some one on the left wing who was said to have been wounded by an arrow, did any Hellene in this battle suffer a single hurt.

Cyrus, seeing the Hellenes conquering, as far as they at any rate were concerned, and in hot pursuit, was well content; but in spite of his joy and the salutations offered him at that moment by those about him, as though he were already king, he was not led away to join in the pursuit, but keeping his squadron of six hundred horsemen in close order, waited and watched to see what the king himself would do. The king, he knew, held the centre of the Persian army. Indeed it is the fashion for the Asiatic monarch to occupy that position during action, for this twofold reason: he holds the safest place, with his troops on either side of him, while, if he has occasion to despatch any necessary order along the lines, his troops will receive the message in half the time. The king accordingly on this occasion held the centre of his army, but for all that, he was outside Cyrus' left wing; and seeing that no one offered him battle in front, nor yet the troops in front of him, he wheeled as if to encircle the enemy. It was then that Cyrus, in apprehension lest the king might get round to the rear and cut to pieces the Hellenic body, charged to meet him. Attacking with his six hundred, he mastered the line of troops in front of the king, and put to flight the six thousand, cutting down, as is said, with his own hand their general, Artagerses.

But as soon as the rout commenced, Cyrus's own six hundred themselves, in the ardor of pursuit, were scattered, with the exception of a handful who were left with Cyrus himself — chiefly his table companions, so-called. Left alone with these, he caught sight of the king and the close throng about him. Unable longer to contain himself, with a cry, "I see the man," he rushed at him and dealt a blow at his chest, wounding him through the corselet. This according to the statement of Ctesias the surgeon, who further states that he himself healed the wound. As Cyrus delivered the blow, some one struck him with a javelin under the eye severely; and in the struggle which then ensued between the king and Cyrus and those about them to protect one or other, we have the statement of Ctesias as to the number slain on the king's side, for he was by his side. On the other,

Cyrus himself fell, and eight of his bravest companions lay on the top of him. The story says that Artapates, the trustiest esquire among his wand-bearers, when he saw that Cyrus had fallen to the ground, leapt from his horse and threw his arms about him. Then, as one account says, the king bade one slay him as a worthy victim to his brother; others say that Artapates drew his scimitar and slew himself by his own hand. A golden scimitar it is true he had; he wore also a collar and bracelets and the other ornaments such as the noblest Persians wear; for his kindliness and fidelity had won him honors at the hand of Cyrus.

So died Cyrus — a man the kingliest and most worthy to rule of all the Persians who have lived since the elder Cyrus, according to the concurrent testimony of all who are reputed to have known him intimately.

THE FIRST GLIMPSE OF THE SEA

From the Anabasis, Book IV. vii. §§ 19-27.

PASSING on from thence in four stages of twenty parasangs, they reached a large and prosperous well-populated city, which went by the name of Gymnias, from which the governor of the country sent them a guide to lead them through a district hostile to his own. This guide told them that within five days he would lead them to a place from which they would see the sea, "and," he added, "if I fail of my word, you are free to take my life." Accordingly he put himself at their head; but he no sooner set foot in the country hostile to himself than he fell to encouraging them to burn and harry the land; indeed his exhortations were so earnest, it was plain that it was for this he had come, and not out of the good-will he bore the Hellenes.

On the fifth day they reached the mountain, the name of which was Theches. No sooner had the men in front ascended it and caught sight of the sea than a great cry arose, and Xenophon, with the rearguard, catching the sound of it, conjectured that another set of enemies must surely be attacking in front; for they were followed by the inhabitants of the country, which was all aflame; indeed the rearguard had killed some and captured others alive by laying an ambuscade; they had taken also about twenty wicker shields, covered with the raw hides of shaggy oxen.

But as the shout became louder and nearer, and those who from time to time came up began racing at the top of their speed towards the shouters, and the shouting continually recommenced with yet greater volume as the numbers increased, Xenophon settled in his mind that something extraordinary must have happened, so he mounted his horse, and taking with him Lycius and the cavalry, he galloped to the rescue. Presently they could hear the soldiers shouting and passing on the joyful word, *The sea! the sea!*

Thereupon they began running, rearguard and all, and the baggage animals and horses came galloping up. But when they had reached the summit, then indeed they fell to embracing one another, — generals and officers and all, — and the tears trickled down their cheeks. And on a sudden, some one, whoever it was, having passed down the order, the soldiers began bringing stones and erecting a great cairn, whereon they dedicated a host of untanned skins, and staves, and captured wicker shields, and with his own hand the guide hacked the shields to pieces, inviting the rest to follow his example. After this the Hellenes dismissed the guide with a present raised from the common store, to wit, a horse, a silver bowl, a Persian dress, and ten darics; but what he most begged to have were their rings, and of these he got several from the soldiers. So, after pointing out to them a village where they would find quarters, and the road by which they would proceed towards the land of the Macrones, as evening fell he turned his back upon them in the night, and was gone.

PLATO

PLATO was born at Athens in 427 B. C., of a wealthy and aristocratic family which traced its descent from the old kings of prehistoric times, and was connected with the lawgiver Solon. His father was Aristo, and in infancy he himself received his grandfather's name Aristocles, but was afterwards called Plato (*Broad*), from the breadth of his chest, or his forehead, or from the copiousness of his style. His mother was Perictione, sister of Charmides and cousin of Critias, who were prominent among the Thirty Tyrants who for a brief time ruled Athens at the close of the Peloponnesian War, 404 B. C. That he felt the course of Critias and Charmides to be no disgrace but a glory, is shown by his naming a dialogue after each, and he cannot have been in sympathy with the democratic party in his native city.

The youthful Plato is said to have distinguished himself in gymnastics and even to have entered the Isthmian Games at Corinth in competition for a prize. Entirely probable is the story that he had ambitions as a poet, and in particular desired to distinguish himself in tragedy. His dialogues show not only poetic studies and genius, but peculiar interest in tragedy. The occasion and circumstances of his meeting with Socrates are unknown. Very probably he joined the company of Socrates's followers when he was about twenty years old, or in 407 B. C.

On the death of Socrates, in April or May of 399 B. C., Plato withdrew from Athens and spent some time in Egypt. Thence he returned and formed a school, or more strictly, according to Athenian law, a religious society of his followers, first in a gymnasium, and then in a garden of his own, in a grove about a mile west of the city walls sacred to Academus, — his *Academy* in the " grove of Academe." He made more than one visit to Sicily — largely, it would seem, in the hope of persuading the tyrant of Syracuse to become a "philosopher," and thus to have the opportunity of putting in practice some of his political schemes, but he spent his last years at Athens, and died there in 347 B. C.

Plato showed his devotion to his master by making Socrates the chief person in all but one (the *Laws*) of his dialogues, and by keeping himself entirely in the background. Indeed, he mentions himself but twice. We think of him as a writer, but he regarded himself as a teacher, and his writings as secondary in importance to his oral instruction, — useful chiefly as a reminder of what had been uttered in conversation. Some of his dialogues, however, clearly have in mind readers who may not be Athenians. The dialogue form was chosen partly since this was the Socratic method of imparting instruction, but chiefly because this allowed an artistic expression of his thoughts.

Thirty-five dialogues, thirteen letters, some " definitions," and seven minor dialogues, which were considered spurious even in ancient times, have come down to us under the name of Plato. The definitions and some of the letters and dialogues are not authentic. The Platonic authorship of the most important dialogues, however, is vouched for by Aristotle's references to them.

The longest of Plato's dialogues is the *Laws ;* the greatest is the *Republic*, in which he presents his views of the ideal State; the *Phaedo*, the *Symposium*, the *Protagoras*, and the *Gorgias* are highly finished and dramatic. The *Apology* purports to be the speech which Socrates made to the court when on trial for his life.

We are fortunate in having an admirable translation of Plato's works by the late Master of Balliol, Benjamin Jowett, from which the following extracts are taken.

SOCRATES

SOCRATES, the master of Plato, wrote no books himself. He said that he was dissatisfied with books, for books could not answer questions. He was born about 469 B. C., the son of Sophroniscus, a stone-cutter, and he himself was a sculptor during the early part of his life. A group of the Graces which stood on the Acropolis was said to be his work. But he turned from the carving of stone to the moulding of men's minds and the search for truth. As Cicero says, he was the first to call Philosophy down from the clouds to dwell among men. He formed no school and received no pupils, but as he met men on the street and in the market-place, questioned them, and roused them to thought. Gradually a band of followers formed around him, — chiefly young men, among whom Plato, Alcibiades, and Xenophon are best known to us. The character of Socrates had many sides. Plato was his true successor in the search for truth. Xenophon was not a philosopher, but being an intensely practical man was much impressed by his ethical teachings. Socrates's self-control and contempt for physical in comparison with mental and moral pleasures were continued with exaggerations by the Cynics and Stoics.

Alcibiades and others of the young men who had followed Socrates entered upon political courses displeasing to the Athenians, and in the spring of 399 B. C., Socrates was brought to trial on the charge of corrupting the youth and of introducing new divinities. The second "count" of the indictment referred to his belief that a special divine influence (*daemonium*) often restrained him from action, thus guiding him aright. He was condemned to death, and, according to the custom of that time, drank the poison-hemlock (*conium*) in his cell. The *Phaedo* of Plato narrates his life and conversation in the prison on the day of his death, — the heart of the dialogue being devoted to an argument for the immortality of the soul.

THE TRUE POLITICIAN [1]

From the Gorgias, pp. 521, 522.

SOCRATES. CALLICLES.

Socrates. Then to which service of the State do you invite me? determine for me. Am I to be the physician of the State, who will strive and struggle to make the Athenians as good as possible; or am I to be the servant and flatterer of the State? Speak out, my good friend, freely and fairly as you did at first and ought to do again, and tell me your entire mind.

Callicles. I say, then, that you should be the servant of the State.

Socrates. The flatterer? well, sir, that is a noble invitation.

Callicles. The Mysian,[2] Socrates, or what you please. For if you refuse, the consequences will be —

Socrates. Do not repeat the old story — that he who likes will kill me and get my money; for then I shall have to repeat the old answer, that he will be a bad man and will kill the good, and that the money will be of no use to him, but he will wrongly use that which he wrongly took, and if wrongly, basely, and if basely, hurtfully.

Callicles. How confident you are, Socrates, that you will never come to harm! You seem to think that you are living in another country, and can never be brought into a court of justice, as you very likely may be brought by some miserable and mean person.

Socrates. Then I must indeed be a fool, Callicles,

[1] In this is a distinct reference to Socrates's position before his judges.

[2] A barbarian. He means, "Call me the lowest kind of slave, or anything you like."

if I do not know that in the Athenian State any man may suffer anything. And if I am brought to trial and incur the dangers of which you speak, he will be a villain who brings me to trial — of that I am very sure, for no good man would accuse the innocent. Nor shall I be surprised if I am put to death. Shall I tell you why I anticipate this?

Callicles. By all means.

Socrates. I think that I am the only, or almost the only, Athenian living who practices the true art of politics; I am the only politician of my time. Now, seeing that when I speak, my words are not uttered with any view of gaining favor, and that I look to what is best and not to what is most pleasant, having no mind to use those arts and graces which you recommend, I shall have nothing to say in the justice court. And you might argue with me, as I was arguing with Polus; I shall be tried just as a physician would be tried in a court of little boys at the indictment of the cook. What would he reply under such circumstances, if some one were to accuse him, saying, " O my boys, many evil things has this man done to you: he is the death of you, especially of the younger ones among you, cutting, and burning, and starving, and suffocating you, until you know not what to do; he gives you the bitterest potions, and compels you to hunger and thirst. How unlike the variety of meats and sweets on which I feasted you!" What do you suppose that the physician would be able to reply when he found himself in such a predicament? If he told the truth he could only say, " All these evil things, my boys, I did for your health." And then would there not just be a clamor among a jury like that? How they would cry out!

Callicles. I dare say.

Socrates. Would he not be utterly at a loss for a reply?

Callicles. He certainly would.

Socrates. And I too shall be treated in the same way, as I well know, if I am brought before the court. For I shall not be able to rehearse to the people the pleasures which I have procured for them, and which, although I am not disposed to envy either the procurers or enjoyers of them, are deemed by them to be benefits and advantages. And if any one says that I corrupt young men, and perplex their minds, or that I speak evil of old men, and use bitter words towards them, whether in private or public, it is useless for me to reply, as I truly might: "All this I do for the sake of justice, and with a view to your interest, my judges, and to nothing else." And therefore there is no saying what may happen to me.

Callicles. And do you think, Socrates, that a man who is thus defenceless is in a good position?

Socrates. Yes, Callicles, if he have that defence which, as you have often acknowledged, he should have — if he be his own defence, and have never said or done anything wrong, either in respect of gods or men; and this has been repeatedly acknowledged by us to be the best sort of defence. And if any one could convict me of inability to defend myself or others after this sort, I should blush for shame, whether I was convicted before many, or before a few, or by myself alone; and if I died from want of ability to do so, that would indeed grieve me. But if I died because I have no power of flattery or rhetoric, I am very sure that you would not find me repining at death. For no man who is not an utter fool and coward is afraid of death itself, but he is afraid of doing wrong. For to go to the world below having one's soul full of injustice is the last and worst of all evils.

CRITO

SOCRATES.   CRITO.

SCENE. — *The Prison of Socrates.*

Socrates. Why have you come at this hour, Crito? it must be quite early?
Crito. Yes, certainly.
Socrates. What is the exact time?
Crito. The dawn is breaking.
Socrates. I wonder that the keeper of the prison would let you in.
Crito. He knows me because I often come, Socrates; moreover, I have done him a kindness.
Socrates. And are you only just arrived?
Crito. No, I came some time ago.
Socrates. Then why did you sit and say nothing instead of at once awakening me?
Crito. I should not have liked myself, Socrates, to be in such great trouble and unrest as you are — indeed I should not: I have been watching with amazement your peaceful slumbers; and for that reason I did not awake you, because I wished to minimize the pain. I have always thought you to be of a happy disposition; but never did I see anything like the easy, tranquil manner in which you bear this calamity.
Socrates. Why, Crito, when a man has reached my age he ought not to be repining at the approach of death.

Crito. And yet other old men find themselves in similar misfortunes, and age does not prevent them from repining.

Socrates. That is true. But you have not told me why you come at this early hour.

Crito. I come to bring you a message which is sad and painful; not, as I believe, to yourself, but to all of us who are your friends, and saddest of all to me.

Socrates. What? Has the ship come from Delos, on the arrival of which I am to die?

Crito. No, the ship has not actually arrived, but she will probably be here to-day, as persons who have come from Sunium [1] tell me that they left her there; and therefore to-morrow, Socrates, will be the last day of your life.

Socrates. Very well, Crito; if such is the will of God, I am willing; but my belief is that there will be a delay of a day.

Crito. Why do you think so?

Socrates. I will tell you. I am to die on the day after the arrival of the ship.

Crito. Yes; that is what the authorities say.

Socrates. But I do not think that the ship will be here until to-morrow; this I infer from a vision which I had last night, or rather only just now, when you fortunately allowed me to sleep.

Crito. And what was the nature of the vision?

Socrates. There appeared to me the likeness of a woman, fair and comely, clothed in bright raiment, who called to me and said : " O Socrates,

"'The third day hence to fertile Phthia thou shalt go.'" [2]

Crito. What a singular dream, Socrates!

[1] Southern promontory of Attica.   [2] Homer, Iliad, ix. 363.

Socrates. There can be no doubt about the meaning, Crito, I think.

Crito. Yes, the meaning is only too clear. But O, my beloved Socrates, let me entreat you once more to take my advice and escape. For if you die I shall not only lose a friend who can never be replaced, but there is another evil: people who do not know you and me will believe that I might have saved you if I had been willing to give money, but that I did not care. Now, can there be a worse disgrace than this — that I should be thought to value money more than the life of a friend? For the many will not be persuaded that I wanted you to escape, and that you refused.

Socrates. But why, my dear Crito, should we care about the opinion of the many? Good men, and they are the only persons who are worth considering, will think of these things truly as they occurred.

Crito. But you see, Socrates, that the opinion of the many must be regarded, for what is now happening shows that they can do the greatest evil to any one who has lost their good opinion.

Socrates. I only wish it were so, Crito, and that the many could do the greatest evil; for then they would also be able to do the greatest good — and what a fine thing this would be! But in reality they can do neither; for they cannot make a man either wise or foolish; and whatever they do is the result of chance.

Crito. Well, I will not dispute with you; but please to tell me, Socrates, whether you are not acting out of regard to me and your other friends: are you not afraid that if you escape from prison we may get into trouble with the informers for having stolen you away, and lose either the whole or a great part of our property; or that even a worse evil may happen to us? Now, if you fear on our account, be at ease; for in order to save you, we ought surely to run this, or even a greater risk; be persuaded, then, and do as I say.

Socrates. Yes, Crito, that is one fear which you mention, but by no means the only one.

Crito. Fear not — there are persons who are willing to get you out of prison at no great cost; and as for the informers, they are far from being exorbitant in their demands — a little money will satisfy them. My means, which are certainly ample, are at your service, and if you have a scruple about spending all mine, here are strangers who will give you the use of theirs; and one of them, Simmias the Theban, has brought a large sum of money for this very purpose; and Cebes and many others are prepared to spend their money in helping you to escape. I say, therefore, do not hesitate on our account, and do not say, as you did in the Court, that you will have a difficulty in knowing what to do with yourself anywhere else. For men will love you in other places to which you may go, and not in Athens only; there are friends of mine in Thessaly, if you like to go to them, who will value and protect you, and no Thessalian will give you any trouble. Nor can I think that you are at all justified, Socrates, in betraying your own life when you might be saved; in acting thus you are playing into the hands of your enemies, who are hurrying on your destruction. And further I should say that you are deserting your own children; for you might bring them up and educate them; instead of which you go away and leave them, and they will have to take their chance; and if they do not meet with the usual fate of orphans, there will be small thanks to you. No man should bring children into the world who is unwilling to persevere to the end in their nurture and education. But you appear to be choosing the easier part, not the better and manlier, which would have been more becoming in one who professes to care for virtue in all his actions, like yourself. And indeed, I am ashamed not only of you, but of us who are your friends, when I reflect that the whole business will be attributed entirely to our want of courage. The trial need never have come on, or might have been managed differently; and this last act, or crowning folly, will seem to have occurred through our negligence and cowardice, who might have saved you, if we had been good for anything; and you might have saved yourself, for there was no difficulty at all. See now, Socrates, how sad and discreditable are the consequences, both to us and you. Make up your mind then, or rather have your mind already made up, for the time of deliberation is over, and there is only one thing to be done, which must be done this very night, and if we delay at all will be no longer practicable or possible; I beseech you therefore, Socrates, be persuaded by me, and do as I say.

Socrates. Dear Crito, your zeal is invaluable, if a right one; but if wrong, the greater the zeal the greater the danger; and therefore we ought to consider whether I shall or shall not do as you say. For I am and always have been one of those natures who must be guided by reason, whatever the reason may be which upon reflection appears to me to be the best; and now that this chance has befallen me, I cannot repudiate my own words: the principles which I have hitherto honored and revered I still honor, and unless we can at once find other and better principles, I am certain not to agree with you; no, not even if the power of the multitude could inflict many more imprisonments, confiscations, deaths, frightening us like children with hobgoblin terrors. What will be the fairest way of considering the question? Shall I return to your old argument about the opinions of men? — we were saying that some of them are to be regarded, and others not. Now were we right in maintaining this before I was condemned? And has the argument which was once good now proved to be talk for the sake of talking — mere childish nonsense? That is what I want to consider with your help, Crito: — whether, under my present circumstances, the argument appears to be in any way different or not; and is to be allowed by me or disallowed. That argument, which, as I believe, is maintained by many persons of authority, was to the effect, as I was saying, that the opinions of some men are to be regarded, and of other men not to be regarded. Now you, Crito, are not going to die to-morrow — at least, there is no human probability of this — and therefore you are disinterested, and not liable to be deceived by the circumstances in which you are placed. Tell me then, whether I am right in saying that some opinions, and the opinions of some men only, are to be valued, and that other opinions, and the opinions of other men, are not to be valued. I ask you whether I was right in maintaining this?

Crito. Certainly.

Socrates. The good are to be regarded, and not the bad?

Crito. Yes.

Socrates. And the opinions of the wise are good, and the opinions of the unwise are evil?

Crito. Certainly.

Socrates. And what was said about another matter? Is the pupil who devotes himself to the practice of gymnastics supposed to attend to the praise and blame and opinion of every man, or of one man only — his physician or trainer, whoever he may be?

Crito. Of one man only.

Socrates. And he ought to fear the censure and welcome the praise of that one only, and not of the many?

Crito. Clearly so.

Socrates. And he ought to act and train, and eat and drink, in the way which seems good to his single master who has understanding, rather than according to the opinion of all other men put together?

Crito. True.

Socrates. And if he disobeys and disregards the opinion and approval of the one, and regards the opinion of the many who have no understanding, will he not suffer evil?

Crito. Certainly he will.

Socrates. And what will the evil be, whither tending and what affecting, in the disobedient person?

Crito. Clearly, affecting the body; that is what is destroyed by the evil.

Socrates. Very good; and is not this true, Crito, of other things which we need not separately enumerate? In questions of just and unjust, fair and foul, good and evil, which are the subjects of our present consultation, ought we to follow the opinion of the many and to fear them; or the opinion of the one man who has understanding? ought we not to fear and reverence him more than all the rest of the world: and if we desert him shall we not destroy and injure that principle in us which may be assumed to be improved by justice and deteriorated by injustice;—there is such a principle?

Crito. Certainly there is, Socrates.

Socrates. Take a parallel instance: if, acting under the advice of those who have no understanding, we destroy that which is improved by health and is deteriorated by disease, would life be worth having? And that which has been destroyed is the body?

Crito. Yes.

Socrates. Could we live, having an evil and corrupted body?

Crito. Certainly not.

Socrates. And will life be worth having, if that higher part of man be destroyed, which is improved by justice and depraved by injustice? Do we suppose that principle, whatever it may be in man, which has to do with justice and injustice, to be inferior to the body?

Crito. Certainly not.

Socrates. More honorable than the body?

Crito. Far more.

Socrates. Then, my friend, we must not regard what the many say of us; but what he, the one man who has understanding of just and unjust, will say, and what the truth will say. And therefore you begin in error when you advise that we should regard the opinion of the many about just and unjust, good and evil, honorable and dishonorable. "Well," some one will say, "but the many can kill us."

Crito. Yes, Socrates; that will clearly be the answer.

Socrates. And it is true; but still I find with surprise that the old argument is unshaken as ever. And I should like to know whether I may say the same of another proposition — that not life, but a good life, is to be chiefly valued.

Crito. Yes, that also remains unshaken.

Socrates. And a good life is equivalent to a just and honorable one — that holds also?

Crito. Yes, it does.

Socrates. From these premises I proceed to argue the question whether I ought or ought not to try and escape without the consent of the Athenians; and if I am clearly right in escaping, then I will make the attempt; but if not, I will abstain. The other considerations which you mention, of money and loss of character, and the duty of educating one's children, are, I fear, only the doctrines of the multitude, who would be as ready to restore people to life, if they were able, as they are to put them to death — and with as little reason. But now, since the argument has thus far prevailed, the only question which remains to be considered is, whether we shall do rightly either in escaping or in suffering others to aid in our escape and paying them in money and thanks, or whether in reality we shall not do rightly; and if the latter, then death or any other calamity which may ensue on my remaining here must not be allowed to enter into the calculation.

Crito. I think that you are right, Socrates; how then shall we proceed?

Socrates. Let us consider the matter together, and do you either refute me if you can, and I will be convinced; or else cease, my dear friend, from repeating to me that I ought to escape against the wishes of the

Athenians: for I highly value your attempts to persuade me to do so, but I may not be persuaded against my own better judgment. And now please to consider my first position, and try how you can best answer me.

Crito. I will.

Socrates. Are we to say that we are never intentionally to do wrong, or that in one way we ought and in another way we ought not to do wrong, or is doing wrong always evil and dishonorable, as I was just now saying, and as has been already acknowledged by us? Are all our former admissions which were made within a few days to be thrown away? And have we, at our age, been earnestly discoursing with one another all our life long only to discover that we are no better than children? Or, in spite of the opinion of the many, and in spite of consequences, whether better or worse, shall we insist on the truth of what was then said, that injustice is always an evil and dishonor to him who acts unjustly? Shall we say so or not?

Crito. Yes.

Socrates. Then we must do no wrong?

Crito. Certainly not.

Socrates. Nor when injured injure in return, as the many imagine; for we must injure no one at all?

Crito. Clearly not.

Socrates. Again, Crito, may we do evil?

Crito. Surely not, Socrates.

Socrates. And what of doing evil in return for evil, which is the morality of the many — is that just or not?

Crito. Not just.

Socrates. For doing evil to another is the same as injuring him?

Crito. Very true.

Socrates. Then we ought not to retaliate or render evil for evil to any one, whatever evil we may have suffered from him. But I would have you consider, Crito, whether you really mean what you are saying. For this opinion has never been held, and never will be held, by any considerable number of persons; and those who are agreed and those who are not agreed upon this point have no common ground, and can only despise one another when they see how widely they differ. Tell me, then, whether you agree with and assent to my first principle, that neither injury, nor retaliation, nor warding off evil by evil is ever right. And shall that be the premises of our argument? Or do you decline and dissent from this? For so I have ever thought and continue to think; but, if you are of another opinion, let me hear what you have to say. If, however, you remain of the same mind as formerly, I will proceed to the next step.

Crito. You may proceed, for I have not changed my mind.

Socrates. Then I will go on to the next point, which may be put in the form of a question: Ought a man to do what he admits to be right, or ought he to betray the right?

Crito. He ought to do what he thinks right.

Socrates. But if this is true, what is the application? In leaving the prison against the will of the Athenians, do I wrong any? or rather do I not wrong those whom I ought least to wrong? Do I not desert the principles which were acknowledged by us to be just — what do you say?

Crito. I cannot tell, Socrates; for I do not know.

Socrates. Then consider the matter in this way: Imagine that I am about to play truant (you may call

the proceeding by any name which you like), and the
laws and the government come and interrogate me:
"Tell us, Socrates," they say, "what are you about?
are you not going by an act of yours to overturn us —
the laws and the whole State, as far as in you lies?
Do you imagine that a State can subsist and not be
overthrown, in which the decisions of law have no
power, but are set aside and trampled upon by individuals?" What will be our answer, Crito, to these
and the like words? Any one, and especially a rhetorician, will have a good deal to say on behalf of the
law which requires a sentence to be carried out. He
will argue that this law should not be set aside; and
shall we reply, "Yes; but the State has injured us and
given an unjust sentence." Suppose I say that?

Crito. Very good, Socrates.

Socrates. "And was that our agreement with you?"
the law would answer; "or were you to abide by the
sentence of the State?" And if I were to express my
astonishment at their words, the law would probably
add: "Answer, Socrates, instead of opening your eyes
— you are in the habit of asking and answering questions. Tell us, — what complaint have you to make
against us which justifies you in attempting to destroy
us and the State? In the first place did we not bring
you into existence? Your father married your mother by our aid and begat you. Say whether you have
any objection to urge against those of us who regulate
marriage?" "None," I should reply. "Or against
those of us who after birth regulate the nurture and
education of children, in which you also were trained?
Were not the laws, which have the charge of education, right in commanding your father to train you
in music and gymnastic?" "Right," I should reply.

"Well then, since you were brought into the world and nurtured and educated by us, can you deny in the first place that you are our child and slave, as your fathers were before you? And if this is true you are not on equal terms with us; nor can you think that you have a right to do to us what we are doing to you. Would you have any right to strike or revile or do any other evil to your father or your master, if you had one, because you have been struck or reviled by him, or received some other evil at his hands?—you would not say this? And because we think right to destroy you, do you think that you have any right to destroy us in return, and your country as far as in you lies? Will you, O professor of true virtue, pretend that you are justified in this? Has a philosopher like you failed to discover that our country is more to be valued and higher and holier far than mother or father or any ancestor, and more to be regarded in the eyes of the gods and of men of understanding? Also to be soothed, and gently and reverently entreated when angry, even more than a father, and either to be persuaded, or if not persuaded, to be obeyed? And when we are punished by her, whether with imprisonment or stripes, the punishment is to be endured in silence; and if she lead us to wounds or death in battle, thither we follow, as is right; neither may any one yield or retreat or leave his rank, but whether in battle or in a court of law, or in any other place, he must do what his city and his country order him; or he must change their view of what is just; and if he may do no violence to his father or mother, much less may he do violence to his country." What answer shall we make to this, Crito? Do the laws speak truly, or do they not?

Crito. I think that they do.

Socrates. Then the laws will say : " Consider, Socrates, if we are speaking truly that in your present attempt you are going to do us an injury. For, having brought you into the world, and nurtured and educated you, and given you and every other citizen a share in every good which we had to give, we further proclaim to any Athenian by the liberty which we allow him, that if he does not like us when he has become of age and has seen the ways of the city, and made our acquaintance, he may go where he pleases and take his goods with him. None of us laws will forbid him or interfere with him. Any one who does not like us and the city, and who wants to emigrate to a colony or to any other city, may go where he likes, retaining his property. But he who has experience of the manner in which we order justice and administer the State, and still remains, has entered into an implied contract that he will do as we command him. And he who disobeys us is, as we maintain, thrice wrong; first, because in disobeying us he is disobeying his parents; secondly, because we are the authors of his education; thirdly, because he has made an agreement with us that he will duly obey our commands ; and he neither obeys them nor convinces us that our commands are unjust; and we do not rudely impose them, but give him the alternative of obeying or convincing us ; that is what we offer, and he does neither.

" These are the sort of accusations to which, as we were saying, you, Socrates, will be exposed if you accomplish your intentions ; you, above all other Athenians." Suppose now I ask, " Why I rather than anybody else ? " they will justly retort upon me that I above all other men have acknowledged the agreement. " There is clear proof," they will say, " Socrates, that we and the city were not displeasing to you. Of all Athenians, you have been the most constant resident in the city, which, as you never leave, you may be supposed to love. For you never went out of the city either to see the games, except once when you went to the Isthmus, or to any other place unless when you were on military service; nor did you travel as other men do. Nor had you any curiosity to know other States or their laws: your affections did not go beyond us and our State; we were your special favorites, and you acquiesced in our government of you; and here in this city you begat your children, which is a proof of your satisfaction. Moreover, you might in the course of the trial, if you had liked, have fixed the penalty at banishment; the State which refuses to let you go now would have let you go then. But you pretended that you preferred death to exile, and that you were not unwilling to die. And now you have forgotten these fine sentiments, and pay no respect to us the laws, of whom you are the destroyer; and are doing what only a miserable slave would do, running away and turning your back upon the compacts and agreements which you made as a citizen. And first of all answer this very question: Are we right in saying that you agreed to be governed according to us in deed, and not in word only? Is that true or not?" How shall we answer, Crito? Must we not assent?

Crito. We cannot help it, Socrates.

Socrates. Then will they not say: " You, Socrates, are breaking the covenants and agreements which you made with us at your leisure, not in any haste or under any compulsion or deception, but after you have had seventy years to think of them, during which time you were at liberty to leave the city, if we were not to your mind, or if our covenants appeared to you to be unfair. You had your choice, and might have gone either to Lacedaemon or Crete, both which States are often praised by you for their good government, or to some other Hellenic or foreign State. Whereas you, above all other Athenians, seemed to be so fond of the state, or, in other words, of us her laws (and who would care about a State which has no laws?) that you never stirred out of her; the halt, the blind, the maimed were not more stationary in her than you were. And now you run away and forsake your agreements. Not so, Socrates, if you will take our advice; do not make yourself ridiculous by escaping out of the city.

"For just consider, if you transgress and err in this sort of way, what good will you do either to yourself or to your friends? That your friends will be driven into exile and deprived of citizenship, or will lose their property, is tolerably certain; and you yourself, if you fly to one of the neighboring cities, as, for example, Thebes or Megara, both of which are well governed, will come to them as an enemy, Socrates, and their government will be against you, and all patriotic citizens will cast an evil eye upon you as a subverter of the laws, and you will confirm in the minds of the judges the justice of their own condemnation of you. For he who is a corrupter of the laws is more than likely to be a corrupter of the young and foolish portion of mankind. Will you then flee from well-ordered cities and virtuous men? And is existence worth having on these terms? Or will you go to them without shame, and talk to them, Socrates?

And what will you say to them? What you say here about virtue and justice and institutions and laws being the best things among men? Would that be decent of you? Surely not. But if you go away from well-governed states to Crito's friends in Thessaly, where there is great disorder and license, they will be charmed to hear the tale of your escape from prison, set off with ludicrous particulars of the manner in which you were wrapped up in a goatskin or some other disguise, and metamorphosed as the manner is of runaways; but will there be no one to remind you that in your old age you were not ashamed to violate the most sacred laws from a miserable desire of a little more life? Perhaps not, if you keep them in a good temper; but if they are out of temper you will hear many degrading things. You will live, but how? — as the flatterer of all men, and the servant of all men; and doing what? — eating and drinking in Thessaly, having gone abroad in order that you may get a dinner. And where will be your fine sentiments about justice and virtue? Say that you wish to live for the sake of your children — you want to bring them up and educate them — will you take them into Thessaly and deprive them of Athenian citizenship? Is this the benefit which you will confer upon them? Or are you under the impression that they will be better cared for and educated here if you are still alive, although absent from them; for your friends will take care of them? Do you fancy that if you are an inhabitant of Thessaly they will take care of them, and if you are an inhabitant of the other world that they will not take care of them? Nay; but if they who call themselves friends are good for anything, they will — to be sure they will.

"Listen, then, Socrates, to us who have brought you up. Think not of life and children first, and of justice afterwards, but of justice first, that you may be justified before the princes of the world below. For neither will you nor any that belong to you be happier or holier or juster in this life, or happier in another, if you do as Crito bids. Now you depart in innocence, a sufferer and not a doer of evil; a victim, not of the laws, but of men. But if you go forth, returning evil for evil, and injury for injury, breaking the covenants and agreements which you have made with us, and wronging those whom you ought least of all to wrong, that is to say, yourself, your friends, your country, and us, we shall be angry with you while you live, and our brethren, the laws in the world below, will receive you as an enemy; for they will know that you have done your best to destroy us. Listen, then, to us and not to Crito."

This, dear Crito, is the voice which I seem to hear murmuring in my ears, like the sound of the flute in the ears of the mystic; that voice, I say, is humming in my ears, and prevents me from hearing any other. And I know that anything more which you may say will be vain. Yet speak, if you have anything to say.

Crito. I have nothing to say, Socrates.

Socrates. Leave me, then, Crito, to fulfil the will of God, and to follow whither he leads.

THE DEATH OF SOCRATES

From the Phaedo, pp. 115-118.

Scene. — *The Prison.*

The story is supposed to be told by Socrates's young friend Phaedo, his "beloved disciple," to Echecrates and a company of philosophers in Phlius.

"Wherefore,[1] Simmias, seeing all these things, what ought not we to do that we may obtain virtue and wisdom in this life? Fair is the prize, and the hope great!

"A man of sense ought not to say, nor will I be very confident, that the description which I have given of the soul and her mansions is exactly true. But I do say that, inasmuch as the soul is shown to be immortal, he may venture to think, not improperly or unworthily, that something of the kind is true. The venture is a glorious one, and he ought to comfort himself with words like these, which is the reason why I lengthen out the tale. Wherefore, I say, let a man be of good cheer about his soul, who having cast away the pleasures and ornaments of the body as alien to him and working harm rather than good, has sought after the pleasures of knowledge; and has arrayed the soul, not in some foreign attire, but in her own proper jewels, temperance, and justice, and courage, and nobility, and truth — in these adorned she is ready to go on her journey to the world below, when her hour comes. You, Simmias and Cebes, and all other men, will depart at some time or other. Me already, as a

[1] Socrates is just concluding his discussion of the immortality of the soul.

tragic poet would say, the voice of fate calls. Soon I must drink the poison; and I think that I had better repair to the bath first in order that the women may not have the trouble of washing my body after I am dead."

When he had done speaking, Crito[1] said: "And have you any commands for us, Socrates — anything to say about your children, or any other matter in which we can serve you?"

"Nothing particular, Crito," he replied; "only, as I have always told you, take care of yourselves; that is a service which you may be ever rendering to me and mine and to all of us, whether you promise to do so or not. But if you have no thought for yourselves, and care not to walk according to the rule which I have prescribed for you, not now for the first time, however much you may profess or promise at the moment, it will be of no avail."

"We will do our best," said Crito; "and in what way shall we bury you?"[2]

"In any way that you like; but you must get hold of me, and take care that I do not run away from you." Then he turned to us and added with a smile: "I cannot make Crito believe that I am the same[3] Socrates who has been talking and conducting the argument; he fancies that I am the other Socrates whom he will soon see, a dead body — and he asks, How shall he bury me? And though I have spoken many words in the endeavor to show that when I have drunk the poison I shall leave you and go to the joys of the blessed, — these words of mine, with which I

---

[1] Crito had been a friend of Socrates from boyhood. He was present not as a philosophical follower but as his oldest friend.

[2] I. e. Do you wish to be cremated or buried?

[3] Rather, *this* Socrates.

was comforting you and myself, have had, as I perceive, no effect upon Crito. And therefore I want you to be surety for me to him now, as at the trial he was surety to the judges for me; but let the promise be of another sort; for he was surety for me to the judges that I would remain, and you must be my surety to him that I shall not remain, but go away and depart; and then he will suffer less at my death, and not be grieved when he sees my body being burned or buried. I would not have him sorrow at my hard lot, or say at the burial, 'Thus we lay out Socrates,' or, 'Thus we follow him to the grave,' or 'bury him;' for false words are not only evil in themselves, but they infect the soul with evil. Be of good cheer, then, my dear Crito, and say that you are burying my body only, and do with that whatever is usual, and what you think best."

When he had spoken these words, he arose and went into a chamber to bathe; Crito followed him, and told us to wait. So we remained behind, talking and thinking of the subjects of discourse, and also of the greatness of our sorrow; he was like a father of whom we were being bereaved, and we were about to pass the rest of our lives as orphans. When he had taken the bath his children were brought to him (he had two young sons and an elder one); and the women of his family also came, and he talked to them and gave them a few directions in the presence of Crito; then he dismissed them and returned to us.

Now the hour of sunset was near, for a good deal of time had passed while he was within. When he came out, he sat down with us again after his bath, but not much was said. Soon the jailer, who was the servant of the Eleven,[1] entered and stood by him, saying: "To you, Socrates, whom I know to be the noblest and gentlest and best of all who ever came to this place, I will not impute the angry feelings of other men, who rage and swear at me, when, in obedience to the authorities, I bid them drink the poison — indeed, I am sure that you will not be angry with me; for others, as you are aware, and not I, are to blame. And so fare you well, and try to bear lightly what must needs be — you know my errand." Then bursting into tears, he turned away and went out.

Socrates looked at him and said: "I return your good wishes, and will do as you bid." Then turning to us, he said, "How charming the man is! since I have been in prison he has always been coming to see me, and at times he would talk to me, and was as good to me as could be, and now see how generously he sorrows on my account. We must do as he says, Crito; and therefore let the cup be brought, if the poison is prepared; if not, let the attendant prepare some."

"Yet," said Crito, "the sun is still upon the hilltops,[2] and I know that many a one has taken the draught late, and after the announcement has been made to him, he has eaten and drunk, and enjoyed the society of his beloved; do not hurry — there is time enough."

Socrates said: "Yes, Crito, and they of whom you speak are right in so acting, for they think that they will be gainers by the delay; but I am right in not following their example, for I do not think that I should gain anything by drinking the poison a little

[1] "The Eleven" at Athens were in charge of the prisons and of all executions.
[2] The sentence was that the prisoner should die on that day, and the day ended with sunset.

later ; I should only be ridiculous in my own eyes for sparing and saving a life which is already forfeit. Please then to do as I say, and not to refuse me."

Crito made a sign to the servant, who was standing by; and he went out, and having been absent for some time, returned with the jailer carrying the cup of poison. Socrates said: "You, my good friend, who are experienced in these matters shall give me directions how to proceed." The man answered: "You have only to walk about until your legs are heavy, and then to lie down, and the poison will act." At the same time he handed the cup to Socrates, who in the easiest and gentlest manner, without the least fear or change of color or feature, looking at the man with all his eyes, Echecrates, as his manner was, took the cup and said: "What do you say about making a libation out of this cup to any god? May I, or not?" The man answered: "We only prepare, Socrates, just so much as we deem enough." "I understand," he said, "but I may and must ask the gods to prosper my journey from this to the other world — even so — and so be it according to my prayer." Then raising the cup to his lips, quite readily and cheerfully he drank off the poison. And hitherto most of us had been able to control our sorrow; but now when we saw him drinking, and saw too that he had finished the draught, we could no longer forbear, and in spite of myself my own tears were flowing fast; so that I covered my face and wept, not for him, but at the thought of my own calamity in having to part from such a friend. Nor was I the first; for Crito, when he found himself unable to restrain his tears, had got up, and I followed; and at that moment, Apollodorus, who had been weeping all the time, broke out in a loud and passionate cry which made cowards of us all. Socrates alone retained his calmness. "What is this strange outcry?" he said. "I sent away the women mainly in order that they might not misbehave in this way, for I have been told that a man should die in peace. Be quiet then, and have patience." When we heard his words we were ashamed, and refrained our tears; and he walked about until, as he said, his legs began to fail, and then he lay on his back, according to the directions, and the man who gave him the poison now and then looked at his feet and legs; and after a while he pressed his foot hard and asked him if he could feel; and he said, "No;" and then his leg, and so upwards and upwards, and showed us that he was growing cold and stiff. And he felt them himself, and said: "When the poison reaches the heart, that will be the end." He was beginning to grow cold about the groin, when he uncovered his face, for he had covered himself up, and said — they were his last words — he said: "Crito, I owe a cock to Asclepius;[1] will you remember to pay the debt?" "The debt shall be paid," said Crito; "is there anything else?" There was no answer to this question; but in a minute or two a movement was heard, and the attendants uncovered him; his eyes were set, and Crito closed his eyes and mouth.

Such was the end, Echecrates, of our friend; concerning whom I may truly say, that of all the men of his time whom I have known, he was the wisest and justest and best.

[1] A cock was sacrificed to Asclepius (Aesculapius) on recovery from illness; thus Socrates means, "I have been released from the ills and sufferings of life."

THE SHIP OF STATE

THE TRUE PHILOSOPHER

From the Republic, Book VI. 488-492.

SOCRATES. ADEIMANTUS.

Socrates. Imagine, then, a fleet or a ship in which there is a captain [1] who is taller and stronger than any of the crew, but he is a little deaf and has a similar infirmity in sight, and his knowledge of navigation is not much better. The sailors are quarrelling with one another about the steering — every one is of opinion that he has a right to steer, though he has never learned the art of navigation and cannot tell who taught him or when he learned, and will further assert that it cannot be taught, and they are ready to cut in pieces any one who says the contrary. They throng about the captain, begging and praying him to commit the helm to them; and if at any time they do not prevail, but others are preferred to them, they kill the others or throw them overboard, and having first chained up the noble captain's senses with drink or some narcotic drug, they mutiny and take possession of the ship and make free with the stores; thus, eating and drinking, they proceed on their voyage in such manner as might be expected of them. Him who is their partisan and cleverly aids them in their plot for getting the ship out of the captain's hands

[1] A more accurate translation would be *ship-owner*, who of course has the right to appoint the commander of his ship. He corresponds to the common people of Athens, who have the right to appoint the ruler. The sailors are the politicians. The *steering* is the command of the ship. The philosopher is able to command, but is not skilled in persuading the people to allow him to rule; so he is called a stargazer and visionary by the politicians.

into their own, whether by force or persuasion, they compliment with the name of sailor, pilot, able seaman, and abuse the other sort of man, whom they call a good-for-nothing; but that the true pilot must pay attention to the year and seasons and sky and stars and winds, and whatever else belongs to his art, if he intends to be really qualified for the command of a ship, and that he must and will be the steerer, whether other people like or not — the possibility of this union of authority with the steerer's art has never seriously entered into their thoughts or been made part of their calling. Now in vessels which are in a state of mutiny and by sailors who are mutineers, how will the true pilot be regarded? Will he not be called by them a prater, a star-gazer, a good-for-nothing?

Of course, said Adeimantus.

Then you will hardly need, I said, to hear the interpretation of the figure, which describes the true philosopher in his relation to the State; for you understand already.

Certainly.

Then suppose you now take this parable to the gentleman who is surprised at finding that philosophers have no honor in their cities; explain it to him, and try to convince him that their having honor would be far more extraordinary.

I will.

Say to him, that, in deeming the best votaries of philosophy to be useless to the rest of the world, he is right; but also tell him to attribute their uselessness to the fault of those who will not use them, and not to themselves. The pilot should not humbly beg the sailors to be commanded by him, — that is not the order of nature; neither are "the wise to go to the doors of the rich" — the ingenious author of this saying told a lie — but the truth is, that, when a man is ill, whether he be rich or poor, to the physician he must go, and he who wants to be governed, to him who is able to govern. The ruler who is good for anything ought not to beg his subjects to be ruled by him; although the present governors of mankind are of a different stamp; they may be justly compared to the mutinous sailors, and the true helmsman to those who are called by them good-for-nothings and star-gazers.

Precisely so, he said.

For these reasons, and among men like these, philosophy, the noblest pursuit of all, is not likely to be much esteemed by those of the opposite faction; not that the greatest and most lasting injury is done to her by her opponents, but by her own professing followers, the same of whom you suppose the accuser to say that the greater number of them are arrant rogues, and the best are useless; in which opinion I agreed.

Yes.

And the reason why the good are useless has now been explained?

True.

Then shall we proceed to show that the corruption of the majority is also unavoidable, and that this is not to be laid to the charge of philosophy any more than the other?

By all means.

And let us ask and answer in turn, first going back to the description of the gentle and noble nature. Truth, as you will remember, was his leader, whom he followed always and in all things; failing in this, he was an impostor, and had no part or lot in true philosophy.

Yes, that was said.

Well, and is not this one quality, to mention no others, greatly at variance with present notions of him?

Certainly, he said.

And have we not a right to say in his defence, that the true lover of knowledge is always striving after being — that is his nature; he will not rest in the multiplicity of individuals, which is an appearance only, but will go on — the keen edge will not be blunted, nor the force of his desire abate until he have attained the knowledge of the true nature of every essence by a sympathetic and kindred power in the soul, and by that power drawing near and mingling and becoming incorporate with every being, having begotten mind and truth, he will have knowledge and will live and grow truly, and then, and not till then, will he cease from his travail.

Nothing, he said, can be more just than such a description of him.

And will the love of a lie be any part of a philosopher's nature? Will he not utterly hate a lie?

He will.

And when truth is the captain, we cannot suspect any evil of the band which he leads?

Impossible.

Justice and health of mind will be of the company, and temperance will follow after?

True, he replied.

Neither is there any reason why I should again set in array the philosopher's virtues, as you will doubtless remember that courage, magnificence, apprehension, memory, were his natural gifts. And you objected that, although no one could deny what I then said, still, if you leave words and look at facts, the persons who are thus described are some of them manifestly useless, and the greater number utterly depraved; we were then led to inquire into the grounds of these accusations, and have now arrived at the point of asking why are the majority bad, which question of necessity brought us back to the examination and definition of the true philosopher.

Exactly.

And we have next to consider the corruptions of the philosophic nature, why so many are spoiled and so few escape spoiling, — I am speaking of those who were said to be useless but not wicked, — and when we have done with them, we will speak of the imitators of philosophy, what manner of men are they who aspire after a profession which is above them and of which they are unworthy, and then, by their manifold inconsistencies, bring upon philosophy, and upon all philosophers, that universal reprobation of which we speak.

What are these corruptions? he said.

I will see if I can explain them to you. Every one will admit that a nature having in perfection all the qualities which we required in a philosopher, is a rare plant which is seldom seen among men.

Rare indeed.

And what numberless and powerful causes tend to destroy these rare natures!

What causes?

In the first place, there are their own virtues, their courage, temperance, and the rest of them, every one of which praiseworthy qualities (and this is a most singular circumstance) destroys and distracts from philosophy the soul which is the possessor of them.

That is very singular, he said.

Then there are all the ordinary goods of life — beauty, wealth, strength, rank, and great connections in the State — you understand the sort of things — these also have a corrupting and distracting effect.

I understand; but I should like to know more precisely what you mean about them.

Grasp the truth as a whole, I said, and in the right way; you will then have no difficulty in apprehending the preceding remarks, and they will no longer appear strange to you.

And how am I to do so? he asked.

Why, I said, we know that all plants or seeds, whether vegetable or animal, when they fail to meet with proper nutriment or climate or soil, in proportion to their vigor, are all the more sensitive to the want of a suitable environment, for evil is a greater enemy to what is good than to what is not.

Very true.

There is reason in supposing that the finest natures, when under alien conditions, receive more injury than the inferior, because the contrast is greater.

Certainly.

And may we not say, Adeimantus, that the most gifted minds, when they are ill-educated, become pre-eminently bad? Do not great crimes and the spirit of pure evil spring out of a fulness of nature ruined by education rather than from any inferiority, whereas weak natures are scarcely capable of any very great good or very great evil?

There I think that you are right.

And our philosopher follows the same analogy —

THE SHIP OF STATE

he is like a plant which, having proper nurture, must necessarily grow and mature into all virtue, but, if sown and planted in an alien soil, becomes the most noxious of all weeds, unless he be preserved by some divine power. Do you really think, as people so often say, that our youth are corrupted by Sophists, or that private teachers of the art corrupt them in any degree worth speaking of? Are not the public who say these things the greatest of all Sophists? And do they not educate to perfection young and old, men and women alike, and fashion them after their own hearts?

When is this accomplished? he said.

When they meet together, and the world sits down at an assembly, or in a court of law, or in a theatre, or a camp, or in any other popular resort, and there is a great uproar, and they praise some things which are being said or done, and blame other things, equally exaggerating both, shouting and clapping their hands, and the echo of the rocks [1] and the place in which they are assembled redoubles the sound of the praise or blame — at such a time will not a young man's heart, as they say, leap within him? Will any private training enable him to stand firm against the overwhelming flood of popular opinion? or, will he be carried away by the stream? Will he not have the notions of good and evil which the public in general have — he will do as they do, and as they are, such will he be?

Yes, Socrates, necessity will compel him.

And yet, I said, there is a still greater necessity, which has not been mentioned.

---

[1] The great theatre at Athens was at the foot of the Acropolis, on the southeastern slope.

What is that?

The gentle force of attainder or confiscation, or death, which, as you are aware, these new Sophists and educators, who are the public, apply when their words are powerless.

Indeed they do; and in right good earnest.

Now what opinion of any other Sophist, or of any private person, can be expected to overcome in such an unequal contest?

THE ALLEGORY OF THE CAVE
From the Republic, Book VII. 514–519.
SOCRATES. GLAUCON.

Socrates. And now, I said, let me show in a figure how far our nature is enlightened or unenlightened: Behold human beings living in an underground den, which has a mouth open towards the light and reaching all along the den; here they have been from their childhood, and have their legs and necks chained so that they cannot move, and can only see before them, being prevented by the chains from turning round their heads. Above and behind them a fire is blazing at a distance, and between the fire and the prisoners there is a raised way; and you will see, if you look, a low wall built along the way, like the screen which marionette players have in front of them, over which they show the puppets.

I see.

And do you see, I said, men passing along the wall, carrying all sorts of vessels, and statues [1] and figures of animals made of wood and stone and various ma-

---

[1] Thus the prisoners see only shadows cast by images of real things, — not even shadows cast by real things themselves.

terials, which appear *over* the wall? Some of them are talking, others silent.

You have shown me a strange image, and they are strange prisoners.

Like ourselves, I replied; and they see only their own shadows, or the shadows of one another, which the fire throws on the opposite wall of the cave?

True, he said; how could they see anything but the shadows if they were never allowed to move their heads?

And of the objects which are being carried in like manner they would only see the shadows?

Yes, he said.

And if they were able to converse with one another, would they not suppose that they were naming what was actually before them?

Very true.

And suppose further that the prison had an echo which came from the other side, would they not be sure to fancy when one of the passers-by spoke that the voice which they heard came from the passing shadow?

No question, he replied.

To them, I said, the truth would be literally nothing but the shadows of the images.

That is certain.

And now look again, and see what will naturally follow if the prisoners are released and disabused of their error. At first, when any one of them is liberated and compelled suddenly to stand up and turn his neck round and walk and look towards the light, he will suffer sharp pains; the glare will distress him, and he will be unable to see the realities of which in his former state he had seen the shadows; and then conceive some one saying to him that what he saw before was an illusion, but that now, when he is approaching nearer to being and his eye is turned towards more real existence, he has a clearer vision, — what will be his reply? And you may further imagine that his instructor is pointing to the objects as they pass and requiring him to name them, — will he not be perplexed? Will he not fancy that the shadows which he formerly saw are truer than the objects which are now shown to him?

Far truer.

And if he is compelled to look straight at the light, will he not have a pain in his eyes which will make him turn away to take refuge in the objects of vision which he can see, and which he will conceive to be in reality clearer than the things which are now being shown to him?

True, he said.

And suppose once more, that he is reluctantly dragged up a steep and rugged ascent, and held fast until he is forced into the presence of the sun himself, is he not likely to be pained and irritated? When he approaches the light his eyes will be dazzled, and he will not be able to see anything at all of what are now called realities.

Not all in a moment, he said.

He will require to grow accustomed to the sight of the upper world. And first he will see the shadows best, next the reflections of men and other objects in the water, and then the objects themselves; then he will gaze upon the light of the moon and the stars and the spangled heaven; and he will see the sky and the stars by night better than the sun or the light of the sun by day?

Certainly.

Last of all he will be able to see the sun, and not mere reflections of him in the water, but he will see him in his own proper place, and not in another; and he will contemplate him as he is.

Certainly.

He will then proceed to argue that this is he who gives the season and the years, and is the guardian of all that is in the visible world, and in a certain way the cause of all things which he and his fellows have been accustomed to behold?

Clearly, he said, he would first see the sun and then reason about him.

And when he remembered his old habitation, and the wisdom of the den and his fellow-prisoners, do you not suppose that he would felicitate himself on the change, and pity them?

Certainly, he would.

And if they were in the habit of conferring honors among themselves on those who were quickest to observe the passing shadows and to remark which of them went before, and which followed after, and which were together; and who were therefore best able to draw conclusions as to the future, do you think that he would care for such honors and glories, or envy the possessors of them? Would he not say with Homer, "Better to be the poor servant of a poor master," and to endure anything, rather than think as they do and live after their manner.

Yes, he said, I think that he would rather suffer anything than entertain these false notions and live in this miserable manner.

Imagine once more, I said, such an one coming suddenly out of the sun to be replaced in his old situation; would he not be certain to have his eyes full of darkness?

To be sure, he said.

And if there were a contest, and he had to compete in measuring the shadows with the prisoners who had never moved out of the den, while his sight was still weak, and before his eyes had become steady (and the time which would be needed to acquire this new habit of sight might be very considerable), would he not be ridiculous? Men would say of him that up he went and down he came without his eyes; and that it was better not even to think of ascending; and if any one tried to loose another and lead him up to the light, let them only catch the offender and they would put him to death.

No question, he said.

This entire allegory, I said, you may now append, dear Glaucon, to the previous argument; the prison-house is the world of sight, the light of the fire is the sun, and you will not misapprehend me if you interpret the journey upwards to be the ascent of the soul into the intellectual world according to my poor belief, which, at your desire, I have expressed — whether rightly or wrongly God knows. But, whether true or false, my opinion is that in the world of knowledge the idea of good appears last of all, and is seen only with an effort; and, when seen, is also inferred to be the universal author of all things beautiful and right — parent of light and of the lord of light in this visible world, and the immediate source of reason and truth in the intellectual; and that this is the power upon which he who would act rationally either in public or private life must have his eye fixed.

I agree, he said, as far as I am able to understand you.

Moreover, I said, you must not wonder that those who attain to this beatific vision are unwilling to descend to human affairs; for their souls are ever hastening into the upper world where they desire to dwell; which desire of theirs is very natural, if our allegory may be trusted.

Yes, very natural.

And is there anything surprising in one who passes from divine contemplations to the evil state of man, misbehaving himself in a ridiculous manner; if, while his eyes are blinking and before he has become accustomed to the surrounding darkness, he is compelled to fight in courts of law, or in other places, about the images or shadows of images of justice, and is endeavoring to meet the conceptions of those who have never yet seen absolute justice?

Anything but surprising, he replied.

Any one who has common sense will remember that the bewilderments of the eyes are of two kinds, and arise from two causes, either from coming out of the light or from going into the light, which is true of the mind's eye, quite as much as of the bodily eye; and he who remembers this when he sees any one whose vision is perplexed and weak, will not be too ready to laugh; he will first ask whether that soul of man has come out of the brighter life, and is unable to see because unaccustomed to the dark, or having turned from darkness to the day is dazzled by excess of light. And he will count the one happy in his condition and state of being, and he will pity the other; or, if he have a mind to laugh at the soul which comes from below into the light, there will be more reason in this than in the laugh which greets him who returns from above out of the light into the den.

That, he said, is a very just distinction.

But then, if I am right, certain professors of education must be wrong when they say that they can put a knowledge into the soul which was not there before, like sight into blind eyes.

They undoubtedly say this, he replied.

Whereas, our argument shows that the power and capacity of learning exists in the soul already; and that just as the eye was unable to turn from darkness to light without the whole body, so too the instrument of knowledge can only by the movement of the whole soul be turned from the world of becoming into that of being, and learn by degrees to endure the sight of being, and of the brightest and best of being, or in other words, of the good.

Very true.

And must there not be some art which will effect conversion in the easiest and quickest manner; not implanting the faculty of sight, for that exists already, but has been turned in the wrong direction, and is looking away from the truth?

Yes, he said, such an art may be presumed.

And whereas the other so-called virtues of the soul seem to be akin to bodily qualities, for even when they are not originally innate they can be implanted later by habit and exercise, the virtue of wisdom more than anything else contains a divine element which always remains, and by this conversion is rendered useful and profitable; or on the other hand, hurtful and useless. Did you never observe the narrow intelligence flashing from the keen eye of a clever rogue — how eager he is, how clearly his paltry soul sees the way to his end; he is the reverse of blind, but his keen eyesight is forced into the service of evil, and he is mischievous in proportion to his cleverness?

Very true, he said.

But what if there had been a circumcision of such natures in the days of their youth; and they had been severed from those sensual pleasures, such as eating and drinking, which, like leaden weights, were attached to them at their birth,[1] and which drag them down and turn the vision of their souls upon the things that are below — if, I say, they had been released from these impediments and turned in the opposite direction, the very same faculty in them would have seen the truth as keenly as they see what their eyes are turned to now.

Very likely.

Yes, I said; and there is another thing which is likely, or rather a necessary inference from what has preceded, — that neither the uneducated and uninformed of the truth, nor yet those who never make an end of their education, will be able ministers of State; not the former, because they have no single aim of duty which is the rule of all their actions, private as well as public; nor the latter, because they will not act at all except upon compulsion, fancying that they are already dwelling apart in the islands of the blest.

Very true, he replied.

---

[1] Plato means: "If the soul should be freed from the tendencies to the world of *change* (the world of 'becoming') which have become attached to the soul by the pleasures of eating and drinking, and hold it down like leaden weights," etc.

Then, I said, the business of us who are the founders of the State will be to compel the best minds to attain that knowledge which we have already shown to be the greatest of all — they must continue to ascend until they arrive at the good; but when they have ascended and seen enough we must not allow them to do as they do now.

What do you mean?

I mean that they remain in the upper world; but this must not be allowed; they must be made to descend again among the prisoners in the den, and partake of their labors and honors, whether they are worth having or not.

But is not this unjust? he said; ought we to give them a worse life, when they might have a better?

You have again forgotten, my friend, I said, the intention of the legislator, who did not aim at making any one class in the State happy above the rest; the happiness was to be in the whole State, and he held the citizens together by persuasion and necessity, making them benefactors of the State, and therefore benefactors of one another; to this end he created them, not to please themselves, but to be his instruments in binding up the State.

DEMOSTHENES

DEMOSTHENES, the world's greatest orator, was born near Athens, 384 B. C., probably in the same year as the philosopher Aristotle, and two years before the birth of Philip of Macedon, against whom many of his most important political measures were directed. He died in 322 B. C., within a month or two of Aristotle and a little more than a year after the death of Philip's son, Alexander the Great. When he was seven years of age his father died, leaving his son and a still younger daughter, with considerable property, to the care of guardians, who were unfaithful and seem not only to have neglected the children's interests, but also to have taken wrongful possession of much of their property. Since Athenian law required that each suitor at law should plead his own cause before the court, the young Demosthenes was forced to study and practice rhetoric and law, in order to secure his rights from his guardians. His success as an orator in these suits seems to have turned the current of his life, and he appeared as a statesman before the great assembly of the Athenian people when he was thirty years of age.

In the conflict between free Greece and the king of Macedon, Demosthenes was on the losing side, the side of the lighter battalions, and the Macedonians prevailed. Greece had been exhausted by the civil wars, which had continued for nearly a century, in which its best blood had been spilt. The younger generation was thoroughly demoralized. Union against the Persian invaders, near the opening of the fifth century, had been glorious, but difficult: now effective union against the Macedonians was impossible.

The chief Athenian leader of the pro-Macedonian party, Demosthenes' ablest rival and opponent, was Aeschines. In the spring of 336 B. C., a certain Ctesiphon had proposed that a golden crown be awarded to Demosthenes for his public services, and that this crown be proclaimed in the theatre, at the great Dionysiac festival. Aeschines attacked this measure as unconstitutional, and prosecuted Ctesiphon, in whose defence, as well as in behalf of his own fame, Demosthenes delivered his *Oration on the Crown*, from which these extracts are taken, — reviewing his whole public life and policy. The case came to trial six years after the accusation, in August 330 B. C., before a court of at least five hundred citizens. Many other Athenians, and Greeks from other cities, were present, and the orator often speaks as if he were addressing the whole body of his fellow citizens. Aeschines received less than one fifth of the votes of the court, and withdrew from Athens in humiliation.

The translation here used is that of the English statesman, Lord Brougham, — himself an orator of no mean power, but not wholly successful as a translator.

ORATION ON THE CROWN

§§ 42–53.

I NOW return to the proof that the corruption and profligacy of these men was the cause of our present condition.

When you were circumvented by Philip through those hirelings of his whom you had sent as ambassadors, and who never made you any true report, and when the miserable Phocians were also circumvented, and had their cities razed to the ground,[1] what followed? The despicable Thessalians and the senseless

[1] In 346 B. C.

Thebans looked upon Philip as their friend, benefactor, savior; he was all in all with them: if any one thought of saying anything to the contrary, not a word would they hear. You, on the other hand, though these transactions awakened your suspicions, and caused some impatience, still kept the peace (nor indeed could you help it, standing single as you did); and the other Greeks, as well as you, cheated and deluded in their hopes, strictly observed the peace, though already in some sort attacked by Philip. For when he was striding all around, subduing the Illyrians and Triballians,[1] and even some of the Greek states; when he was acquiring large accessions to his power; and when some persons under cover of the peace were proceeding from different cities on a visit to be corrupted by him, Aeschines among the rest,— then I maintain that all the powers against whom he was making such preparations were actually attacked. If they did not themselves perceive it, that is another thing, and no concern of mine, for I foretold it, and testified to it both here to you, and wherever else I was sent as ambassador. But all the states were infatuated, and while the ministers and magistrates of some were corrupted and bought with a price, in others neither individuals nor the people showed any provident circumspection, but all were taken with the ephemeral bait of indolence and ease, and all the states became so stricken with infatuation as to believe that nothing could befall themselves, but that they could work out their own safety by other people's perils. It thus came to pass, as I conceive, that the people lost their independence through extreme and inopportune sloth, while the leading men,

[1] A Thracian people; see page 276. In 345 B. C.

and they who designed to sell everything but themselves, were found to have sold themselves first of all. Instead of friends and guests, names which they prostituted for lucre of gain, they must now be content to hear themselves called parasites, persons accursed, and whatever else fits them best. And justly! For no one, Athenians, when he bribes ever looks to the benefit of the traitor; nor, when once possessed of the bribe-worthy service, do we ever after trust the traitor. If we did, nothing could be more fortunate than the traitor's position. But it is not so by any means. How should it be? It is quite the reverse. No sooner has an ambitious usurper accomplished his purpose than he becomes master of those who have sold their country; and, thoroughly acquainted with their villainy, he detests them, and distrusts them, and loads them with insults. For, observe — if the events themselves are past and gone by, yet the opportunity of reflecting upon them is ever present to the wise. Time was that Philip called Lasthenes his friend, until he had betrayed Olynthus; time was that he thus termed Timolaus, till he had overthrown Thebes; and Eudicus and Simus, of Larissa, until they had surrendered Thessaly to his arms. Then, when they were chased away, and covered with indignities, and there was no maltreatment that they had not to endure, the whole habitable world was filled with traitors. How fared Aristratus, in Sicyon? How Perilaus, at Megara? Are they not doomed to utter execration? From whence any one may clearly perceive that whoso most stoutly defends his country, and most vehemently resists such men as those, supplies to you traitors and mercenaries, Aeschines, the means of being bribed; and it is because such patriots are numerous and oppose your councils that you can receive your hire in safety; for as far as depended on yourselves you must long since have perished.

And now, although I have much more to say touching these transactions, yet I rather think I have dwelt too long upon them. But he is to blame for it; his having poured out in our faces the crapulous remains of his own profligacy and crimes made it indispensably necessary that I should justify myself in the eyes of persons who have been born since those transactions. Perhaps, however, you are fatigued with the subject, as before I had spoken a word you were aware of his mercenary conduct. That, indeed, he terms friendship and hospitality; and in one part of his speech he described me as having considered Alexander's hospitality a shame. I speak of Alexander's hospitality to you! Whence did you derive it, or how earn it? Nor Philip's guest, nor Alexander's friend should I ever think of calling you; I am not so senseless; unless, indeed, we are to call reapers and others who work for hire the friends and guests of those who pay them wages. But it is not so; nothing of the kind! Why should it be? Quite the reverse. But I and all here present call you the hireling, formerly of Philip, now of Alexander. If you doubt it, ask them. But I had rather do that for you. Men of Athens! whether do you consider Aeschines as the hireling or the guest of Alexander? — Do you hear what they say? — I now then proceed to answer this charge and to explain my conduct, in order that Aeschines, though he is well aware of the whole, may also hear my own statement of my just title, both to the honors decreed, and to far greater than these.

§§ 168–179.

Having thus set the different states at variance with each other by the agency of these men,[1] Philip, elated with those decrees and those answers, advanced with his army and occupied Elatea, as if assured that, come what might, you and the Thebans never would agree. The consternation into which the city was instantly thrown, you all know; but it may be as well you should hear the most important particulars. It was evening. A messenger came to acquaint the Prytanes that Elatea was taken; whereupon some of them, instantly starting from the table at which they were sitting, cleared the booths in the Forum, and set fire to their wicker coverings; others summoned the Generals of the State, and ordered the alarum to be sounded. The city was filled with consternation. When the next day broke, the Prytanes[2] convoked the Senate in the Senate House; you repaired to your own assembly, and before they[3] could adopt any measure, or even enter upon their deliberations, the whole people had seated themselves upon the hill. And now, when the Senators came forth, and the Prytanes announced the intelligence, and presented the bearer of it, and he had himself related it, the herald made proclamation, If any one desired to be

[1] The orator has told the story of the opening of this war. The congress of the Amphictyonic Council, which met at Delphi, had been persuaded by Aeschines to adopt measures which led to a conflict and then to a war which Philip was invited to lead on behalf of the Amphictyons. But, entering Greece (in the autumn of 339 B. C.), Philip neglected the work to which he was summoned, and seized Elatea, a Phocian town of great military importance.

[2] The Prytanes were a sort of executive committee of the Senate, serving for a month, and continually in session.

[3] I. e., the Senate, who had the right of initiative.

heard? No man stood forward. He repeated the proclamation again and again. No person rose the more, though all the Generals and all the Orators were present, and though the cries of our common country were heard, imploring some one to lift his voice and save her. For the voice of the herald, in the solemn form ordained by law, may well be deemed the general voice of the country. And truly, if the only qualification to come forward then had been an anxiety for the public safety, all of you, and every other Athenian too, would have risen and ascended the Bema;[1] for I am well aware that all were anxious to save the State. If wealth had been the qualification, we might have had the three hundred; if both wealth and patriotism, those who, in the sequel, became such ample voluntary contributors. But that was, manifestly, the crisis, — that the day not merely for a wealthy and patriotic individual to bear a part, but for one who had, from the very first, kept pace with the progress of affairs, and happily penetrated the motives of the conduct and the designs of Philip. For a man unacquainted with these — one who had not anxiously watched them from their first appearance — might be ever so rich and ever so zealous, and yet be none the more likely to descry the best course, and to give you the soundest counsel. In that day, then, such a man was I, — and standing up, I spoke to you, what you must once more attentively listen to, with two views: first, that you may perceive how, alone, of all the Orators and Statesmen, I did not abandon the post of Patriotism in the hour of peril, but, both by my words and my actions, discharged my duty to you in the last emergency;

[1] The *tribune*, the standing-place of the speaker.

next, that, at the expense of a little time, you may acquire a fuller insight into our whole polity for the future.

I conceived, then (I said), that those who were in so great a consternation at the idea of the Thebans being friendly to Philip were unacquainted with the real state of affairs; for I knew full well that, were this apprehension well founded, we should not now hear of him being in Elatea, but upon our own frontiers; I knew for certain, however, that he was come to get matters in Thebes ready for him. But how the case stands, said I, hear now from me. All those Thebans whom he has been able either to bribe by gold or delude by craft, he has at his command; but those who, from the first, have resisted him, and are now opposing him, he can in no way move. What, then, does he now meditate, and with what view has he seized on Elatea? It is that, displaying his forces in our neighborhood, and marching up his troops, he may at once elevate and inspirit his friends, and strike terror into his adversaries, and that they, being overawed, may be induced, or may be compelled, to make concessions which they now refuse. If then, I said, we are, in these circumstances, resolved to bear in mind whatever wrongs the Thebans may have done us aforetime, and to distrust them as taking part with our enemies, we shall in the first place be doing the very thing that Philip is praying for, and next, I fear me lest they who now are his adversaries may join him, and, all Philippizing after the same fashion, both Thebans and Philip may invade Attica. But if you will be advised by me, and consider well what I am about to state instead of quarrelling with it, then it may come to pass, I conceive, both that you should approve of my councils, and that I should dispel the dangers which surround the country. What, then, do I recommend? First of all, to dissipate the prevailing alarm; then to change its direction, and all be alarmed about the Thebans, for they are far nearer a catastrophe than we, and the peril is much closer upon them than upon us; and then, that the young men and the cavalry marching upon Eleusis,[1] should prove to all Greece that you are in arms, and that your partisans at Thebes may have an equal power to maintain their cause when they find you are as ready and as willing to succor the asserters of liberty, if attacked, as Philip was to aid with his forces in Elatea those who were selling their country to him. Next, I require that the ten Ambassadors be chosen by vote, and that they, with the Commanders, have authority to determine the time both of their arrival and of their setting out. But when the Ambassadors come to Thebes, how do I recommend that they should conduct the affair? Give me now your whole attention. Require nothing of the Thebans (for at this time it would be shameful), but promise whatever succor they demand, they being in the most extreme danger, and we better able than they to foresee the result; so that, if they agree with us and take our advice, we shall both carry our point and act upon a plan worthy of the State; but if we should happen to fail in this object, then they will have themselves to blame for their errors, and by us nothing base, nothing unworthy, will have been done.

Having said thus much, and more to the like effect, I sat down. All assenting, no one saying one word to

[1] I. e., to Eleusis. Eleusis is about fifteen miles from Athens, on the bay of Salamis, and on one of the better routes to Thebes.

the contrary, not only did I make this speech, but I propounded a decree; not only did I propound a decree, but I went ambassador; not only went ambassador, but I persuaded the Thebans; and from the first, throughout the whole transaction, down to the end, I persevered, and gave myself up, in your service, without any reserve, to confront the perils that surrounded the country.

§§ 297–305

Then you ask what is my title to public honors? I will tell you. It is, that while the statesmen of Greece, beginning with yourself, Aeschines, were all corrupted — first by Philip and then by Alexander, — over me neither opportunity, nor fair speeches, nor lavish promises, nor hopes, nor fears, nor favors, nor any other earthly consideration ever prevailed, seducing or driving me to betray in any one particular what I deemed the rights and the interests of my country. Never did I, like you, and such as you, incline my councils as if weighed in a balance towards the side that paid the best; but my whole conduct was formed by a righteous, and just, and incorruptible soul; and having borne the most forward part among the men of my times in administering the mightiest affairs, my whole policy has ever been sound and honest and open. For these things I claim to be honored.

But this repair of the walls and the fosses which you revile, I deem to merit favor and commendation: wherefore should I not? Yet I certainly place this far below my administration of public affairs. For I have not fortified Athens with stone walls and tiled roofs:[1] no, not I! Neither is it on deeds like these that I plume myself. But would you justly estimate my outworks, you will find armaments and cities, and settlements, and harbors, and fleets, and cavalry, and armies raised to defend us: — these are the defences that I drew around Attica, as far as human prudence could defend her, and with such outworks as these I fortified the country at large, not the mere circuit of the arsenal[2] and the city! Nor was it I that succumbed to Philip's policy and his arms; very far otherwise! but the captains and the forces of your allies yielded to his fortune. What are the proofs of it? They are manifest and plain, and you shall see them. For what was the part of a patriotic citizen? What the part of him who would serve his country with all earnestness, and zeal, and honesty of purpose? Was it not to cover Attica, on the seaboard with Euboea — inland with Boeotia — on Peloponnesus, with the adjoining territories? Was it not to provide for making the corn trade secure, that every coast our ships sailed along till they reached the Piraeus might be friendly to us? Was it not to save some points of our dominion, such as Proconnesus, the Chersonese, Tenedos, by dispatching succors, and making the necessary statements, and proposing the fit decrees? Was it not to secure from the first the coöperation and alliance of other states, Byzantium, Abydos, Euboea? Was it not to wrest from the enemy his principal forces? Was it not to supply what this country most wanted? Then all these things were effected by my

[1] I. e., the defences which Demosthenes threw around Athens, and for which he claims glory, were not mere walls of stone or brick, — though as commissioner he had erected such walls for the city.

[2] The Piraeus, the chief harbor of Athens, about five miles from the City.

Decrees, and my measures. All these things, Athenians, if any one chooses to examine the matter without prejudice, he will find both correctly advised by me, and executed with perfect integrity; and that no opportunity was lost by me, through carelessness, or through ignorance, or through treachery, nor anything neglected which it could fall within the power and the wisdom of one man to do. But if the favor of some Deity, or of Fortune, or the remissness of commanders, or the wickedness of traitors like you, Aeschines, in different states, or if all these causes together have embarrassed our whole affairs, and brought them to ruin — wherein has Demosthenes been to blame? But if there had been found in any [1] Greek State one man such as I have been in my sphere among you, rather, if Thessaly had only possessed a single man, and if Arcadia had possessed any one of the same principles with me, none of all the Greeks, whether within Thermopylae [2] or without, would have been suffering their present miseries; but all remaining free, and independent, and secure from alarm, would in perfect tranquillity and prosperity have dwelt in their native land, rendering thanks to you and the rest of the Athenian people for so many and such signal blessings conferred on them through me. That you may perceive how much smaller my words are than my works, through fear of misconstruction, read [3] now and recite the account of the succors sent in pursuance of my decrees.

[1] Rather, in *each*.
[2] This famous pass led from Thessaly into Locris. "Within Thermopylae" thus means "south of Thessaly."
[3] This direction is addressed to the clerk of the court.

THEOCRITUS

THEOCRITUS was the greatest of all pastoral or bucolic poets, and was the real founder of this branch of literature, though he lived in the midst of the formal conventional life of courts and students. He was born about 315 B. C. in Sicily, the land of flocks and herds, but his early training was under Philetas, a poet of the island Cos, near the southwest corner of Asia Minor. Before 280 he returned to Sicily, and sought the favor of Hiero the younger, the king of Syracuse, by a poem which was imitated by Spenser in his *Shepherd's Calendar, October*. In this he asks, "Who of all those who dwell under the bright Dawn will open his doors and receive our Graces to his home?" Failing to secure Hiero as his patron, he turned to Ptolemy Philadelphus at Alexandria, the enlightened ruler of Egypt, who had been a pupil of Philetas not long before him. Two of the extant idyls are in honor of Ptolemy, and another clearly was composed to please Ptolemy's queen and sister, Arsinoë. Of the thirty poems which are extant under the name of Theocritus, only one third are strictly bucolic. Two are love songs. Three are *mimes* or little dramas, of which no other specimens were known to the modern world until in 1891 some of the mimes of Herodas (or Herondas) were published from a papyrus roll found in a tomb in Egypt. Two of the idyls are *encomia*, one is a hymn to the Dioscuri, another is a hymn to Dionysus, two are little epic scenes, one is a picture of the life of fishermen, eight are generally rejected or are at least of suspected authenticity. Of twenty-six epigrams, eight are generally accepted as from Theocritus. He seems to have died at Alexandria.

IDYL I. THE DEATH OF DAPHNIS.

Thyrsis. A Goatherd.

Thyrsis. Sweet are the whispers of yon pine that makes
Low music o'er the spring, and, Goatherd, sweet
Thy piping; second thou to Pan alone.
Is his the hornèd ram? then thine the goat.
Is his the goat? to thee shall fall the kid; 5
And toothsome is the flesh of unmilked kids.
    Goatherd. Shepherd, thy lay is as the noise of streams
Falling and falling aye from yon tall crag.
If for their meed the muses claim the ewe,
Be thine the stall-fed lamb; or if they choose 10
The lamb, take thou the scarce less-valued ewe.
    Thyrsis. Pray, by the nymphs, pray, Goatherd, seat thee here
Against this hill-slope in the tamarisk shade,
And pipe me somewhat, while I guard my goats.
    Goatherd. I durst not, shepherd, O I durst not pipe
At noontide; fearing Pan, who at that hour 16
Rests from the toils of hunting. Harsh is he;
Wrath at his nostrils aye sits sentinel.
But, Thyrsis, thou canst sing of Daphnis' woes;
High is thy name for woodland minstrelsy: 20
Then rest we in the shadow of the elm
Fronting Priapus and the Fountain-nymphs.[1]
There, where the oaks are and the shepherd's seat,
Sing as thou sang'st erewhile, when matched with him

---

[1] That is the rude wooden statues of these garden and field divinities.

IDYL I. THE DEATH OF DAPHNIS

Of Libya, Chromis; and I'll give thee, first, 25
To milk, ay thrice, a goat — she suckles twins,
Yet ne'ertheless can fill two milk pails full;—
Next, a deep drinking-cup, with sweet wax scoured,
Two-handled, newly-carven, smacking yet
O' the chisel. Ivy reaches up and climbs 30
About its lip, gilt here and there with sprays
Of woodbine, that enwreathed about it flaunts
Her saffron fruitage. Framed therein appears
A damsel ('t is a miracle of art)
In robe and snood: and suitors at her side 35
With locks fair-flowing, on her right and left,
Battle with words, that fail to reach her heart.
She, laughing, glances now on this, flings now
Her chance regard on that; they, all for love
Wearied and eye-swoln, find their labor lost. 40
Carven elsewhere an ancient fisher stands
On the rough rocks: thereto the old man with pains
Drags his great casting-net, as one that toils
Full stoutly: every fibre of his frame
Seems fishing; so about the gray-beard's neck 45
(In might a youngster yet) the sinews swell.
Hard by that wave-beat sire a vineyard bends
Beneath its graceful load of burnished grapes;
A boy sits on the rude fence watching them.
Near him two foxes; down the rows of grapes 50
One ranging steals its ripest; one assails
With wiles the poor lad's scrip, to leave him soon
Stranded and supperless. He plaits meanwhile
With ears of corn a right fine cricket-trap,
And fits it on a rush: for vines, for scrip, 55
Little he cares, enamored of his toy.

The cup is hung all round with lissom briar,
Triumph of Aeolian art, a wondrous sight,

It was a ferryman's of Calydon:
A goat it cost me, and a great white cheese. 60
Yet ne'er my lips came near it, virgin still
It stands.   And welcome to such boon art thou,
If for my sake thou 'lt sing that lay of lays.
I jest not: up, lad, sing: no songs thou 'lt own
In the dim land where all things are forgot. 65
    Thyrsis (sings). Begin, sweet Maids, begin the woodland song.
The voice of Thyrsis, Aetna's Thyrsis I.
Where were ye, Nymphs, oh where, while Daphnis pined?[1]
In fair Penëus' or in Pindus' glens?
For great Anapus'[2] stream was not your haunt, 70
Nor Aetna's cliff, nor Acis' sacred rill.
    (*Begin, sweet Maids, begin the woodland song.*)
O'er him the wolves, the jackals howled o'er him;
The lion in the oak-copse mourned his death.
    (*Begin, sweet Maids, begin the woodland song.*) 75
The kine and oxen stood around his feet,
The heifers and the calves wailed all for him.
    (*Begin, sweet Maids, begin the woodland song.*)
First from the mountain Hermes came, and said,
"Daphnis, who frets thee?   Lad, whom lov'st thou so?" 80
    (*Begin, sweet Maids, begin the woodland song.*)
Came herdsmen, shepherds came, and goatherds came;
All asked what ailed the lad.   Priapus came
And said, "Why pine, poor Daphnis, while the maid
Foots it round every pool and every grove? 85
    (*Begin, sweet Maids, begin the woodland song.*)
"O lack-love and perverse, in quest of thee;

[1] Milton had this in mind in his *Lycidas*, and Shelley in his *Adonais*.
[2] The Anapus is the small river near Syracuse.

IDYL I. THE DEATH OF DAPHNIS

Herdsman in name, but goatherd rightlier called.
With eyes that yearn the goatherd marks his kids
Run riot, for he fain would frisk as they: 90
 (Begin, sweet Maids, begin the woodland song.)
"With eyes that yearn dost thou too mark the laugh
Of maidens, for thou may'st not share their glee."
Still naught the herdsman said: he drained alone
His bitter potion, till the fatal end. 95
 (Begin, sweet Maids, begin the woodland song.)
Came Aphrodité, smiles on her sweet face,
False smiles, for heavy was her heart, and spake:
"So, Daphnis, thou must try a fall with Love!
But stalwart Love hath won the fall of thee." 100
 (Begin, sweet Maids, begin the woodland song.) [1]
Then "Ruthless Aphrodité," Daphne said,
"Accursed Aphrodité, foe to man,
Say'st thou my hour is come, my sun hath set?
Dead as alive, shall Daphnis work Love woe." 105
 (Begin, sweet Maids, begin the woodland song.)
"Fly to Mount Ida, where the swain (men say)
And Aphrodité — to Anchises fly:
There are oak-forests; here but galingale,
And bees that make a music round the hives. 110
 (Begin, sweet Maids, begin the woodland song.)
"Adonis owed his bloom to tending flocks
And smiting hares, and bringing wild beasts down.
 (Begin, sweet Maids, begin the woodland song.)
"Face once more Diomed:[2] tell him 'I have slain 115
The herdsman Daphnis; now I challenge thee.'
 (Begin, sweet Maids, begin the woodland song.)

---

[1] Anchises, the Trojan, won the love of Aphrodite (Venus), who bore to him Aeneas, who was the founder of the Roman people.

[2] In the *Iliad*, Diomed wounds Aphrodite on the field of battle, and she flees in distress. The injunction here is ironical.

"Farewell, wolf, jackal, mountain-prisoned bear!
Ye 'll see no more by grove or glade or glen
Your herdsman Daphnis! Arethuse, farewell,   120
And the bright streams that pour down Thymbris' side.
  (*Begin, sweet Maids, begin the woodland song.*)
"I am that Daphnis, who lead here my kine,
Bring here to drink my oxen and my calves.
  (*Begin, sweet Maids, begin the woodland song.*) 125
"Pan, Pan, O whether great Lyceum's crags
Thou haunt'st to-day, or mightier Maenalus,
Come to the Sicel isle! Abandon now [1]
Rhium and Helicé, and the mountain-cairn
(That e'en gods cherish) of Lycaon's son!   130
  (*Forget, sweet Maids, forget your woodland song.*)
"Come, king of song, o'er this my pipe, compact
With wax and honey-breathing, arch thy lip:
For surely I am torn from life by Love.
  (*Forget, sweet Maids, forget your woodland song.*)
"From thicket now and thorn let violets spring,   135
Now let white lilies drape the juniper,
And pines grow figs, and nature all go wrong:
For Daphnis dies. Let deer pursue the hounds,
And mountain owls out-sing the nightingale."   140
  (*Forget, sweet Maids, forget your woodland song.*)
So spake he, and he never spake again.
Fair Aphrodité would have raised his head,
But all his thread was spun. So down the stream [2]
Went Daphnis: closed the waters o'er a head   145
Dear to the Nine,[3] of nymphs not unbeloved.
  Now give me goat and cup, that I may milk
The one and pour the other to the Muse.
Fare ye well, Muses, o'er and o'er farewell!
I 'll sing strains lovelier yet in days to be.   150

[1] Leave Arcadia.   [2] The Styx.   [3] Muses.

IDYL VII. HARVEST HOME 435

Goatherd. Thyrsis, let honey and the honeycomb
Fill thy sweet mouth, and figs of Aegilus:
For ne'er cicala [1] trilled so sweet a song.
Here is the cup: mark, friend, how sweet it smells:
The Hours,[2] thou 'lt say, have washed it in their
    well.   155
Hither, Cissaetha! [3]   There, go milk her! Kids,
Be steady, or your pranks will rouse the ram.
                    Translated by Charles Stuart Calverley.

IDYL VII. HARVEST HOME.

ONCE on a time did Eucritus and I [4]
(With us Amyntas) to the riverside
Steal from the city. For Lycopeus' sons
Were that day busy with the harvest-home, —
Antigenes and Phrasidemus, sprung   5
(If aught thou holdest by the good old names)
By Clytia from great Chalcon — him who erst
Planted one stalwart knee against the rock,
And lo, beneath his foot Buriné's rill
Brake forth, and at its side poplar and elm   10
Showed aisles of pleasant shadow, greenly roofed
By tufted leaves. Scarce midway were we now,
Nor yet descried the tomb of Brasilas:
When, thanks be to the Muses, there drew near
A wayfarer from Crete, young Lycidas.[5]   15
The horn'd herd was his care; a glance might tell
So much: for every inch a herdsman he.

[1] The shrill chirping noise made by the wings of the male cicala (or cicada) was much admired by the Greeks.
[2] The goddesses, daughters of Zeus and Themis, who ushered in the four seasons.   [3] His goat.
[4] With the Introduction compare Tennyson's *Gardener's Daughter.*
[5] Milton took the name for his *Lycidas* from this.

Slung o'er his shoulder was a ruddy hide
Torn from a he-goat, shaggy, tangle-haired,
That reeked of rennet yet: a broad belt clasped 20
A patched cloak round his breast, and for a staff
A gnarled wild-olive bough his right hand bore.
Soon with a quiet smile he spake — his eye
Twinkled, and laughter sat upon his lip:
" And whither ploddest thou thy weary way 25
Beneath the noontide sun, Simichidas?
For now the lizard sleeps upon the wall,
The crested lark folds now his wandering wing.
Dost speed, a bidden guest, to some reveller's board ?
Or townward to the treading of the grape? 30
For lo! recoiling from thy hurrying feet
The pavement-stones ring out right merrily."
Then I: " Friend Lycid, all men say that none
Of haymakers or herdsmen is thy match
At piping: and my soul is glad thereat. 35
Yet, to speak sooth, I think to rival thee.
Now look, this road holds holiday to-day:
For banded brethren solemnize a feast
To richly-dight Demeter, thanking her
For her good gifts: since with no grudging hand 40
Hath the boon goddess filled the wheaten floors.
So come. The way, the day, is thine as mine:
Try we our woodcraft — each may learn from each.
I am, as thou, a clarion-voice of song;
All hail me chief of minstrels. But I am not, 45
Heaven knows, o'ercredulous: no, I scarce can yet
(I think) outvie Philetas,[1] nor the bard
Of Samos, champion of Sicilian song.
They are as cicadas[2] challenged by a frog."

[1] Poet of Cos, and teacher of Theocritus.
[2] See page 435, note 1.

I spake to gain mine ends; and laughing light   50
He said: "Accept this club, as thou 'rt indeed
A born truth-teller, shaped by heaven's own hand!
I hate your builders who would rear a house
High as Oromedon's mountain-pinnacle:
I hate your song-birds too, whose cuckoo-cry   55
Struggles (in vain) to match the Chian bard.[1]
But come, we 'll sing forthwith, Simichidas,
Our woodland music: and for my part I —
List, comrade, if you like the simple air
I forged among the uplands yesterday."   60

(*His Song.*)

He spake and paused; and thereupon spake I.
"I too, friend Lycid, as I range the fells,
Have learned much lore and pleasant from the Nymphs,
Whose fame mayhap hath reached the throne of Zeus.
But this wherewith I 'll grace thee ranks the first: 65
Thou listen, since the Muses like thee well."

(*The Song.*)

I ceased. He smiling sweetly as before,
Gave me the staff, "the Muses' parting gift,"
And leftward sloped tow'rd Pyxa. We the while,
Bent us to Phrasydeme's, Eucritus and I,   70
And baby-faced Amyntas: there we lay
Half-buried in a couch of fragrant reed
And fresh-cut vine-leaves, who so glad as we?
A wealth of elm and poplar shook o'erhead;
Hard by, a sacred spring flowed gurgling on   75
From the Nymph's grot, and in the sombre boughs
The sweet cicada chirped laboriously.
Hid in the thick thorn-bushes far away

[1] Homer.

The tree-frog's note was heard; the crested lark
Sang with the gold-finch; turtles made their moan, 80
And o'er the fountain hung the gilded bee.
All of rich summer smacked, of autumn all:
Pears at our feet, and apples at our side
Rolled in luxuriance; branches on the ground
Sprawled, overweighed with damsons; while we brushed 85
From the cask's head the crust of four long years.
Say, ye who dwell upon Parnassian peaks,
Nymphs of Castalia,[1] did old Chiron e'er
Set before Heracles a cup so brave
In Pholus' cavern[2] — did as nectarous draughts 90
Cause that Anapian shepherd, in whose hand
Rocks were as pebbles, Polypheme the strong,[3]
Featly to foot it o'er the cottage lawns, —
As, ladies, ye bid flow that day for us
All by Demeter's shrine at harvest-home? 95
Beside whose cornstacks may I oft again
Plant my broad fan: while she stands by and smiles,
Poppies and corn-sheaves on each laden arm.

Translated by Charles Stuart Calverley.

IDYL XV. THE FESTIVAL OF ADONIS.

"Somewhere about two hundred and eighty years before the Christian era, a couple of Syracusan women staying at Alexandria, agreed, on the occasion of a great religious solemnity, — the feast of Adonis, — to go together to the

---

[1] I. e. the Muses, who alone could tell of mythical events.

[2] Chiron was the "schoolmaster" of the mythical period, the only centaur that was not wild and untamed. He opened for Heracles a cask of wine kept in the cave of Pholus, and presented to him by Dionysus, the god of wine, himself. Attracted by the scent of the wine, the centaurs rushed upon the cave and were killed by Heracles.

[3] The Cyclops Polyphemus. See page 36.

IDYL XV. THE FESTIVAL OF ADONIS

palace of King Ptolemy Philadelphus, to see the image of Adonis, which the Queen Arsinoë, Ptolemy's wife, had had decorated with peculiar magnificence. A hymn, by a celebrated performer, was to be recited over the image. The names of the two women are Gorgo and Praxinoë; their maids, who are mentioned in the poem, are called Eunoë and Eutychis. Gorgo comes by appointment to Praxinoë's house to fetch her, and there the dialogue begins."

(MATTHEW ARNOLD.)

Gorgo. Is Praxinoë at home?

Praxinoë. My dear Gorgo, at last! Yes, here I am. Eunoë, find a chair, — get a cushion for it.

Gorgo. It will do beautifully as it is.

Praxinoë. Do sit down.

Gorgo. O, this gad-about spirit! I could hardly get to you, Praxinoë, through all the crowd and all the carriages. Nothing but heavy boots, nothing but men in uniform. And what a journey it is! My dear child, you really live *too* far off.

Praxinoë. It is all that insane husband of mine. He has chosen to come out here to the end of the world, and take a hole of a place, — for a house it is not, — on purpose that you and I might not be neighbors. He is always just the same; — anything to quarrel with one! anything for spite!

Gorgo. My dear, don't talk so of your husband before the little fellow. Just see how astonished he looks at you. Never mind, Zopyrio, my pet, she is not talking about papa.

Praxinoë. Good heavens! the child does really understand.

Gorgo. Pretty papa!

Praxinoë. That pretty papa of his the other day (though I told him beforehand to mind what he was about), when I sent him to a shop to buy soap and rouge, brought me home salt instead; — stupid, great, big, interminable animal!

Gorgo. Mine is just the fellow to him. . . . But never mind now, get on your things and let us be off to the palace to see the Adonis. I hear the queen's decorations are something splendid.

Praxinoë. In grand people's houses everything is grand. What things you have seen in Alexandria! What a deal you will have to tell to anybody who has never been here!

Gorgo. Come, we ought to be going.

Praxinoë. Every day is holiday to people who have nothing to do. Eunoë, pick up your work; and take care, lazy girl, how you leave it lying about again; the cats find it just the bed they like. Come, stir yourself, fetch me some water, quick! I wanted the water first, and the girl brings me the soap. Never mind; give it me. Not all that, extravagant! Now pour out the water; — stupid! why don't you take care of my dress? That will do. I have got my hands washed as it pleased God. Where is the key of the large wardrobe? Bring it here — quick!

Gorgo. Praxinoë, you can't think how well that dress, made full, as you 've got it, suits you. Tell me, how much did it cost? — the dress by itself, I mean.

Praxinoë. Don't talk of it, Gorgo: more than eight guineas of good hard money. And about the work on it I have almost worn my life out.

Gorgo. Well, you could n't have done better.

Praxinoë. Thank you. Bring me my shawl (*to Eunoë*), and put my hat properly on my head, — properly. No, child (*to her little boy*), I am not going to take you; there's a bogy on horseback, who bites. Cry as much as you like; I'm not going to have you lamed for life. Now we'll start. Nurse, take the little one and amuse him; call the dog in, and shut the street-door. (*They go out.*) Good heavens! what a crowd of people! How on earth are we ever to get through all this? They are like ants: you can't count them. — My dearest Gorgo, what will become of us? here are the royal Horse Guards. My good man, don't ride over me! Look at that bay horse rearing bolt upright; what a vicious one! Eunoë, you mad girl, do take care! — That horse will certainly be the death of the man on his back. How glad I am now that I left the child safe at home!

Gorgo. All right, Praxinoë, we are safe behind them; and they have gone on to where they are stationed.

Praxinoë. Well, yes, I begin to revive again. From the time I was a little girl I have had more horror of horses and snakes than of anything in the world. Let us get on; here's a great crowd coming this way upon us.

Gorgo (*to an old woman*). Mother, are you from the palace?

Old Woman. Yes, my dears.

Gorgo. Has one a tolerable chance of getting there?

Old Woman. My pretty young lady, the Greeks got to Troy by dint of trying hard; trying will do anything in this world.

Gorgo. The old creature has delivered herself of an oracle and departed.

Praxinoë. Women can tell you about everything, Jupiter's marriage with Juno not excepted.

Gorgo. Look, Praxinoë, what a squeeze at the palace-gates!

Praxinoë. Tremendous! Take hold of me, Gorgo; and you, Eunoë, take hold of Eutychis! — tight hold, or you 'll be lost. Here we go in all together. Hold tight to us, Eunoë! O dear! O dear! Gorgo, there 's my scarf torn right in two. For heaven's sake, my good man, as you hope to be saved, take care of my dress!

Stranger. I 'll do what I can, but it does n't depend upon me.

Praxinoë. What heaps of people! They push like a drove of pigs.

Stranger. Don't be frightened, ma'am, we are all right.

Praxinoë. May you be all right, my dear sir, to the last day you live, for the care you have taken of us! What a kind, considerate man! There is Eunoë jammed in a squeeze. Push, you goose, push! Capital! We are all of us on the right side of the door, as the bridegroom said when he had locked himself in with the bride.

Gorgo. Praxinoë, come this way. Do but look at that work, how delicate it is! — how exquisite! Why, they might wear it in heaven.

Praxinoë. Heavenly patroness of needlewomen, what hands were hired to do that work? Who designed those beautiful patterns? They seem to stand up and move about, as if they were real; — as if they were living things, and not needlework. Well, man is a wonderful creature! And look, look, how charming he lies there on his silver couch, with just a soft down on his cheeks, that beloved Adonis, — Adonis, whom one loves, even though he is dead!

Another Stranger. You wretched woman, do stop your incessant chatter! Like turtles, you go on for-

IDYL XV. THE FESTIVAL OF ADONIS

ever. They are enough to kill one with their broad lingo, — nothing but *a, a, a*.

Gorgo. Lord, where does the man come from? What is it to you if we *are* chatterboxes? Order about your own servants! Do you give orders to Syracusan women? If you want to know, we came originally from Corinth, as Bellerophon did; we speak Peloponnesian. I suppose Dorian women may be allowed to have a Dorian accent.

Praxinoë. O honey-sweet Proserpine, let us have no more masters than the one we've got![1] We don't the least care for *you;* pray don't trouble yourself for nothing.

Gorgo. Be quiet, Praxinoë! That first-rate singer, the Argive woman's daughter, is going to sing the *Adonis* hymn. She is the same who was chosen to sing the dirge last year. We are going to have something first-rate from *her*. She is going through her airs and graces ready to begin.

(*The Hymn to Adonis.*)

Gorgo. Praxinoë, certainly women are wonderful things. That lucky woman to know all that![2] and luckier still to have such a splendid voice! And now we must see about getting home. My husband has not had his dinner. That man is all vinegar, and nothing else; and if you keep him waiting for his dinner he's dangerous to go near. Adieu, precious Adonis, and may you find us all well when you come next year!

Translated by Matthew Arnold.

---

[1] Ptolemy Philadelphus, the king.
[2] I. e., to be able to compose such a poem.

LUCIAN

LUCIAN, "the first of the moderns," was born more than three hundred years after Theocritus, about 125 A. D. He was not a Greek by birth, but a Syrian of Samosata, near Antioch. He prepared himself to be a sculptor, but in a dream, he tells us, Culture appeared to him and persuaded him to take up the profession of Sophist. After studying and practising eloquence at home for some time, he travelled from city to city through Asia Minor, Greece, Italy, and Gaul, delivering lectures with great success. At the age of forty he established himself for a time in Athens, and devoted himself to literature. When he was already old, he was compelled by poverty to take a minor office in a court of law, and died in Egypt at an advanced age.

The writings of Lucian are sermons on the vanities of human life. He belongs to no school of philosophy, but mocks at all schools. He derides alike the ancient gods of the Pantheon and the new doctrine of Christianity; he scoffs at the ignorance in the past and the rising science of this present time. But he uses his weapons of ridicule and satire, not for the mere joy of using them, no matter against what, but with the definite purpose of wounding all that he believes rotten or false in the men and doctrines of the time. In one of his Dialogues, the sequel to the *Sale of the Philosophers*, when he is arraigned for judgment before Philosophy itself, he says in his own defence: —

"I make it my business to hate quacks, hate jugglery, hate lies, and hate conceit, and I hate every such class of wicked men. . . . Yet, in spite of this, I have a very precise knowledge of the opposite sentiment also. . . . For I'm a lover of truth, a lover of beauty, and a lover of simplicity, and whatever else has to do with loving. Albeit, very few are worthy of this profession, while those ranged under the opposite head and better suited to be objects of one's hate, are legion. I am, therefore, in danger of soon forgetting the former art for want of practice, but am likely to attain a thorough understanding of this latter. . . . My practice, however, is of this sort — namely, to hate the bad, and praise and love the good."

This impartiality and ability to see all sides of a question made his work of real value in his own time and of real interest in ours. His works have been copied and imitated by satirists from Rabelais down to the present day, but he still stands unapproached in his own field, at the side of his great predecessor Aristophanes.

The following passages are quoted by the kind permission of their translator, Winthrop Dudley Sheldon, Vice-President of Girard College.

TIMON OF ATHENS.[1] ACT III

SCENE I. — *A desert place. Timon digs up the treasure. The false friends of former days — Gnathonides, Philiades, Demeas, Thrasycles, Blepsias, Laches,* and *Gniphon,* and a crowd of others — hear of his good fortune and hasten to greet him.

Timon (alone). Come now, O mattock, take courage for the nonce, I pray you, and don't tire of calling Thesaurus forth from the depths into the light. (*The strokes of his mattock suddenly revealing the treasure.*) O Zeus, god of marvels, and ye beloved priests of Cybele, and Hermes, bestower of treasure trove — whence comes so much gold? Can it be that it's a dream? At any rate, I'm afraid I shall

[1] Timon the Misanthrope appears first in Aristophanes. He is best known to the modern world through Shakespeare's *Timon of Athens.*

awake and find only coals. Yet truly it is gold coin, reddish, heavy, and in appearance perfectly exquisite.

O gold, the fairest blessing by mortal men possessed!
Thou strik'st the eye both night and day, just like a flaming fire.

Come, dearest and most lovely being! Now, indeed, I can believe that even Zeus once upon a time turned into gold. For what maiden would not welcome with open arms so fair a lover, though he dropped down through the roof?[1] O Midas and Croesus, and ye votive offerings in Delphi,[2] how utterly insignificant, after all, were ye in comparison with Timon and Timon's wealth, to whom, in fact, not even the king of the Persians is equal! O mattock and dearest leathern frock, it will be a graceful thing to dedicate you to Pan here. As for myself I'll purchase at once all the land on the border and build a little tower over my treasure, big enough for me to live in by myself; and I think when I die, I'll have the same as my tomb also. Be this irrevocably decreed and ordained by law for the rest of my life — no intercourse or acquaintance with anybody, and contempt for all. Be friend, guest, companion, or Mercy's altar an utter absurdity; and to pity one in tears, or help one in need, shall be held a transgression of law and a breach of manners. My mode of life shall be solitary, just like that of wolves, and Timon my only friend. Let all others be regarded as enemies and plotters. It shall be defilement even to hold intercourse with any of them; and if I merely catch sight of a man, it shall be a day of ill omen. In a word, let men be to me just the same as statues of marble or of bronze. I shall receive no messenger from them and make no

[1] Cf. the story of Danaë. See the extract from *Simonides*, p. 70.
[2] I. e. at the Pythian oracle.

treaty. Let the wilderness be my boundary, so far as they are concerned. The terms, fellow-tribesmen, fellow-clansmen, fellow-citizens, and the very name fatherland shall be frigid, useless appellations, and objects of rivalry among men of no understanding. Timon shall have the exclusive enjoyment of his wealth and look down upon all; he shall fare sumptuously apart by himself, free from flattery and wearisome compliments, and sacrifice to the gods and feast with nobody but himself as neighbor and boon companion, a great way off from everybody else. Be it decreed once for all that he alone bid himself farewell, and when he must needs die, place a garland upon his brow. "The Misanthrope" shall be my most agreeable name; and peevishness, roughness of manner, and awkwardness, anger and dislike of men, shall be tokens of my character. If I should see a man burning up and imploring me to put the fire out, be it decreed to quench it with pitch and oil. And if a winter torrent should carry a man past me and he should stretch out his arms and beg me to give him a helping hand, be it ordained to push even such a one away, and plunge him in head-foremost, that he may not be able to pop up again. For thus they would receive an impartial fate. Timon, son of Echecratides, of the township of Collytus, proposed this law; the same Timon put the question to the assembly. Amen! Let this stand as our decree, and let us in manly fashion abide by it. Albeit I should lay great stress upon having the fact that I am again rolling in wealth pretty well known to all men. For that would answer as well as a hanging for them. — But what does this mean? Heavens! what hurrying! From all quarters people are rushing hither in such haste as to be covered with dust and gasping for breath. I don't understand whence they got scent of the gold. Shall I then mount this rocky hill and drive them off by pelting them at a distance with these stones from overhead, or shall I transgress my law to this extent at least and consort with them for this once, in order that they may be more annoyed at being treated with contempt? This plan, I think, is even better than the other. So then let me show a bold front and receive them on the spot. Come, let me see! Who is that foremost one among them? Gnathonides, the parasite, who, on my asking him lately for a friendly loan, handed me that halter, though he had often made himself sick when dining at my house by swilling down entire jars of wine. Well! it was very kind of him to be the first to arrive. For he shall howl before the others.

Enter GNATHONIDES.

Gnathonides. Did n't I tell you the gods would n't be neglectful of so excellent a man as Timon? Good-day, Timon! What's the good word with you, my *beau idéal* of grace and charm, jolliest of boon companions?

Timon. Humph! Good-day to you, too, Gnathonides, the most gluttonous of the whole brood of vultures, and the biggest rogue among men!

Gnathonides. Really, you always did have a *penchant* for cracking jokes. But where do you keep wassail? For I've got here a brand-new lyric ode, made up of dithyrambs, only just brought out.

Timon. Yes, and, besides, I'll make you chant an elegy right pathetically to the accompaniment of this mattock here. (*Striking* GNATHONIDES.)

Gnathonides. What means this, Timon? How dare you strike? I protest. Heracles! Oh! Oh! I cite you before the court of Areopagus for assault and battery.

Timon. Well, if you linger here a moment longer, I shall have to be indicted pretty soon for murder. (*Still beating him.*)

Gnathonides. Don't! Don't! But really, you'd effect a complete cure of the wound by scattering a little of your gold upon it. For that's a potent remedy for staunching blood.

Timon. What! Are you still hanging around?

Gnathonides. Well, I'll go. But you shall repent having become such a boor, from being the kindly fellow you once were.

[*Exit* GNATHONIDES.

Timon (*seeing some one else approaching*). Who's this man coming toward me — he with the bald head? It's Philiades, of all flatterers the most disgusting. He received from me a whole estate and two talents as dowry for his daughter, as a reward for his compliments, when he alone amid the general silence indulged in fulsome praise of my singing, declaring with an oath that I was more musical than the swans. But when he recently saw me ailing, and I went up to him with the request for help, he laid all the more blows upon me — the generous fellow!

Enter PHILIADES.

Philiades (*seeing* GNATHONIDES *departing*). Oh, what impudence! Do you now presume to be acquainted with Timon? Is Gnathonides now his friend and boon companion? So then the fellow has got his deserts — such an ingrate is he. But we, though old acquaintances of Timon's, companions of his in youth and of the same township, are nevertheless moderate in our demands, that we may not appear to be rushing upon him full tilt. (*Addressing* TIMON.) Good-day, my lord! Take care and be on your guard against these foul parasites, mere trencher friends, who, for the rest, differ not at all from carrion-crow. 'T won't do to trust any of the men of the present day any more. They are all base ingrates. *I was en route* with a talent for you, that you might have it to use for your pressing wants, and when almost here, I heard that you had become immensely wealthy. I 've come, accordingly, to give you this piece of advice. And yet you are so wise that perhaps you don't need any words from me, for you could recommend even to Nestor what should be done.

Timon. Thank you, Philiades! Only come forward, and I 'll give you an affectionate greeting with my mattock. (*Strikes him.*)

Philiades. O sirs, I 've got my skull cracked by this ingrate, all because I was for giving him some good advice.

[*Exit* PHILIADES.

Timon. See, there 's the third one coming, the orator, Demeas, with a decree in his right hand and affirming that he is a kinsman of mine. This man in one day paid the city in full of all demands sixteen talents out of my purse — for he had had judgment given against him, and in default of payment, had been bound with fetters, and I took pity on him and set him free. But when recently it fell to his lot to apportion the theoric fund to the tribe of Erechtheïs, and I went and asked him for my proper share, he declared he did n't recognize me as a citizen.

TIMON OF ATHENS. ACT III   451

Enter DEMEAS.

Demeas. Hail, Timon! Thou very flower of race, support of the Athenians! bulwark of Greece! In sooth, the people in assembly and both councils have been long awaiting your presence. But first hear the decree which I have proposed in your behalf: —

"Since Timon — the son of Echecratides, of the township of Collytus — not only the *beau idéal* of a man, but also wiser than anybody else in Greece, is all the time doing continually what is best for the city, and in one day has been victor at Olympia in boxing, wrestling, and in racing both with a four-in-hand of full-grown coursers and with a pair of fillies " —

Timon. Nay, but I've never been at Olympia, even as a looker-on.

Demeas. What's the odds? You will be by and by, and it's better that many such specifications be added. (*Proceeding with the decree.*) "Moreover also by proposing measures, by giving advice and acting as general, he has rendered the city services of no small moment. In return for all this, be it decreed by the Senate, the assembled Commons, and the Supreme Court, voting by tribes, and by all the townships individually and in concert, to set up a golden statue of Timon alongside the Athene upon the Acropolis, with a thunderbolt in his right hand and seven lightning rays upon his head, and to crown him with chaplets of gold, and that the chaplets be proclaimed by the herald to-day at the feast of Dionysus, when the new tragedies are brought out — for in his honor the Dionysia is to be celebrated to-day. Demeas, the orator, being his next of kin and his pupil, made the motion, for Timon is also a most excellent orator and everything else he would like to be." So here's your decree! I also wanted to introduce to you my son, whom I have christened "Timon" after your name.

Timon. How can that be? Seeing you've not even got married — at least so far as I know.

Demeas. But I'm going to take a wife next year — God willing — and shall have offspring, and I'll at once name my prospective child "Timon," for it will be a son.

Timon. Well! I don't know as you will any longer have a chance to get married — you fellow there — after receiving a good sound castigation from me. (*Strikes.*)

Demeas. Mercy on us! What does this mean? Timon, are you aiming at absolute power and striking freemen, when not even you yourself are a genuine freeman? But you shall speedily pay the proper penalty for your other crimes, and in particular for setting the Acropolis on fire.

Timon. But, you blackguard, the Acropolis has not been set on fire. Plainly, then, you are accusing me falsely.

Demeas. At least, you've got rich by digging your way into the treasury.

Timon. Neither has that been entered with the spade. And so this charge also of yours is unlikely.

Demeas. It will be dug into hereafter. But you've already got everything there was in it.

Timon. There! take another whack! (*Dealing him a second blow.*)

Demeas. Oh! Oh! My back! (*Putting his hands behind him.*)

Timon. Have done with your bawling, or I'll let

you have a third. For I should become a perfect laughing-stock, if unarmed I cut to pieces two battalions of Lacedaemonians, but failed to crush one beastly pygmy of a fellow. Why, all in vain would have been my victories in the Olympic contests at fisticuffs and wrestling. [*Exit* DEMEAS.

A DIALOGUE OF THE DEAD

MENIPPUS [1] AND HERMES.[2]

Menippus. Look here, Hermes, where are the handsome men and women? Show me the lions — I'm a new-comer in these parts.[3]

Hermes. I've no time to spare, Menippus. However, just look over there to your right. There are Hyacinthus, Narcissus, Nireus, and Achilles, and Tyro, Helen, and Leda — in fine, all the old-time beauties.

Menippus. I see nothing but bones and skulls, with not a scrap of flesh upon them — the most of them just alike.

Hermes. In sooth, they are what all the poets admire — these bones, which you appear to think slightly of.

Menippus. All the same, show me Helen, for I at least should n't know her from the others.

Hermes. That skull there is Helen.

Menippus. Was it, then, for this that the thousand ships were manned from all Greece, and Greeks and

---

[1] A cynic philosopher, represented by Lucian as always jesting at serious things.
[2] Hermes (*Mercury*) conducted the shades of the dead to the lower world. See page 228.
[3] I. e., the lower world.

barbarians fell in such numbers, and so many cities were destroyed?

Hermes. But, Menippus, you did n't see the woman alive. Else you, too, would have declared it a blameless thing " to suffer ills so long a time for such a lady's sake." [1] For, take the case of flowers that are withered; if one should look at them, now that they have lost their color, to him no doubt they will seem unsightly. When, however, they are in blossom and have their proper hue, they are in the highest degree beautiful.

Menippus. Therefore, Hermes, I 'm amazed at this, that the Greeks did n't perceive that they were straining every nerve over a thing so ephemeral and easily fading away.

Hermes. Well, Menippus, I have n't any leisure for arguing the matter with you. So select a spot wherever you please, and lay yourself down and stay there. For I must go at once and fetch the rest of the dead.

PEREGRINUS

"Peregrinus Proteus, who burned himself alive at the Olympic games in A. D. 165, — Lucian himself being present, — had been a Christian before he became a Cynic." This selection contains §§ 11–13 of the letter of Lucian which give an account of Peregrinus's death.

AT this time also he [2] made himself proficient in the marvellous wisdom of the Christians by keeping company, around about Palestine, with their priests and scribes. Yes, and would you believe it? — in a short

[1] Homer's *Iliad*, III. 157.   [2] Peregrinus.

time he made them out to be mere children in comparison with himself, who united in his own person alone the offices of prophet, master of ceremonies, head of the synagogue, and everything. And of their books he explained and interpreted some, and many he himself also wrote, and they came to look upon him as a god, made him their law-giver, and chose him as their patron. At all events, they still worship that extraordinary man, who was crucified in Palestine for introducing into the world this new religious sect.

Just about this time Peregrinus Proteus was seized on this account and thrown into prison, which very circumstance procured for him no small honor during his subsequent career, and the reputation for wonderful powers, and the popularity of which he was passionately fond. However, now that he had been put in bonds, the Christians, looking upon the thing as a misfortune, left no stone unturned in their efforts to secure his release. Then, when this proved to be impracticable, they all the time zealously rendered him ministries of every other sort. From earliest dawn aged widows and orphan children were to be seen waiting at the door of the prison; and men of rank among them even obtained the privilege of sleeping with him within by bribing the prison guards. Then they were wont to bring in all manner of viands and read their sacred Scriptures, and our most excellent Peregrinus — for that was still his name — was dubbed by them a new Socrates.

Moreover, there came certain even from the cities of Asia, sent by the Christians at the common charge, to help the man, and advocate his cause, and comfort him. They exhibit extraordinary activity, whenever some such thing occurs affecting their common interest. In short, they are lavish of everything. And what is more, on the pretext of his imprisonment, many contributions of money from them came to Peregrinus at that time, and he made no little income out of it. Why, these poor wretches have persuaded themselves that they are going to be every whit immortal and live forever; wherefore they both despise death and voluntarily devote themselves to it — the most of them. Moreover, their first law-giver persuaded them that they all are brethren one of another, when once they come out and reject the gods of the Greeks, and worship that crucified sophist, and live according to his requirements. Therefore they esteem all things alike as of small account, and regard their property as common, having received such ideas from others, without any adequate basis for their faith. If, then, any cheat came among them and a trickster able to manage things, in a very short time he got ever so rich, laughing in his sleeve at these unsophisticated folk.

Lightning Source UK Ltd.
Milton Keynes UK
UKHW040601061219
354855UK00001B/71/P